CONTEMPORARY ISSUES
IN THE POST-CRISIS
REGULATORY LANDSCAPE

CONTEMPORARY ISSUES IN THE POST-CRISIS REGULATORY LANDSCAPE

Imad A. Moosa

Royal Melbourne Institute of Technology, Australia

World Scientific

NEW JERSEY · LONDON · SINGAPORE · BEIJING · SHANGHAI · HONG KONG · TAIPEI · CHENNAI · TOKYO

Published by

World Scientific Publishing Co. Pte. Ltd.

5 Toh Tuck Link, Singapore 596224

USA office: 27 Warren Street, Suite 401-402, Hackensack, NJ 07601

UK office: 57 Shelton Street, Covent Garden, London WC2H 9HE

Library of Congress Cataloging-in-Publication Data
Names: Moosa, Imad A., author.
Title: Contemporary issues in the post-crisis regulatory landscape / Imad A. Moosa
    (Royal Melbourne Institute of Technology, Australia).
Description: New Jersey : World Scientific, 2016. | Includes bibliographical references.
Identifiers: LCCN 2016013140 | ISBN 9789813109285 (hc : alk. paper)
Subjects: LCSH: Finance--Government policy. | Financial institutions--Government policy. |
    Banks and banking--Government policy.
Classification: LCC HG173 .M63798 2016 | DDC 332--dc23
LC record available at https://lccn.loc.gov/2016013140

British Library Cataloguing-in-Publication Data
A catalogue record for this book is available from the British Library.

Desk Editors: Anthony Alexander/Pui Yee

Typeset by Stallion Press
Email: enquiries@stallionpress.com

Printed in Singapore

To Ryan

Preface

Eight years after the global financial crisis, we are still waiting for regulators and politicians to endorse and implement drastic measures to put an end to abusive behavior and malpractices of those running financial institutions (the financial oligarchs). Instead we only hear about half-hearted measures justified by the claims that the clock cannot be turned back and that regulation will kill "financial innovation". As a result, the bonus culture is thriving once more and the credit rating agencies (CRAs) are back in business as usual. Even worse, the monetary authorities in the US, UK and the European Union are indulged in quantitative easing to maintain ultra-low interest rates, the very same policy that caused the global financial crisis. The power of the financial oligarchy is quite evident.

One bright spot in all of this is Iceland, where offending financial oligarchs have been put behind bars, as opposed to major financial centers (such as London and New York) where the financial oligarchs still demand and obtain bonuses and golden parachutes. The Icelanders have demonstrated courage by contemplating plans to deprive bankers from the ability to create money by moving from a system of fractional reserve banking to a system of sovereign money — in effect nationalizing the money supply process. The Icelanders have also shown the rest of the world that there is no such thing as a too big to fail (TBTF) bank as they allowed three banks to fail although these banks were huge, some 11 times the size of the economy. In other places, bankers are still calling the shots.

This book is about financial regulation in the post-crisis era, in which a proposition is put forward that the main justification for financial regulation is the rampant corruption and fraud in the financial sector and that fraud causes financial insatiability. This proposition is presented in Chapter 3 following two chapters on the post-crisis regulatory landscape and a discussion of important regulatory issues in the aftermath of the crisis. Two chapters are devoted to the "war on regulation" in terms of theories, hypotheses and doctrines, including rational expectations, the Washington Consensus, the Great Moderation, the trickle-down effect and the weapon of mass destruction, the efficient market hypothesis. Particular regulatory issues are discussed in separate chapters, including the regulation of remuneration in the financial sector, shadow banking and CRAs. Two chapters are devoted to the regulatory implications of quantitative easing and financial reform in Iceland. In the last chapter we conclude that tweaking around the edges will not work and that drastic actions are needed to take us back to "boring banking".

Writing this book would not have been possible without the help and encouragement I received from family, friends and colleagues. My utmost gratitude must go to my wife and children (Afaf, Nisreen and Danny) who are my source of joy. I would also like to thank my colleagues and friends, including John Vaz, Kelly Burns, Vikash Ramiah, Mike Dempsey, Larry Li, George Tawadros, Liam Lenten and Brien McDonald. In preparing the manuscript, I benefited from an exchange of ideas with members of the Table 14 Discussion Group, and for this reason I would like to thank Bob Parsons, Greg O'Brien, Greg Bailey, Bill Breen, Paul Rule, Peter Murphy, Bob Brownly and Tony Paligano. My thanks also go to friends and former colleagues who live far away but provide help via means of telecommunication, including Kevin Dowd (whom I owe intellectual debt), Razzaque Bhatti, Ron Ripple, Bob Sedgwick, Sean Holly, Dan Hemmings and Ian Baxter. Last, but not least, I thank Dal Singh, Rodrigo Olivares and Ray LaBrosse for making me increasingly interested in financial regulation.

Naturally, I am the only one responsible for any errors and omissions that may be found in this book. It is dedicated to my grandson, Ryan Imad Longhurst, on the occasion of his first birthday.

Imad A. Moosa
January, 2016

About the Author

Imad Moosa is currently a Professor of Finance at RMIT, Melbourne. Before taking on the present position, he was a Professor of Finance at Monash University and La Trobe University, and a Lecturer in Economics and Finance at the University of Sheffield. Prior to becoming an academic in 1991, he was a professional Economist and a Financial Journalist for over 10 years, and he also worked as an Economist at the Financial Institutions Division of the Bureau of Statistics, the International Monetary Fund (Washington DC). Professor Moosa has published 21 books and over 200 papers in scholarly journals. He has served in a number of advisory positions, including his role as an economic advisor to the US Treasury.

Contents

List of Figures

List of Abbreviations/Acronyms

ABCP	Asset-backed commercial paper
ABN	Algemene Bank Nederland
ABS	Asset-backed security
AC	Average cost
ACFE	Association of Certified Fraud Examiners
AIG	American International Group
AR	Average revenue
ARM	Adjustable rate mortgage
BBA	British Bankers' Association
BBC	British Broadcasting Corporation
BCBS	Basel Committee on Banking Supervision
BIS	Bank for International Settlements
CBO	Collateralized bond obligation
CD	Certificate of deposit
CDO	Collateralized debt obligation
CDS	Credit default swap
CEO	Chief Executive Officer
CFA	Chartered financial analyst
CFO	Chief financial officer
CFTC	Commodity Futures Trading Commission
CLO	Collateralized loan obligation
CMBS	Commercial mortgage-backed securities

CMO	Collateralized mortgage obligation
CNBC	Consumer News and Business Channel
CPDO	Constant proportion debt obligation
CPI	Consumer price index
CRA	Credit rating agency
DDT	Dichloro Diphenyl Trichloroethane
DEA	Drug Enforcement Agency
DOJ	Department of Justice
D-SIB	Domestic systemically important bank
ECB	European Central Bank
EMH	Efficient market hypothesis
ESMA	European Securities and Markets Authority
EU	European Union
EUIBOR	Euro interbank offered rate
FBI	Federal Bureau of Investigation
FCA	Financial Conduct Authority
FCIC	Financial Crisis Inquiry Commission
FDIC	Federal Deposit Insurance Corporation
FOA	Friends of Angelo
FOMC	Federal Open Market Committee
FPU	Financial Products Unit
FSA	Financial Services Authority
FSB	Financial Stability Board
GDP	Gross domestic product
GM	Great Moderation
G-SIB	Global systemically important bank
HEL	Home equity loan
HFT	High-frequency trading
HSBC	Hong Kong and Shanghai Banking Corporation
IBA	International Bar Association
ICAP	Intercapital
IMF	International Monetary Fund
IPO	Initial public offering
ISK	Icelandic krona
IT	Information technology
KPMG	Klijnveld Peat Marwick Goerdeler

LIBOR	London interbank offered rate
LTCM	Long-Term Capital Management
MBS	Mortgage-backed security
MC	Marginal cost
MIT	Massachusetts Institute of Technology
MMMF	Money market mutual fund
MP	Member of Parliament
MR	Marginal revenue
MSNBC	Microsoft/National Broadcasting Company
NASA	National Aeronautics and Space Administration
NBER	National Bureau of Economic Research
NBFI	Non-bank financial intermediary
NFB	Narrow funding bank
NFL	National Football League
NIIP	Net international investment position
NINJA	No income, no job and no assets
NRSRO	Nationally recognized statistical rating organization
NSB	Narrow saving bank
NY-LON	New York-London
NYSE	New York Stock Exchange
OECD	Organization for Economic Co-operation and Development
OFIs	Other financial intermediaries
OTC	Over-the-counter
PIIGS	Portugal, Italy, Ireland, Greece and Spain
PIMCO	Pacific Investment Management Company
PRA	Prudential Regulation Authority
PWC	Price Waterhouse Coopers
QE	Quantitative easing
QE1	Quantitative easing (round one)
QE2	Quantitative easing (round two)
QE3	Quantitative easing (round three)
QE4	Quantitative easing (round four)
RBS	Royal Bank of Scotland
REH	Rational Expectations Hypothesis
RMBS	Residential mortgage-backed securities

S&L	Savings and loan (crisis)
S&P	Standard and Poor's
SEC	Securities and Exchange Commission
SFT	Securities financing transaction
SIC	Special Investigation Commission
SIFI	Systemically important financial institution
SIFMA	Securities Industry and Financial Markets Association
SIV	Special investment vehicle
SPV	Special purpose vehicle
TARP	Troubled asset relief program
TBTF	Too big to fail
TLAC	Total loss absorption capacity
UBS	Union Bank of Switzerland
VAR	Vector autoregression
VW	Volks Wagen
WC	Washington Consensus
WTO	World Trade Organization

Chapter 1

The Post-Crisis Regulatory Landscape: An Overview

1. Free Marketeers and the Dislike of Regulation

Free marketeers hate regulation in any shape or form — and this is not surprising at all. What is surprising, however, is that this stance has not changed despite the destruction inflicted on humanity by the global financial crisis as people lost their homes, jobs and retirement funds in the name of the free market. In the aftermath of the crisis free marketeers who oppose regulation and advocate deregulation came in three categories. Category one are those who claim that the crisis was caused by excessive regulation. Category two comprises those who suggest that deregulation was not a cause of the crisis. The most outrageous claim, however, is made by category three free marketeers who suggest that no major deregulation has taken place in the last 30 years or so. One can only wonder if category three free marketeers are talking about Planet Earth, but more likely they are in a state of denial.

One of the free marketeers belonging to category one is Senator John Ensign, chairman of the National Republican Senatorial Committee, who went on *Face the Nation* to put forward his diagnosis of the economic meltdown. He said: "Unfortunately, it was allowed to be portrayed that this was a result of deregulation, when in fact it was a result of overregulation" (Huffington, 2008). Another example is Ambler (2011) who contends that "the 2008 financial crash was not caused by a lack of regulation" and that "an excess of regulation was a larger factor, creating as it did the illusion of security". However, the facts on the ground tell a different story — one example would suffice at this stage (but we will come across many more examples as we move on). Had over-the-counter (OTC) derivatives been regulated as suggested by Brooksley Born in the 1990s, we would have gone a long way in at least reducing the effects of the global financial crisis. As early as 1997, the then Fed Chairman, Alan Greenspan, fought to keep the derivatives market unregulated. On the advice of the President's Working Group on Financial Markets, the Congress and President allowed the so-called "self-regulation" of the OTC derivatives market when they enacted the Commodity Futures Modernization Act of 2000 (Summers *et al.*, 1999).[1]

As for category two, we have the dissenting voices of members of the Financial Crisis Inquiry Commission (FCIC, 2011). In their dissenting statement, Commissioner Keith Hennessey, Commissioner Douglas Holz-Eakin and Vice Chairman Bill Thomas rejected what they call the "too simplistic the hypothesis that too little regulation caused the crisis". They argued against the proposition that "the crisis was avoidable if only the US had adopted across-the-board more restrictive regulations, in conjunction with more aggressive regulators and supervisors". Instead they adopt

---

[1] Brooksley Born was the chairperson of the Commodity Futures Trading Commission (CFTC) between 26 August 1996 and 1 June 1999. While she held that position, Born attempted to regulate OTC derivatives, only to find herself the target of bullying by Robert Rubin and Larry Summers (both former US Treasury secretaries) as well as the former Fed chairman, Alan Greenspan. Acting on behalf of the financial oligarchy, the trio won and Born had to resign. In reference to the trio, Born is known to have said the following: "They totally opposed to it [regulation]. That puzzled me. What was it in this market that had to be hidden" (http://www.pbs.org/wgbh/pages/frontline/warning/view/#morelink). It is ironic, to say the least, that the trio appeared on the cover of the 15 February 1999 issue of *Time* and described as the "Committee to Save the World".

what they call a "global perspective", arguing that a credit bubble appeared in both the US and Europe and that large financial firms failed in Iceland, Spain, Germany and the UK, where stricter regulation was in operation. Hence they rule out as causes of the crisis the political influence of the financial sector in Washington, the "runaway mortgage securitization train", the corporate and regulatory structures of investment banks and Alan Greenspan's deregulatory ideology. The fact of the matter is that Iceland, Spain and the UK were hurt badly by the crisis because they followed the American model and allowed their financial oligarchies to run the show. Germany as a whole was not affected as badly by the crisis because the Germans proved to be wise enough not to follow the American model and abandon manufacturing industry, neither did they adopt the British motto of "who needs manufacturing industry when we have the City?" Germany is mentioned here perhaps because some German banks and pension funds collapsed as they took the bait and accumulated US-manufactured junk assets.

Under category three we have two members of the FCIC with dissenting voices: Peter Wallison and Arthur Burns who dismiss as causes of the global financial crisis deregulation or lax regulation. They argue that "explanations that rely on lack of regulation or deregulation as a cause of the financial crisis are also deficient". Against the facts on the ground they suggest that no significant deregulation of financial institutions occurred in the last 30 years. Specifically they contend that the repeal of the Glass–Steagall Act (which is the prime example of deregulation) had no role in the crisis.

2. The Facts on the Ground

Common sense and an ideological free consideration of the facts on the ground would tell us that deregulation was a major cause of the crisis and that wholesale deregulation has taken place since the early 1980s. The contribution of regulatory failure and deregulation to the eruption of the global financial crisis is emphasized by the FCIC (2011). In its report on the crisis, the Commission declared:

> There was an explosion in risky subprime lending and securitization, an unsustainable rise in housing prices, widespread reports of egregious and predatory lending practices, dramatic increases in household mortgage debt, and exponential growth in financial firms' trading activities, unregulated derivatives, and short-term "repo" lending markets, among many other red flags. Yet there was pervasive permissiveness; little meaningful action was taken to quell the threats in a timely manner.

The report refers in particular to the "pivotal failure" of the Fed to stem the flow of toxic mortgages, which it could have done by setting prudent mortgage lending standards. Reference to the contribution of deregulation is made at the outset as follows:

> More than 30 years of deregulation and reliance on self-regulation by financial institutions, championed by former Federal Reserve chairman Alan Greenspan and others, supported by successive administrations and Congresses, and actively pushed by the powerful financial industry at every turn, had stripped away key safeguards, which could have helped avoid catastrophe.

The Commission also refers to failure to use existing regulation:

> Yet we do not accept the view that regulators lacked the power to protect the financial system. They had ample power in many arenas and they chose not to use it. To give just three examples: the Securities and Exchange Commission could have required more capital and halted risky practices at the big investment banks. It did not. The Federal Reserve Bank of New York and other regulators could have clamped down on Citigroup's excesses in the run-up to the crisis. They did not. Policy makers and regulators could have stopped the runaway mortgage securitization train. They did not.

The Commission argues that the financial industry itself played a key role in weakening regulatory constraints on institutions, markets and products. The FCIC's report makes it explicit that regulators have been captured by big financial institutions, arguing that it was not surprising that "an industry of such wealth and power would exert pressure on policy makers and regulators", pointing out that "from 1999 to 2008, the financial sector spent $2.7 billion in reported federal lobbying expenses, while individuals and political action committees in the sector made more than $1 billion in campaign contributions".

Spaventa (2009) points out that regulators were caught by the crisis with their eyes wide shut, having resisted attempts to allow regulation to keep pace with financial innovation. He presents his view as follows:

> This was coherent with the prevailing creed: that markets were self-regulating and only required the lightest possible public touch; that self-interest would lead to proper risk assessment; that capital deepening was always good for growth, no matter how.

Deregulation becomes the law of the land when regulators argue against regulation. In a 2003 speech, Fed Vice Chairman Roger Ferguson praised "the truly impressive improvement in methods of risk measurement and the growing adoption of these technologies by mostly large banks and other financial intermediaries". His boss, Alan Greenspan, is quoted as saying that "the real question is not whether a market should be regulated" but "the real question is whether government intervention strengthens or weakens private regulation". Richard Spillenkothen, the Fed's director of Banking Supervision and Regulation from 1991 to 2006, is quoted as saying that "supervisors understood that forceful and proactive supervision, especially early intervention before management weaknesses were reflected in poor financial performance, might be viewed as (i) overly-intrusive, burdensome and heavy-handed, (ii) an undesirable constraint on credit availability, or (iii) inconsistent with the Fed's public posture" (FCIC, 2011).

Regulation by an external agent is needed because "private regulation" and "self-regulation" do not work in an industry where business is motivated primarily by greed. In Oliver Stone's 1987 movie *Wall Street*, Gordon Gekko spells it out on the role of greed in the finance industry by saying the following:

> Greed, for lack of a better word, is good. Greed is right. Greed works. Greed clarifies, cuts through, and captures, the essence of the evolutionary spirit. Greed, in all of its forms; greed for life, for money, for love, knowledge, has marked the upward surge of mankind and greed, you mark my words, will not only save Teldar Paper, but that other malfunctioning corporation called the USA.

It is true that Gordon Gekko is a fictitious character, but what he said is a true representation of what motivates the financial oligarchy. While greed cannot be regulated, it leads to something that can and should be regulated: fraud and corruption. In this book an argument will be made repeatedly, that corruption and fraud provide the best justification for regulation.

3. Boom and Bust

The regulatory landscape should be shaped by what is needed to avoid another crisis aided by the lessons learned from the last crisis. Dozens of studies have been conducted to determine the causes of the global financial crisis, in which case there is no need to repeat the exercise here. However, it is useful to recount what happened and how the boom (or bubble) in asset markets was followed by a big bust. Emphasis is placed on two observations: (i) the boom and bust cycle starts with deregulation and regulatory failure and (ii) every boom involves elements of corruption, fraud and greed.

Figure 1.1 is a schematic representation of the boom. The starting point is deregulation and regulatory failure. For 50 years following the implementation of the Glass–Steagal Act in 1933, financial stability prevailed, but that came to an end with the advent of the savings and loan crisis of the 1980s, which was a direct result of the wholesale deregulation initiated by a champion free marketeer, Ronald Reagan. The wave of deregulation continued into the 1990s,

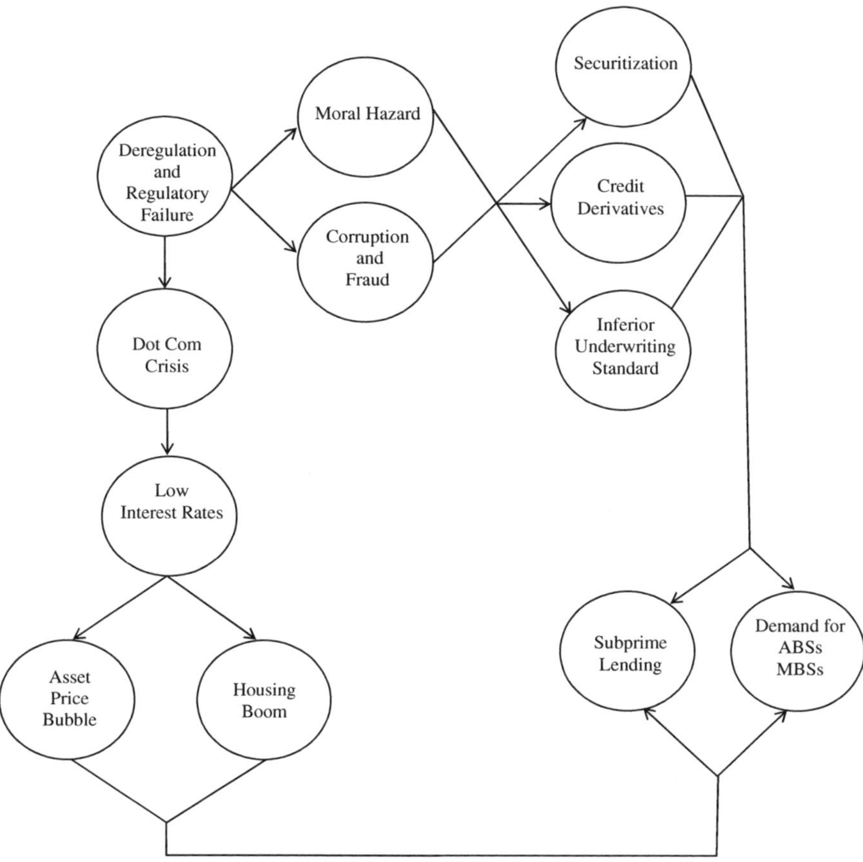

Figure 1.1:   The Boom

culminating with the abolition of the Glass–Steagal Act, which gave bankers a free hand to do as they pleased and led to the creation of jumbo financial institutions that were allowed to gamble with depositors' money. We did not have to wait long after that to witness the bursting of the dot-com bubble, causing the recession of the early 2000s. In response to the recession, the Fed reacted by reducing interest rates to stimulate the economy, a policy that was in place for too many years. Under an environment of low interest rates, people rushed to buy houses on a massive scale, using adjustable-rate mortgages as they were led (by mortgage brokers) to believe that it was a great deal. A housing market boom was initiated and so was a general asset price bubble, particularly in the stock market.

Deregulation and regulatory failure enhanced moral hazard and provided the right environment for rampant greed-driven corruption and fraud. By securitizing every cash flow under the sun, bankers invented the Frankenstein financial assets of asset-backed securities (ABSs), mortgage-backed securities (MBSs), collateralized debt obligations (CDOs) and their variants such as CDO squared. Another "great" invention was an insurance policy called credit default swaps (CDSs) intended to hedge the risk of default faced by the holders of the Frankenstein securities. Together with predatory lending and inferior underwriting standards, these securities and derivatives were used as a conduit for fraud, particularly because no one understood how they worked and not even their inventors could estimate the degree of risk embodied in them (this is not to say that the inventors and their bosses did not realize that they were junk securities). The ABSs, MBSs and CDOs were given the AAA designation by the credit rating agencies (CRAs) which encouraged demand for these toxic assets by the world investment community.[2] This wave of "financial innovation" led to rapid growth in subprime lending, which was enhanced on the demand side by the housing boom and general asset price bubble. While the party lasted everyone was happy. Mortgage lenders were happy to lend and keep subprime loans off their books via securitization. Issuers of ABSs were happy to get their commissions. Borrowers were happy to get loans without scrutiny. Investors were happy to acquire assets that were "risk-free" and offered a return of hundreds of basis points over that offered by US Treasuries. Members of the financial oligarchy (bankers and financiers) were happy to receive billions of dollars worth of bonuses without any contribution to human welfare. The situation was simply an orgy of hubris and excesses.

---

[2]It was like the scene of young people queuing overnight in front of a shop, competing to be the first to get one of the newest apple phones.

Like every party, this party came to an end, a very unhappy end. Figure 1.2 represents how the bust materialized — that is, how the party came to a very unhappy end. Just like the boom started with low interest rates, the bust started when the Fed embarked on a tight policy whereby the official interest rate was raised 17 times during the period 2004–2006. As a result, payments on adjustable rate mortgages started to rise, leading to a slowdown in the demand for houses and massive defaults on mortgage payments. The defaults experienced far exceeded what was predicted by the risk models used by financial institutions, including those based on the Gaussian Copula (see, for example, Reid, 2015). As a result, ABSs, MBSs and CDOs lost their appeal as the return on these assets dwindled. Being the backward-looking institutions they are, the CRAs downgraded these assets, leading to a tightening of leveraged positions as hedge funds and banks had to meet margin calls. To raise capital, banks and hedge funds started to sell off liquid assets. A liquidity squeeze ensued as the interbank market dried up and financial institutions became reluctant to lend to each other. Insolvencies arose and stock markets took a nose-dive. The crisis was in full swing as Lehman Brothers filed for bankruptcy and American International Group (AIG) found itself unable to meet demand for payoffs on CDSs.[3]

The policy response was shaped by the desire to save big financial institutions, those that are too politically connected to fail and those that owed money to those that are too politically connected to fail (such as AIG owing billions of dollars to Goldman Sachs). A bailout program was approved to save AIG and major banks. The response to the Great Recession took the shape of quantitative easing, a policy whereby the central bank prints new money to finance the purchase of government securities and toxic assets from

---

[3] AIG did not have adequate capital to pay claims on CDSs, originally bought from AIG to protect the holders of junk securities against default. The company operated without adequate capital only because the CRAs blessed it (just like it had blessed Enron) with the AAA designation. In any case, the people running AIG thought it would never come to that because house price could not fall nationwide the way they actually did.

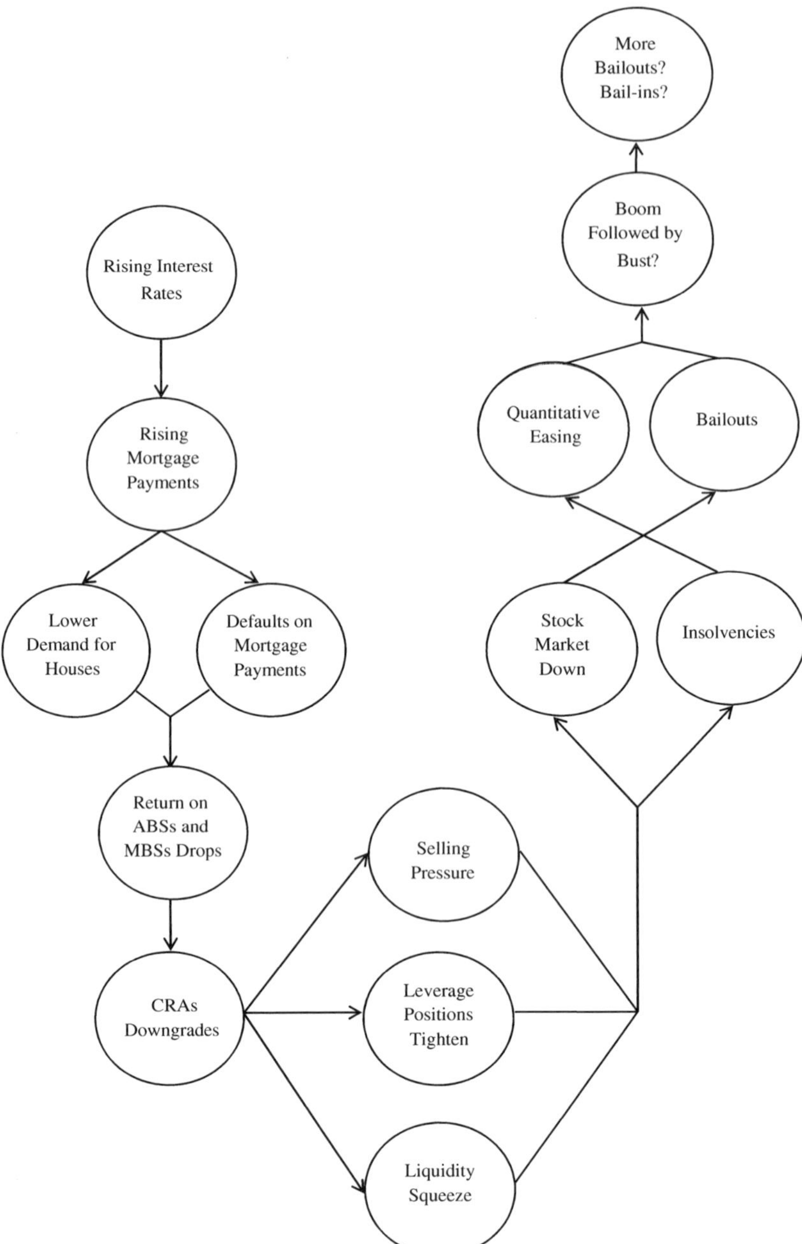

Figure 1.2:   The Bust

financial institutions. Both bailouts and quantitative easing amount to sowing the seeds of the next crisis. Bailouts enhance moral hazard and excessive risk-taking. Quantitative easing not only enhances moral hazard but it is also a very bad policy from a macroeconomic perspective. It has inflationary implications, it punishes savers (with bad consequences for economic growth) and it creates asset price bubbles, with adverse distributional consequences. We should not forget that the low interest rates maintained over a long period of time played a big role in the initiation of the crisis, so it is fair to conclude that the current environment of low interest rates maintained through quantitative easing may lead to the next crisis. If and when another crisis causes the failure of financial institutions, the government will respond with more bailouts. The fear now is that governments may resort to bail-ins, refinancing banks by confiscating (more appropriately, stealing) depositors' money.[4]

4. Key Players and Culprits

Although the global financial crisis was American in origin, non-American contributors played a role, mainly by emulating the American model of financial *laissez faire* and by accumulating toxic assets manufactured by US investment banks. Moreover, lax regulation outside the US allowed financial institutions to indulge in parasitic and fraudulent activities. For example, the Financial Products Unit (FPU) of AIG, the manufacturer of CDSs, was operating out of London, as the lax regulation of the City of London (its source of pride) allowed the FPU to inflict so much damage on the rest of the world.

Many key players and culprits contributed to the advent of the global financial crisis. US financial regulators made their

---

[4] In 2013, Cypriot banks were bailed in. What makes bail-ins a reality is that they are more politically acceptable than bailouts. The underlying idea is that if you put your money in a bank, you are taking risk, just like when you buy shares. Bank depositors are then given the choice between losing their money completely and receiving shares that are worth close to nothing in the recapitalized banks. Naturally, bankers will still get their bonuses.

contribution through regulatory failure and capture. Regulators from other countries failed because they copied US regulators blindly. The Federal Reserve failed by ignoring asset price bubbles and engaging in faulty policies that caused the bubbles (and still does). Like regulators from other countries, the central banks of other countries failed by copying Fed policies blindly. Investment banks invented toxic assets and conspired with the CRAs to sell these assets to their customers on the grounds that they were low-risk high-return assets (one particular bank that sold toxic assets bet against its own clients without disclosing the conflict of interest). The CRAs failed for giving toxic assets top ratings. Academia played the role of a hired gun by providing the intellectual justification for deregulation on the basis of the notorious efficient markets hypothesis. Investment analysts used flawed asset pricing and risk models that led to underpricing of risk, producing disastrous results. Motivated by greed and the desire to maximize bonuses, members of the financial oligarchy turned a blind eye (perhaps even encouraged) fraud and indulged in short-termism at the expense of the long-term stability of their firms. Boards of directors failed to preserve sound corporate governance and to protect shareholders against excessive executive compensation, the very reason for the rise of moral hazard. Fund managers failed to do their homework before advising their clients on bad investments (they even acted as marketing agents for the issuers of junk securities). Mortgage brokers sold loans to unqualified borrowers in order to collect commissions. Home buyers inflicted damage on themselves by following the advice of unscrupulous mortgage brokers and taking loans that they could not afford to pay back. Last, but not least, the US government (and the governments of the other so-called "western countries") failed by yielding to pressure from the financial oligarchy to deregulate the economy and bailout financial institutions. Lobbyists were allowed a free hand to act on behalf of bankers. Members of the oligarchy or their lieutenants were hired for senior government posts and anti-regulation free marketeers were appointed in regulatory positions.

It must be pointed out here that the word "failure" is used to mean or encompass negligence, incompetence and fraud. Indeed the biggest culprit was not a person or an entity but rather the fraud committed by individuals and institutions. This is why it may be unfair to label home buyers as culprits because they were mostly victims of fraudulent behavior. Fraud and misconduct took many shapes and forms — the following are just examples:

- The conversion and packaging of home, car, student and other loans into junk securities that were sold as investment-grade assets.
- Convincing potential home buyers who are not qualified for loans (subprime borrowers) to borrow on the grounds that the housing boom will in itself provide the financing.
- The role played by the CRAs in promoting junk securities.
- Insurance companies selling insurance to the holders of the junk securities to protect them against potential losses. Investors were under the illusion that their investments were highly secure. The scheme went further when the insurers allowed other investors to buy insurance on securities they did not own. All of that happened when insurers did not hold enough capital to cover claims.
- Lobbyists, hired politicians and people inside the government acted on behalf of the financial oligarchy by opposing regulation and encouraging deregulation. Regulators were effectively captured by the supposedly regulated institutions.

What is worse than fraud is failure to prosecute fraud. Even if markets are not regulated, common law should punish fraud and the misleading of clients by knowingly selling bad securities and loans to clients without disclosing risk. Nothing much has happened on this front. While Tom Hayes has been put behind bars for manipulating London Interbank Offered Rates (LIBORs), tens of the likes of Tom Hayes are still at large. We will come back to fraud and corruption over and over again.

5. Good Regulation versus Bad Regulation

The debate on regulation has been centered on the choice between a free market (economy) and a regulated market (economy). However, the global financial crisis has taught us a lesson the hard way, the lesson that corruption, fraud and greed are rampant in the finance industry and that these should be regulated to avoid another crisis. The financial oligarchs should never be given a free hand to do as they please, and this is where regulation comes in. Alan Greenspan, the former chief of the Fed, once said that there is no need for the regulation of fraud because if a stock broker indulges in fraudulent activity he will be recognized by the financial community and no one will deal with him (Roig-Franzia, 2009). Obviously, the victims of Bernie Madoff do not sympathize with this view, but while Greenspan has since changed his mind about the charm of the free market, some "die-hard" free marketeers still advocate the idea that free markets provide the only salvation.

The real question, particularly in the aftermath of the global financial crisis, is not if financial regulation is needed but whether a particular set of regulatory measures are good or bad. In other words, the debate should be about the distinction and choice between good regulation and bad regulation. However, this issue is hardly dealt with, perhaps because of the extreme view expressed by free marketeers that no regulation is good regulation and any regulation is bad regulation, which triggers a debate on more regulation or more deregulation. The proposition that the debate should be about good regulation versus bad regulation seems to be assuming increasing acceptance, even by the general public. The debate should be about quality, not (or not only) about quantity. It is rather refreshing to see an internet debate on this issue, in which the main question asked is the following: do any of you make a distinction between regulations that are actually useful or needed versus those that are harmful? The person raising this question suggests the following[5]:

---

[5] Good Regulation versus Bad Regulation (how much, companies, economic, government) http://www.city-data.com/forum/politics-other-controversies/1011716-good-regulation-vs-bad-regulation.html.

I generally support regulation in the form of oversight to bring about transparency that deals with reducing shady or abusive business practices. But I don't support regulations that have a distorting affect on economic activity like price controls for example. This is why I don't support regulation just for the sake of regulation. If the regulation is about oversight then I'am for it but if the regulation is about trying to control the market to bring about a certain outcome then it's this regulation that seems to cause the most problems.

This statement has some merits. Regulation should never be for the sake of regulation, in the sense that it is a pure compliance exercise. And regulation should be about oversight. The contradiction in the statement is that it indicates firm belief in the ability of the almighty market to solve our problems. Rejecting price controls under any circumstances means rejecting the regulation of the predatory business of payday loans. Furthermore, arguing against "trying to control the market to bring about a certain market outcome" because this regulation "seems to cause the most problems" implies that we should allow polluters to produce the level of output dictated by market forces without any consideration given to externalities. Does not "oversight" imply that we should not allow something like this to happen? There is inconsistency between believing in oversight and leaving it all to market forces.

There is no question that regulation is a mixed blessing. Regulation serves a vital role in improving social, environmental and economic standards. Regulation defines and enforces property rights, which are the basis for economic exchange.[6] Regulation also gives government bureaucrats the power to flex their muscles on ordinary people. The dark side of regulation is that it may be used

---

[6] It is often thought that the industrial revolution started in Britain in the 18th century because of technology and technology alone — that is, because Britain was more technologically advanced than the rest of the world. This begs the question as to why no industrial revolution erupted in China hundreds of years earlier when China was ahead of the rest of the world in terms of technology. The difference is that Britain had in place an advanced system of property rights and patents, which China did not have.

to serve the interest of a small minority at the expense of the majority, which typically occurs under conditions of regulatory capture. Even well-intentioned regulation can bring problems of its own. This is why the costs associated with regulation have to be balanced against potential benefits. In general terms, good regulation should produce benefits that outweigh the costs.

Attempts have been made to identify the characteristics of good regulation. Banks (2003) lists the following characteristics: (i) it must have a sound rationale and be shown to bring a net benefit to society; (ii) it must be better than any alternative regulation or policy tool; (iii) it must be robust to errors in the assumptions underlying it, (iv) it should not be immortal in the sense that it should be dismantled when it is no longer required; (v) it should state (*ex ante*) what it is going to do and establish verifiable performance criteria; (vi) it should be clear and concise; (vii) it must be enforceable and (viii) it needs to be administered by accountable bodies in a fair and consistent manner. Likewise, Thomadakis (2007) argues that "good regulation must start with a clear understanding of the objective — and this necessitates a trilateral dialogue between regulators, the regulated community, and the beneficiaries of regulation". For him, "good regulation serves the public interest through supporting ongoing confidence in processes, such as the market process, in which the public participates in activities, such as auditing, on which the public relies". He also identifies some criteria for good regulation: necessity, transparency, proportionality, effectiveness and flexibility. D'Arcy (2004) suggests another list of criteria for good regulation: fair (applied equally), simple, inexpensive, enforceable, targeted and proportional.

Good financial regulation is any regulation that helps reduce the incidence of financial crises and provides consumer protection from rampant fraud and corruption in the finance industry. Because fraud and corruption contribute to the advent of financial crises, good regulation combats corruption and protects the vulnerable without imposing excessive costs on the society. Good regulation should have a positive balance in terms of costs and benefits. Bad regulation, on the other hand, can be bad because it represents capture, which may take the form of erecting barriers to maintain the competitive position of existing firms. Goldman Sachs (dubbed the "bank that rules the world") likes regulation that keeps competitors at bay. The Goldman CEO, Lloyd Blankfein, explains how higher regulatory costs are crushing competition by saying that a "more intense regulatory and technology requirements have raised the barriers to entry higher than at any other time in modern history" and that "this (banking) is an expensive business to be in, if you don't have the market share in scale". He also says that Goldman is "prepared to have this relationship with our regulators" and that "the regulators are prepared to have a deep relationship with Goldman for a long time".

It has been argued that distinguishing between good regulation and bad regulation is not an exact science, which makes it rather difficult to judge a piece of regulation as good or bad. Furchtgott-Roth (2000) writes the following on this issue:

> Chemists use precise tests to detect and identify the component elements of different substances. Physicists have methods to examine objects, both large and small. Biologists can discern much information about the basic building blocks of life from genetic material. Scientists have many techniques to answer fundamental questions about the world, but can those techniques enable them to distinguish a good government regulation from a bad one? Labeling some regulations "good" and others "bad" may seem simple, but what distinguishes one from the other?

However, two criteria can be used to determine whether a piece of regulation is good or bad, particularly financial regulation. If the objective of regulation is to combat fraud and corruption then the first criterion is its effectiveness in doing so. The second criterion is that the regulation pays off in terms of costs and benefits. Each piece of regulations has arguments for and against, so good regulation must have more arguments for than against. This is some sort of a qualitative approach to cost-benefit analysis. The following are examples of good regulation and bad regulation.

An example of good regulation is the regulation of payday loans. The arguments against this kind of regulation are typically based on the free market doctrine, while the arguments for are based on consumer protection and morality — but then morality means nothing for free marketeers. The main argument against payday loans is that since payday loan providers charge higher interest rates than mainstream financial institutions, they have the effect of depleting the assets of low-income communities. The arguments for and against payday loans amount to the free market doctrine (the so-called efficiency) versus morality, equity and the protection of the vulnerable. Arguing against the regulation of payday loans is allowing the market to erode morals. The regulation of payday loans is good regulation because it combats greed and pays off in terms of costs and benefits.

Another example of good regulation is that of insider trading. The main argument against the regulation of insider trading, which for most people is a criminal offense, is that regulation reduces market efficiency and transparency. Without regulation (more specifically, the prohibition of insider trading), insiders (a very small minority) have an unfair advantage over all other investors, as they utilize a privileged access to information that allows them to make lucrative profit. Insider trading is not desirable, not only because it is a form of corruption but also because it has other adverse effects (see, for example, Moosa, 2015a). The main issue remains that insider trading is a form of corruption whether it is based on negative or positive information — hence it should be prohibited. Other examples of good regulation include the regulation of OTC derivatives, leverage, liquidity and shadow banking.

An example of bad regulation is the regulation of short selling. Good regulation should be effective, fair, implementable, non-discriminatory and feasible in terms of costs and benefits. Regulatory measures taken against the short selling of stocks (particularly the imposition of a total or partial ban) do not satisfy any of these criteria. They are ineffective, as the empirical evidence tells us, because a market decline may be due to reasons other than short selling. A ban on naked short selling is not easily implementable or enforceable because of the practical difficulty of distinguishing between covered and naked short selling. A (selective) ban discriminates against traders with bearish views of the market, those who short stocks as opposed to other financial assets and other means of shorting, non-market makers as opposed to market makers, and the shorting of financial stocks as opposed to other stocks. In terms of costs and benefits, the regulation of short selling is not feasible because it kills the contribution of short sellers to the functioning of the stock market without achieving any tangible result.

Another example of bad regulation is that of high-frequency trading (HFT), which is problematical because the practice cannot be defined precisely. Some of the justifications for the regulation of HFT pertain to activities that are somehow classified under HFT or some malpractices that are not necessarily an integral part of HFT. Apart from that, calls for the regulation of HFT are based on the allegation that high-frequency traders make obscene profit by using state-of-the-art technology and that it caused the flash crash of 2010. The facts on the ground indicate that HFT did not cause the flash crash and that HFT is not as profitable as it is portrayed to be. The regulation of HFT is bad regulation, except when it involves fraud. One form of fraud is that an HFT trader gains access to trading information before other traders. This is as fraudulent as insider trading. Another example is when a high-frequency trader attracts funds under management by convincing potential clients that this style of trading produces extraordinary returns. These kinds of fraud should be prevented whether they are associated with high-frequency or low-frequency trading.

6. The *Status Quo*

This book is about how negligence, incompetence, complacency and fraud on the part of many players has created the mess we are in now as legislators in many countries are threatening that next time a too big to fail (TBTF) bank fails, the bosses will get their bonuses out of the confiscated deposits (the so-called bail-in). Nothing much has changed as regulators keep looking after the financial oligarchy, granting them concessions and talking about things like "ring-fencing" and "total loss absorption capacity" without any substantive measures to rein in the financial oligarchy. One exception to this state of affairs is the brave measures taken by the Icelandic government to put bankers where they belong. The Icelandic experience will be described in Chapter 10.

Chapter 2

Regulatory Issues in the Aftermath of the Crisis

1. Introduction

We have learned a number of lessons from the global financial crisis, but whether or not these lessons have been translated into appropriate regulatory actions is a different issue. The Basel Committee on Banking Supervision has responded by introducing provisions for leverage and liquidity into Basel III but these provisions are flawed. In the US the Dodd–Frank Act has been introduced but some of its provisions are inconsistent with the Basel accords (for example, the use of credit rating agencies (CRAs) scores to assign risk weights). Furthermore, the provisions are inadequate to deal with shadow banking and over-the-counter (OTC) derivatives. The introduction of the Volcker rule is a positive step in the endeavor to curb the tendency of banks to gamble with depositors' money, but it falls short of the reintroduction of the Glass–Steagall Act. The new regulatory proposals of ring-fencing and total loss absorption capacity (TLAC) are halfhearted measures which are likely to be watered down.[1] In general, the regulatory response to

---

[1] A discussion of ring-fencing and TLAC can be found in Chapter 11.

the global financial crisis leaves a lot to wish for. In the rest of this chapter we will deal with some of the lessons, the issues and what ought to be done to avoid another crisis.

2. Securitization

The term "securitization" emerged in the 1980s to refer to the tendency to raise capital by issuing bonds (securities) than by borrowing from banks. However, the term as used in conjunction with the global financial crisis refers to the process of bundling different financial assets (such as mortgages, loans and corporate bonds) together and converting them into new types of securities such as mortgage-backed securities (MBSs) and collateralized debt obligations (CDOs). These securities are essentially debt instruments that allow the holder to claim fixed payments financed by the cash flows arising from repayments on a large number of loans. An MBS, for example, might contain several 1,000 mortgages, and a CDO might contain over 100 MBSs. With time the securities became increasingly complex — for example, some CDOs were constructed out of existing ones, creating the so-called CDOs squared. When the manufacturers ran out of the real product (genuine CDOs), they resorted to the production of cheaper synthetic CDOs — composed not of real mortgage securities but of bets on other mortgage products. Overall, the whole business was, and still is, a scam. This is how Hutchinson (2008) describes the situation:

> Even the doziest mortgage broker can originate subprime mortgages for even the least creditworthy borrowers. The fact that the borrowers are incapable of making payments on the mortgage will magically be priced into the mortgage by the securitization process, which will bundle the mortgage with other mortgages originated by a similarly lax process and sell the lot to an unsuspecting German Landesbank attracted by the high initial yield. Everyone will make fees on the deal, everyone will be happy.

We have learned from the global financial crisis that securitization boosts moral hazard and allows banks to indulge in excessive risk taking. Securitization also played a major role in spreading financial risk globally because MBSs and CDOs were sold to central banks, private banks, local governments and pension funds around the world. Therefore, it makes a lot of sense to prevent, or at least put a limit on, an activity whereby unreliable streams of cash flows are converted into marketable securities. Banks like securitization also because it enables them to generate fees over and above what they earn from arranging mortgages. Presumably, the arrangement of a mortgage is a commercial banking function while securitization is an investment banking function. Banks these days, particularly since the abolition of the Glass–Steagall Act, can indulge in both of these activities, which makes mortgage underwriting and the subsequent securitization a double whammy. Vince Cable once said that "putting investment bankers in charge of high-street banks is like putting mice in charge of cheese supplies" (Cable, 2012).

Banks perform a vital function by providing credit and the means of payment, which makes them some sort of public utilities. They are supposed to serve public good, and this is why they are granted access to government guarantees, government bailouts and central bank lending. It makes sense, therefore, to argue that banks should not be permitted to indulge in securitization because it undermines the quality of underwriting. To combat moral hazard, banks should be required to hold loans until maturity as there is no legitimate reason why they should move assets off their balance sheets. This is not to say that securitization should be outlawed as banks with no access to government guarantees should be allowed to securitize if they wish, provided that they do not indulge in the con job of selling junk securities to their customers. Banks, which are still a power to be reckoned with, love securitization because it is a profitable activity but they also want government rescue when securitization leads them astray. If commercial banks are not allowed to securitize loans while investment banks are allowed to do so under scrutiny, separation between commercial and investment banking becomes inevitable. It is refreshing, therefore, to hear that regulators are talking about "ring-fencing" to shield the retail banking units of large banks from their investment banking units. However, banks are already receiving concessions on ring-fencing (see, for example, Binham and Dankley, 2015).

It is unfortunate, therefore, that securitization is coming back "from the dead", as *The Economist* (2014a) puts it. Ironically, politicians and regulators are happy about the resurrection of securitization. *The Economist* quotes Andy Haldane, an official at the Bank of England, as praising securitization, describing it as "a financing vehicle for all seasons" that should no longer be thought of as a "bogeyman". The comeback is welcomed by the European Central Bank and the Basel Committee as the rules that threaten to stifle securitization are watered down. Justification for the welcome back comes in various shapes and forms — for example, "it was the stuff that was put into the vehicles (i.e. dodgy mortgages) that was toxic, not securitization itself". This is like saying that Jack the Ripper should not be blamed for serial killing but rather the knives he used to commit murder. Furthermore, regulators argue that things have changed, and this is why they are enthusiastic about the return of securitization. For example, those involved in creating securitized products will have to retain some of the risk linked to the original loan, which means that they would abandon the underwriting practices used in the run-up to the global financial crisis. Another tightening of the rules makes it more difficult to indulge in resecuritization to produce the likes of CDO-squared.

According to *The Economist* (2014a), the biggest change is that the rating agencies are behaving themselves because they are aware of the reputational risks of messing up again.[2] The Economist believes that the revival of securitization "should be welcomed, for it is probably essential to continued economic recovery, particularly in Europe" but this welcome back banner is accompanied by a

---

[2]Behaving properly for fear of the loss of reputation is a myth, at least when applied to the CRAs. In general, this argument is not valid for a firm with a monopolistic or oligopolistic power, which is what the agencies have. This issue will be elaborated on in Chapter 8.

warning banner that says "used recklessly, though, securitization can be dangerous". The return of securitization with vengeance is yet another victory for banks and the loss of an opportunity for regulators to redeem themselves. Securitization 2.0 is unlikely to be different from securitization 1.0, because securitizers are still the same securitizers. Have bankers given us any reason to make us believe that they will behave less recklessly next time?

3. Inferior Underwriting Standards

The lack of underwriting checks opened the way to endemic fraud in the mortgage industry. In 2006, for example, there was no verification of key underwriting data in almost half of the subprime loans and the category of loans in between prime and subprime loans. At the same time, about 40% of mortgage loans were non-prime loans (Black, 2010; Faber, 2009; Zandi, 2009). The terms of subprime mortgages were conducive to large defaults when interest rates rose or the housing bubble burst. "Innovative" new mortgage products included the "liar loan" where borrowers could simply state their income without providing any evidence of it, the "piggyback loan" in which a borrower takes out two mortgages to eliminate the need for any down payment, the "teaser" loan where initial low interest rates reset to higher rates after two years which the borrower cannot afford, and "NINJA" loans made to people with no income, no job and no assets.

In 2004, the Federal Bureau of Investigation (FBI) warned of an epidemic of fraud in the mortgage industry (Frieden, 2004). When the staff of the Fitch Ratings Agency (2007) checked a small sample of non-prime loans, they found "the appearance of fraud or misrepresentation in almost every file". Mortgage lenders were estimated to have initiated fraud in about 80% of cases, primarily so that those in charge could maximize their "reported income and their executive compensation" (Black, 2009, 2010). The annual volume of subprime loans increased from $145 billion in 2001 to $625 billion in 2005, making up over 20% of total loans, with over a third of these loans being for 100% of the house value (Morris, 2009).

There was no effective response to this kind of fraudulent activity from the Fed or the Securities and Exchange Commission (SEC). The fraudulent loans were used for the purpose of securitization to produce junk securities. Had we learned anything from the savings and loan crisis and taken proper regulatory action, this scandalous enterprise would not have evolved and flourished.

The Financial Crisis Inquiry Commission (FCIC) interviewed Richard Bowen on events during his tenure as the chief underwriter for correspondent lending at Citigroup (where he was responsible for over 220 professional underwriters). In his testimony he suggested that by the final years of the US housing bubble (2006–2007), the collapse of mortgage underwriting standards was endemic. He revealed that by 2006, 60% of the mortgages purchased by Citi from some 1,600 mortgage companies (to be securitized) were "defective" (were not underwritten to rules, or did not contain all required documents) although each of these 1,600 originators was contractually responsible (certified via representations and warrantees) that its mortgage originations met Citi's standards. In another testimony to the Commission, officers of Clayton Holdings (the largest residential loan due diligence and securitization surveillance company in the US and Europe) declared that of over 900,000 mortgages issued during the period between January 2006 and June 2007, some 54% of the loans did not meet their originators' underwriting standards. The analysis showed that 28% of the sampled loans did not meet the minimal standards of any issuer. The analysis further showed that 39% of those loans (the loans that did not meet any issuer's minimal underwriting standards) were subsequently securitized and sold to investors as top-notch investment vehicles.

4. Low Interest Rates and Leverage

In late 2000, the Federal Reserve cut short-term interest rates to stimulate the economy in the aftermath of the dot-com collapse. From 2000 to 2003 the Fed took the federal funds rate from 6.5% down to 1%, creating a low interest rate environment that prevailed until mid-2004. As early as 2002, it was apparent that credit was fueling housing instead of business investment. The free cash used by consumers from home equity extraction doubled from $627 billion in 2001 to $1,428 billion in 2005 as the housing bubble built, a total of nearly $5 trillion over the period (Reuters, 2007; Seeking Alpha, 2007). US home mortgage debt relative to gross domestic product (GDP) increased from an average of 46% during the 1990s to 73% during 2008, reaching a total of $10.5 trillion (Barr, 2009). US household debt as a percentage of annual disposable personal income was 127% at the end of 2007, compared with 77% in 1990. In 1981, US private debt was 123% of GDP but by the third quarter of 2008, it was 290% (Financial Times, 2009).

In an environment of low interest rates, financial institutions (particularly hedge funds) found it tantalizing to borrow and use the borrowed funds to boost return on shareholders' equity. The Royal Bank of Scotland, for example, became the largest company in the world through debt-financed mergers and acquisitions. Low interest rates also fueled the housing bubble (and asset price bubbles in general) and encouraged subprime lending and securitization. As Morris (2009) puts it, "when money is free, and lending is costless and riskless, the rational lender will keep lending until there is no one else to lend to". By the end of 2007, Morgan Stanley and Bear Stearns had reached asset to equity ratios of 33: 1 (Crotty, 2008). Likewise, commercial banks were highly leveraged but this was not apparent because they kept a large proportion of their assets, in some cases more than half, off their balance sheets — that is, by using shadow financial institutions. Much of this leverage was attained by using complex financial instruments such as off-balance sheet securitization and derivatives, which made it difficult for creditors and regulators to monitor.

Nouriel Roubini, who is often credited as having predicted the global financial crisis, explains how easy and risky it was to develop very high levels of leverage (Roubini, 2007):

Any wealthy individual can take $1 million and go to a prime broker and leverage this amount three times; then the resulting

$4 million ($1 equity and $3 debt) can be invested in a fund of funds (an investment fund that has a portfolio of other investment funds) that will in turn leverage these $4 millions three or four times and invest them in a hedge fund; then the hedge fund will take these funds and leverage them three or four times and buy some very junior tranche of a CDO that is itself levered nine or 10 times. At the end of this credit chain, the initial $1 million of equity becomes a $100 million investment out of which $99 million is debt (leverage) and only $1 million is equity.

With a leverage ratio of 100: 1, a 1% fall in the price of the final investment wipes out the initial capital. High levels of leverage made the financial sector increasingly fragile and vulnerable to a breakdown and a systemic crisis. It seems that nothing has been learned from the failure of Long-Term Capital Management (LTCM), which was leveraged 100:1 when it collapsed in 1998. Excessive leverage symbolizes greed, bad risk management and weak regulation, but this is not to say that reasonable debt financing is not useful and beneficial.

5. Liquidity

The global financial crisis has taught us a number of lessons about the importance of liquidity. During the crisis, financial institutions came under severe pressure to maintain adequate liquidity, but they found out that liquidity risk can proliferate quickly with funding sources dissipating and concerns arising about asset valuation and capital adequacy. They also realized that an important relation exists between funding risk and market liquidity (involving the efficient conversion of assets into liquid funds at a given price). In August 2007, funding from the interbank loan and asset-backed commercial paper (ABCP) markets suddenly dried up, soon followed by a breakdown in secured money markets. Short-term funding was severely disrupted as securitization markets (particularly the market for ABCP) collapsed and interbank markets froze. In September 2007, the British banking system experienced its first bank run in over 100 years when Northern Rock, a large mortgage lending institution (previously a building society), encountered difficulties in rolling over its short-term debt as the demand for MBSs dwindled and fund providers vanished. The end result was a run on the bank and a consequent government bailout. This episode raised the question of whether Northern Rock experienced insolvency or illiquidity (or perhaps both).

Kowalik (2013) argues that "the distress in funding markets was amplified by preceding changes in the liquidity management practices of financial institutions, changes that had accelerated in the decade leading up to the crisis". These changes occurred on the assets side because financial institutions relied increasingly on securities that were liquid in good times but could become illiquid under market-wide stress. They occurred on the liabilities side because financial institutions relied increasingly on short-term money market funding, such as overnight repurchase agreements (repos), to fund long-term assets. The practice, according to Goldstein (2008), has been "just-in-time" borrowed liquidity for major players instead of an adequate reserve of own liquidity.

The debate on whether the global financial crisis was a liquidity crisis or a solvency crisis is still alive. A liquidity crisis occurs when financial institutions are solvent, in the sense that their assets are greater than their liabilities, but they are so short of cash that they cannot meet their short-term obligations (loan repayments and cash withdrawals). A solvency crisis, on the other hand, occurs when financial institutions are actually bankrupt because there is a shortfall of assets compared to liabilities (negative net worth). The difference between liquidity and solvency crises has important policy implications. If a financial institution is illiquid but solvent, the central bank may help by performing the function of a lender of last resort. If it is insolvent, the institution has to be bailed out or file for bankruptcy. Based on the Diamond–Dybvig (1983) model of bank runs, some economists suggest that the global financial crisis was a liquidity crisis. Gorton and Metrick (2010a), Lucas and Stokey (2011) and Cochrane (2013) argue that instead of people rushing to the bank to withdraw their deposits, repo customers conducted a fire sale of repo securities, curtailing the power of banks to borrow short-term funds. Liquidity does matter, which makes one wonder why the Basel rules did not cover liquidity until the destructive power of illiquidity was demonstrated during the global financial crisis.[3]

6. Deregulation and Regulatory Failure

Inadequacy of financial regulation takes three forms: (i) deregulation, lack of regulation and regulatory failure. The most prominent example of deregulation is the repeal of the Glass–Steagall Act, which was introduced in 1933 to separate commercial and investment banking. The underlying idea was that when they are allowed to indulge in investment banking operations, commercial banks may use depositors' money to make bad loans or for bailing out their insolvent investment banking affiliates. In general terms the separation is essential if bankers are to be prevented from gambling with depositors' money. Furthermore, the separation is required to avoid the conflict of interest arsing from serving two customers with different needs. For example, conflict of interest arises when a bank grants a loan to a customer on the condition that the customer uses part of the loan to participate in an initial public offering arranged by the bank for a firm. The conflict of interest arises because the bank serves the borrower by extending credit (a commercial banking function) and the issuer of securities (the firm initiating the IPO). This situation involves some sort of blackmail as the bank makes the granting of a loan conditional upon the acceptance of the customer to buy securities whether he likes it or not. Recently, the Bank of England proposed "ring-fencing" rules to separate investment banking and commercial (retail) banking. The rules, which are intended to be put in place by 2019, are being resisted by big banks with large investment banking divisions (see, for example, Binham and Dunkley, 2015).[4]

---

[3] Basel I and Basel II did not have provision for liquidity. Basel III does.

[4] More will be said about ring-fencing in Chapter 11.

Other examples of deregulation include the gradual removal of selective credit controls requiring minimum down payments and maximum periods of repayment for various types of loans and the decision taken by the Securities and Exchange Commission to relax the capital-base and leverage restrictions on large investment banks in 2004. This allowed banks to use their capital for new activities and to choose their own leverage ratios based on their own models of risk. The result was a big rise in the banks' leverage ratios and the transfer of capital to CDOs.

Parts of the financial sector have been unregulated or subject to minimal regulation. There was (and still is) virtually no regulation of the so-called "shadow banking system" consisting of non-bank financial institutions, such as bank-created special investment vehicles, private equity funds and hedge funds. Regulators have failed to supervise banks properly, to understand the poor risk management practices of private lenders, to take action against predatory lending practices on high interest payday loans and subprime mortgages, and to act on warnings of looming financial and economic mishaps. The failure of regulators and regulatory bodies can be explained, in part, by the significant degree of regulatory capture, which arises when regulators look after the interests of the institutions they are supposed to regulate. This is evident in the way senior personnel from the financial sector with anti-regulatory views and agendas came to hold top positions in key institutions, such as the Treasury and Federal Reserve. Alan Greenspan left JP Morgan Bank to become chairman of the Federal Reserve in 1987, and both Robert Rubin and Henry Paulson left Goldman Sachs to head the US Treasury under Bill Clinton and George W. Bush, respectively. Greenspan and Rubin, among other things, used their positions to prevent the regulation of the shadow banking system before returning to lucrative positions in the financial sector. According to Johnson (2009) the personal connections between the financial sector and politics "were multiplied many times over at the lower levels of the past three presidential administrations, strengthening the ties between Washington and Wall Street".

As we mentioned earlier, two members of the FCIC with dissenting voices, Peter Wallison and Arthur Burns, suggested that no significant deregulation of financial institutions occurred in the last 30 years. Specifically they contend that the repeal of the Glass–Steagall Act (which is the prime example of deregulation) had no role in the crisis. However, four major deregulatory acts were implemented in 1980, 1982, 1999 and 2000. In 1980, the Depository Institutions Deregulation and Monetary Control Act was used to phase out a number of restrictions on banks' financial practices. In October 1982, Ronald Reagan signed into law the Garn-St. Germain Depository Institutions Act, which provided for adjustable-rate mortgage loans and contributed to the savings and loan crisis. In November 1999, Bill Clinton signed into law the Gramm–Leach–Bliley Act, which repealed part of the Glass–Steagall Act of 1933. Subsequently, Clinton signed the Commodity Futures Modernization Act of 2000 that allowed the so-called "self-regulation" of the OTC derivatives market.

In a meeting held in Washington in May 2015, Brookesley Born, a former chairperson of the Commodity Futures Trading Commission (CFTC) who advocated the regulation of OTC derivatives, criticized the notion of self-regulation. In that meeting Born said that "Wall Street had poured billions of dollars into deregulation lobbying which was supported by the fallacious beliefs championed notably by Alan Greenspan that financial markets and financial firms are capable of policing themselves" (Martens and Martens, 2015). In 1999, Born lost the battle against the Greenspan–Rubin–Summers alliance, which allowed for the implementation of the Commodity Futures Modernization Act. It is therefore preposterous to suggest that no deregulatory measures were introduced in the past 30 years. However, it is not easy to believe that Wallison and Burns truly think that there has been no deregulation. More likely, what they say is rhetoric in defence of the free market ideology.

7. Predatory Lending

Predatory lending occurs when unscrupulous lenders entice borrowers to enter into loans of suspicious quality for inappropriate purposes. Typically, these loans were written into extensively detailed contracts, and swapped for more expensive loans just before closing the deal. Invariably customers took the bait. While the underlying interest rate may be advertised to be 1% or 1.5%, the effective rate (typically adjustable) would be much higher. These loans give rise to "negative amortization", which the borrower might not notice until long after the loan agreement had been signed. When house prices started to decline, holder of adjustable rate mortgages had little incentive to make their monthly payments, since their home equity had disappeared, causing the collapse of Countrywide, among other mortgage lenders.

In 2006, Countrywide financed 20% of all mortgages in the US, about 3.5% of GDP, a higher percentage than any other single mortgage lender. This is also the same company from which numerous politicians had received mortgage financing at non-competitive rates because they were FOAs — that is, "Friends of Angelo" (Countrywide's chief executive Amgelo Mozilo). The company was founded in 1968 and by 1992 it had become the largest originator of single-family mortgages in the US. Following its collapse, the company was acquired by Bank of America for $4 billion (a year earlier the company's market value was $25 billion). On the eve of the trial of Angelo Mozilo in October 2010, a statement was announced to declare that Mozilo would pay a $67.5 million penalty and accept a permanent ban from serving as an officer or director of a public company. Mozilo has been excoriated as "one of the real villains of the subprime scandal" (Osler, 2010).

8. Financial Innovation and Financial Engineering

The so-called "financial innovation" and "financial engineering" involve parasitic activities that have led to the explosive growth of financial markets. Instead of producing tools for risk management, financial engineers have been producing tools for more risk exposure, tools that can hardly be understood by anyone. In his review of Gillian Tett's book, *Fool's Gold*, Dominic Lawson (2009) tells a story about an e-mail sent by one of the inventors of complex credit derivatives to one of his colleagues. The e-mail said: "What kind of monster has been created here? It's like you've raised a cute kid who then grew up and committed a horrible crime". Lawson also argues that these derivatives were invented by JP Morgan, and this is why Morgan was much more cautious about exposure to the subprime mortgage-based instruments that brought up the demise of Merrill Lynch, Lehman Brothers and Bear Stearns.

As financial assets became more complex and harder to price, investors who were oblivious to the impending disaster were reassured by the rating agencies and regulators (who rely on these agencies) that some complex models provided by the issuers of securities predicted nothing to worry about (Norris, 2008). Commenting on this state of affairs, George Soros (2008) wrote:

> The super boom got out of hand when the new products became so complicated that the authorities could no longer calculate the risks and started relying on the risk management methods of the banks themselves. Similarly, the rating agencies relied on the information provided by the originators of synthetic products. It was a shocking abdication of responsibility.

Derivatives, the products of financial innovation and financial engineering, can bankrupt countries and destroy the lives of their citizens. Greece, for example, got itself in deep financial trouble because the Greek government was at one time persuaded by some unscrupulous bankers to use derivatives to accumulate enormous and unsustainable debt while avoiding external scrutiny. In early 2010, worries over Greece rattled world markets as its debt exceeded by far the limits imposed by the European Union. According to the *New York Times*, "instruments (some exotic swaps) developed by Goldman Sachs, JP Morgan and a wide range of other banks enabled politicians to make additional borrowing in Greece, Italy and possibly elsewhere" (Story *et al.*, 2010). In this sense, banks (with the help of financial innovation) enabled Greece to borrow beyond its means. In 2001, the Greek government paid Goldman $300 million in fees for arranging such deals. The *New York Times* states that "such derivatives, which are not openly documented or disclosed, add to the uncertainty over how deep the troubles go in Greece". In effect, Greece held a "garage sale", mortgaging airports and highways (as well as revenue from taxes on national lottery) in return for immediate cash.

Teather (2008) argues that if, as Warren Buffett believes, derivatives are "weapons of mass destruction", then Blythe Masters is "one of the destroyers of the World". Masters, according to *The Guardian*, is a member of an elite group dubbed the "JP Morgan Mafia" that invented the complex credit derivatives that lie at the heart of the global financial crisis. After the fact, Masters was unapologetic about the Frankenstein-like creation. In an exchange of e-mails with *The Guardian*, Masters blamed it on the misuse of derivatives, not on the very essence of the derivatives. With respect to credit default swaps, she said: "I do believe that credit default Swaps (CDSs) have been miscast, as much as workmen tend to blame their tools" (Teather, 2008).

One argument against the regulation of shadow banking, which in effect is no different from the underground economy, is that regulation will stifle financial innovation, because most of the innovation takes place in shadow banking away from the scrutiny of the regulators. Wallison (2012) argues that regulation amounts to buying stability at the expense of an innovative and diverse system of financing that has proven itself over the last 35 years to be far more efficient and stable than deposit banking. This is the argument of "boring banking" and innovation. Some observers think that the only way out is to go back to "boring banking" and forget about "innovation". Moosa (2015b) describes this argument as "ludicrous" because "impeding and containing financial innovation may be the right thing to do". One can only wonder what has been the contribution to human welfare of those "innovators" who invented synthetic CDOs and CDO squared, because these "inventions" serve no purpose whatsoever (apart from the generation of revenue for the inventors and their bosses). Wallison's argument is confused: if the objective of regulating shadow banking is "buying stability", this means that shadow banking is unstable whereas he argues that it is stable.

The terms "financial innovation" and "financial engineering" represent an insult to both innovation and engineering (and to innovators and engineers). Innovation is good when it serves human needs and bad when it involves some bright ideas that do not work (such as DDT, Microsoft Bob, Asbestos, the electric facial mask and the tanning bed).[5] Innovation can be useless if it is innovation for the sake of innovation. Financial innovation is worse than bad and useless because it serves one purpose only, fraud. The world will be a better place if financial engineers can be converted into mechanical, civil, electrical or chemical engineers, and if they are taken away from dealing rooms and sent to labs and factories.

9. Underpricing of Risk

As financial assets became increasingly complex and harder to value, investors were reassured of the validity of the prediction of complex mathematical models that (theoretically, of course) risk was much smaller than what it turned out to be. However, mortgage risks were underestimated by every institution in the chain from originators to investors by underweighting the possibility of falling house prices based on historical trends of the previous 50 years. Limitations of default and prepayment models, the core of pricing models, led to overvaluation of mortgage and asset-backed products and their derivatives by originators, securitizers, broker-dealers, rating agencies, insurance underwriters and investors (Samuelson, 2011; Kourlas, 2012).

A question has been raised as to whether or not the risk models used by financial institutions are any good. Dowd (2014) contends that "in the last two decades or so, there have been major problems with financial modeling, not least because faulty financial models were a big contributor to the recent financial crisis". He defines a risk model as "a computer algorithm that projects possible future financial outcomes and perhaps their

---

[5] See the World's 50 Worst Inventions http://content.time.com/time/specials/packages/completelist/0,29569,1991915,00.html.

associated probabilities". Risk models are used to manage risk, guide investment decisions, and give a sense of potential exposure to future losses. Furthermore they are used to determine capital requirements, such that if the risk model is wrong, the risk estimates can be too low, which means that the underlying bank is undercapitalized and more vulnerable to failure. Dowd (2014) views a risk model as a "black box based on calibrated data that spews out loss risk forecasts or loss projections, usually known as risk measures", then he identifies three sources of the problems associated with using models to estimate risk: (i) the black box or model itself; (ii) the model's input — that is, the data used to calibrate it and (iii) the model's output, the risk measure. Some of the problems identified by Dowd are (i) inability to identify the true loss distribution; (ii) unavailability of reliable data to calculate the probability of default, correlation and events like a housing market collapse; and (iii) inadequacy of the most common risk measure, value at risk.

A major problem with the mathematical models used by financial institutions is that they ignore history and human nature. *The Economist* (2012a) makes the same point by referring to the models used by the hedge fund LTCM in the 1990s, which predicted the impossibility of divergence between the yields on bonds issued by countries like Russia and the US, and the models (used by American International Group, Inc. (AIG) among others) that predicted the impossibility of a simultaneous collapse of house prices across the US. In both cases, it is pointed out, "financial firms quickly found themselves racking up daily losses that the computer said should occur only once in millions of years".

When it comes to the inadequacy of the models used as the basis of risk management in financial institutions, no one puts it better than Dowd (2009b) who argues that these models are based on implausible assumptions. This is what he says:

> They assume that financial risks follow Gaussian distributions (and so ignore "fat tails" which really matter); they assume that correlations are constant (and ignore the fact that correlations

tend to radicalize in crises and so destroy the portfolio diversification on which a risk management strategy might be predicted); and they make assumptions about market liquidity that break down when they are most needed.

Dowd adds that risk models are focused far too much on normal market conditions, which do not matter, at the expense of ignoring the abnormal conditions that do. Dowd *et al.* (2011a) argue that internal models offer a very shaky foundation for either capital adequacy or good risk management — one reason being that the processes governing the operations of financial markets (as social systems) are not immutable to the laws of physics. Likewise, Smith (2010) suggests that the financial models used for risk management underestimate tail risk and they are based on the implausible and dangerous assumption that correlations between different types of exposure and asset types are stable and that markets are continuous (always liquid). It remains to say that internal models are typically developed by academics who are happy to receive consultancy fees and conduct experiments on these models using other people's money, but they will never bet their superannuations on the predictions of their models. This is why Taleb (2009) calls for the marginalization of the economics and business school establishments and abolishing the Nobel Prize in economics.[6]

Dowd (2014) is also skeptical of the models used by regulators to conduct "stress tests" for the purpose of determining regulatory capital, arguing that while stress tests were intended to make the financial system safe, they have instead created a "potential for a new systemic financial crisis". Specifically, he argues that markets are not "mathematizable", which gives rise to several problems with stress testing. According to Dowd, the Fed's regulatory stress tests are problematical because they (i) ignore well-established weaknesses in risk modeling and violate the core principles of good stress testing; (ii) expose the whole financial system to the weaknesses in the Fed's models and greatly boost systemic risk;

---

[6] More will be said about the Nobel Prize in Economics in Chapter 11.

(iii) impose a huge and growing regulatory burden; (iv) are undermined by political factors; (v) fail to address the major risks identified by independent experts and (vi) fail to embody lessons to be learned from the failures of other regulatory stress tests. The solution, according to Dowd (2014), is to "establish a simple, conservative capital standard for banks based on reliable capital ratios instead of unreliable models".

10. The Shadow Banking System

There is strong evidence indicating that the riskiest, worst performing mortgages were funded through the shadow banking system and that competition from shadow banking may have pressured more traditional institutions to lower their own underwriting standards and originate riskier loans (Simkovic, 2013). Shadow banking entities are vulnerable because of maturity mismatch, meaning that they borrow short-term in liquid markets to purchase long-term, illiquid and risky assets. This means that disruptions in credit markets would make them subject to rapid deleveraging, selling their long-term assets at depressed prices. Krugman (2009) describes the run on the shadow banking system as the "core of what happened" to cause the crisis. He referred to this lack of controls as "malign neglect" and argues that regulation should have been imposed on all banking-like activity. The regulation of shadow banking is discussed in detail in Chapter 7.

11. Financialization and the Financial Oligarchy

Financialization is a process whereby the financial oligarchy gains greater influence over economic policy and economic outcomes, in the process transforming the functioning of economic systems at both the macro and micro levels. Palley (2007) identifies the following "principal impacts" of financialization: (i) elevating the significance of the financial sector relative to the real sector, (ii) transferring income from the real sector to the financial sector and (iii) aggravating income inequality and contributing to wage stagnation. Financialization, according to Palley (2007), operates through three different conduits: changes in the structure and operation of financial markets, changes in the behavior of non-financial firms, and changes in economic policy. Epstein (2001) defines financialization as the "increasing importance of financial markets, financial motives, financial institutions, and financial elites in the operation of the economy and its governing institutions, both at the national and international level".

Financial institutions are no longer, as they are supposed to be, humble intermediaries that channel funds from lenders to borrowers and from savers to investors. They have become the means for a small group of people (the financial oligarchs) to earn fat bonuses and amass huge individual fortunes by taking excessive risk with other people's money while counting on government bailouts when things go wrong. What they have been doing is a clear manifestation of "heads I win big, tails you lose it all".

Since the beginning of the 1980s, the financial sectors of most advanced countries have grown more rapidly than other sectors of the economy to grab an ever increasing share of total corporate profit although its contribution to aggregate output is small.[7] Indeed, the financial sector has become a world of its own, an entity that exists for its own sake, not for the purpose of supporting real economic activity (the production of goods and services that we need or want). It has become an end — not the means to achieve the end of lubricating economic activity by providing credit, liquidity and means of payment. The financial sector as a whole has become much larger than what can be justified on the basis of its main function of supporting real economic activity, perhaps too big for the good of the economy — or "too big for its boots", as *The Economist* (2009a) puts it and it has become the jewel in the crown of the economy. This is why some scholars use the term "financialization of the economy" (Metais, 2009).

---

[7]Some figures on the share of the financial sector in corporate profit and its contribution to GDP can be found in Chapter 6.

Morris (2009) quotes Martin Wolf of the *Financial Times* as saying that "over the very long term global financial services profits are about twice as high as those in the rest of the industry", which "runs counter to a fundamental proposition of free market economics, that profits across enterprises should even out over time". Morris attributes what he calls "the permanent advantage of financial services" to the fact that "they don't really compete in free markets". This is how he explains what he calls the "inordinate privileges of financial services":

> They (financial institutions) earn high profits because they take big risks, as evidenced by their very high degree of leverage compared to other industries. In truly free markets, however, periods of high risks and high profits are offset by periods of large losses. But in financial services, although the high profits accrue to managers and shareholders, their losses are usually partly socialized.

The finance industry, particularly in the US, has lifted itself to super stardom by creating an image, boosted by group think, that a flourishing financial sector necessarily means a flourishing economy. Politicians, including law makers and those in government, have not only embraced this image of the finance industry but also reinforced it. This is strange, given that most of what happens in the finance industry constitutes a parasitic activity. Johnson (2009) wonders whether modern finance is more like electricity or junk food. "It is more like junk food", Johnson (2009) believes. He points out that "there is growing evidence that the vast majority of what happens in and around modern financial markets is much more like junk food — little nutritional value, bad for your health, and a hard habit to kick".

The Economist (2009a) suggests that "the (finance) industry's profitability allows it to gain political influence, either through the funding of candidates or via the desire of the government to protect taxpaying businesses". Johnson (2009) points out that although the finance industry has become one of the top contributors to political campaigns, at the peak of its influence it did not have to buy favors in the same way tobacco companies or military contractors might have to. Johnson argues that the finance industry "benefited from the fact that Washington insiders already believed that large financial institutions and free-flowing capital markets were crucial to America's position in the world". Another explanation for the love affair between the US government and the finance industry is the "revolving door" between the government and the financial sector, which is what Jagdish Bhagwati (2009) calls "the Wall Street-Treasury Complex".

Palley (2007) contends that "there are reasons to believe that financialization may put the economy at risk of debt deflation and prolonged recession". For this and other reasons financialization must be controlled by (i) restoring policy control over financial markets, (ii) challenging the neoliberal economic policy paradigm encouraged by financialization, (iii) making firms responsive to the interests of stakeholders other than just financial markets and (iv) reforming the political process so as to diminish the influence of corporations and wealthy elites. Financialization is different from the Dutch disease only in as far as the economy depends on the financial sector rather than natural resources. In Chapter 10, we will see how the financialization of the Icelandic economy led to a disaster. Iceland followed the British motto of "who needs manufacturing industry when we have the City" by adopting the motto "who needs fishing when Reykjavik can be converted into an international financial centre".

12. The Failure of Corporate Governance

A major lesson to draw from the financial crisis is that corporate governance does matter. Corporate governance pertains to how firms operate, their motives and principles, their reporting lines, who they are accountable to, and how they manage profit, remuneration and, in the case of many financial firms, other people's money. The principal agent problem is at its height in financial institutions, as there is a big wedge between management and shareholders, with management having the upper hand. Shareholders have no say in executive pay although executives pay themselves out of shareholders money. This is so much worse because there is no relationship between pay and performance. As a matter of fact, some executives were rewarded handsomely for destroying shareholders values and bringing the firms they managed down to their knees. All that happened with autocratic behavior of CEOs, the "king of the mountain" mentality. It has become apparent that compensation practices played a role in promoting the accumulation of risk that led to the crisis, that boards of directors have failed to protect the rights (and wealth) of shareholders from the predatory practices of the executives motivated primarily by greed, and that shareholders are typically kept in the dark.

The FCIC emphasizes the failure of corporate governance and the consequent risk taking as a cause of the crisis. In its final report the Commission says the following (FCIC, 2011):

> We conclude dramatic failures of corporate governance and risk management at many systemically important financial institutions were a key cause of this crisis. ... Too many of these institutions acted recklessly, taking on too much risk, with too little capital, and with too much dependence on short-term funding. In many respects, this reflected a fundamental change in these institutions, particularly the large investment banks and bank holding companies, which focused their activities increasingly on risky trading activities that produced hefty profits.... Too often, risk management became risk justification. Compensation systems — designed in an environment of cheap money, intense competition, and light regulation — too often rewarded the quick deal, the short-term gain — without proper consideration of long-term consequences. Often, those systems encouraged the big bet — where the payoff on the upside could be huge and the downside limited. This was the case up and down the line — from the corporate boardroom to the mortgage broker on the street. Our examination revealed stunning instances of governance breakdowns and irresponsibility.

Dowd (2009a) blames it all on the very nature of the joint stock company and limited liability, which (according to him) is why "the buck stops with the senior management and risk management will only ever really work if senior executives have an incentive to make it work". Adam Smith recognized the short-comings in *The Wealth of Nations*, when he wrote the following (Smith, 1776):

> The directors of such companies ... being the managers of other people's money than their own, it cannot well be expected that they should watch over it with the same anxious vigilance. ... Negligence and profusion must always prevail, more or less, in the management of such a company.

The adverse effects of limited liability are recognized by Campbell and Griffin (2006) in the aftermath of the Enron scandal. This is what they write:

> One has to stretch the point to say that the executives of large public companies are exposed to the economic risks of failure in any significant way, and certainly they are more or less com-pletely cocooned from the most fundamental market pressure, fear of personal bankruptcy. By in this way distancing directors from the downside of their decisions, the public company based on incorporation and limited liability severely handicaps or even eliminates the core function of the market.

Cox (1857) went as far as arguing that limited liability deprives people of their common law right "to recover their debts, enforce their contracts, or obtain redress for injuries". Dowd (2009a) raises the question of alternatives to limited liability, an issue that it attracting attention. For example, Anderson (2006) examines the option of imposing liability on directors for creditor losses when a company is unable to pay its debts, concluding that "imposing liability on directors appears to be a superior way in which to ensure creditor protection because it not only potentially gives creditors access to funds for compensation but also deters the adverse behavior which may be a cause of loss to creditors". In general terms, Dowd (2009a) suggests that "if I take risk at your expense, then that's moral hazard and that's bad". One lesson learned in this respect is that something must be done so that the financial oligarchy will not be in a position to say "the bad news is that we have lost a lot of money, but the good news is that it is not our money".

13. The Failure of Capitalism

Some left-wing economists suggest another explanation for the global financial crisis, considering it to be a symptom of another, deeper crisis, which is a systemic crisis of capitalism itself. Batra (2011) suggests that growing inequality of financial capitalism produces speculative bubbles that burst and result in depression and major political changes. Bogle (2005a) argues that a series of unresolved challenges face capitalism that have contributed to past financial crises and have not been sufficiently addressed. He writes:

> Corporate America went astray largely because the power of managers went virtually unchecked by our gatekeepers for far too long…. They failed to 'keep an eye on these geniuses' to whom they had entrusted the responsibility of the management of America's great corporations.

Bogle raises particular issues such as "manager's capitalism", which has replaced "owners' capitalism", meaning that managers run firms for their benefit rather than the benefit of the shareholders, a variation on the principal-agent problem. He also mentions the burgeoning executive compensation and the management of earnings, mainly a focus on share price rather than the creation of genuine value. He refers to the failure of gatekeepers, including auditors, boards of directors, Wall Street analysts and career politicians.

14. The Failure of Neoclassical Financial Economics

The financial crisis was not widely predicted by mainstream economists, who believed (and still believe) in the Great Moderation and the efficient market hypothesis, both of which imply that there is nothing to worry about. The Great Moderation refers to a reduction in the volatility of business cycle fluctuations starting in the mid-1980s, believed to have been caused by institutional and structural changes that occurred in the later part of the 20th century. The efficient market hypothesis states that prices cannot diverge significantly and for a long period of time from fundamental values, which means that bubbles could not occur. Both of these principles are taken to imply "leave the market alone — it will fix everything".

Quiggin (2009) points out that "the failure of the efficient markets hypothesis will have ramifications throughout economics and finance, and will require a thorough rethinking of the analysis of financial regulation". He also talks about the Great Moderation and the other principles that have been guiding economic policy such as central bank independence, trickle-down, the case for privatization and individual retirement accounts. Spaventa (2009) explains the lack of concern for financial variables in modern macro-modeling in terms of the acceptance of the efficient market hypothesis and of neutrality theorems and the illusion that the volatility of financial markets had come to an end with the Great Moderation.

Not all economists were oblivious to the advent of the global financial crisis. Nouriel Roubini warned of a looming crisis as early as September 2006, when he declared in a meeting at the International Monetary Fund that he expected a bleak sequence of events: a housing bust, mortgage defaults, a collapsing market for MBSs, declining consumer confidence and deep recession (Mihm, 2008). The audience at the IMF meeting were skeptical, even dismissive. When Anirvan Banerji delivered his response to Roubini's talk, he noted that Roubini's predictions did not make use of mathematical models and dismissed his hunches as those of a "career naysayer". According to *The Guardian*, Roubini was ridiculed for predicting a collapse of the housing market and worldwide recession (Brockes, 2009). Robert Shiller wrote an article a year before the collapse of Lehman Brothers in which he predicted that a slowing US housing market would cause the housing bubble to burst, leading to financial collapse (Shiller, 2007). Nassim Taleb, author of *The Black Swan*, spent years warning against the breakdown of the banking system in particular and the economy in general. According to David Brooks of the *New York Times*, "Taleb not only has an explanation for what's happening, he saw it coming" (Brooks, 2008). The majority of economists did not predict the crisis because of their firm belief in neoclassical economics, which tells us that everything will be fine if the market is put in charge and that the economy adjusts very quickly to shocks. They had to believe that because their mathematical models told them that a crisis on the scale witnessed in 2008 can only happen once every few billion years.

15. Conclusion

Operational risk is the risk of losses resulting from the failure of people, processes, systems and from external events (factors). The sinking of the Titanic was a catastrophic operational loss event, resulting from the failure of people (Captain Smith, the sailors and the boss, J.B. Ismay), systems and processes (life boats and evacuation procedures) and one external factor, the iceberg. Likewise, the global financial crisis can be viewed as a catastrophic operational loss event. The failure of people (which can be triggered by ignorance, incompetence and/or fraud) encompasses, among others, those identified in Chapter 1, including the financial oligarchs, regulators, academics, investment analysts, boards of directors, fund managers, mortgage brokers, credit raters and politicians. The processes and systems that failed include, among others, securitization, underwriting standards, economic policy, regulatory policy, risk models, financialization, corporate governance, capitalism and neoclassical financial economics. The external event was the collapse of the housing market. All of these points will be dealt with in detain in the remaining chapters of this book.

Chapter 3

Financial Regulation as a Response to Corruption and Fraud

1. Introduction

Financial regulation can be justified on several grounds, one of which is the objective of maintaining financial stability. If corruption and fraud cause financial boom and bust, regulation against malpractices and fraudulent behavior in the financial sector can contribute to financial stability. Another motive for regulation in general is consumer protection — for example, doing what it takes to prevent unscrupulous entrepreneurs from selling horse meat as beef. This is fraud triggered by greed, the equivalent of which in the financial sector is selling risky junk securities as safe, investment-grade assets. Regulation can be directed at preventing the selling of horse meat as beef and junk securities as high-quality assets in terms of risk and return.

Transparency International (2015) suggests that "corruption in the banking sector has manifested itself in many scandals involving money laundering, rate rigging and tax evasion, all of which undermine the public's trust in financial institutions". Excessive risk taking with other peoples' money is fraud. As Dewatripont and Freixas (2012) put it, "it has been noted that risk taking is intrinsically involved in the business of banking and that this can lead to unethical conduct at the expense of the public interest".

Some free marketeers argue against regulation because it is easy to circumvent, choosing to overlook the fact that Bernie Madoff managed to engage in fraudulent activity on a massive scale for such a long time only because regulators turned a blind eye to what he was doing.

At the outset, it may be useful to define the terms "corruption" and "fraud", which are often used interchangeably.[1] Defining corruption is certainly not an easy task, but in general it involves the offering, giving, receiving or soliciting, directly or indirectly, of anything of value to influence improperly the actions of another party. The underlying conduct typically involves the use of improper means (such as bribes and kickbacks) by someone to induce another person to act or to refrain from acting in the exercise of his duties, in order to obtain or retain business, or to obtain an undue advantage. For example, regulatory capture is a form of corruption as the regulator acts in the best interest of the regulated firms in return for a lucrative job in the same firm when the regulator leaves public service. Gardiner (2002) argues that "if an act is harmful to the public interest, it is corrupt even if it is legal; if it is beneficial to the public, it is not corrupt even if it violates the law". A concise definition is that corruption is "an abuse of entrusted powers for private gains", where abuse is any conduct that deviates from the formal or informal rules generally accepted in society (Boehm, 2007). The entrusted powers subject to abuse may be acquired by merit or by delegation (that is, administration in the public sector, management in the private sector and election in the case of politicians).

Fraud, on the other hand, involves an action or omission (including misrepresentation) that knowingly or recklessly misleads (or attempts to mislead) a party to obtain a financial benefit or to avoid an obligation. A reckless action, omission or misrepresentation must involve reckless indifference as to whether it is true or false, but simple negligence on its own does not constitute a "fraudulent practice". We have already come across examples of

---

[1]See, for example, the definitions adopted by the World Bank http://siteresources.worldbank.org/INTDOII/Resources/INT_inside_fraud_text_090909.pdf.

financial fraud, including the selling of junk securities as investment grade assets and the practices followed by mortgage underwriters in the run-up to the global financial crisis. The question of whether or not the credit rating agencies (CRAs) committed fraud by endorsing junk securities as AAA depends on whether or not they knew the truth about the inferiority of securities, whether or not they cared as long as they got paid, and whether or not they made an honest mistake — just an opinion as they typically claim. Corruption is a broader concept that encompasses fraud.[2]

2. The History and Extent of Corruption in the Financial Sector

Corruption in the financial sector is not a new phenomenon — it is certainly not a phenomenon of the 20th or 21st century. Misconduct and criminal behavior are entrenched in the operations conducted in the financial sector. In 1721, formal investigations exposed a web of deceit, corruption and bribery that led to the prosecution of many of the major players in the crisis following the South Sea bubble of 1720, including both company and government officials. Many members of parliament took bribes in the South Sea Company stock and traded in the stock on insider information (Painter, 2006). Financial fraud goes even further back as Chakrabarty (2013) points out:

> We all know that fraud, and more so, the financial frauds have been in existence for a very long time. Some may be surprised,

---

[2]A related term is that of "white-collar crime", which refers to financially motivated non-violent crime committed by business and government professionals. The term is attributed to Edwin Sutherland who defined the term as "a crime committed by a person of respectability and high social status in the course of his occupation" (see, for example, Sutherland, 1949). Typical white-collar crimes include fraud, bribery, Ponzi schemes, insider trading, embezzlement, cybercrime, copyright infringement, money laundering, identity theft and forgery. The Federal Bureau of Investigation (FBI) defines white-collar crime simply as "lying, cheating and stealing" (https://www.fbi.gov/about-us/investigate/white_collar).

but, it is interesting to note that Kautilya, in his famous treatise "Arthashastra" penned down around 300 BC, painted a very graphic detail of what we, in modern times, term as "fraud". Kautilya describes 40 ways of embezzlement, some of which are: "what is realized earlier is entered later on; what is realized later is entered earlier; what ought to be realized is not realized; what is hard to realize is shown as realized; what is collected is shown as not collected; what has not been collected is shown as collected; what is collected in part is entered as collected in full; what is collected in full is entered as collected in part; what is collected is of one sort, while what is entered is of another sort". As you would all agree, some of the above actions continue to be the modus operandi adopted in many instances of financial fraud that have hit the headlines in recent times.

The Basel Committee on Banking Supervision (BCBS) identifies two kinds of fraud in banking: internal fraud and external fraud (see, for example, Moosa, 2007). Internal fraud is committed by insiders (such as employees), including account takeover and impersonation, forgery, credit fraud, extortion, embezzlement, and unauthorized and unreported transactions. External fraud, on the other hand, is committed by outsiders, including computer hacking, forgery and theft (including theft of information). This is not what we are concerned with here — rather, we are concerned with the fraud committed by the financial oligarchy against their clients, the government and the community at large. The fraud committed by insiders and outsiders against financial institutions is a drop in the ocean compared to the fraud committed by financial institutions against the community. In committing fraud, the financial oligarchy is armed with "creative" accounting, financial "innovation", computer models and a diversified set of gimmicks and marketing tricks.

The extent of corruption on Wall Street is best described by Snyder (2010) as follows:

If you ask most Americans, they will agree that the financial system is corrupt. It is generally assumed that just like most politicians, most big bankers are corrupt by nature. The truth is that the vast majority of Americans have no idea just how corrupt the US financial system has become. The corruption on Wall Street has become so deep and so vast that it is hard to even find the words to describe it. It seems that the major financial players will try just about anything these days — as long as they think they can get away with it but in the process they are contributing to the destruction of the greatest economic machine that the planet has ever seen.

Some observers go further than Snyder. An anonymous reader of *The Economist* posted a comment on the magazine's website where he said the following: "Yes, Wall Street is essentially criminal — a large criminal enterprise which works in close partnership with that other large criminal enterprise — America's elected legislatures".[3] Kaufman (2009) describes as a myth that "corruption is a challenge mainly for public officials in developing countries and that it is unrelated to the current global crisis". He argues strongly that "corruption is not unique to developing countries, nor has it declined on average".[4] The difference may be trivial: in a developing country a corrupt official may be paid for his services by receiving an envelope full of cash; in a developed country, the payment is more subtle — for example, the promise of a lucrative job in the future.

Corruption is more rampant in the financial sector than in other sectors of the economy, because the commodity traded in the financial sector is money, which makes it more tantalizing to commit fraud. Moreover, fraud in the financial sector can be very difficult to detect, given that "financial innovation" has created so much complexity that, together with the so-called "creative accounting", makes the detection of fraud a difficult task. Hutton (2010) argues that London and New York have become the center of an

---

[3] http://www.economist.com/node/21600090/comments.

[4] Some developing countries, such as Chile and Botswana, exhibit lower levels of corruption than some fully industrialized countries. And countries like Colombia and Liberia have made gains in recent years.

international financial system in which the purpose of banking is to make money out of money — and where the complexity of the "innovation" allows extensive fraud and deception. It is also the case that the financial oligarchy is so powerful and intertwined with the government that those committing fraud are rarely brought to justice. Typically a financial institution caught in action is given a fine and perhaps a slap on the wrist but even a hefty fine is affordable for financial institutions that can easily retrieve the amount by passing on the cost to customers through fees and commissions and by committing even more fraud. Black (2005) makes the interesting remark that "one of the great advantages that white-collar criminals have over blue-collar criminals is "the ability to use top lawyers even before criminal investigations begin".[5]

The finance literature deals extensively with incentives to commit fraud and when fraud is most likely to occur. Bebchuk and Bar-Gill (2002) present a model in which firms may commit fraud to obtain better terms when they issue shares to raise funds to finance further investments.[6] Goldman and Slezak (2006) present a model in which optimal managerial pay-for-performance contracts balance incentives to exert effort against incentives to commit fraud. Subrahmanyam (2005) presents a model in which more intelligent managers are better both at running firms and at committing successful (undetected) fraud. Noe (2003) analyzes situations when managers effectively steal value from their firms.

However, reality is more powerful than the analysis of fraud presented in published papers. The 2014 *Global Fraud Study*, conducted by the Association of Certified Fraud Examiners, reveals that the Australian financial sector experienced a greater number of fraud incidents than any other sector (ACFE, 2014). Fraud includes scandals perpetrated by financial planners, mortgage

---

[5] The US hosts 25% of the world's prison population. Black men jailed for petty crimes are over-represented while people convicted for white-collar crimes are extremely under-represented.

[6] The incentive to commit fraud intensifies if managers can sell some of their own shares in the short run or if accounting and legal rules are lax.

fraud, insider trading and kickbacks. Jones (2015) argues that "the Australian banking sector is dominated by corrupt organizations that also run banks on the side, supported by a craven, supplicant media and political establishment".[7] Strubel (2014) describes the financial sector as the "greatest parasite in human history". Drum (2012) thinks that fraud in the financial sector is getting worse, suggesting that one reason why "the financial sector is still trading at less than book value" is that "the number investors who trust the banks is now zero". Kaufman (2009) suggests that the study of corruption ought to include acts that may be legal in a strict narrow sense but where the rules of the game have been bent, arguing that this broader view of corruption would make the scale of fraud in the financial sector even greater than what it appears to be. The situation is succinctly described by Schechter (2010) who suggests that "the 'F Word' (for fraud) is back in polite conversation on Wall Street" and that "fraud and financial crime are slowly becoming part of the debate over what must be done to restore confidence in what has so plainly been a confidence game".

One tends to think that financial institutions would be more reluctant to commit fraud in the post-crisis era. Unfortunately, this is only wishful thinking because the financial oligarchs are back in business as usual. Post-2008 scandals have erupted, involving the manipulation of interest rates (LIBOR) and the rigging of commodity and foreign exchange markets. In a conference on finance and society held in May 2015, Brooksley Born declared that the dangers of fraud have only grown since the collapse (Martens and Martens, 2015). She said the following:

> The power and influence of the financial sector threatens a continuation of the regulatory capture that contributed to the

---

[7] So, it is not only the Wall Street firms that make money by committing fraud. But surely Wall Street and the City of London provide a role model in this respect. Morck (2005) argues that London and New York share "a strong tradition of economic and political liberalism, a fertile ground for belief in the self-regulation of business and finance, as well as corporate governance and accounting standards geared towards business owners rather than other stakeholders".

financial crisis. Financial firms, too often, have significant say in the appointment of high regulatory officials. The tendency of some former government officials to obtain highly lucrative positions in the financial sector after leaving government may well act as an inducement to those remaining in government to serve the interest of the financial sector rather than those of the public.

She reminded the audience that since the enactment of the Dodd–Frank financial reform legislation, the US has witnessed more frauds, manipulations and reckless behavior on the part of the very same financial firms.

3. Moral Hazard and Greed

Corruption is linked to moral hazard, a term that is frequently used in the finance literature. Dowd (2009a) describes moral hazard as a situation where one party is responsible for the interests of another, but has an incentive to put his or her interests first. As examples, Dowd refers to situations where someone sells a financial product (such as a mortgage) to a person while knowing that it is not in his (the buyer's) interest. Another example is a business executive paying himself a big bonus in return for managing shareholders' funds. The same executive may take risks that the shareholders have to bear.

Peston (2008) describes as a "greed game" the arrangement between the partners of equity and hedge funds and their clients. This situation is what Dowd (2009a) calls "subsidized risk taking: heads I win, tails you lose". A typical arrangement between the partners and their clients involves a compensation scheme whereby the partners would receive 20% of the gains (plus a 2% annual management charge). Any losses, however, will be borne by the clients and by them alone. This is a clear case of moral hazard that leads to excessive risk taking and significant leverage. If the market is booming and the fund generates $500 million in gains, the partners will receive $110 million, including $10 million in management fees. If there was a loss of $500 million — well, the partners lose nothing. Peston (2008) writes the following:

Structured finance was revolutionary financial technology for transforming poor quality loans into high-quality investments. There was an epidemic of Nelsonian Eye Syndrome on Wall Street and London. Bankers, private equity partners and hedge fund partners acknowledge — or at least some do — that the cause was good, old-fashioned greed induced by a turbocharged remuneration system that promised riches in return for minimal personal risk.

The clients accept this kind of rip-off when they see a good track record, and a good track record can be obtained with excessive leverage in a bull market. What makes things even worse, according to Dowd (2009a), is that "this absence of any deferred compensation gives fund managers an incentive to focus only on the period to the next bonus". In the case of a loss, the attitude of the fund managers is as follows: "the bad news is that we have lost a lot of money; the good news is that it is not our money". Dowd argues that the absence of deferred remuneration institutionalizes short-termism and undermines the incentive to take a more responsible longer-term view. Wolf (2008a) describes this situation by suggesting that no other industry but finance "has a comparable talent for privatizing gains and socializing losses". Dowd describes this kind of corruption as follows:

> Instead of "creating value", as we were repeatedly assured, the practices of financial engineering (including structured finance and alternative risk transfer), huge leverage, aggressive accounting and dodgy credit rating have enabled their practitioners to extract value on a massive scale — while being unconstrained by risk management, corporate governance and financial regulation.

The "talent" argument is typically used as a justification for ripping off clients and shareholders. One talented practitioner was Bernie Madoff, who ended up taking not only the agreed upon fess and bonuses but the whole lot while the clients lost the whole lot. Taleb (2009) makes an interesting remark by saying "do not let someone making an incentive bonus manage a nuclear plant — or your financial risk" because "odds are he would cut every corner on safety to show profits while claiming to be conservative".

Because of the corruption involved in the money "mismanagement" business, Partnoy (2010) recommends a return to 50 years ago when 97% of individual investors invested in the stock market directly without going through mutual funds. He argues that investors are better off with a passive approach, such as investing in an index, because returns are not obtained by trading too much and by trying to pick stocks. Investing in an index is a simple buy and hold of a diversified portfolio. He also argues that mutual funds have proven disastrous for investors, simply because fund managers trade too much or try to pick stocks. Even funds that are advertized as index funds are really actively managed funds in disguise. According to Partnoy (2010) "the vast majority of actively traded mutual funds have underperformed market indexes, because of their high costs and relatively low comparative advantage".[8] Taleb (2009) shares the sentiment as he argues that "citizens should not depend on financial assets or fallible 'expert' advice for their retirement" and that "economic life should be definancialized". He further argues that we should learn not to use markets as storehouses of value because they do not harbor the certainties that normal citizens require" and that "citizens should experience anxiety about their own businesses (which they control), not their investments (which they do not control)".

People, including retirees, with funds under management are ripped off through an extensive menu of fees: termination fees, investment switching fees, annuity fess, low account preservation

---

[8] This should not be taken as an endorsement of the efficient market hypothesis. The average investor is better off with the index because she saves on management fees, circumvents the potential problems of incompetence and moral hazard on the part of the fund manager, and avoids the effects of firm-specific information and unfair competition from insider traders. There is also the benefit of diversification associated with trading the index. But for someone like Warren Buffet, whose performance provides evidence against the EMH, investment in an index does not pay off.

fess, issuer fees, establishment fees, performance fees, buy and sell fees, expense recovery fess, insurance fees, administration fees and advisory service fees. This is why John Bogle, an opponent of active trading, argues that "the financial services sector as a whole is chasing short-term gains and in the process saddling investors with the costs of higher trading volumes and often not acting in their best interest" (Corbin, 2014). Bogle (2013) writes the following about active fund managers:

> They are offended by the idea that if you pay less for investment management, you receive a larger share of stock market returns. Managers believe that they can, by dint of intelligence, street smarts, strategy, stock selection, etc., add value that will exceed the total management fees, portfolio turnover costs, and sales commissions that their investors pay.

Bogle's case against active trading is not based on the efficient market hypothesis but rather on what he calls the "cost matters hypothesis". Bogle (2014a) identifies three factors that influence a fund's "all-in" costs, including (i) cash drag; (ii) portfolio turnover and (iii) fees for brokers, advisors and sales loads. He demonstrates that the costs associated with an index fund are lower by 2.21% compared with an actively managed fund. This is why he calls for less trading and higher fiduciary bar.

Let us once more ask the question why investors take the bait and pay exuberant fees, despite the logic of "those who know do not tell and those who tell do not know". *The Economist* (2015a) presents an explanation based on the misuse of statistics. Investors may be lured by investment advisors by the following strategy:

> Each week you will receive a share recommendation from a fund manager, telling you whether the stock's price will rise or fall over the next week. After 10 weeks, if all the recommendations are proved right, then you should be more than willing to hand over your money for investment. After all, there will be just a one in a thousand chance that the result is down to luck. Alas, this is a well-known scam. The promoter sends out 100,000 e-mails,

picking a stock at random. Half the recipients are told that the stock will rise; half that it will fall. After the first week, the 50,000 who received the successful recommendation will get a second e-mail; those that received the wrong information will be dropped from the list and so on for 10 weeks. At the end of the period, just by the law of averages, there should be 98 punters convinced of the manager's genius and ready to entrust their savings.

This line of reasoning is based on a paper by Harvey and Liu (2014) who reach the conclusion that "most of the empirical research in finance, whether published in academic journals or put into production as an active trading strategy by an investment manager, is likely false", which implies that "half the financial products (promising out performance) that companies are selling to clients are false". *The Economist* (2015a) concludes that clients of the investment industry "need to be much more sceptical about the brilliant trading strategies that fund managers try to sell them".

4. Corruption as a Cause of Financial Crises

Corruption is a cause of financial instability and crises. The results of a 1986 Federal Deposit Insurance Corporation (FDIC) survey show that criminal misconduct by insiders was a major contributing factor in 45% of bank failures (Sprague, 1986). The last three major crises (the savings and loan crisis, the subprime crisis and the global financial crisis) were caused predominantly by greed driven fraud and corruption. This is not to say that there was a single cause for the global financial crisis but the facts on the ground imply that corruption must come on top.

Crises involve booms followed by busts, in which corruption plays a role. It has been found that booms encourage and conceals financial fraud, which is exposed by the subsequent busts. Povel *et al.* (2007) argue that firms commit fraud by altering publicly reported information to be more favorable, that fraud is most likely to occur in relatively good times, and that the link between fraud and good times becomes stronger as monitoring costs decline.

They provide an explanation for why fraud peaks toward the end of a boom and is then revealed in the subsequent bust. In fact, some observers suggest that fraud played a role in the 1929 crisis and the Great Depression. In this section, we discuss how corruption and fraud played a role in these crises.

4.1. The 1929 crisis

In the 1930s, the Senate Banking Committee, led by its Chief Counsel Ferdinand Pecora, reached the conclusion that fraud and corruption led to the crash of 1929 and the subsequent Great Depression (Kuttner, 2011). The Committee's findings helped change the political mood and laid the foundation for the sweeping financial reforms of Roosevelt's New Deal. Roosevelt depended on Pecora's work to build public support for regulation and appointed him to the newly created Securities and Exchange Commission.

The original Pecora investigation established that conflicts of interest and fraud were common among elite finance and government officials and that the financial sector and its political allies were corrupt. Nothing much has changed since — in fact, the similarities between what happened in the 1920s and the recent crisis are obvious. In the introduction to his father's (John Kenneth Galbraith) study of the Great Depression (*The Great Crash*, 1929), James Galbraith wrote the following (Galbraith, 2009):

> The main relevance of *The Great Crash*, 1929 to the great crisis of 2008 is surely here. In both cases, the government knew what it should do. Both times, it declined to do it. In the summer of 1929 a few stern words from on high, a rise in the discount rate, a tough investigation into the pyramid schemes of the day, and the house of cards on Wall Street would have tumbled before its fall destroyed the whole economy. In 2004, the FBI warned publicly of "an epidemic of mortgage fraud" but the government did nothing, and less than nothing, delivering instead low interest rates, deregulation and clear signals that laws would not be enforced. The signals were not subtle: on one occasion the

director of the Office of Thrift Supervision came to a conference with copies of the Federal Register and a chainsaw. There followed every manner of scheme to fleece the unsuspecting.

Corruption that led to the crash of 1929 took many shapes and forms, most notably insider trading. Robert Shiller, for example, argues that "the scandal in which it has come to light that the biggest banks have routinely mishandled homeownership documents, putting the legality of foreclosures and related sales in doubt — is a replay of the 1930s, when Americans lost faith that institutions such as business and government were dealing fairly" (Washington's Blog, 2010). Another form was the use of depositors' money for speculative purposes, which led to the implementation of the Glass–Steagall Act. The Congressional Research Service notes the following (Washington's Blog, 2009):

> In the Great Depression after 1929, Congress examined the mixing of the "commercial" and "investment" banking industries that occurred in the 1920s. Hearings revealed conflicts of interest and fraud in some banking institutions' securities activities. A formidable barrier to the mixing of these activities was then set up by the Glass–Steagall Act.

4.2. The savings and loan crisis

In his book, *The Best Way to Rob a Bank is to Own One*, William Black describes in detail the complex network of collusion between bankers, regulators and legislators that brought about the savings and loan crisis of the 1980s (Black, 2005). Black obtained an insider's knowledge of many details not generally known because he was a lawyer working for the Federal Home Loan Bank Board during the presidency of the big deregulator, Ronald Reagan. In his book, Black identifies the villains as Charles Keating of Lincoln Savings, the king of junk bonds, Michael Milken and former speaker of the House Jim Wright (who was subsequently forced to resign in disgrace). The fraud was enabled by accounting conventions whose fraud friendly rules helped hide the true extent of the collapse for a long period. The episode involves a Ponzi scheme that was in operation as bad banks were allowed to buy other banks, using phantom capital.

Ironically, it was a Reagan appointee and a deregulation advocate, Edwin Gray, who ultimately revealed and stopped the fraud. Gray was an enthusiastic deregulator until he saw the consequences in the form of Ponzi schemes, real estate bubbles, and derelict construction projects. Black believes that Gray's reregulation agenda averted a national real estate bubble and saved the taxpayer an enormous amount of money. He explains why and how the Reagan administration and Congress covered up the depth of the savings and loan insolvency and why the conventional wisdom about the crisis is fallacious, when lessons could have been learned that might have prevented the global financial crisis. He also explains why private market discipline does not prevent widespread fraud of this type (again, self-regulation does not work).

Black (2005) argues that without the regulatory response, and despite the interference that tempered the response, the systemic risk generated by fraud would have spread through the economy and a global debacle similar to the global financial crisis might have materialized. In the aftermath of the savings and loan crisis he thought that US regulators had learned a lesson and would vigorously enforce anti-fraud regulation, but that did not happen as crises with similar causes occurred subsequently. He suggests that regulators failed in their responsibility to protect the public from fraud. Calavita *et al.* (1997) compare the actions of the principals involved in the crisis to organized crime. They also argue that fraud was a significant factor in the crisis to the extent that it was present in the majority of institutions that went bankrupt. Francis (2010) argues that the crisis provided a model of the use of bank loans for fraud.

Gray was not reappointed on the expiry of his term — rather he was replaced by Danny Wall who had no experience in supervision and believed that the financial institutions involved in the crisis could grow out of their solvency problem and worked to delay regulatory intervention, hoping (as any free marketeers would) that the market would sort things out. Despite the prosecution of some of the most high-profile operators of insolvent institutions, Calavita *et al.* (1997) express concern that revisionist economics has de-emphasized the role of fraud, instead blaming the economic environment, poor regulation and poor (but not intentionally fraudulent) management. They provide statistics to support their claim that fraud was a major, if not the major, factor in the savings and loan crisis, concluding that "corrupting government by influencing the legislative and regulatory process was an integral part of the fraud". Both Calavita *et al.* (1997) and Black (2005) warn that failure to regulate against fraud creates an environment that is conducive to the materialization of fraud.

It must be mentioned here that the expression "the best way to rob a bank is to own one" was popularized by William Crawford, the California savings and loan commissioner who testified before Congress on the savings and loan crisis on 13 June 1987. In his testimony, he said the following (House Committee on Government Operations, 1988):

> We build thick walls, we have cameras, we have time clocks on the vaults; we have dual control — all these controls were to protect against somebody stealing the cash. Well, you can steal far more money, and take it out the back door. The best way to rob a bank is to own one.

Obviously this statement is not only associated with the S&L crisis, but it represents a general description of the state of affairs in the financial sector. It also shows that owning a bank and robbing it is a much better strategy in terms of risk and return than digging a tunnel to reach the vault.

4.3. The subprime crisis

During the subprime crisis, which Dowd (2009a) describes as a "giant Ponzi scheme", fraud took the form of undermining underwriting standards by fraudulent means, and this is why Stiglitz (2010) describes the "wheelings and dealings of the mortgage industry" as "the great scam of the early 21st century". This is what Das (2006) says about the rip-off:

> Dealers began seeking new ways to improve profitability and started marketing structured products directly to retail customers, the widows and orphans of legend … Structured product marketers set out into suburbs and strip malls. The logic was compelling — you had less sophisticated clients, the margins would be richer. In short, you could rip them off blind.

First-person evidence of mortgage related fraud is supplied by Richard Bitner, who was a subprime lender for five years during the heyday of subprime lending (Bitner, 2008). He sold his share in a mortgage business in 2005 when he noticed a marked deterioration in the quality of loans. As he was leaving the subprime lending business he noticed that about 70% of mortgage applications contained some misrepresentation (hence, fraud). In his book, Bitner describes the deceptive tactics brokers used to get loans approved and the methods used by brokers and mortgage banks to subvert conventional underwriting criteria. On 1 November 2008, a *New York Times* reporter, Gretchen Morgenson, told a story of a senior underwriter at Washington Mutual who at the height of the bubble was pressured to approve loans that she thought were flawed, and in some cases fraudulent (Morgenson, 2008). Levin (2010) observes that two of WaMu's "most prolific and highly praised underwriters" were found by an internal audit to have violated the company's underwriting standards and that they "had an extremely high incidence of confirmed fraud". Finally, an audit performed by Fitch on a sample of subprime loans revealed fraud in the overwhelming majority, including 16% where identity fraud was indicated (Francis, 2010).

4.4. The global financial crisis

Corruption is perceived as a cause of the global financial crisis just as it was a cause of its prelude, the subprime crisis. Rakoff (2014) reaches the conclusion that "in the aftermath of the financial crisis, the prevailing view of many government officials was that the crisis was in material respects the product of intentional fraud". In 2010, William Black gave an interview to the Real News Network, providing his perspective on the global financial crisis, which he sees as being eerily similar to previous collapses.[9] In the interview, Black explained how the crisis resulted from fraudulent schemes orchestrated by top people on Wall Street, with the simple aim of enriching themselves. In an internet survey conducted by Francis (2010), the participants were asked to rank the importance of fraud in the global financial crisis on a scale from 1 to 10, with 1 being the highest — the average score was 3.5. According to Hutton (2010), the global financial crisis was caused "not just by the bankers' colossal mismanagement" but it was also due to "the new financial complexity offering up the opportunity for widespread, systemic fraud". Fraud did not only involve mortgage lending and mortgage lenders. Hutton (2010) argues that financial complexity was used to deceive borrowers and investors in a scheme that also involved the so-called "independent experts"(such as lawyers, accountants, rating agencies and portfolio managers) to validate the deception.

In its final report on the crisis, the FCIC (2011) uses variants of the word "fraud" over 150 times to describe what led to the crisis". One of the conclusions reached by the Commission is that "there was a systemic breakdown in accountability and ethics". This is what the Commission had to say:

> We witnessed an erosion of standards of responsibility and ethics that exacerbated the financial crisis. This was not universal, but these breaches stretched from the ground level to the corporate suites. They resulted not only in significant financial consequences but also in damage to the trust of investors, businesses, and the public in the financial system.

---

[9] http://therealnews.com/t2/index.php?option=com_content&task=view&id=31 &Itemid=74&jumival=4937. The title of the interview was "To Rob a Country, Own a Bank".

Appelbaum (2015) suggests that the crisis was caused in part by fraud, particularly mortgage fraud, which took the form of overstating the borrower's income to obtain a larger loan. While this may sound as if financial institutions are the victims of fraud, Applebaum argues that "it is far-fetched to think that most borrowers would have known what lies to tell, or who, without inside help". He quotes James Vanasek, the chief risk officer at Washington Mutual from 1999 to 2005, as saying that "some fraud was clearly collaborative" in the sense that "brokers and borrowers worked together to game the system". Vanasek adds that "at times borrowers were coached to fill out applications with overstated incomes or net worth to meet the minimum underwriting requirements". Applebaum declares that "some of America's largest lenders, including Countrywide, Wells Fargo and Ameriquest, overstated the incomes of borrowers — without telling them — to qualify them for larger loans than they could afford".

Wray (2011) puts a very strong case for the role of fraud in the global financial crisis, which he characterizes as a solvency rather than liquidity crisis. However, he recognizes a run on liquidity, which he describes as a "refusal to refinance one's fellow crooks", adding that "criminal enterprise always relies on trust, and when that breaks down, war breaks out". He refers to a small time bank robber, Willy Sutton, who responded to the question why he robbed banks by saying "because that's where the money is". Wray describes the global financial crisis as "the biggest scandal in human history" but then he qualifies his statement. This is what he says:

> It is apparent that fraud became normal business practice. I have compared the home finance food chain to Shrek's onion: every layer was not only complex, but also fraudulent, from the real estate agents to the appraisers and mortgage brokers who overpriced the property and induced borrowers into terms they could not afford, to the investment banks and their subsidiary trusts that securitized the mortgages, to the credit ratings agencies and accounting firms that validated values and practices, to the servicers and judges who allow banks to steal homes, and on to

Chief executive officers (CEOs) and lawyers who signed off on the fraud. To say that this is the biggest scandal in human history is an understatement and the fraudsters are still running the institutions.

Mortgage fraud was not the only form of corruption that led to the eruption of the global financial crisis as fraud took many shapes and forms. Investors were led to believe that mortgage-backed securities (MBSs) were high quality assets. Financial institutions collected commissions from collaterized debt obligations (CDOs), then from CDO squared based on the original CDOs. A particular insurance company sold billions of dollars worth of insurance policies against default without having the money to meet claims. Investors were persuaded to buy junk securities by an institution that knew with a high degree of confidence that these securities would lose value over night, then took a bet on the collapse. Does anyone not agree that this is the biggest scandal in human history?

5. Regulatory Capture as a Form of Corruption

One form (perhaps the worst and most damaging form) of corruption is regulatory capture. Baxter (2011) presents a working definition of capture as follows: "regulatory capture (is) present whenever a particular sector of the industry, subject to the regulatory regime, has acquired persistent influence disproportionate to the balance of interests envisaged when the regulatory system was established". George Stigler once said the following: "… as a rule, regulation is acquired by the industry and is designed and operated primarily for its benefits" (Stigler, 1971). Regulatory capture is not readily observable and any action motivated by capture can be justified otherwise, which makes it "one neglected dimension of political corruption"as described by Kaufman (2009).[10] Capture occurs

---

[10] For example, bailing out a failed financial institution may be justified in terms of fear of a systemic collapse. Another example is that erecting barriers to preserve the oligopolistic position of the CRAs may be justified in terms of the desire to maintain the quality of ratings.

when powerful companies (or individuals) bend the rules for their private benefit by using high-level bribery, lobbying or influence peddling. Banks and major financial institutions fit this description more than other firms. Green and Nader (1973) suggest that capture is enhanced by the exchange of personnel, arguing that "a kind of regular personnel interchange between (regulatory) agency and industry blurs what should be a sharp line between regulator and regulatee, and can compromise independent regulatory judgment". Baxter (2011) emphasizes the "revolving door" as follows:

> As both our need for expert regulators and the skill of regulators increase, the doors between regulators and the industry will spin faster. If we are to engage in technical regulation at all, this is not only unavoidable, but sometimes even desirable. Revolving doors are also dangerous: many current examples vividly highlight the unseemly appearance, if not reality, of an incestuous relationship between regulators and industry that must surely risk fostering an improper influence of industry over the regulators.

This again is more valid for financial institutions than other firms — no more so than Goldman Sachs. In Figure 3.1, we see a list of names of some of those who worked for Goldman Sachs and assumed public office, in many cases as regulators. Ironically, perhaps, most of these individuals assumed public office in the Obama administration.[11]

Regulatory capture played a big role in the advent of the global financial crisis. According to Kaufman (2009), capture was the main reason for the systemic failure of oversight, regulation and disclosure in the financial sector. To support his argument, Kaufman lists just a few examples of how regulatory capture contributed to the eruption of the crisis:

- Freddie Mac and Fannie Mae spent millions of dollars lobbying some influential members of Congress in exchange for, among other things, lax capital and reserve requirements.

---

[11] Details and comments are available on http://www.softpanorama.org/Skeptics/ Financial_skeptic/Casino_capitalism/Systemic_instability_of_financial_sector/ TBTF/Goldman_Sachs/index.shtml.

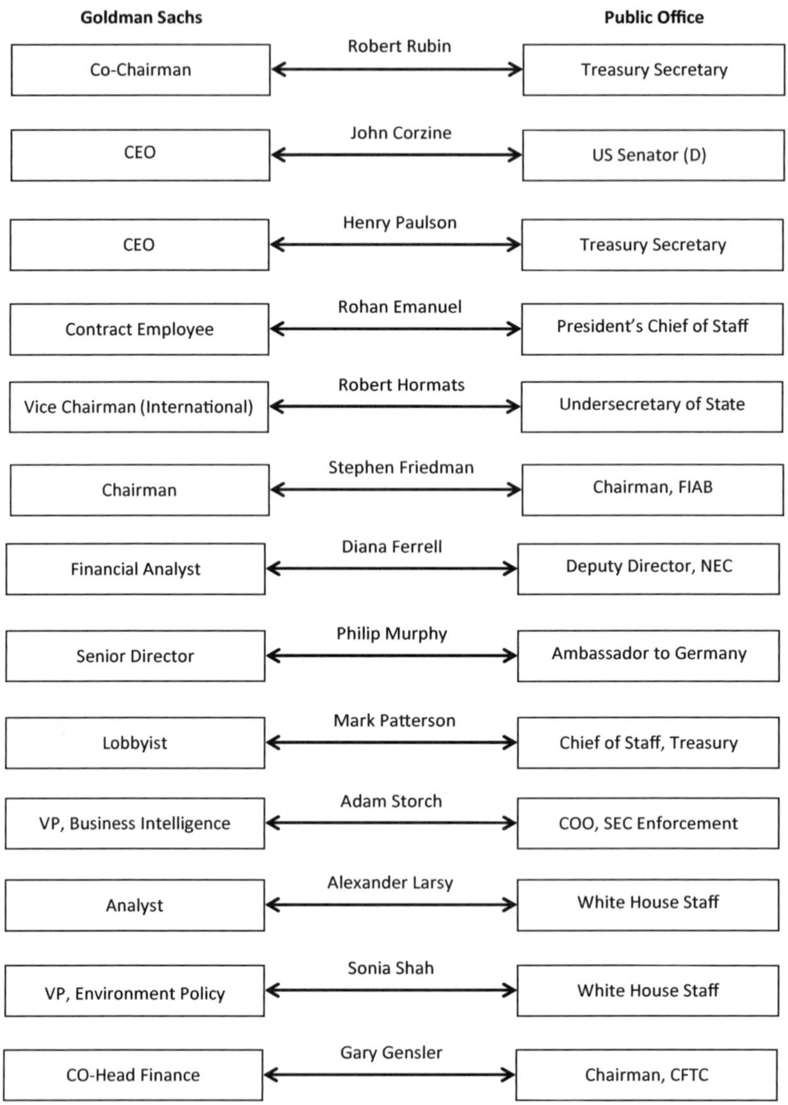

Figure 3.1: **The Revolving Door: From Goldman to Public Office and Vice Versa**

- Capture-driven lax regulatory oversight allowed a small unit of American International Group, Inc. (AIG) to obscure its accounts and take inordinate risks that effectively brought down AIG's empire of 100,000 employees in 130 countries. Despite the damage inflicted by AIG, regulators decided to finance its bailout.
- Giant mortgage lenders such as Countrywide Financial switched regulators in order to fall under the lax oversight of the Office of Thrift Supervision, which was funded by fees paid by regulated banks (and which also supervised AIG's derivative unit).
- During a 55 minute long meeting held in April 2004 at the Securities and Exchange Commission (SEC), the largest investment banks persuaded the SEC to relax its regulatory stance and allow them to take on much larger amounts of debt.
- For a long time the SEC knew that Bernie Madoff, who had served on the Commission's own advisory committee, was involved in multiple violations and was misleading it by misrepresenting how he managed his customers' funds. Yet the SEC chose to fail in unmasking the Ponzi scheme. We have in this case a star fraudster advising a regulatory body on matters that include financial fraud.

Furthermore, regulatory capture is the cause of what Johnson and Boone (2010) call the "doomsday cycle", which is illustrated in Figure 3.2. The implicit and explicit subsidies granted to financial institutions deemed too big to fail (TBTF) or systemically important financial institutions (SIFIs) encourages excessive risk taking and moral hazard, which would eventually result in loss-making bets. Regulation is imposed to discourage excessive risk taking, but the regulators are captured by loss-making financial institutions. When those institutions fail, the regulators come to the rescue through bailout (stealing taxpayers money), bail-in (stealing depositors money), or/and quantitative easing (printing money and giving it away at zero interest rate). These are the subsidies that encourage excessive risk taking — and so the process repeats itself for the benefit of the financial oligarchy at the expense of taxpayers, depositors and the middle class at large.

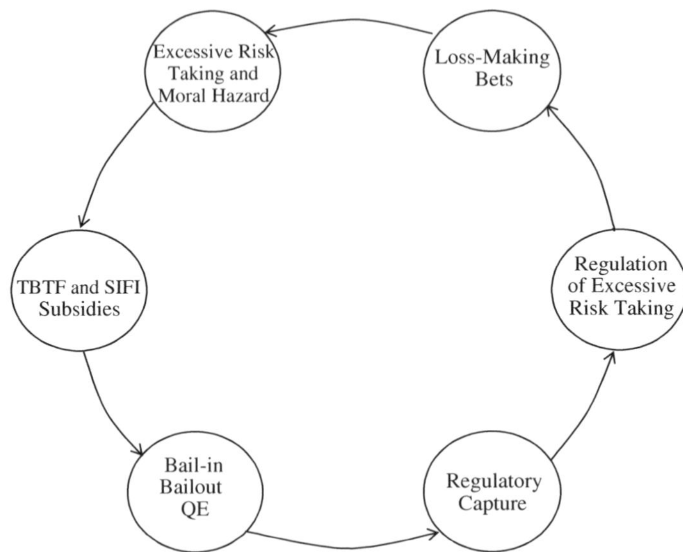

Figure 3.2:   The Doomsday Cycle

In the remainder of this section we describe some cases of regulatory capture to demonstrate how financial institutions capture their supposed regulators.

5.1. The commodity futures trading commission

Under the leadership of Brooksley Born, who headed the Commodity Future Trading Commission (CFTC) in the period 1996–1999, the CFTC was at the front of calls to take the necessary regulatory action to combat financial fraud, specifically the fraud associated with over-the-counter (OTC) derivatives. Since she was toppled by free marketeers (she resigned, according to the official story), things have changed for the benefit of the financial oligarchy.

Hilzenrath (2010) tells a story about the capture of the CFTC. In October 2010, George Painter retired as one of the two CFTC administrative law judges. In the process, Painter requested that his cases not to be assigned to the other judge, Bruce Levine. The reason

Painter gave for his request was that Judge Levine had promised Wendy Gramm (then the chairperson of the Commission) that he would never rule in favor of a complainant, a promise that was fulfilled as a review of Levine's rulings would indicate. Gramm was accused of helping Goldman Sachs, Enron and other large firms gain influence over commodity markets. Interestingly, Wendy Gramm joined the board of Enron after leaving the CFTC.

5.2. The SEC

Taibbi (2011) accuses the SEC of acting in the interest of Wall Street banks and hedge funds and of dragging its feet or refusing to investigate cases or bring charges for fraud and insider trading. In September 2005, the SEC dismissed an employee because he was critical of his superiors' refusal to pursue John Mack who was suspected of giving insider information to Arthur Samberg, head of Pequot Capital Management, which was once one of the world's largest hedge funds. The list of officials who have left the SEC for highly lucrative jobs in the private sector includes Arthur Levitt, Robert Khuzami, Linda Thomsen, Richard Walker, Gary Lynch and Paul Berger.[12]

In an interview on his article "Why isn't Wall Street in Jail" Matt Taibbi (2011) describes the SEC as a classic case of regulatory capture. The SEC has also been described as "an agency that was set up to protect the public from Wall Street, but now protects Wall Street from the public" (Bauder, 2011). On 17 August 2011, Taibbi reported that in July 2001, a preliminary fraud investigation against Deutsche Bank was stymied by Richard Walker, a former SEC enforcement director, who began working as general counsel for Deutsche Bank in October 2001. Darcy Flynn, an SEC lawyer and the whistleblower who exposed this case, revealed that for 20 years, the SEC had been routinely destroying documents related to

---

[12]On these stories, see SEC (2009), Bogdanich and Morgenson (2006), *New York Times* (2001) and Abelson (1996).

thousands of preliminary inquiries that were closed rather than proceeding to formal investigation.

In a comment made on 9 April 2014 and posted on *The Economist's* website, an anonymous reader said the following[13]:

> A trial attorney from the SEC said his bosses were too tentative and fearful to bring many Wall Street leaders to heel ... James Kidney, who joined the SEC in 1986 and retired this month, offered the critique in a speech at his goodbye party ... The SEC has become "an agency that polices the broken windows on the street level and rarely goes to the penthouse floors".... On the rare occasions when enforcement does go to the penthouse, good manners are paramount. Tough enforcement, risky enforcement, is subject to extensive negotiation and weakening. Kidney said his superiors were more focused on getting high-paying jobs after their government service than on bringing difficult cases. The agency's penalties, Kidney said, have become "at most a tollbooth on the bankster turnpike".

A former SEC chairman, Chris Cox, appeared on the *Time* list of the "25 People to Blame for the Financial Crisis". Although the magazine mentions Cox's "blindness to repeated allegations in the Madoff scandal", he was put on the list for "his lax enforcement (of the rules)". For example, "the SEC had plenty of power to go after big investment banks like Lehman Brothers and Merrill Lynch for better disclosure, but he chose not to".

5.3. The Federal Reserve Bank of New York

Johnson (2014) tells a story involving a whistleblower under the heading "Federal Reserve Covers up Banker Crimes". This is the story of a former bank examiner, Carmen Segarra, who (as he puts it) exposed "how the privately owned and controlled Federal Reserve covers up criminal practices of the world's wealthiest elites". In 2011, Ms. Segarra was hired by the Federal Reserve Bank of New York

---

[13] http://www.economist.com/node/21600090/comments.

as a bank examiner and assigned the task of monitoring a TBTF bank in the process of implementing regulatory measures put in place as the result of the Dodd–Frank Act. Under the new rules, investment bankers were expected to address conflicts of interest with respect to dealing with clients. As a result of an investigation, it was concluded that the bank "fell far short of the new legal requirements". When these revelations were brought to the attention of the New York Fed, Ms. Segarra was taken aside and pressured to change her position. When she refused to do that she was fired.

5.4. International organizations

On the international level, the World Trade Organization (WTO) is a captured regulator. Faunce *et al.* (2009) argue that the WTO's non-violation nullification of benefits claims, particularly when inserted in bilateral trade agreements, can facilitate intense lobbying by the industry, which can result in effective regulatory capture of large areas of governmental policy. The WTO has done a good job protecting the privileges of multinationals.

The same goes for the Basel Committee on Banking Supervision (BCBS), which seems to be captured by big banks. Indicative of capture is that the Committee allows self-regulation because big banks are permitted to calculate their regulatory capital by using internal models and because new regulatory rules are relaxed and watered down over time. On 12 January 2014, the BCBS released new rules whereby big European banks were allowed off the hook of having to raise $96 billion in capital. Although they still have to meet a leverage ratio (the ratio of equity to assets) of at least 3%, the formula used for the calculation has been softened. The BCBS had originally suggested obliging banks to hold equity (the loss-absorbing capital put up by investors) of at least 3% of assets. In theory, the standards still apply, but the Committee has come up with various revisions to how the ratio is to be calculated, in effect making the rules less restrictive. The new rules allow banks to off-set some derivatives against one another and to exclude some assets from the calculation altogether, thus making their exposure seem smaller. Analysts at Barclays characterized the concession as a "substantial loosening", while Citibank called it "significant regulatory forbearance". The stock prices of big European banks, such as Barclays and Deutsche Bank, surged to their highest level in nearly three years on the news (*The Economist*, 2014b).

6. Two Crisis-Related Fiascos

The proposition that financial boom encourages fraud, which is uncovered by the subsequent bust is valid for two "events": the Goldman Sachs hedging scandal and the Bernie Madoff Ponzi scheme. These fiascos are discussed in turn.

6.1. The Goldman Sachs "hedging" fiasco

Snyder (2010) puts the case against Goldman Sachs very strongly by arguing that "corruption at Goldman Sachs is very deep and very entrenched, but they will never be fully investigated because they have such close ties to the US government". Taibbi (2009) describes Goldman as "a great vampire squid wrapped around the face of humanity, relentlessly jamming its blood funnel into anything that smells like money". This criticism was triggered by a scandal when Goldman advised their unsuspecting clients to do something while doing exactly the opposite. Goldman knew with a high degree of confidence that their clients would incur losses by following the advice — otherwise they (Goldman) would have acted on similar lines.

In fact, some observers believe that it was intentional and that the CDOs they sold were inferior by design. According to Eisinger and Bernstein (2010), "Goldman Sachs allowed hedge fund manager Paulson to design sure to fail synthetic CDOs that Goldman sold to its own customers, allowing both Goldman and Paulson to use credit default swaps (CDSs) to bet on failure". Hutton (2010) describes the scam as follows: "Goldman's Vice President Fabrice Tourre created a dud financial instrument packed with valueless subprime mortgages at the instruction of hedge fund client Paulson, sold it to investors knowing it was valueless, and then allowed Paulson to profit from the dud financial instrument". He responds to Goldman's claim that the buyers were "among the most sophisticated mortgage investors in the world" by describing the situation as a "used car salesman flogging a broken car he's got from some wide boy pal to some driver who can't get access to the logbook".[14]

The top brass at Goldman justify their action on the grounds that it was "hedging", which is preposterous. Hedging entails taking a position on an asset and an opposite position on a hedging instrument, but both of these positions belong to the hedger. You do not hedge by taking an opposite position to that of your clients' position, a position that you have advised them to take. What Goldman did was not hedging — it was speculation, betting on a market downturn. Goldman correctly anticipated a downturn but did not convey that message to their clients so that those victims would continue buying junk securities from Goldman.

In a formal reaction to this fiasco, Goldman Sachs issued a letter to shareholders alongside the 2009 annual report, declaring that the bank did not "bet against its clients" when it changed its position in the housing market in 2007, shortly before prices began to collapse. The letter contained a detailed defence of the $12.9 billion payout that Goldman received from AIG after the failed insurance company was bailed out by the US government (more specifically, by a previous Goldman CEO, Hank Paulson, in his capacity as the then Treasury Secretary). As a matter of fact, Goldman was the biggest beneficiary of the AIG bailout. Eliot Spitzer, the former governor of New York, called Paulson's decision to fulfil AIG's CDO

---

[14] Hutton (2010) claims that Paulson identified some of the "dud subprime mortgages" that he wanted Tourre to put into the CDO and that Tourre could see what was coming. In one email in January 2007 Tourre wrote the following: "more and more leverage in the system. The whole building is about to collapse anytime now … only potential survivor, the fabulous Fab rice Tourre … standing in the middle of all these complex highly leveraged exotic trades he created without necessarily understanding all of the implications of those monstrosities".

contracts in full a "disgrace" (Wearden, 2010). Perhaps "disgrace" is an "understatement".

The Goldman bosses deny any wrongdoing, arguing that various "sophisticated" investors simply took differing views. This is how Goldman defended the indefensible in that notorious letter:

> Although Goldman Sachs held various positions in residential mortgage-related products in 2007, our short positions were not a 'bet against our clients'. Rather, they served to offset our long positions. Our goal was, and is, to be in a position to make markets for our clients while managing our risk within prescribed limits.

True, the action was not a bet against the clients *per se*. It was a bet against the market, which they took because they correctly believed that the market was heading south. "Making markets for our clients" means selling junk securities to the clients while conveying the message that conditions were so bright that long positions on junk securities are extremely profitable. Then why did Goldman choose to offset their long positions (which means that they were anticipating a declining market) while advising their clients to keep going long by accumulating more rotten eggs? Contrary to what the Goldman bosses claim, Francis (2010) asserts that Goldman had conspired with the Paulson (John, not Hank) hedge fund such that Paulson would select assets for inclusion in CDOs based on their low quality. This is the ultimate double crossing: sell rotten eggs and then bet that no one would eat them.

Whenever the term "rent-seeking" is mentioned, the name "Goldman Sachs" invariably crops up. In an article entitled "Goldman Critics versus Little Goldmans", Kurdas (2009) defends Goldman by arguing that (i) investment banking is profitable, and if it does not happen in the US it will happen elsewhere; (ii) Goldman paid back public money that the government insisted it takes when the failure of Lehman Brothers paralyzed the markets and (iii) there is no problem with bonuses as they are like retained earnings. This is actually the first time that I hear that Goldman was forced to take taxpayers' money in what sounds like a gesture of goodwill towards taxpayers (who would have been really disappointed if their beloved Goldman had refused to accept the "gift"). I am not sure how the government could have forced Goldman to take the money, had they said "no". Then, how is it that bonuses are like retained earnings? While retained earnings are used instead of borrowing to finance corporate operations, bonuses are used to finance the luxury life style of bonus recipients. There is nothing wrong with making profit and accumulating wealth, provided that fraud, deception and dishonesty are not involved. Bill Gates has become the richest man in the world not by selling rotten eggs but by selling fresh eggs that people around the world want to buy. Investment banking is more profitable than the business of Bill Gates because fraud is extremely profitable.

Kurdas's passionate defence of Goldman brought about some comments from the readers of the blog. In a response to these claims, a commentator argues that Kurdas seems oblivious to the fact that a principal source of Goldman's profit is rent-seeking through intimate connections with top Treasury and Fed officials. Another commentator agrees with the rent-seeking proposition, arguing that there is evidence for the "cosy" relationship with the government: "the Paulson/Goldman Moscow meeting, the exclusive AIG/Treasury/Goldman negotiations in which Goldman had a $20 billion stake, Paulson's phone logs from his Goldman days showing contact communication with Bush and Bernanke, and Goldman front-running trades with special the New York stock exchange (NYSE) access". Yes, the US government has a love affair with Goldman, and this is why Goldman will always be in a good shape.

6.2. The Bernie Madoff fiasco

The Bernie Madoff Ponzi scheme fits the description of Povel *et al.* (2007) that financial fraud tends to occur during bubbles and gets exposed when the bubble bursts. The scheme flourished in the 1990s and 2000s and collapsed in late 2008 as the demand for cash by investors intensified during the global financial crisis. For a long time, Bernie Madoff was widely considered to have a magic touch as a money manager, which made his hedge fund, Ascot Partners, a magnate for investors including celebrities. Ascot's monthly reports were voluminous, showing numerous transactions in and out of the market every day. Madoff was supposed to have some "black box" model that generated buy and sell signals — he was one of the most active traders in the market (as that was the impression he gave).

Ascot Partners was offering stable double-digit returns, with a distribution that resembles nothing else (Francis, 2010). The descriptive statistics of those returns deviated sharply from returns on other assets, as they exhibited a very small fraction of negative values. They showed no correlation with the S&P 500 when the fund invested in a combination of the S&P 500 index and some options to limit downside and upside returns. In reality, however, Madoff was running a Ponzi scheme whereby he would distribute dividends to old clients from the fresh money received from new clients while syphoning millions and billions of dollars to the unknown. For a long time the SEC knew that Bernie Madoff, who had served on the Commission's own advisory committee, committed multiple violations and misled the Commission on how he managed his clients' funds. Yet the SEC failed in unmasking Madoff's giant scam. Warning signals were abundant — for example, it is virtually impossible to have the kind of returns that Madoff reported. If Madoff had not faced $7 billion in redemptions, his Ponzi scheme might have survived longer.

If $50 billion was lost (which is what Madoff gained), this Ponzi scheme is indeed the largest such fraud in history, and one that might even put to shame the conman whose name (Ponzi) is attached to this brand of deception. In 1920, Charles Ponzi claimed in public that he could make a 50% return for investors in 45 days, which was tantalizing for those who mortgaged their homes and invested their life savings with him. A similar story is that of Ivar Kreuger who shot himself in the head in March 1932. He had cooked the books of his match manufacturing business and forged $142 million of bonds. It was reported that he may have burned through $400 million of investors' money by falsifying the accounts of 400 separate companies.

In May 2014, a fund established to compensate Madoff's victims received 51,700 claims for more than $40 billion. Richard Breeden, appointed by the US Department of Justice to oversee the Madoff Victim Fund, said that at least twice as many investors as previously thought lost money in Madoff's fraud (Stempel, 2014). It is interesting to note that claimants came from 119 countries as disparate as Kazakhstan, Madagascar and Vietnam. A former chairman of the US SEC said in a phone interview that "the fact we have victims in 119 countries makes this a very unique process". He also said: "I can't think of any situation where there has been such a widespread distribution of a fraud". The US accounts for 58% of the claimed losses and 38% of claimants whereas Germany, Italy and France provide the next most claimants. About 78% of the claimants reported losses of $500,000 or less. These things are not supposed to happen in the presence of a regulator such as the SEC unless, of course, the regulator is captured or regulation is lax. Is it not strange that a crook like Madoff served as an adviser to the SEC? This is like a drug lord sitting on an advisory committee of the Drug Enforcement Administration (DEA).

7. Market Manipulation and Fraudulent Accounting Practices

In the aftermath of the global financial crisis and the massive bailouts of failed financial institutions, one would tend to think that these institutions would behave themselves and refrain from indulging in fraudulent activities. Yet three major scandals have surfaced, involving the manipulation of commodity prices (precious meals, to be exact), exchange rates and interest rates. One would tend to think that a bank that is mostly owned by taxpayers (the Royal Bank of Scotland) would be the last institution to be involved in these scandals, but that is not the case. Executives at the RBS have been demanding bonuses for losing $5 billion, not $10 billion, rather than paying back taxpayers money. Perhaps they thought that by making more money through fraud, they can justifiably claim bonuses. In this section, we describe the three scandals. Furthermore, financial institutions still practice fraudulent accounting, *a la* Lehman Brothers.

7.1. Manipulation of the prices of gold and silver

In November 2009, Andrew Maguire, a former silver trader in Goldman Sach's London office, contacted the CFTC's Enforcement Division to report that traders at JPMorgan Chase were indulged in illegal manipulation of the silver market. He told the CFTC how silver traders at JPMorgan Chase openly bragged about their misconduct, including how they sent signals to the market in advance so that other traders could make profit during price suppression episodes. Traders would recognize these signals and, following the lead of JPMorgan, make money by taking short positions on precious metals. Maguire exposed the practice of manipulating the market at the time of option expiries, during non-farm payroll data releases, during commodities exchange contract rollovers, and at other times if it was deemed necessary. On 25 July 2014, a lawsuit was filed in New York against Deutsche Bank, Bank of Nova Scotia and HSBC for allegedly manipulating silver bullion prices, both in the physical market and the futures market.[15]

Another form of manipulation of the price of gold and silver (commodities in general) takes place via the use of futures contracts (derivatives again). Roberts and Kranzler (2015) suggest that the price of gold and silver in the futures markets is inconsistent with the conditions of supply and demand in the market for physical bullion. They describe as "fraudulent" the practice of driving down the price in the futures market by increasing the supply of "paper bullion" (futures contracts) despite high demand for and constrained supply of bullion in the physical market. As an indication of the surge in demand for the physical

---

[15]Free marketeers hate regulation because it interferes with the working of the market mechanism. Price manipulation is also interference with the working of the price mechanism. It follows that any regulation against price manipulation is bound to boost the "freedom" of the market, in which case it is not clear why free marketeers oppose regulation, at least in this case.

commodity, the US Mint announced on 7 July 2015 that due to a "significant" increase in demand, it had sold out of Silver Eagles (one ounce silver coin) and was suspending sales until sometime in August. The financial press and mainstream media in general attribute the drop in precious metals prices to a "surge in global demand for coins", which makes no sense because if demand increases, price goes up, not down. Those who provided this explanation obviously do not know the difference between a change in demand and a change in the quantity demanded. For Roberts and Kranzler (2015), manipulation is the only possible explanation for observing a high demand for the physical metal under conditions of constrained supply and a simultaneous decline in futures prices.

7.2. The forex scandal

The forex scandal refers to the revelation that banks colluded to manipulate exchange rates for their own financial gain. In June 2013, Bloomberg reported that currency dealers had been "front-running" client orders and rigging the foreign exchange benchmark rates by colluding and pushing through trades before and during the 60 second windows when the benchmark rates are set (Vaughan *et al.*, 2013). At the center of the investigation are the transcripts of electronic chatrooms in which senior currency traders from various banks declare the types and volume of the trades they planned to place. The electronic chatrooms had names such as "The Cartel", "The Bandits' Club", "One Team, One Dream" and "The Mafia" (see, for example, Vaughan *et al.*, 2013; Martin and Enrich, 2013). The discussions in the chatrooms were interspersed with jokes about manipulating the foreign exchange market and repeated references to alcohol, drugs and women (Enrich and Martin, 2013). In November 2014, the UK's Financial Conduct Authority (FCA) gave some examples of how traders calling themselves names such as "the players", "the three musketeers", "one team, one dream" and "the A-team" attempted to manipulate foreign exchange markets (Chrispin, 2015).

To understand how the scam works we have to understand the meaning of front-running and the benchmark fix. Front-running is an illegal practice whereby a foreign exchange dealer executes orders for own account while taking advantage of advance knowledge of pending orders from customers. A dealer involved in front-running may buy for own account before filling customer buy orders, causing price to go up, or sells for own account before filling customer sell orders, thus driving prices down. In both cases the dealer makes profit at the expense of customers. The benchmark fix involves the calculation of a set of exchange rates at a particular time, typically 4 pm London time — this is called the "London fix", which is published by WM/Reuters (WMRs).[16] A dealer may obtain confidential information about something that is about to happen and could change prices — this information may pertain to clients' orders and trading positions. This trader could then place own orders to profit from subsequent movement in prices. With respect to the 4 pm fix, the dealer may place an order before 4 pm because he knows that something will happen at around 4 pm. It is easier to move prices if several market participants work together. By agreeing to place orders at a certain time or sharing confidential information, it is possible to move prices more sharply. Collusion can be active, with traders speaking to each other on the phone or on internet chatrooms. It can also be "implicit", when traders do not speak to each other but they are still aware of what other people in the market are planning to do.

According to settlements announced by the Justice Department in Washington on 20 May 2015, Citicorp, JPMorgan Chase, Barclays, RBS and UBS agreed to plead guilty to felony charges of conspiring to manipulate exchange rates (McLaughlin *et al.*, 2015). They were accused of colluding to influence benchmark rates by aligning positions and pushing transactions through at the same time.

---

[16] WM publishes reference rates throughout the course of the day. The London 4 pm rate is by far the most heavily used. There are a number of other reference rates, with the 2.15 pm Central European Time (CET) rates published by the European Central Bank (ECB) quite widely used.

Other banks are also involved as the investigation goes on. It is ironic that the RBS, which was saved by British taxpayers and is struggling to recover from the mismanagement that brought it down, is involved in yet another scandal. The RBS has apologized after agreeing a new penalty over the rigging of foreign exchange markets, bringing the total bill to over £800 million (Herald Scotland, 2015). Naturally, this scandal will not prevent the RBS executives from demanding bonuses.

7.3. The LIBOR manipulation scandal

In 2012, an international investigation into the manipulation of the London interbank offered rate (LIBOR) revealed a widespread plot undertaken by several banks (most notably Barclays, UBS, Rabobank and the RBS). Regulators in the US, UK and EU fined banks more than $6 billion for participating in the rigging scheme. Barclays agreed in late June 2012 to pay a $453 million fine to settle allegations that it had systematically manipulated LIBOR between 2005 and 2009. The bank was also fined for "misconduct" related to the European equivalent of LIBOR, the Euro interbank offered rate (EUIBOR). By November 2013, RBS, UBS, Rabobank and the British broker ICAP had to pay large fines, bringing the total penalties paid in LIBOR settlements to more than $3.7 billion. According to Talley (2013) the scandal may go down as one of the most significant and far reaching events associated with the global financial crisis.

Banks worldwide use LIBOR as a base rate for setting interest rates on consumer and corporate loans. Indeed, hundreds of trillions of dollars in securities and loans are linked to LIBOR, including car and home loans. Talley (2013) puts the figure at $350 trillion worth of notional value in global financial contracts, ranging from mortgages to credit cards to corporate debt securities to countless financial derivatives. When LIBOR rises, rates and payments on loans often rise, and vice versa. LIBOR is used for a range of retail products such as adjustable-rate mortgages and student loans, as well as interest rate futures and options. Barclays reportedly manipulated LIBOR for the first time in 2005 so that its traders could make profit on derivatives pegged to the base rate. Swap traders often asked the Barclays employees who submitted the rates to provide figures that would benefit the traders, instead of submitting the rates the bank would actually pay to borrow money. Moreover, traders at Barclays coordinated with other banks to alter their rates. Manipulation may involve upward and downward adjustment of LIBOR, depending on a trader's position.

Talley (2013) argues that "the scandal is now thought to have been so broad as to involve coordinated practices between banks (not just within them), resulting in some additional allegations of racketeering and/or antitrust violations". This kind of malpractice distorts trust in the market because participants cannot trust the rates at which banks are lending to one another and because trillions of dollars of financial instruments are priced at the wrong rate. A conspiracy theory that sounds realistic is that regulators had some knowledge of what was going on but did little, perhaps because they wanted to boost confidence in banks amid the financial crisis. Talley (2013) argues that the manipulation of LIBOR represents "strategic shading by banks attempting to elude the scrutiny of regulators or other financial market watchdogs at moments of maximal economic uncertainty". Is it a good idea to allow this malpractice in the name of free market, deregulation and self-regulation?

In August 2015, former UBS and Citigroup trader, Tom Hayes, was sentenced to 14 years in prison after being found guilty of conspiracy to rig LIBOR, following a week of deliberations (Finch and Vaughan, 2015). As the judge handed in the sentence, he said that "a message needs to be sent to the world of banking". Prosecutors said during the nine-week trial that Hayes was the "ringmaster" of a global network of 25 traders and brokers from at least 10 firms who tried to manipulate LIBOR on an industrial scale and that "he would bribe, bully, cajole and reward his contacts for their help in skewing the benchmark". Hayes's lawyers reiterated their defense that benchmark manipulation was widespread in the industry and that "the conduct Mr. Hayes has been convicted of was prevalent" for at least five years prior to his joining UBS. So, where are the others who should also be held accountable? Fines on their own will not work.

As bad as the 2012 LIBOR scandal was, it is nothing compared to the real LIBOR scandal that is brewing but receiving little attention. Jesse Colombo, who describes himself as "an economic analyst who is warning of dangerous post-2009 bubbles", believes that the "real" LIBOR scandal is keeping LIBOR at record low levels, "which is helping to fuel the entire world that will end in a devastating financial crisis that will be even worse than the global financial crisis" (Colombo, 2014). The scandal referred to here is not the making of private financial institutions but that of central banks, particularly the Federal Reserve and now the ECB, which have been engaged in what will prove to be a devastating policy called quantitative easing. For some observers, quantitative easing is a policy conducted for the benefit of bankers and the rich — it is regulatory capture all over again.[17]

7.4. Fraudulent accounting practices

Quinn (2010) points out that several major Wall Street banks are using accounting techniques similar to those utilized by Lehman Brothers in its final days to mask the size of their balance sheets at the end of reporting periods. He refers to a study conducted by the *Wall Street Journal* showing that 18 major banks were, on average, able to reduce the debt levels used to fund securities trades by 42% by using repurchase agreements (repos). Lehman had used "Repo 105", which is an accounting trick whereby a short-term repo is classified as a sale. The cash generated by the "sale" is used to pay back debt. Following the publication of financial reports, the company borrows cash and repurchases its original assets.

Repo 105 allowed Lehman to claim liabilities that were $50 billion lower than what they actually were by May 2008, just months

---

[17]Max Keiser holds strong views in this respect. See, for example, https://www.youtube.com/watch?v=lRJmTsj2s_8.

before the bank collapsed. When short sellers found out that Lehman was using fraudulent accounting they attacked it, and justifiably so, but the Lehman boss blamed the collapse on short sellers, not on mismanagement and fraud. Quinn (2010) suggests that the latest revelations about the extent of the use of repo-financing should worry investors in the financial sector, as it suggests that banks are continuing to take pre-crisis level risks in spite of the global financial crisis.

Robert Reich, the former Clinton Labor Secretary, thinks that not only Lehman indulged in this malpractice. He is quoted by Schechter (2010) as saying the following:

> Lehman's practices couldn't have been all that different from those of every other big bank on the Street. After all, they were all competing for the same business, and using many of the same techniques. Lehman was just the first to go under, causing a financial run that led George W. to warn "this sucker could go down" unless the federal government came up with hundreds of billions to bailout the others".

Reich suggests that the accounting fraud at Lehman involved shifting liabilities off its books at the end of each quarter. Interestingly, Ernst and Young approved of the (mal) practice against the advice of its own whistleblower, who was fired by the accounting firm. Does this remind anyone of Enron and Arthur Andersen?

8. Concluding Remarks

Why is corruption rampant in the finance industry? Partnoy (2010) provides an answer to this question by suggesting that it is the absence of fear of punishment. For example, regulators were tipped off to the fraud committed by Bernie Madoff, but nothing happened for a long time, either because regulators did not understand the tip or because they did not have the political will to bring a case. People are deterred from engaging in criminal activity either because they believe it is immoral or because the expected punishment, if caught, exceeds the expected benefits. Partnoy makes it clear that "in financial markets, the question of whether an action is morally wrong is typically irrelevant; the relevant consideration is profit". For example, Partony suggests that "if the gains from cooking the books is substantial, and the probability of punishment is zero, the rational strategy is to cook, cook, cook". What is important is the probability of punishment, not what the punishment is. In 2002, the US Congress doubled the maximum prison sentence for financial fraud, but that made no dent whatsoever in criminal behavior in the finance industry. Partnoy makes the interesting remark that "legislators might as well have added the death penalty, given the low probability of conviction for complex financial fraud".

What is important to remember is that fraud in the financial sector is not a phenomenon that is associated with "few rotten apples" — rather it is endemic, entrenched in the very culture that governs behavior in the financial sector. In a comment on the LIBOR scandal, Vince Cable once wrote the following (Cable, 2012):

> Last week's banking scandals demolished a convenient myth: that the banking crash was all the fault of a few colourful rogues like Fred the Shred of RBS and Adam Applegarth of Northern Rock. We have been reminded, instead, that the rot was far more widespread. Incompetence, corruption and greed have been endemic in British banking.

On the bright side, there is hope that misbehaving bankers may (only may) be prosecuted. On 10 June 2015, Mark Carney, the governor of the Bank of England, declared that "the age of irresponsibility is over" (*The Economist*, 2015b). But surely, more than one person were involved in the LIBOR scandal, so why is it that only one person, Tom Hayes, has been put behind bars?

Chapter 4

The War on Regulation

1. Introduction

Financial deregulation has benefited the financial elite and their hired guns, those who provide the political and intellectual justification for deregulation. In a sense, a war was declared on regulation in the early 1980s, and despite the catastrophic outcomes of this war, it is still going on. This war is justified, not on the basis of regime change or introducing democracy in this country or that (as in recent wars), but rather in defense of the almighty market. This war is motivated by the belief that only when market forces operate freely, without the intervention of regulators, can efficiency be achieved (and efficiency is all that matters). The free market ideology has been promoted by the potential beneficiaries of *laissez faire*, who always find support from politicians and academics providing justification for the war on regulation.

A variety of "weapons" have been used to kill regulation — all of these weapons emanate from the right-wing free market ideology. These weapons are essentially, theories, propositions, doctrines and philosophies that have been put forward to demonstrate that regulation is bad and deregulation is good. They include the rational expectations hypothesis and its offspring, the policy ineffectiveness proposition, which have been used to demonstrate that government intervention in economic activity is at best useless and at worst harmful and destabilizing. Then came the Washington Consensus, a collection of pro-market principles used to argue for liberalization, privatization and deregulation, everything that free marketeers like. Another draconian principle is that of the trickle-down effect, which is used to justify poverty, inequality and the obscene amounts paid to the financial oligarchs. The Great Moderation is a principle used to convey the message that the move to free market policies has put an end to business fluctuations, which demonstrates that the market is looking after us. The most draconian doctrine is that of the efficient market hypothesis that has been used to justify financial deregulation in particular. Although all of these doctrines should have gone the way of the dinosaurs following the hard lessons we learned from the global financial crisis, the die-hard free and efficient marketeers have not given any concessions, and they are still in the business of calling for more deregulation. The war on regulation is still going on.

The objective of this chapter is to describe the doctrines that have been used as weapons in the war on regulation. Since the efficient market hypothesis is of particular importance, it will be discussed in much more detail in Chapter 5, where it is described as a "weapon of mass destruction".

2. The Rational Expectations Hypothesis

In the 1980s, some political leaders on both sides of the Atlantic wanted to initiate a program of wholesale deregulation and diminished government intervention in economic activity. In his inaugural address on 20 January 1981, Ronald Reagan declared that "in this present crisis, government is not the solution to our problem; government is the problem". The intellectual justification for this doctrine was provided by Robert Lucas, Tom Sargent and Neil Wallace who somehow twisted a proposition that had been put forward by John Muth (1961) and proved, with the help of formidable mathematics and incredibly unrealistic assumptions, that government intervention does no good (see, for example, Lucas and Sargent, 1981; Sargent and Wallace, 1976). Somehow they managed to move from Muth's proposition that rational agents do not make systematic expectation errors to the impotence of government intervention in economic activity. However, no sophisticated mathematics is needed to realize that when you cut yourself shaving you do not need the intervention of a doctor because the body can heal itself from a scratch or a minor wound. This does not apply to someone who gets shot and does not die immediately — this person needs the intervention of a surgeon or else he dies. Depending on the nature and magnitude of the shock, government intervention in economic activity may be necessary.

Prior to the work of Lucas, Sargent and Wallace, macroeconomic models were largely based on the adaptive expectations hypothesis in which economic agents are backward looking. In the pre-Lucas–Sargent–Wallace models, agents revise their expectations on the basis of past expectation errors, which means that they can make systematic errors. Those models embodied the adaptive expectations hypothesis, which holds that agents do not revise their expectations even if the government announces a policy that involves increasing the money supply beyond its expected growth rate. Revisions would only be made after the increase in money supply has occurred, and even then agents would react gradually. Therefore equilibrium in the economy would only be converged upon and never reached, in which case the government would be able to maintain employment above its natural level and easily manipulate the economy. Under rational expectations, on the other hand, agents are rational and forward looking — they collect all available information to form expectations. They do not make systematic errors, which means that eventually they converge on the right model governing the economy and financial markets. By applying rational expectations within a macroeconomic framework, Sargent and Wallace (1976) produced the policy ineffectiveness proposition, according to which the government could not intervene successfully in the economy by attempting to manipulate output. If the government employed monetary expansion in order to boost output, agents would foresee the effects and consequently revise wage and price expectations upward. As a result, real wages remain constant and so does output, as money illusion does not occur. Only stochastic shocks to the economy can cause deviations in employment from its natural level.

The policy ineffectiveness proposition has been criticized by a wide range of economists who have questioned the validity of the rational expectations assumption. Grossman and Stiglitz (1980) argued that even if agents had the cognitive ability to form rational expectations, they would be unable to profit from the resultant information since their actions would then reveal their information to others, implying that agents would not expend the effort or money required to become informed — as a result, government policy remains effective. Fischer (1977) and Phelps and Taylor (1977) assumed that workers sign nominal wage contracts that last for more than one period, which makes wages "sticky". If the assumption of wage stickiness is used in the analysis, the underlying model will show that government policy is fully effective because even if workers expect the outcome of a change in policy rationally, they are unable to respond to it as they are locked into expectations formed when they signed their wage contract. It is both possible and desirable for government policy to be used effectively. The government is in a position to respond to stochastic shocks in the economy (which agents are unable to react to) and by doing that, output and employment can be stabilized. Davidson (1982) argues that the rational expectations hypothesis is a poor guide to real world economic behavior because it assumes that market participants passively forecast events rather than actively causing them.

It has been established conclusively that the idea of rational expectations in financial markets is bizarre, to say the least. To start with, the rational expectations hypothesis precludes heterogeneity in favor of the representative agent hypothesis. The literature disputes the validity of this hypothesis, rejecting it in favor of heterogeneity on the grounds that the former is inconsistent with observed trading behavior and the existence of active and volatile financial markets. Indeed, it is arguable that there would be no incentive to trade if all market participants were identical with respect to information, endowments and trading strategies (Frechette and Weaver, 2001). Brock and Hommes (1997), Cartapanis (1996) and Dufey and Kazemi (1991) have demonstrated that persistence of heterogeneity can result in boom and bust behavior under incomplete information. Furthermore, Harrison and Kreps (1978), Varian (1985), De Long *et al.* (1990), Harris and Raviv (1993) and Wang (1998) have shown that heterogeneity can lead to market behavior that is similar to what is observed empirically.

In response to concerns about the representative agent hypothesis, financial economists started to model the behavior of traders in speculative markets in terms of heterogeneity. Chavas (1999) views market participants to fall in three categories in terms of how they form expectations: naïve, quasi-rational and rational. Weaver and Zhang (1999) allow for a continuum of heterogeneity in expectations and explain the implications of the extent of heterogeneity for price level and volatility in speculative markets. Frechette and Weaver (2001) classify market participants by the direction of bias in their expectations, their bullish or bearish sentiment, rather than by how they form expectations. He (2012) surveys recent developments on heterogeneous beliefs and adaptive behavior of financial markets, arguing that growing evidence indicates that the traditional view of homogeneity and perfect rationality in finance and economics faces a number of limitations theoretically and challenges empirically. As Heckman (2001) puts it, "the most important discovery was the evidence on pervasiveness of heterogeneity and diversity in economic life", arguing that "when a full analysis was made of heterogeneity in response, a variety of candidate averages emerged to describe the average person, and the longstanding edifice of the representative consumer was shown to lack empirical support". The message that comes out of this research is loud and clear: homogeneity is conducive to the emergence of one-sided markets, whereas heterogeneity is more consistent with behavior in speculative markets characterized by active trading and volatility.

The rational expectations hypothesis has since lost its appeal because economists have come back to their senses and decided that the hypothesis is implausible and counterfactual. For example, Syll (2010) argues that "rational expectations could only apply to a fictitious, ergodic world governed by stable and stationary stochastic processes". In a world characterized by uncertainty, structural breaks and regime shifts it is quite possible for agents to make systematic errors.

3. The Washington Consensus

The Washington Consensus, a term that was originally coined by Williamson (1989), is a set of 10 policy prescriptions that is considered to constitute the "standard" reform package promoted by institutions based in Washington, primarily the International Monetary Fund (IMF), World Bank and US Treasury. The prescriptions cover issues such as macroeconomic stabilization, openness with respect to trade and investment, and the expansion of market forces within the domestic economy. These prescriptions formed the basis of the advice given to third world countries to promote "economic progress".[1] Right from the beginning, therefore, a significant element of the Washington Consensus was to give market forces a bigger role. Subsequently, the term "Washington Consensus" was used in a "broader sense", to refer to a more general orientation toward a strongly market-based approach (sometimes described as market fundamentalism or neoliberalism).

As originally put forward by Williamson, the Washington Consensus consisted of the following policy recommendations:

(1) Fiscal policy discipline, including the avoidance of large fiscal deficits relative to gross domestic product (GDP).
(2) Redirection of public spending from subsidies (particularly indiscriminate subsidies) toward broad-based provision of

---

[1] Third world countries are constantly lectured by "western" countries on the benefits of free trade. However, when "western" countries were at an early stage of development, they practiced protectionism on a massive scale.

key pro-growth, pro-poor services like primary education, primary health care and infrastructure investment.

(3) Tax reform to achieve a broad tax base and adopt moderate marginal tax rates.

(4) Maintaining market-determined interest rates at a moderate level in real terms.

(5) Maintaining "competitive" exchange rates.

(6) Trade liberalization, including the liberalization of imports in the sense of eliminating quantitative restrictions while using "relatively low uniform tariffs" for the purpose of trade protection.

(7) Liberalization of inward foreign direct investment.

(8) Privatization of state enterprises.

(9) Deregulation, including the abolition of regulations that impede market entry or restrict competition, except for those justified on safety, environmental and consumer protection grounds, and prudential oversight of financial institutions.

(10) Legal security for property rights.

While there are some good policy prescriptions in these principles, they are overwhelmingly market-oriented, intended to serve the interest of multinationals, particularly those involving the liberalization of trade and direct investment and the privatization of state enterprises. The promotion of these ideas in developing countries was aimed mainly at encouraging privatization, so that multinationals can get great deals when public assets are sold (to maximize efficiency, of course). As far as regulation is concerned, deregulation has always been on the agenda, while paying lip service to regulation aimed at consumer protection, including a prudential oversight of financial institutions. When it comes to financial regulation, the word "oversight" is used instead of "regulation". It means allowing financial institutions to do as they please but watch them carefully, which never works.

Williamson opposes the alternative use of the term "Washington Consensus" to cover market fundamentalism in a manner that is consistent with the neoliberal agenda (for example, Naim, 1999).

In particular, he opposes the ideas of capital account liberalization, monetarism, supply-side economics, and the notion of a minimal state that does not indulge in welfare provision and income redistribution — these are neoliberal ideas. According to Williamson (2002), "these ideas have rarely dominated thought in Washington and certainly never commanded a consensus there or anywhere much else". More specifically, Williamson argues that the first three of his 10 prescriptions (fiscal policy discipline, redirection of public spending away from subsidies and tax reform) are uncontroversial, but the others have evoked some controversy.[2] For example, he argues that the redirection of spending to infrastructure, health care and education, has often been neglected. He also argues that, while the prescriptions were focused on reducing certain functions of the government (such as ownership of productive enterprises), they were also about strengthening the ability of the government to support education and health. Williamson (2000) claims that he does not endorse market fundamentalism and argues that the Consensus prescriptions, if implemented correctly, would benefit the poor. Furthermore, a proposal has been put forward calling for an expanded reform agenda, emphasizing crisis-proofing of economies, "second-generation" reforms, and policies addressing inequality and social issues (Kuczynski and Williamson, 2003).

Many commentators see the Consensus, particularly if interpreted in the broader sense of the term, as having been at its strongest during the 1990s. Some would argue that the Consensus in this sense ended at the turn of the century, or at least that it became less influential after about the year 2000 (for example, Narayana, 2010). More commonly, commentators suggest that the Consensus in its broader sense survived until the onset of the global financial crisis (for example, Skidelsky, 2009). The crisis demonstrated the carnage

---

[2]Even the original principles are controversial. Does fiscal policy discipline mean that deficit spending is undesirable even in response to a severe downturn? Is a subsidy on flour a bad idea? Tax reform should be more about plugging loopholes and preventing tax evasion than about maintaining "moderate tax rates". What are "competitive exchange rates"? There are a lot of question marks on liberalization, privatization and deregulation.

inflicted by market failure and the necessity of government intervention in economic activity, which convinced a number of journal-
ists, politicians and senior officials that the Washington Consensus
was dead (for example, Cooper and Savage, 2008; Painter, 2009).
Following the 2009 G-20 London summit, former British Prime
Minister Gordon Brown declared that "the old Washington
Consensus is over" (Sky News, 2009). On that occasion, John
Williamson was asked by *The Washington Post* (2009a) whether or
not he agreed with Gordon Brown that the Washington Consensus
was dead. He responded as follows:

> It depends on what one means by the Washington Consensus.
> If one means the 10 points that I tried to outline, then clearly it's
> not right. If one uses the interpretation that a number of people —
> including Joe Stiglitz, most prominently — have foisted on it, that
> it is a neoliberal tract, then I think it is right.

The term "Washington Consensus" has become associated with
neoliberal policies in general, embodying the right-wing ideology
of the free market and diminishing role of the government in economic activity. On an international level, the philosophy behind
the Washington Consensus is used to justify globalization and US
hegemony. Rodrik (2006) views the Consensus as "stabilize, privat-
ize, and liberalize", which became the mantra of a generation of
technocrats who cut their teeth in the developing world and of the
political leaders they counseled.[3] He points out that while China
and India increased their economies' reliance on free market forces
to a limited extent, their general economic policies remained the
exact opposite to the main recommendations of the Washington
Consensus. Both countries have high levels of protectionism, no
privatization, extensive industrial policies planning, and lax fiscal
and financial policies through the 1990s. Had there been dismal

---

[3]Rodrik is right in arguing that the Consensus involves privatization and
liberalization, but he is wrong about "stabilization". Justifying privatization and
liberalization is easier under unstable conditions. The argument then would be
that privatization and liberalization are needed for the purpose of stabilization.

failures they would have presented strong evidence in support of the recommended Washington Consensus policies. However, they turned out to be successes. According to Rodrik, "while the lessons drawn by proponents and skeptics differ, it is fair to say that nobody really believes in the Washington Consensus anymore". The question now, he argues, "is not whether the Washington Consensus is dead or alive; it is what will replace it".

4. The Great Moderation

The "Great Moderation" is a phrase coined by Bernanke (2004) to describe his interpretation of the evidence presented by Blanchard and Simon (2001) showing that the volatility of output had declined over time. A variety of explanations have been put forward for the phenomenon. Summers (2005) explains the Great Moderation in terms of better monetary policy, structural changes in inventory management, and good luck. As far as monetary policy is concerned, lower output volatility is "a result of central bankers' greater emphasis on, and success at, controlling inflation". Summers argues that while monetary policy has not directly reduced output volatility, it "may have been important in reducing output volatility to the extent that policy changes have resulted in lower and more stable inflation". As for inventory management, "the widespread adoption of information technology enabled fundamental changes in the nature of production and distribution processes, and their relationship to final sales, especially for durable goods". Good luck pertains to the absence of large adverse events hitting several countries simultaneously and causing widespread volatility (good luck is the result of the absence of bad luck as represented, for example, by massive oil price shocks).

To the extent that the Moderation has been seen as more than a run of good luck, it has been explained by improvement in macroeconomic management associated with, or as result of, the benefits of economic liberalism — again the notions of free market and deregulation. One of the explanations is that the deregulation of financial markets had a damping effect on the fluctuations of the business cycle. These changes gave consumers a vast range of financial instruments (such as credit cards and home equity loans) that enabled them to match their spending with changes in their incomes over long periods. Cecchetti *et al.* (2006) find evidence for the role played by financial innovation, arguing that financial development, as measured by the importance of bank lending, is linked to real economic stability. However, they also add that their results are based on correlation rather than causation. This is what they say:

> We should note that what we have done is established a set of correlations … What we have not done is show causal links. It is surely possible, for example, that financial systems are more prone to develop in countries that are more stable and that less stable countries may trade more.

If anything, financial innovation and development caused the Great Recession, which means that the Great Moderation was shattered by the global financial crisis. Quiggin (2009) argues that the collapse of the Great Moderation has destroyed the pragmatic justification that, whatever the inequities and inefficiencies involved in the process, the shift to economic liberalism since the 1970s delivered sustained prosperity. As a weapon used in the war on regulation, the Great Moderation means that market forces ensure that nothing drastic will hit the economy. Nothing can be further away from the truth. While he believes in "the ability of markets to allocate resources efficiently and to act as effective shock absorbers", Thoma (2007) does not endorse the proposition that "economists are in broad agreement that the Great Moderation is due primarily to the liberation of markets". To the contrary, he argues that this proposition is "based more upon an attempt to sell an ideological point about free markets than an honest presentation of the evidence".

5. The Trickle-Down Effect

The term "trickle-down" originated in US politics, although it has been attributed to humorist Will Rogers, who said during the Great Depression that "money was all appropriated for the top in hopes that it would trickle down to the needy" (Sims and Boyle, 2009; Giangreco and Moore, 1999). In more recent history, the phrase is most closely identified with critics of "Reaganomics". Reagan's budget director, David Stockman, championed Reagan's tax cuts at first, but subsequently he became critical of them. He told journalist William Greider that "supply-side economics is the trickle-down idea" and that "it's kind of hard to sell 'trickle-down', so the supply-side formula was the only way to get a tax policy that was really 'trickle-down'" (Greider, 1981, 1982). John Kenneth Galbraith noted the following:

> "Trickle-down economics" had been tried before in the US in the 1890s under the name "horse and sparrow theory." … Mr. David Stockman has said that supply-side economics was merely a cover for the trickle-down approach to economic policy — what an older and less elegant generation called the horse and sparrow theory: "If you feed the horse enough oats, some will pass through to the road for the sparrows".

Galbraith actually claimed that the horse and sparrow theory was partly to blame for the panic of 1896 (Galbraith, 1982).

The underlying idea is that policies designed to benefit the wealthy, such as financial deregulation and favorable tax treatment of capital income, will "ultimately" benefit everybody. It is the proposition that the benefits of growth will "eventually" trickle-down even to the poor or that high tide carries all boats". This notion, according to Quiggin (2009), is one of the casualties of the global financial crisis. The problem is that "eventually" and "ultimately" may never come (they have not yet). This is the same idea as the "American dream" — that is, no one should worry about poverty because eventually beggars become billionaires. The trickle-down effect is particularly relevant to the divide between the financial oligarchs, who benefit from deregulation, and the rest of the society. The spectacular growth in the share of income accruing to the financial oligarchs has been justified on the grounds that all members of the community would "eventually" benefit from this process. The argument goes as follows: rewarding the financial oligarchs and members of the upper 1% generously will enhance productivity, leading to the provision of goods and services at a lower cost and to higher demand for the services of the common person who will therefore earn higher wages.

The notion of trickle-down has been criticized severely. In the 1992 presidential election, Independent candidate, Ross Perot, called trickle-down economics "political voodoo".[4] In New Zealand, Labor Party MP Damien O'Connor has, in the Labor Party campaign launch video for the 2011 general election, described trickle-down economics as "the rich pissing on the poor".[5] A 2012 study by the Tax Justice Network indicates that wealth of the super-rich does not trickle-down to improve the economy, but tends to be amassed and sheltered in tax havens with a negative effect on the tax bases of the home economy (Stewart, 2012).[6] Chang (2011) criticizes trickle-down policies, citing examples of "slowing job growth in the last few decades, rising income inequality in most rich nations, and the inability to raise living standards across all income brackets rather than at the top only". In a 2015 report published by the International Monetary Fund, Dabla-Norris *et al.* (2015) reach the conclusion that there is no trickle-down effect as the rich get richer. This is what the report says:

> If the income share of the top 20% (the rich) increases, then GDP growth actually declines over the medium term, suggesting that the benefits do not trickle down. In contrast, an increase in the income share of the bottom 20% (the poor) is associated with higher GDP growth.

---

[4] This was in an advertisement by Perot. http://www.livingroomcandidate.org/commercials/1992/trickle-down.

[5] http://www.stuff.co.nz/national/politics/5870477/Labour-campaign-video-harks-back-to-history.

[6] The study found that $21 trillion worth of assets have been lost to tax havens. If taxed, that could have been enough to put Africa back on its feet — and even solve the euro crisis.

The financial sector is the obvious test case for this theory because incomes in the financial sector have risen more rapidly than in any other part of the economy. According to the trickle-down theory, the growth in income accruing to the financial sector has benefited the US population as a whole in three main ways (Quiggin, 2009). First, the facilitation of takeovers, mergers and buyouts by private equity firms offered the opportunity to boost the efficiency with which capital was used, and the productivity of the economy as a whole. Second, expanded provision of credit to households allowed higher standards of living to be enjoyed, as households could ride out fluctuations in income, bring forward the benefits of future income growth and draw on the capital gains associated with rising prices for stocks, real estate and other assets. Third, there is the classic "trickle-down" effect in which the wealth of the financial sector generates demand for luxury goods and services of all kinds, thereby benefiting workers in general, or at least those in cities with high concentrations of financial activity such as London and New York.

Nothing can be further away from the truth. The explosion in the pay of the financial elite has contributed to the advent of the global financial crisis, which has left no less than 50 million people living below the poverty line in the US alone. There is no evidence for enhanced productivity growth as a result of mergers and acquisitions. Take, for example, the worst corporate deal in history, the takeover by the Royal Bank of Scotland of ABN Amro at the cost of $50 billion. That brought nothing but disaster for the British taxpayers. The expansion in credit and diversity of financial services offered to consumers has produced nothing but enormous private debt — the alleged beneficiaries live on a day-to-day basis by borrowing on one credit card to pay the bill for another. There is certainly no evidence for rising standard of living as real wages for the majority have been stagnant at a time when financial innovation has produced bubbles, crashes and crises that have made the poor poorer. As for the third argument, it is exactly the opposite of the truth because the concentration of wealth has an adverse effect on consumption. How many Rolex watches does an individual buy?

Are we supposed to believe that if the financial oligarchs get bonuses out of taxpayers, depositors or shareholders, these stakeholders will be better off eventually? This is a travesty because the only beneficiary will be tax havens and Swiss banks as the oligarchs have a marginal propensity to consume of zero.

6. Concluding Remarks

Opposition to government intervention by the advocates of free market or *laissez faire* economics is based on the view that government intervention is generally harmful, due to the law of unintended consequences and because the government is unable to manage economic affairs effectively. For example, government officials tend to be naturally disposed to seek more power and authority, and this quest often takes the form of economic interventionism which they then seek to justify. So, the story goes as follows: those who work for the government are incompetent and corrupt, while those working for the private sector are smart and honest. It is true that some government bureaucrats flex their muscles on people — go through any airport these days and you are bound to come across someone who bosses you around in the name of national security. However, this does not make Al Capone a good guy and Nelson Mandela a bad guy. We cannot complain about police brutality (which is real) and forget about the brutality of the Mafia or drug cartels. At least those in government are accountable and can lose their positions when they are voted out. The financial oligarchs are not accountable to anyone.

The law of unintended consequences, which is used to argue against government intervention in economic activity, means that actions taken by the government always have effects that are unanticipated or unintended. Why is it that only government actions produce unintended consequences, not the actions taken by the private sector? It gets even better because one argument put forward by free marketeers is that the private sector's actions have positive unintended consequences, one of which is Adam Smith's "invisible hand". Smith (1776) argued that each individual, seeking only his own gain, "is led by an invisible hand to promote an end which was no part of his intention", that end being public interest. "It is not from the benevolence of the butcher, or the baker, that we expect our dinner", Smith wrote, "but from regard to their own self-interest". Does this mean that when the financial oligarchs give themselves bonuses they act in the public interest and contribute to social welfare?

It is not clear why, for free marketeers, government intervention is always counterproductive. After all, the government is elected by people to act in the public interest, but this is not to say that a bad government cannot act against public interest, by looking at the interest of a minority as in the capture theory of regulation. This is bad government intervention as exemplified by actions such as bailing out failed financial institutions and the policy of quantitative easing. Corruption is not found only in the public sector. The bad government of Boris Yeltsen privatized the Russian economy in the early 1990s, which was effectively stealing from the people at large to give to a minority of oligarchs. For that, free marketeers loved him and he became the darling of the "west", but the Russian oligarchs did not produce any trickle-down effect as they migrated to London and elsewhere. When the government of Vladimir Putin did the right thing by putting some oligarchs behind bars for tax evasion, he was condemned by the "western" countries. On this occasion, and as far as most people are concerned, Putin is the good guy and the oligarchs are the bad guys.

Chapter 5

The Efficient Market Hypothesis as a Weapon of Mass Destruction

1. Introduction

In Chapter 4, we examined several weapons used in the war on regulation, including the rational expectations hypothesis, the Washington Consensus, the Great Moderation and the trickle-down effect. A weapon of mass destruction has been used in the war on financial regulation, the efficient market hypothesis (EMH), which is basically the rational expectations hypothesis (REH) as applied to financial markets. While the REH has been largely ignored, enthusiasm for the EMH is still alive because it is used to justify the drive for financial deregulation.

The efficient market hypothesis tells us that the market is efficient in the sense that market-determined financial prices (stock prices in particular) reflect all available information.[1] Since information arrives randomly, it follows that financial prices move in a random and an unpredictable manner — in other words, financial prices tend to follow a random walk process. The EMH is closely

---

[1] If the information pertains to the historical price behavior, then we have weak-form efficiency. If the information includes all public announcements and news, that gives semi-strong-form efficiency. If insider and private information is also considered, the market becomes efficient in a strong form.

linked to the rational expectations hypothesis, which postulates that market participants collect and process all of the information relevant to market prices (and any other macroeconomic and financial variable) such that they eventually converge on the correct underlying model or data generating process. One can see how the EMH is related to rational expectations from another description of the EMH: by using available information, all market participants arrive at rational forecasts of stock prices, which means that these forecasts become fully reflected in market prices (Shostak, 1997).

For a long time, the EMH dominated the thinking of finance academics to the extent that it was (and still is for the true believers) something like a heresy to question its validity. An enthusiastic efficient marketeer, Michael Jensen, went as far as claiming that "there is no other proposition in economics which has more solid empirical evidence supporting it than the efficient market hypothesis" (Jensen, 1978). Like many other economists, Jensen has since changed his mind about the empirical validity of the EMH. In 1985 Andrei Shleifer presented a paper in the annual meeting of the American Finance Association, in which he presented compelling evidence against the EMH. In a comment on the presentation, Myron Scholes described what Shleifer said as "rabbi economics" (Fox, 2009). Scholes was referring to his rabbi who would "tell a story about something that happened to his family, then go on to generalize the story to some big moral about the whole world". He was accusing Shleifer, who has since become a leading proponent of behavioral finance (hence an antagonist of the EMH), of following the same logic as the rabbi. If anything, recent events provide credibility for Shleifer rather than Scholes.

The opponents of the EMH, and most neutral observers, believe that the hypothesis provides the intellectual underpinning for embracing financial deregulation, which is widely and justifiably believed to have been a cause of the global financial crisis. The hypothesis was used to justify all of the excesses of the financial oligarchs (such as obscene bonuses and the cancerous growth in derivatives) and led to complacency with respect to asset price bubbles (since efficient marketeers do not believe in bubbles). The connection is simple: in an efficient market, the price of a complex derivative or a securitized asset must be right, the bonuses represent a true reflection of the performance of the recipients, and bubbles do not form. In this sense the EMH was a cause of the global financial crisis — this is a charge to which efficient marketers plead "not guilty".

In another sense, however, the EMH is a casualty of the crisis. With the benefit of hindsight, we know that financial and housing markets were experiencing bubbles that eventually burst and that bonus recipients did not perform that well to deserve the bonuses. We also know that complex derivatives and securities were extremely overvalued to the extent that some smart people managed (by exploiting overvaluation) to make enormous profit, which is an outcome that defies the EMH. The crisis, therefore, exposed the implausibility of the EMH, put it under scrutiny and forced economists and regulators (except the true believers, the enthusiastic efficient marketeers) to reexamine their faith in the hypothesis.

2. Origin, Evolution and Implications

Hilsenrath (2004) traces Eugene Fama's belief in market efficiency to his work as an undergraduate student in the late 1950s at Tufts University when he was hired to contribute to a market forecasting newsletter. While doing that work, he observed that strategies designed to beat the market did not work well in practice. By the time he enrolled at the University of Chicago in 1960, (neoclassical) economists started to view individuals as rational, which means that their behavior could be predicted by mathematical models. In a 1965 paper, Fama argued that stock prices follow a random walk process because the information that affects prices arise in a random manner and that in an efficient market, the actual price of a security at any point in time is a good estimate of its intrinsic value (Fama, 1965). In 1973, Burton Malkiel published a popularized discussion of the EMH, which brought the Chicago idea to the average person (Malkiel, 1973).

The efficient market hypothesis has played an extraordinarily big role in shaping mainstream thinking in financial economics, with significant practical implications. Since investors respond rationally to available information, as reflected in financial prices, they sell when prices are too high, and vice versa. In other words, one implication of the EMH is that assets and markets cannot be overvalued or undervalued and that market-determined prices are always at the right level. Any deviation of the price of an asset from its intrinsic value is eliminated very quickly. What does not make sense here is the rational expectations idea that every market participant believes that an asset is overvalued or otherwise (and to the same extent). This idea is ludicrous, to say the least. If they all want to sell an overvalued asset, who is going to buy? There is simply no such thing as a "representative agent" or a typical trader behaving in a standardized and predictable manner.

A related implication is that financial prices should exhibit no pattern and move randomly because information arrives in a random manner and gets reflected in prices almost instantly. Therefore the EMH lies at the heart of neoclassical thinking that the market takes care of things, restoring equilibrium on its own. This, of course, leads to the important implication that there is no need for regulation and that deregulation enhances market efficiency. For regulators, therefore, the challenge is to ensure that all investors have access to the same information, which means that regulation should be confined to accounting standards, timely publication of company news and data, disclosure of fees, and full description of financial products. One must admit that it is a noble cause to strive for full disclosure and the provision of a level playing field (as far as information is concerned) as this would kill insider trading. However, restricting regulation in this way leaves significant loopholes in the regulatory framework. Furthermore, private information obtained through research cannot (and should not) be regulated. We cannot possibly force someone to disclose the details of a profitable trading rule — this would be a violation of intellectual property rights. However, the EMH implies that profitable trading rules do not exist in an efficient market.

Yet another implication of the EMH is that the market cannot be outperformed on a consistent basis because all available information is already reflected in financial prices. As Hilsenrath (2004) put it, "markets distil new information with lightning speed and provide the best possible estimate of the underlying value of listed companies". Malkeil (1973) points out that "no technique of selecting a portfolio — neither technical nor fundamental analysis — can consistently outperform a strategy of simply buying and holding a diversified group of securities". He even says that "a blindfolded monkey throwing darts at a newspaper's financial pages could select a portfolio that would do just as well as one carefully selected by the expert". According to Shostak (1997) "the implication of the EMH is destructive for fundamental analysis, for this means that analysis of past data is of little help since whatever information this analysis will reveal is already contained in asset prices". Financial markets, in other words, are rational, which means that the best way to trade is to hold the market index. If the EMH were valid, then an index fund should always outperform managed and actively-traded funds, which is not necessarily the case (Hilsenrath, 2004).

It is true that beating the market is not easy and that most people cannot do that, but casual observation tells us that, more often than never, markets can be outperformed. Warren Buffett's view of the EMH, as expressed by Dehnad (2009), is interesting: the EMH "advocates no due diligence when investing — just buy the market — so it is good for his (Buffett's) business". In fact it has been stated that "unless you're Warren Buffett, an index fund is where you should put your money" (Nocera, 2009). This is strange because even Buffett is not supposed to beat the market since the EMH is a universal "law" of economics. Nocera (2009) also quotes Jeremy Grantham, a market strategist, as advocating index funds for unsophisticated investors who have no hope of beating the market while believing that professionals should do better precisely because, as he puts it, "the market is full of major league inefficiencies". As examples, Grantham refers to "incredible aberrations" such as the US housing market in 2007, Japan in the 1980s and

Nasdaq in 2000. Grantham argues that if professional investors had been willing to acknowledge these aberrations — and trade on the fact that the market was out of whack — they should have been able to beat the market". The global financial crisis produced big winners, those who did their research properly and reached the conclusion that the market for structured products would collapse. By betting on that prediction (for example, by taking short positions on credit default swaps) they made a killing. The majority who lost believed in the EMH, explicitly or implicitly, and followed herd behavior on the grounds that there was no bubble, but there was a bubble and that bubble came to the end of its natural life. So, it is not only Warren Buffet who can outperform the market.[2]

To its benefit, the finance industry interpreted the EMH, with the help and encouragement of academia, to imply that the market is capable of pricing financial assets correctly and that deviations from fundamental values could not persist. The development of financial engineering was propelled by the EMH, in the sense that any complex security can be priced correctly through the market mechanism of arbitrage. As a result, the financial oligarchy convinced politicians, regulators and investors that what they were doing was in the interest of the economy. Belief in the EMH made the authorities reluctant to restrain either the dotcom or the housing and credit bubble (*The Economist*, 2009b).

Fox (2009) suggests that efficient marketeers were originally "on to a good idea", but "sealed off in their academic cocoons — and writing papers in their mathematical jargon — they developed an internal logic quite divorced from market realities". Shojai and Fieger (2010) suggest that "the more one delves into the intricacies of (mainstream) academic finance the more one realizes how little the understanding is among a majority of academics". In the tradition of the EMH, Fama and French (1993, 1996) have created an industry of models (the Fama–French three-factor model and its variants), which have been accepted by finance academics to the

---

[2] Warren Buffet is known to acquire undervalued assets, which do not exist according to the EMH.

extent that no one would dare criticize them.[3] However, these models bear no practical significance and they are typically the product of extensive data mining (see, for example, Moosa, 2013a). It is plausible to argue that the developers of these models are quite happy to test them by using other people's money but they will not bet their superannuation balances on the predictions of the models. One may also suggest that there is inconsistency between the EMH (as developed by Fama) and the Fama–French models that are designed to predict stock returns on the basis of some factors.[4]

For a long time, the EMH was accepted as an undisputed fact of life and imposed on finance students in a vibrant process of indoctrination. Andrew Lo, a financial economist at the Sloan School of Management (MIT), says that "efficient-market theory was the norm" when he was a doctoral student at Harvard and MIT in the 1980s and that "it was drilled into us that markets are efficient". He also says that it took him 5–10 years to change his views (Cassidy, 2010). Richard Posner puts forward a plausible (and sarcastic) explanation for the love affair with the EMH. In reference to finance academics, Posner says the following (Cassidy, 2010):

> Well, one possibility is that they have learned nothing.... because market correctives work very slowly in dealing with academic markets. Professors have tenure. They have lots of graduate students in the pipeline who need to get their PhDs. They have

---

[3]More recently, Fama and French (2014) came up with yet another one of these models, the "five-factor asset pricing model". This model is designed to capture the size, value, profitability and investment patterns in average stock returns. One cannot bet that this would be the last model in this series of models, which have contributed nothing to our understanding of how financial markets work.

[4]What is the deal? Can we or cannot we predict stock prices? The five-factor model is supposed to be better than the three-factor model (in predicting stock prices or returns, I assume). Fama and French (2014) argue that there is evidence that average stock returns are related to book-to-market equity ratio as well as profitability and investment. Does this mean that the availability of information on these factors allows us to predict stock returns and conduct profitable trading?

techniques that they know and are comfortable with. It takes a great deal to drive them out of their accustomed way of doing business.

When interviewed by Cassidy (2010), Fama reacted rather furiously to Posner's comment, claiming that Posner is "not an economist" but rather "he's an expert on law and economics". When Fama was asked about Paul Krugman's criticism of the EMH, he replied by saying: "if you are getting attacked by Krugman, you must be doing something right". This kind of response is more suitable for politicians in a parliamentary debate, not in a debate among intellectuals or between Nobel Prize winners. Fama could not accept any criticism from a brilliant economist like Krugman, yet he complains that Posner is not an economist, most likely because Posner cannot solve partial differential equations. It is the brand of economics that Fama believes in (the physics-like economics) that has created the mess we are in now. It is the brand of economics that Posner believes in that will hopefully get us out of the mess.

Fox (2009) argues that it took a new group of young economists, the behaviorist, to nudge the profession back towards reality (that is, away from the EMH).[5] In the ensuing debate behavioral finance specialists proved to be more humble, less arrogant and more accurate in their predictions and explanations. Robert Shiller, for example, gave an early warning that the US housing market was dangerously overvalued. Unlike the EMH brigade, the behavioral finance mavericks do not believe that investors are rational decision makers and that prices reflect the true and intrinsic value of each trade. Rather, they believe that market participants are human beings who have emotions, fears, greed and hopes. As a result, some decisions and patterns of behavior may appear to be inconsistent and irrational. This perspective is shared

---

[5] In reality people have emotions and biases, which is what behaviorist believe. In the economics of Fama and his advocates people are robots and markets are machines.

by a successful trader who should not exist according to the EMH, George Soros, who argues that "the mathematical tools and techniques that are used to study the markets and investors' behavior miss one important point that human beings can influence the course of events" (Dehnad, 2009). An important policy implication of behavioral finance is that one argument for regulation is the protection of people from themselves, since they do not necessarily act in their own best interest (McDonald, 2009). In neoclassical economics, people do not act except in their best interest, which means that regulation is not required to save people from themselves.

One of the most influential behavioral finance specialists is another Chicago economist, Richard Thaler, who contends that "markets can veer off course when individuals make stupid decisions" (Hilsenrath, 2004). In May 2004, 116 economists and business executives gathered at the University of Chicago Graduate School of Business for a conference organized in Fama's honor. On that occasion, Fama surprised the audience by suggesting that poorly informed investors could theoretically lead the market astray. Stock prices, he said, could become "somewhat irrational". Hilsenrath (2004) describes Fama's statement as an "unexpected concession", suggesting that the "behaviorists" ideas had become mainstream". Indeed he quotes Thaler as saying: "I guess we're all behaviorists now", but Fama cannot be further away in his thinking from the behavioral finance camp. He is quoted by Hilsenrath (2004) as saying that behavioral economists like Thaler "haven't really established anything in more than 20 years of research". In response, Thaler describes Fama as "the only guy on earth who doesn't think there was a bubble in Nasdaq in 2000". For Fama the market is a mechanical or electrical system that has some sort of a control feedback loop or circuit breaker — it cannot go wrong because it is self-correcting.

Robert Shiller has long argued that "efficient-market theorists made one huge mistake: just because markets are unpredictable doesn't mean they are efficient" (Hilsenrath, 2004). Shiller further suggests that the leap in logic was one of "the most remarkable errors in the history of economic thought". Fama responds by saying the following: "behavioral economists made the same mistake in reverse: "the fact that some individuals might be irrational doesn't mean the market is inefficient". Needless to say, Fama does not produce any evidence on the size of the small minority of market participants who "might be" irrational when it is plausible to suggest that for the market to be efficient, the majority of participants must be rational.

The EMH was not only challenged by behavioral finance specialists and not only before the advent of the global financial crisis. The hypothesis has been discredited on both empirical and theoretical grounds. For example, Lo and MacKinlay (1999) find that markets are not completely random and that predictable components do exist in stock and bond returns. They actually invite scholars to reconsider the random walk hypothesis and suggest means for generating long-term investment returns through disciplined active investment management. From a theoretical perspective the EMH, like the rational expectations hypothesis, implies that no trading would take place in financial markets. For example, Shostak (1997) points out that "the major problem with the EMH is that it assumes that all market participants arrive at a rational expectations forecast", which "means that all market participants have the same expectations about future securities returns". He wonders why there should be any trade if participants are alike in the sense of having homogenous expectations.

Another problem with the EMH is the implication that any buy-and-hold strategy is as good as any other. On this point Pasour (1989) points out that the EMH is a version of the zero-profit theorem of competitive equilibrium in the conventional theory of the firm, focusing exclusively on equilibrium outcomes while ignoring the entrepreneurial market process that generates those outcomes. The EMH effectively implies that the stock market is a gambling place that is detached from the real world, but von Mises (1998) suggested that the success or failure of financial investment depends on the same factors that determine the success or failure of the venture capital invested.

The question that arises here is that if the EMH has that many loopholes why was it embraced by academia and the regulatory authorities? One explanation is the prevailing ideology, which has been market-oriented since the early 1980s. Academia, on the other hand, is dominated by confirmation bias and herd behavior (in terms of thinking).[6] It took the global financial crisis to convince some academics and regulators to question the EMH and its implications.

3. The EMH as a Cause of the Global Financial Crisis

There is a widespread belief that blind faith in the EMH was a major reason for the advent of the global financial crisis. Volcker (2011) argues that "it's clear that among the causes of the global financial crisis was an unjustified faith in rational expectations and market efficiencies". Volcker also criticizes the "mathematical precision" associated with the EMH and the explosion of derivatives that were intended to diffuse and minimize risk.[7] Instead, he argues, the vaunted efficiency helped justify an explosion of weak credit and an emphasis on trading along with exceedingly large compensation for traders".

The global financial crisis erupted in an environment characterized, among other factors, by weak credit and large compensations that created moral hazard. Nocera (2009) quotes a market strategist, Jeremy Grantham, as saying that "the EMH did a lot of damage in its heyday — damage that we're still dealing with".

---

[6] Academic economists are more interested in publishing papers in top journals than revealing the truth. It is easier to publish in a top journal by confirming established ideas or the orthodoxy than by challenging them. Moosa (2013b) argues that "confirmation bias boils down to the tendency of individuals to avoid rejecting a prior belief, whether in searching for evidence, interpreting it or recalling it from memory". One academic economist got a paper rejected because one of the reviewers said the following: "It is not wise to criticize other people's work just in case one of them turns out to be a referee". A paper submitted to a top finance journal criticizing the Fama–French five-factor model is very likely to be rejected, simply because it represents a criticism of a well-established orthodoxy. Moosa (2013b) argues that "the best example of these biases in finance research pertains to the now defunct efficient market hypothesis".

[7] Instead of being a risk management tool, derivatives have become a source of risk.

In fact Grantham goes as far as saying that "the efficient market hypothesis is more or less directly responsible for the financial crisis". He further says the following:

> The incredibly inaccurate efficient market theory was believed in totality by many of our financial leaders, and believed in part by almost all. It left our economic and government establishment sitting by confidently, even as a lethally dangerous combination of asset bubbles, lax controls, pernicious incentives and wickedly complicated instruments led to our current plight. 'Surely, none of this could be happening in a rational, efficient world,' they seemed to be thinking and the absolutely worst part of this belief set was that it led to a chronic underestimation of the dangers of asset bubbles breaking.

The EMH has contributed to the advent of the global financial crisis via several channels, the most important of which is that it encouraged deregulation. Other channels include complacency with respect to bubbles, heightened moral hazard, excessive use of complex derivatives and securitization, and the underestimation of risk. We start with the deregulation channel.

For efficient marketeers, the market reflects the true asset values and if left alone it takes care of everything, which means that there is no need for regulation. This implication of the EMH is similar to the implication of the rational expectations hypothesis that government intervention in the economy is ineffective. In fact, it is plausible to argue that both rational expectations and market efficiency were developed to justify *laissez faire* in general. Moving away from this general proposition, we ask the question whether or not deregulation was a cause of the crisis. There is a widespread belief that it was.

Looking at the historical record, we can see that regulation has worked in the past by reducing risk and boosting consumer confidence (Moosa, 2010). Prior to the Great Depression, the US experienced banking panics roughly every 15–20 years. In the 1930s, the Great Depression struck and the banking system nearly collapsed. In response to a dire situation, the Roosevelt administration engineered sweeping regulatory measures, including the introduction of federal deposit insurance, securities regulation, banking supervision, and the separation of commercial and investment banking under the Glass–Steagall Act. These regulatory measures produced a stable US financial system — for some 50 years, no major financial crisis was experienced, the longest such period on record.

Significant financial failures reemerged in the 1980s with the collapse of Continental Illinois, the first major bank to be offered the too big to fail (TBTF) status. According to Sprague (1986), "the combined 200 failures in 1984 and 1985 exceeded the 40 total from the beginning of World War II to the onset of the 1980s". Almost 3,000 commercial banks and thrifts failed in the savings and loan crisis, compared to only 243 banks that had failed between 1934 and 1980. By 1994, one-sixth of the federally insured depository institutions had either closed down or required financial assistance, affecting 20% of the banking system's assets. Long-Term Capital Management (LTCM), an unregulated hedge fund, collapsed in 1998, nearly causing a systemic failure. In the 21st century so far, we have already witnessed the bursting of the tech bubble in 2001, the accounting scandals that destroyed Enron in 2001 and WorldCom in 2002, and the worst crisis since the 1930s, the global financial crisis, which was followed by the European debt crisis.

It is no coincidence that financial crises followed a concerted push by bankers (the ultimate beneficiaries), right-wing economists (who provided the intellectual justification for deregulation, most notably the EMH) and market-loving policy makers to deregulate financial markets and institutions. The contribution of regulatory failure and deregulation to the eruption of the global financial crisis is emphasized by the Financial Crisis Inquiry Commission (FCIC, 2011). In its report, the Commission argued that "little meaningful action was taken to quell the threats in a timely manner".

Another channel whereby the EMH caused the crisis was complacency and failure to deal with asset price bubbles. Efficient marketeers do not believe in bubbles because bubbles represent mispricing and deviation of prices from intrinsic values, which cannot arise in efficient markets. The housing market bubble was fueled by low interest rates and expansion in subprime lending. In an interview with Nocera (2009), Jeremy Grantham said the following: "thanks to the efficient market hypothesis, no one was willing to call a bubble a bubble — because, after all, stock prices were rational". He added:

> Government officials, starting with Alan Greenspan, were unwilling to burst the bubble precisely because they were unwilling to even judge that it was a bubble … Our default reflex is that the world knows what it is doing, and that is extravagant nonsense.

Expansion in the use of credit derivatives was also encouraged by the EMH. American International Group's (AIG's) excessive production of credit default swaps without adequate cover was based on the assumption that the housing market would not collapse — but it did. The moral hazard issue takes several forms. Since the market determines asset prices correctly, there is nothing wrong in accumulating toxic assets, those that were rated AAA and offered several hundred basis points above the risk-free rate. There is nothing wrong with the big bonuses awarded to the financial oligarchs because the market sets the level of bonuses correctly. However, overvalued assets lead to faulty decisions and misallocation of resources, For example, a big lesson from the 1990s was that overpriced stocks could lead to bad decisions such as massive overinvestment in telecommunications during the technology boom.

Strong arguments can be put forward for the proposition that the EMH played a major role in causing the global financial crisis, but efficient marketeers present arguments as to why the EMH had nothing to do with the crisis. Even some of those who have questioned the validity of the EMH argue that it is not guilty beyond reasonable doubt. For example, Nocera (2009) quotes Justin Fox as saying that the question of whether "an academic theory hatched in Chicago led to the financial crisis can never be answered definitively". Needless to say, it is Fama, more than anyone else, who rejects entirely the claim that the EMH was a culprit, but he is not alone.

In an interview with John Cassidy, Fama rejected the very notion of bubble, suggesting that he does not even know what a bubble means (Cassidy, 2010). In fact he said that he became so tired of seeing the word "bubble" in *The Economist* that he did not renew his subscription. Fama claims that the economic slowdown predated the collapse of the mortgage market in 2007. His explanation goes as follows: as job and income growth slowed, some homeowners could not make their monthly payments, particularly the subprime borrowers who had taken out the riskiest mortgages. With delinquencies and foreclosures rising, banks and other financial institutions that had invested heavily in subprime mortgage bonds suffered big losses, which prompted them to reduce their lending to others. What we had, according to Fama, "wasn't really a credit crisis: it was an economic crisis". Cassidy (2010) argues that while Fama's story is logically consistent, it appears to contain a big gap as to what caused the Great Recession. Fama blames the gap on economists who do not know what causes recessions and argues that "debates go on to this day about what caused the Great Depression".

Needless to say, you do not have to be a macroeconomist to realize that financial crises are followed by recessions: the financial and banking crisis of the late 1920s and early 1930s was followed by the Great Depression and the global financial crisis was followed by the Great Recession. Like any faithful efficient or free marketeer, Fama insists that "the real culprit in the mortgage mess was the federal government, which instructed Fannie Mae and Freddie Mac to buy subprime mortgages and mortgage securities". Hence what happened was a government failure, not a market failure — it was the fault of those incompetent and corrupt people working for the government and has nothing to do with the greedy financial oligarchs (because greed is good). Blaming the global financial crisis on Fannie Mae and Freddie Mac only is an oversimplification and a distortion of what actually happened.

Fama said the same thing in a Q and A session with students at the University of Chicago (Dimitrakopoulos, 2011). In that meeting Fama said the following: "although many blame the real estate bubble, and in particular the subprime mortgage financing of real estate as the cause of the crisis and the subsequent recession, it was in fact a policy fostered by the government to allow people to have a mortgage with very little down payment". He also suggested that finance was not to blame and that finance was a casualty of the recession. However, the US government did not tell AIG to indulge in the selling of credit default swaps without having adequate capital to cover potential claims, neither did the US government instruct financial institutions to accumulate toxic assets. The British government did not tell Fred Goodwin, once the glamorous CEO of the Royal Bank of Scotland, to acquire ABN-Amro, which was the worst deal in corporate history. Excesses on the part of the financial oligarchs were caused by, at least in part, complacency resulting from belief in the EMH. However, governments must be blamed for the EMH-motivated deregulation and for allowing the financial oligarchs to capture them.

Yet another free marketeer, Burton Malkiel, said in an interview with the *New York Times* that "it's ridiculous" to blame the financial crisis on the efficient market hypothesis and attributed the failure of Bear Stearns to excessive leverage and maturity mismatch (Nocera, 2009). He echoed Fama by saying that bubbles do not exist. Malkeil is right in his diagnosis of the failure of Bear Stearns, but excessive leverage and maturity mismatch (among other phenomena) were allowed by deregulation on the basis that there is nothing to worry about as the market is efficient. Toxic assets were overvalued relative to the risk embodied in them, but the EMH rules out overvaluation.

If Fama does not know what a bubble is, we should perhaps tell him. A bubble is a sustained rise in financial prices over and above what is implied by fundamental factors — this happens as long as market participants feel that the bubble will not burst soon, which means that they can make profit by buying the asset and selling it later. Blanchard and Watson (1982) conclude that bubbles, in many markets, are consistent with rationality, that phenomena such as runaway asset prices and market crashes are consistent with rational bubbles. In fact, financial markets are characterized by the kind of behavior that involves bubbles followed by crashes (for example, De Grauwe and Grimaldi, 2006). Financial history is full of bubbles, including the bubble associated with the Mississippi Scheme, the South Sea bubble, the bubble in American stocks in the 1920s just before the Great Depression, and the dot-com bubble of the late 1990s. Just because the EMH implies that bubbles do not exist does not mean that they do not exist.

It is strange that Fama claims that economists do not know what causes recessions (including the Great Depression) because Fama's high priest, the late Milton Friedman, explained the Great Depression in terms of the collapse of the money supply (Friedman and Schwartz, 1963). Yes, there is a disagreement but Friedman's explanation is plausible. The Great Recession can be explained on similar lines as suggested by the former chairman of the UK's Financial Services Authority, Lord Turner, who stated in February 2013 that "the financial crisis of 2007 to 2008 occurred because we failed to constrain the financial system's creation of private credit and money" (Turner, 2013). Financial crises cause economic downturns, which makes the real sector of the economy a victim of the financial sector. This is what history tells us, and we should believe history more than a man-made theory like the EMH.

Turner's explanation goes as follows. In the run up to the crisis, banks created huge amounts of new money by making loans, which were used mostly to finance speculative transactions in housing and financial markets (very little of those loans went to businesses outside of the financial sector).[8] As a result, the level of personal debt skyrocketed. Since debt was rising more quickly than incomes, some people became unable to keep up with repayments and banks found themselves in danger of going bankrupt.

---

[8]This is why Turner is an enthusiastic supporter of financial reform in Iceland, aiming at depriving banks from the ability to create credit and money. This is an issue that will be elaborated on in Chapter 10.

This process caused the financial crisis. In the aftermath of the crisis, banks became reluctant to extend new loans to businesses and households. The slowdown in lending caused asset prices to drop, which means that indebted investors had to sell their assets in order to repay their loans. As a result asset prices dropped, the bubble burst and banks panicked and cut lending even further. A downward spiral was initiated and the economy went into recession. This may not be the only explanation for the Great Recession but it is a plausible explanation — indeed it is similar to Friedman's explanation of the Great Depression. Bubbles are followed by crashes and crashes cause recessions. The EMH rules out bubbles, implying that financial hubris does not cause recessions.

Another Chicago advocate of the EMH, Ray Ball, questions the reasoning that those who acted on the assumption of market efficiency felt too little need to look into and verify the true values of traded securities and so failed to detect asset price "bubbles" (he puts the word "bubbles" in quotation marks to imply that no one knows what bubbles are or at least that there is no widespread agreement on the meaning of bubbles) (Ball, 2009). Then he argues that "the claim that it (the EMH) is responsible for the current worldwide crisis seems wildly exaggerated". He puts forward an incredibly naive explanation for why the EMH was not responsible for the crisis, wondering "if the EMH is responsible for asset bubbles .... how bubbles could have happened before the words 'efficient market' were first put in print".

Ball's argument is truly ludicrous — it is not the words, but rather the underlying idea, the idea that markets take care of things. The EMH did not exist in the 18th century, but at that time Adam Smith formalized the idea of *laissez faire*, which implies that markets should be left alone, but when markets are left alone we periodically get the phenomenon of bubbles followed by crashes. In his defense of the argument that deregulation caused the global financial crisis, Richard Posner did not refer to the EMH but to the underlying idea when he said "the movement to deregulate the financial industry went too far by exaggerating the resilience — the

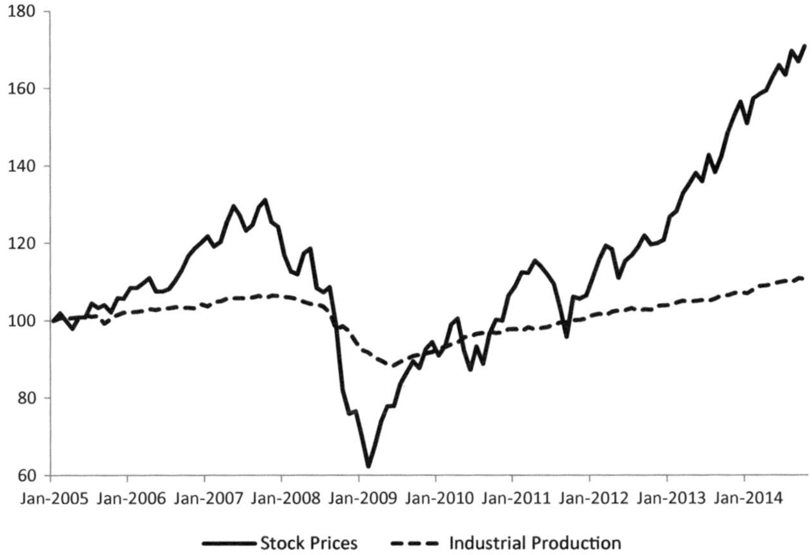

Figure 5.1:   US Stock Prices and Industrial Production

self-healing powers — of *laissez faire* capitalism" (Cassidy, 2010). It is not that a crash will never happen in a regulated market, but regulation has the effect of reducing the frequency and severity of crashes.

The facts and figures do not support the claim made by Fama that the financial sector was a casualty, not the cause, of the crisis. The consensus view on how stock prices are related to economic activity is that stock prices turn before economic activity (that is, stock prices represent a leading indicator of economic activity) but Fama claims that the recession started before the downturn in stock prices. In Figure 5.1, we observe US industrial production and stock prices over the period January 2005–October 2014. We can readily see that stock prices turned before industrial production, both upward and downward. The peak to trough in stock prices occurred between October 2007 and February 2009. The peak to trough in industrial production occurred between November 2007 and June 2009. Fama should have checked the facts and figures before claiming what he claimed.

4. The EMH as a Casualty of the Global Financial Crisis

In 1984, well before the global financial crisis, Robert Shiller described the EMH as "one of the most remarkable errors in the history of economic thought" (Shiller, 1984). At that time, not many economists shared this view, but things have changed as a widely held view is that the crisis has exposed flaws in the EMH. For example, financial journalist Roger Lowenstein blasted the theory, declaring that "the upside of the current Great Recession is that it could drive a stake through the heart of the academic nostrum known as the efficient-market hypothesis (Washington Post, 2009b). The EMH took center stage in the International Organization of Securities Commission's annual conference, held in June 2009, in which Martin Wolf, the chief economics commentator for *Financial Times*, dismissed the hypothesis as being a "useless way to examine how markets function in reality" (Jerusalem Post, 2009). On the same occasion Paul McCulley (managing director of PIMCO) was less extreme in his criticism, saying that the hypothesis had not failed, but was "seriously flawed" in its neglect of human nature. Cohen (2012) quotes Martin Wheatley, head of the consumer and markets business unit at the Financial Services Authority, as saying that the intellectual underpinning for regulation must now be turned on its head. He also quotes Adair Turner, the former chairman of the Financial Services Authority, as saying that regulators need to rethink the assumption that investors, and markets, behave rationally. Turner added that "the pre-crisis delusion was that the financial system, subject to the then defined rules, had an inherent tendency towards efficient and stable risk dispersion".

The EMH is a casualty of the global financial crisis because the collapse of financial markets cannot be explained in terms of the arrival of information. The crisis has dealt a severe blow, not only to the EMH but to the whole discipline of financial economics. Harper and Thomas (2009) suggest that "the disappearance of buyers.... from major financial markets, especially over-the-counter markets for derivatives, reinforces disaffection with efficient market theory". Quiggin (2009) warns of the ramifications of the failure of the efficient markets hypothesis and recommends a thorough rethinking of the analysis of financial regulation. Fox (2009) declares the triumph of the efficient market's critics by showing why traditional market forces can sometimes be just as pervasive as the rational ones.

Naturally, Fama holds a different view. In his interview with John Cassidy (2010), Fama declared that the EMH "did quite well in this episode". He went on to say the following:

> Stock prices typically decline prior to a recession and in a state of recession. This was a particularly severe recession. Prices started to decline in advance of when people recognized that it was a recession and then continued to decline. That was exactly what you would expect if markets are efficient.

This argument is inconsistent with Fama's previous argument that the financial crisis happened because of declining economic activity, meaning that stock prices declined as a result, not in anticipation, of weak economic activity. Fama puts the egg before the chicken in one place and the chicken before the egg in another.

In his defense of the EMH, Siegel (2010) (like others) argues that criticism of the EMH is due primarily to misunderstanding of what it means. In this respect Siegel argues that "no matter what definition is used, the hypothesis does not claim that the market price is always right" and (surprisingly) that "the EMH implies that the prices in the market are mostly wrong". He also says that "ex post rational price would almost always differ from the current market price". The interpretation suggested by Siegel is inconsistent with any of the definitions and descriptions of the EMH, so let us recall some of the definitions stated earlier. These definitions include expressions such as "any deviation of the price of an asset from its intrinsic value is eliminated very quickly", "information gets reflected in prices almost instantly", "markets distil new information with lightening speed", and "deviations from fundamental values could not persist". These expressions are inconsistent with the possibility of persistent deviations of prices from intrinsic values.

Now we are not sure whether the EMH implies that prices are always right, right on average, mostly right or mostly wrong.

5. Conclusion

No less than three Nobel prizes have been awarded for the invention of the efficient market hypothesis and its first cousin, the rational expectations hypothesis — both of which imply that any kind of intervention in the market or economy at large is useless at best and hazardous at worst. The EMH was not developed in a vacuum as an objective description of the behavior of asset prices but rather emerged out of the desire to demonstrate that regulation is bad. It was developed with the specific objective of encouraging deregulation. As a result, the financial stability that followed the regulatory measures of the 1930s has vanished.

The conclusion that can be derived from the arguments and counterarguments presented in this chapter is that the EMH is both a cause and a casualty of the global financial crisis. It is a cause because it encouraged deregulation and provided the justification for all of the excesses of the financial oligarchs in the run up to the global financial crisis. It also gave rise to complacency as bubbles are not supposed to arise. It is a casualty because the crisis has motivated a rethink of the hypothesis. As devastating as it was, it seems that the crisis had a positive by-product, the loss of faith in the EMH.

Chapter 6

The Regulation of Remuneration in the Financial Sector

1. Introduction

Remuneration is the compensation that an employee receives in exchange for work or what may be called "labor services". It takes several forms including wages and salaries, bonuses, golden parachutes, commissions (typically remuneration for sales calculated on the basis of a percentage of the goods sold), stock options (call options on the common stock of the underlying firm), fringe benefits (also called perks, including various types of non-wage compensation) and performance-related incentives.[1] Non-performance related payments may take the form of retention bonuses, payable for the period that an employee stays in the firm by virtue of mere presence. For the purpose of the discussion in this chapter, remuneration components include basic pay, bonuses and golden parachutes. Distinction is also made between cash payments and payments in stocks and stock options.

Remuneration in the financial sector is typically described as a "controversial issue", when in fact there is nothing controversial

---

[1] Performance-related incentives may be different from bonuses on the grounds that a bonus is paid for the performance of the firm as a whole while a performance-related incentive is paid for individual's performance.

about it. It is simply plain fraud involving a reverse Robin Hood transfer of wealth from shareholders and taxpayers to the "masters of the universes", the financial oligarchs. For free marketeers, if a chief executive officer (CEO) pays himself a $100 million bonus, even though the company has endured significant losses under his foresighted leadership, he deserves it because the market says so. It is not obvious how the market expresses an explicit view on the bonus awarded to this CEO and others, but the reasoning is that if this person does not get this bonus from his current employer, he will be able to obtain that amount by moving to another institution that is prepared to pay this kind of bonus, thus depriving the current employer from the opportunity to make things better. This is the twisted logic used by those who oppose the regulation of remuneration in the financial sector. There is no wonder, then, that it is business as usual for the financial oligarchs as they keep on ripping off shareholders, because of the lack of political will to regulate remuneration. This is what Harrington and Hjelt (2001) say in reference to CEO pay, starting with Sandy Weill, who got a pay package worth some $151 million in 2000 for running Citigroup:

> The great CEO pay heist executive compensation has become highway robbery — we all know that. But how did it happen? And why can't we stop it? The answers lie in the perverse interaction of CEOs, boards, consultants, even the Feds.

Yes, the whole scheme is fraud, including regulatory capture. Otherwise it can be put mildly as in Clementi *et al.* (2009) who suggest that to the extent that the pay packages of senior management deviate materially from the long-term financial interests of shareholders, any overcompensation problem is a failure of corporate governance. Several aspects of remuneration in the financial sector can be identified: (i) the exuberant and lavish level of pay, particularly for senior executives, which cannot be justified on any grounds, at least not in terms of economic theory; (ii) the bonus culture that has corrupted the system and provided a boost for moral hazard and (iii) the golden parachute deals offered to executives when they are fired for destroying their companies. These issues and more are discussed in this chapter, including the arguments for and against the regulation of remuneration as well as the proposals that have been put forward for this purpose.

2. Exuberant Remuneration in the Financial Sector

The explosion in executive pay (particularly in the financial sector) has been criticized by the likes of Peter Drucker and Warren Buffett (see, for example, Bogle, 2005b, 2009). It is a predominantly Anglo-American phenomenon, clearly visible in London and New York, the largest two financial centers in the world. For example, The Independent (2014) reported that the London bankers were back to business as usual in 2013 as the number of those earning at least €1 million rose to more than 2,700, in a "new City pay explosion" — this figure is 12 times as big as the pay observed in any other country in the European Union. There is no wonder that Wojcik (2013) suggests that "if global finance is to change, the New York–London axis has to change". Although Wojcik is not referring to remuneration specifically, his statement is particularly valid for this issue.

The proposition that the lavish pay under the alleged pay-for-performance scheme makes sense in terms of economic theory has been questioned by Krugman (2007), who argues that "the idea that huge paychecks are part of a beneficial system in which executives are given an incentive to perform well has become something of a sick joke". These claims are based on the pretext of attracting talent, which is rather ludicrous for at least two reasons. The first reason is that the recipient of the very big pay at the top of the executive ladder are far away from being "talented". This reminds me of the movie "Margin Call", which portrays the finance industry in its true color, where the big boss says the following to one of his technically apt subordinates: "I earn big buck, not because I have the brains". The second reason is that talented mathematicians and physicists should not be working for the financial sector, and they would not be if it were not for the extravaganza of complex derivatives that serve no useful function whatsoever (even worse, they are weapons of mass destruction). Without this extravaganza, those talented people, who solve partial differential equations and grasp topology and measure theory, would be working in laboratories to devise products that make our lives more pleasant, let alone make it possible for humans to land on Mars. The very fact that talented people like these work in dealing rooms rather than laboratories is indicative of the brain drain inflicted by the financial sector on the rest of the economy. True talent in the financial sector is a wasted talent from a national or economy-wide perspective.[2]

The Financial Crisis Inquiry Commission (FCIC) mentions some interesting facts and figures about executive pay in the financial sector (FCIC, 2011):

> As the scale, revenue, and profitability of the firms grew, compensation packages soared for senior executives and other key employees. John Gutfreund, reported to be the highest-paid executive on Wall Street in the late 1980s, received $3.2 million in 1986 as CEO of Salomon Brothers. Stanley O'Neal's package was worth more than $91 million in 2006, the last full year he was CEO of Merrill Lynch. In 2007, Lloyd Blankfein, CEO at Goldman Sachs, received $68.5 million; Richard Fuld, CEO of Lehman Brothers, and Jamie Dimon, CEO of JPMorgan Chase, received about $34 and $28 million, respectively. That year Wall Street paid workers in New York roughly $33 billion in year-end bonuses alone. Total compensation for the major US banks and securities firms was estimated at $137 billion.

---

[2] Talented people in this sense create most of the problems in the financial sector. It is these talented people who designed the toxic assets that brought a large number of financial institutions, hedge funds, pension funds and local authorities to their knees. Let us not forget the story of Long-Term Capital Management (LTCM), which was set up in 1994 by, among others, two extremely talented people, Myron Scholes and Robert Merton. With their work on derivatives, Scholes and Merton seemed to have devised a formula that yielded a safe but lucrative trading strategy. In 1997 they were awarded the Nobel prize. A year later, (LTCM) lost $4.6 billion in less than four months and a bailout was required to avert the threat to the global financial system. Beware of the hazard of employing talented people in the financial sector.

Are these figures justified by economic theory? In terms of marginal analysis, economic theory tells us that the wage rate should be equal to the marginal revenue product. While this condition is satisfied by football players such as Lionel Messi and Cristiano Ronaldo, it is certainly not satisfied by the gentlemen identified by the FCIC as being (or have been) overpaid. Business at the Spanish football clubs, Barcelona and Real Madrid, would be badly affected by the departure of Messi and Ronaldo, respectively, but I doubt very much if the departure of any of the talented gentlemen mentioned above would affect the business of their firms. Unlike Messi and Ronaldo, who are talented, any CEO of a big financial institution can be replaced easily because it does not take much to indulge in parasitic activities and take excessive risk with other people's money. No difference was made by the replacement of the CEOs of major financial institution during the global financial crisis (for example, Citi, Bear Stearns and Merrill Lynch). Interestingly, one of the gentlemen mentioned in the FCIC report defended his big pay by asserting that "if you examine our practices on compensation, you will see a complete correlation throughout our history of having remuneration match performance over the long term" (Aldridge, 2009). I actually like the words "performance", "correlation" and "long term". By observing the facts on the ground we will find that big pay is not related to performance, whether it is long term or short term. The numbers show that correlation is not there.

Based on a study by Bazot (2014), *The Economist* (2014c) considers two explanations for the high incomes earned by bankers and fund managers. The first of these explanations is that they have created a lower cost of capital for businesses in the form of low bond yields and high equity valuations. It is not clear how the paper, which is about the macroeconomic costs of financial crises and the contribution of the financial sector to gross domestic product (GDP), leads to this explanation. In any case, this explanation can be dismissed easily because low bond yields have been the result of expansionary monetary policy (quantitative easing). The other explanation makes sense: bankers and fund managers earn zillions because they are rent seekers and earners (even predators and scavengers). They manage to earn zillions because they are in a privileged position and because the finance industry is protected by the too big to fail (TBTF) doctrine, which even applies to hedge funds if they are well connected politically.

Yet there are those who defend obscene payments to the financial oligarchs because they (the oligarchs) deserve it. For example, the President of the US Chamber of Commerce, Thomas Donohue, defended Wall Street compensation packages in a news conference held on 12 January 2010.[3] Donohue described bonus recipients as "mad scientists", and "very unique people". The irony is that they believe it, which explains why financiers have some sort of an inflated sense of entitlement. They are indeed special and unique because in no other profession do people get paid obscene amounts of money for doing work that is useless at best and destructive at worst. Actually, some of them get paid for spending most of their time playing golf and bridge — their firms (the shareholders, to be more specific) pay for the helicopter ride from the rooftop of their buildings to the golf course or the location of the bridge tournament. Comparing finance gurus to scientists is an absolute insult to science. A disenchanted former computer programmer at Citigroup in Dallas once wrote "I can't help but believe that their (Citi's) financial and upper management gurus are incompetent, narrow-minded and as self-absorbed as the folks who were running the show in their information technology department" (Drum, 2009). Those "mad scientists" are best described by movies like *Margin Call* and *The Wolf of Wall Street*: a bunch of greedy and incompetent people. Greed and incompetence, a lethal combination, brought about the global financial crisis.

The "attracting and retaining talent" argument does not make sense because the talent required to work for NASA is not required to run a financial institution. Basic finance, which is needed to support real economic activity and facilitate the exchange of goods and services, can do without people who are good at solving partial differential equations. Advising a client on how to cover

---

[3] https://self-evident.org/?paged=2.

exposure to foreign exchange risk is not as mentally demanding as the calculations required to make sure that a space shuttle will not burst in flames upon reentry into the Earth's atmosphere. Using complex mathematics to design betting devices (derivatives) is simply an extravaganza with potentially fatal consequences. Dowd (2009a) describes the talent argument sarcastically as follows:

> Again and again, we have business leaders whose sky-high remuneration was said to be based on their superior abilities, the heavy responsibilities they were bearing, and so forth. They then run their businesses onto the rocks, blame bad luck, and ask us to believe that they weren't responsible.

Examples of finance executives who fit the description of Dowd are plentiful. Consider first the Citigroup chief financial officer (CFO) who attributed the large losses announced in November 2007 to the firm being the victim of "unforeseen events". Bonner (2007) makes the following comment:

> No mention was made of the previous five years, when Citi was busily consolidating mortgage debt from people who weren't going to repay, pronouncing it "investment grade," mongering it to its clients and stuffing it into its own portfolio, while paying itself billions in fees and bonuses. No, like the eruption of Vesuvius; even the gods were caught off guard. Apparently, as of 30 September 2007, Citigroup's subprime portfolio was worth every penny of the $55 billion that Citi's models said it was worth. Then, whoa, in came one of those 25-sigma events. Citi was whacked by a once-in-a-blue-moon fat tail. Who could have seen that coming?

Another example is that of Goldman's CFO when Goldman reported heavy losses on one of its hedge funds in August 2007. The CFO explained the event by saying: "we were seeing things that were 25-standard deviation moves, several days in a row" (Larsen, 2007). A single 25-standard deviation event was widely cited in the press as one that we would expect to see one day in 100,000 years — that is, very unlikely. The comment made by the CFO was met with widespread ridicule and achieved instant notoriety (Dowd, 2009a). Goldman must have been very unlucky — or else the talented people running the show were not really talented. As a matter of fact, Dowd *et al.* (2008) suggest that the probability of a 25-sigma event is by far smaller than what is indicated by press estimate of one day in 100,000 years.

Yet another example is the last CEO of Lehman Brothers before its demise, the person who led his firm to the biggest corporate bankruptcy in US history. At a congressional hearing held on 6 October 2008, Congressman Henry Waxman said the following to the CEO:

> You made all this money by taking risks with other people's money. The system worked for you, but it didn't seem to work for the rest of the country and the taxpayers, who now have to pay $700 billion to bailout our economy.

The CEO responded by saying: "I take full responsibility for the decisions that I made and the actions that I took." Dowd's (2009a) interpretation of this response is that the CEO "denied that he had made any errors or misjudgments in the period leading up to the firm's bankruptcy". The CEO even defended why he paid himself about $350 million between 2000 and 2007, attributing the decision to a "compensation committee that spent a tremendous amount of time making sure that the interests of the executives were aligned with shareholders"! It is doubtful that this CEO's interests were aligned with the interests of the shareholders because it is not in the interest of shareholders that the firm went into extinction.[4] According to Dowd (2009a), senior executives at Lehman had

---

[4] It is not obvious why a "tremendous" amount of time is required to make sure that the interests are aligned. They are either aligned or not aligned, and we all know that they are not aligned because of the moral hazard problem. Then why is it that this committee never found the interests to be non-aligned?

been working on their golden parachutes at the same time as they were pleading for federal rescue (meaning taxpayers' money), and it turned out that three departing executives had been paid bonuses just days before the firm collapsed. On this issue, Dowd concludes the following:

> One can only wonder what these people were being paid so much for. Cases such as these give great offence to the public who must pay for them, and the system that gives rise to them is manifestly indefensible…. Indeed, I would go so far as to say that this type of irresponsible behavior on the part of so many senior executives has now become the single biggest challenge to the political legitimacy of the market economy itself.

So much for the talent argument, now what about the profitability argument that finance is a profitable business, which makes people who generate profit eligible for and worthy of a financial reward. No one denies that the financial sector is profitable — the facts and figures confirm this contention. In Figure 6.1, we observe the profit generated by the US financial sector in billions of dollars and as a percentage of total corporate profit. We can see that profit in dollar terms is already above the pre-crisis peak. In terms of percentage, the financial sector claimed more than 40% of total corporate profit in 2002. Although it has declined since, the share of the financial sector of total corporate profit is still around 30%, which is rather high, given that the financial sector constitutes less than 7% of the economy in terms of gross output. In Figure 6.2, we observe how the share of the financial sector of total output has fluctuated narrowly since 1997 — at no time was it as high as 8%. What is amazing about the financial sector is that its share of total profit is not dependent on its share of total output unlike, for example, manufacturing industry. In Figure 6.3, we observe that the share of total profit and share of output are much more strongly correlated in the case of manufacturing industry than the financial sector. In fact the correlation coefficient between the share of profit and the share of output for the financial sector is statistically

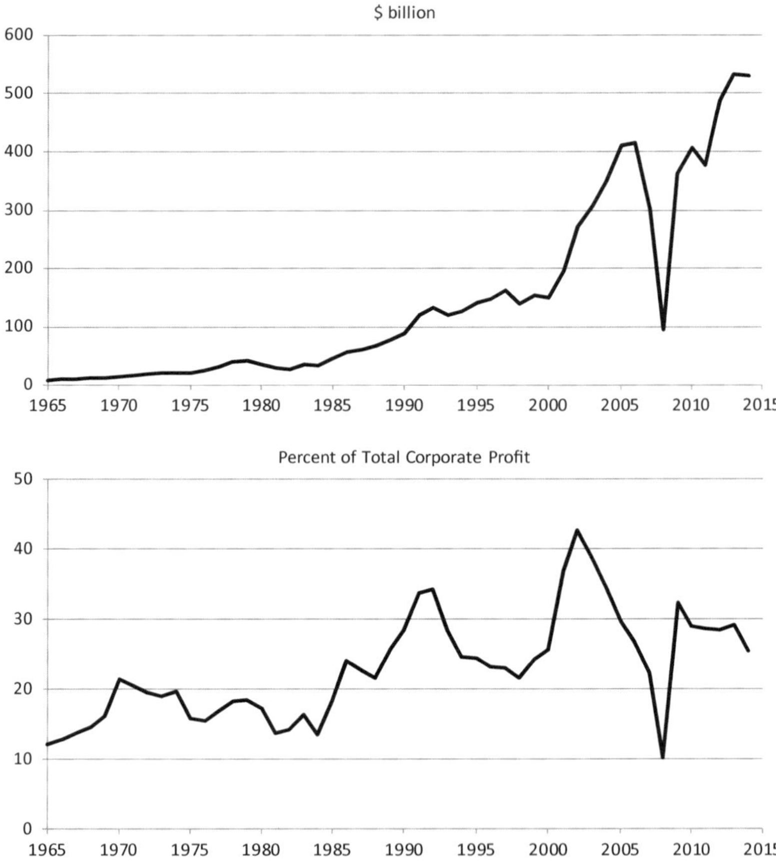

Figure 6.1: Profitability of the US Financial Sector

insignificant.[5] In Figure 6.4, we see that the ratio of the profit share to output share is much higher for the financial sector than manufacturing industry, transportation and wholesale trade. Philippon (2013) believes that total compensation of financial intermediaries (profits, wages, salaries and bonuses) as a fraction of GDP is at an

---

[5] For the financial sector, the null hypothesis that correlation is zero cannot be rejected as the underlying t-statistic is 1.274 with 16 degrees of freedom. For manufacturing, the t-statistic is 5.127, which means that the null is rejected (hence the correlation coefficient is statistically significant).

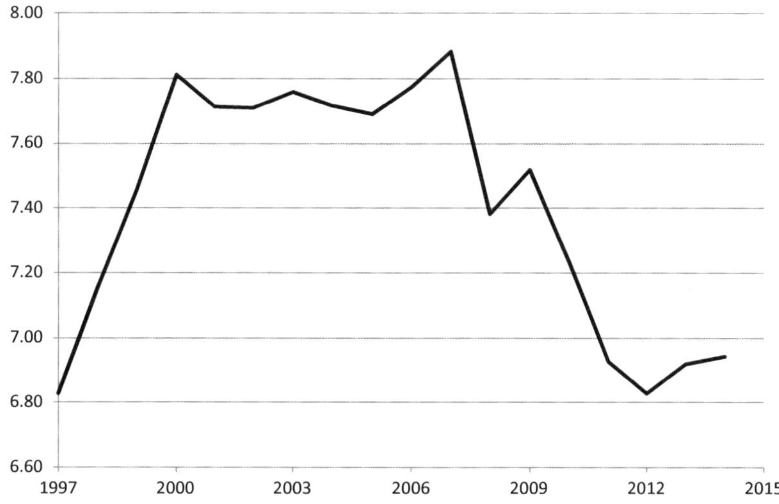

Figure 6.2:　The Share of US Financial Sector in Total Gross Output

all-time high, around 9% of GDP. While Khatiwada (2010) observes the rising incidence of corporate profit across all sectors, he emphasizes the fact that the profit of the financial sector has been growing at a faster rate than the rest of the economy.

It seems therefore that the finance gurus deserve exuberant pay because they generate profit for shareholders. This may be why the Organisation for Economic Co-operation and Development (OECD) found evidence indicating that even the lowest paid finance workers earn 15% more than their counterparts doing similar jobs in other sectors. At the top of the scale, the gap is as wide as 40% (Stewart, 2015). According to Knowledge@Wharton (2010) the compensation of CEOs in the financial services outpaces that of CEOs who head non-financial companies. For example, executives of non-financial companies comprise 3.9% of the people in the top one-tenth of the 1% tax bracket, while investment bankers comprise 5.2% and fund managers 4.8%. The figures obtained from the New York State Comptroller show that Wall Street banks handed out $28.5 billion in bonuses to their 167,800 employees in 2014, up 3% over 2013. To put these figures

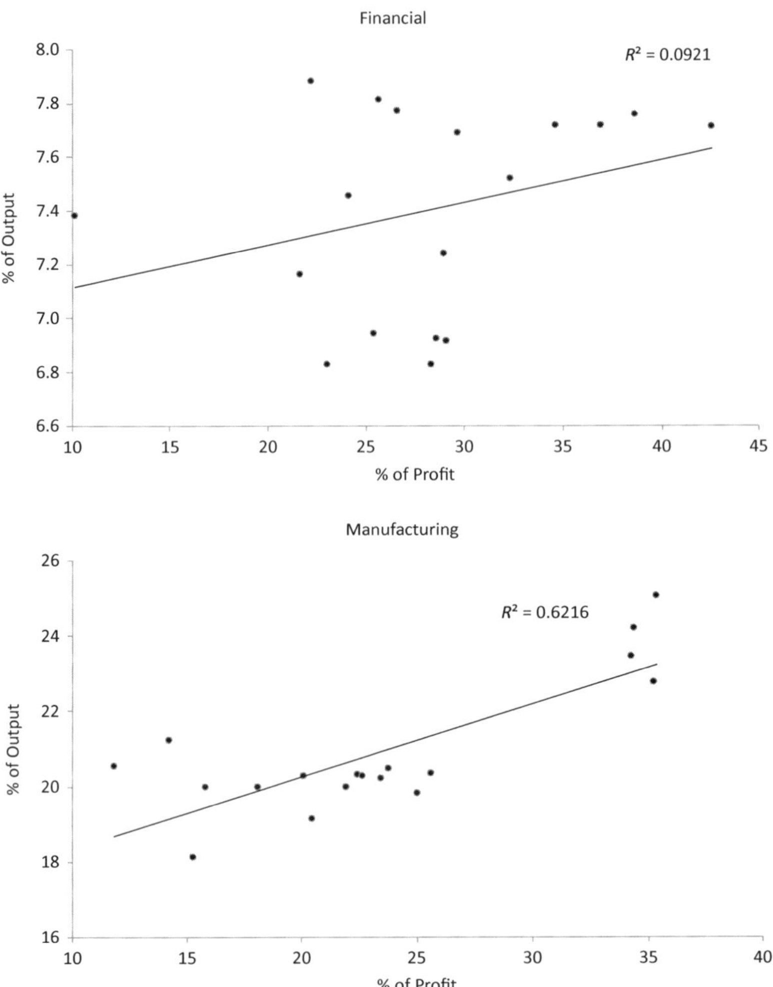

Figure 6.3: **Profit and Output Shares of the US Financial and Manufacturing Sectors**

in perspective, Anderson (2015) compares these payments to low-wage workers' earnings and calculates how much more of a national economic boost would be gained if similar sums were funneled into the pockets of the millions of workers at the bottom end of the pay scale. She demonstrates that the $28.5 billion in bonuses paid out to Wall Street employees is double the annual

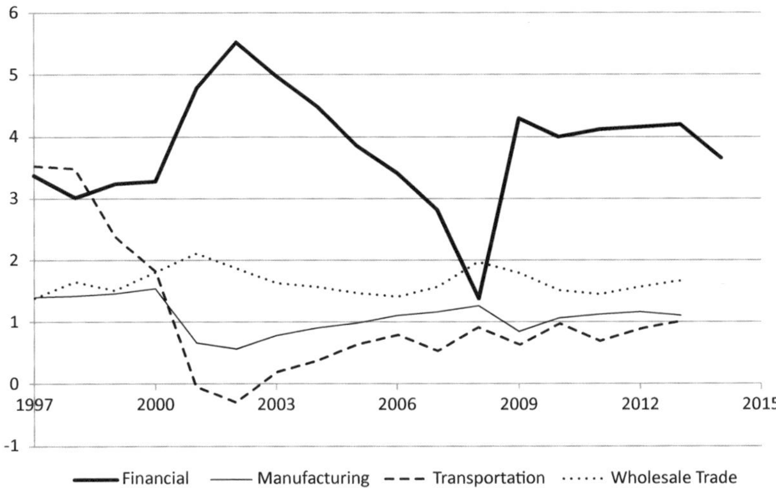

Figure 6.4: **The Ratio of Profit Share to Output Share of US Sectors**

pay for all 1,007,000 Americans who work full-time at the current federal minimum wage of $7.25 per hour.

While it may sound plausible to argue that the financial oligarchs deserve high pay because they generate more profit than those working in other sectors, the figures on their own are deceptive. Yes, financial sector activity generates massive profits but most of what goes on in the financial sector constitute fraud or parasitic activities that produce nothing useful. Consider the following examples of profit generated from fraud or parasitic activity. Why would an executive in a financial institution receive exuberant amounts for the profit generated by fixing London Interbank Offered Rate (LIBOR), manipulating the prices of gold and silver and rigging the foreign exchange market (all of these are criminal offenses)? Is it legitimate that a particular financial institution pays zillions in bonuses out of the profit generated by deceiving clients, telling them to buy certain financial products and betting on a massive decline in the prices of the same products? The same institution generated profit by providing the means whereby a particular European government could escape the scrutiny of the European Union and load up on debt, with disastrous consequences. What is the legitimacy of profit derived from selling junk assets portrayed as AAA assets? What is the legitimacy of the huge profit generated by a small unit of an insurance company by selling insurance against default without having adequate funds to cover claims? The same question can be raised about the profit generated by ripping off clients in terms of fees and commissions. Why would the CEO of a mortgage provider become a quarter billionaire as he was rewarded for the profit generated by extending mortgages to borrowers who were not financially capable of repaying those mortgages, leading to the collapse of the company? I must not forget to mention that accounting fraud is used to manipulate earnings to claim bonuses.

I recall an instance in the movie "Margin Call" when the boss encourages his sales staff to sell huge amounts of junk assets, promising them financial rewards if they achieved certain sales targets. In a nutshell, the profit generated by indulging in con jobs or activities that add nothing to social welfare should not be used to justify exuberant pay for the finance gurus. If activity in the financial sector is restricted to the basic function of supporting economic activity by providing means of payments and credit, the profit generated by the financial sector will be back to a normal level as it is in the case of other sectors of the economy.

Although the financial sector is highly profitable, executive remuneration may not be justifiable in terms of profitability. For example, how is it possible, in any business model, that the wage bill exceeds net income? This actually happens frequently, but one example will suffice. Figure 6.5 shows the wage bill (compensation and benefits) for the Bank of America during the period 2003–2009. With a wage bill like this, what will be left for the shareholders who are supposed to own the company? Why is it that the subordinates (managers) get paid more than the masters (shareholders)? Is not this some sort of a heist? And where is the alignment between the interests of shareholders and senior managers?

Excessively high pay in the financial sector is not only reward for fraud and parasitic activity but it also has other adverse

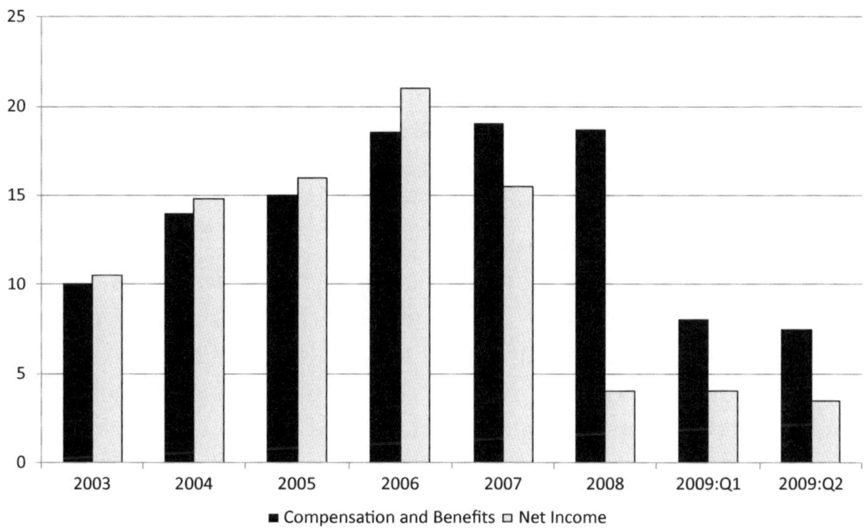

Figure 6.5:　Net Income and the Wage Bill for Bank of America ($ billion)

consequences. First of all, high pay leads to further growth of the financial sector and consequently to more fraud and more parasitic activity. Financialization is already a problem that is no less than the Dutch Disease: as countries become more dependent on the financial sector, they become more vulnerable to financial crises. This is a simple lesson that has not been learned from the global financial crisis. In the US and the UK manufacturing industry has been dwindling as financialization has become a dominant force. In the UK, policy makers have been guided (or rather misguided) by the motto "who needs manufacturing industry when we have the City?". The US economy has changed from a super manufacturing power to one dominated by the financial sector. The reality is that a modern economy cannot be run on a sector that is dominated by parasitic activities, which is exactly what the modern financial sector is all about. While manufacturing industry provides the products of technology in the form consumer goods and machine tools, the financial sector gives us the products of the so-called "financial engineering", including options on futures, futures on options, options on futures on options on swaps, Collaterized debt obligations (CDOs), CDO squared, synthetic CDOs, credit default swaps (CDSs) and so on. This is probably why, based on the analysis of 50 years of data across its 34 member-countries, the OECD has produced evidence indicating that a large financial sector is associated with slow economic growth (Stewart, 2015). The cancerous growth of the financial sector is propelled by high executive pay.

Exuberant remuneration in the financial sector fuels regulatory capture, when regulators become the defendants of the financial institutions they are supposed to regulate and supervise. This is why Brooksley Born warns that "the power and influence of the financial sector threatens a continuation of the regulatory capture that contributed to the financial crisis", suggesting that "the tendency of some former government officials to obtain highly lucrative positions in the financial sector after leaving government may well act as an inducement to those remaining in government to serve the interest of the financial sector rather than those of the public" (Martens and Martens, 2015).[6] As long as the financial sector offers exuberant pay, the problem of regulatory capture will persist. Talk to any regulator these days, and you will hear the same argument in a very apologetic tone, that nothing much can be done to change the *status quo*, which means that regulation can be nothing more than tweaks around the edges of existing rules. Furthermore, as long as pay in the financial sector remains exuberant, fraud will persist and the brain drain will continue. The finance industry has been attracting top-notch mathematicians, physicists and engineers from other sectors of the economy where they have a comparative advantage and where they can produce something useful and advance our knowledge of the world around us. It is never in the interest of the society and economy to convert a mechanical engineer, who could work on the improvement of the fuel efficiency of the internal combustion engine, to a financial engineer working on making derivatives more complex and opaque.

---

[6] In Chapter 3, we presented a number of examples on regulatory capture.

Last, but not least, excessive pay in the financial sector is a major reason for inequality, a proposition that is supported by considerable empirical evidence. The OECD has produced evidence showing that high pay in the financial sector exacerbates inequality (Stewart, 2015). Levy and Temin (2007) demonstrate that the rise of extreme income inequality coincided with a wave of deregulation and financial innovation, marking a shift in official attitudes from a concern for social responsibility and moderation to a championing of individualistic acquisition. Hodgson (2013) attributes income inequality to factors relating to the financial sector, including credit expansion, asset prices, household and corporate debt, and remuneration practices. Hindery (2008) contends that "the disparity in compensation today is an ethical embarrassment to our country, and it is certainly an affront to workers and to shareholders".

Two economists from the Economic Policy Institute, Josh Bivens and Lawrence Mishel, argue that "most of the rise in income inequality over the past few decades is due to the soaring pay of CEOs and Wall Street bankers who are milking money from the markets rather than generating much in the way of economic production" (Gongloff, 2013). Arguing against the proposition that exuberant pay can be justified in terms of economic theory, they suggest that "a substantial part of the extraordinary rise of top 1% incomes is not a result of well-functioning markets allocating pay according to value generated, but instead resulted from shifting institutional arrangements leading to shifting of rents to those at the very top". They point out that "the bulk of the gains by the 1% in the past few decades have been made by people who work on Wall Street" and that "this wouldn't matter if bankers and CEOs were busily adding value to the economy" but "many seem to be busily doing the opposite".

3. The Bonus Culture

A culture is typically defined as encompassing the general customs and beliefs of a particular group of people at a particular point in time. The bonus culture refers to compensation practices that

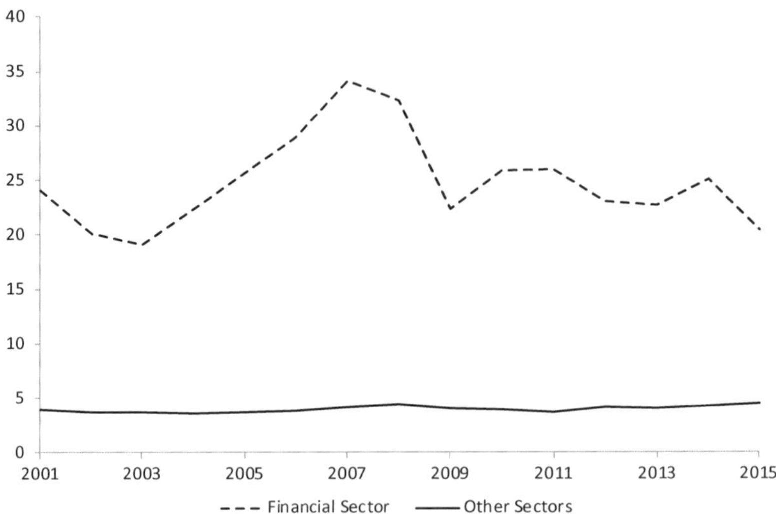

Figure 6.6:   Bonuses as a Percentage of Total Pay in the UK

appeared in the late 1980s, pioneered by big Anglo-American banks and subsequently adopted by financial institutions in the rest of the world. The bonus culture is now so entrenched in financial institutions that it is almost impossible to get rid of it. A bonus has become an acquired right, expected irrespective of performance although in practice bonuses are portrayed as reward for performance. One feature of the bonus system in the financial sector is that it is higher as a percentage of total pay than in other sectors of the economy as shown in Figure 6.6 for the UK.[7] We must remember, however, that these are average figures and that for some individuals bonuses are many multiples of their salaries.

A bonus can be defined as a financial incentive granted to staff in addition to their base pay (salary) in the form of a one-time payment. It can be specified in a particular contract (for example, as a percentage of trading profit), otherwise bonuses are distributed randomly out of a predetermined pool. For trading staff and executives, the bonus is the main component of remuneration as it can be multiple times the basic salary. Practical experience tells us that

---

[7] The figures are from Office for National Statistics (2015).

if bonus payments are linked to performance, measured somehow, it encourages risk taking and fraud. This kind of pay arrangement is responsible for the huge losses incurred by Societe Generale as a trader named Jerome Kerviel indulged in unauthorized trading to maximize profit and hence his bonus. However, Kerviel told investigators that his trading behavior was common and that the management turned a blind eye to any kind of trading behavior.[8] Like Kerviel, his superiors at Societe Generale were motivated by the desire to maximize bonuses, thus allowing adventurous traders to indulge in unauthorized trading and take excessive risk so that the traders and their bosses may hit the jackpot. As it turned out, Kerviel did not hit the jackpot.

Two main economic arguments can be presented for awarding bonuses. The first argument is that a bonus compensation scheme provides financial institutions with a degree of flexibility in their cost structure. This system enables them to adapt to cyclical variations in profits because it is easier to cut bonuses than to reduce salaries when business turns bad. This argument is bogus because casual observation tells us that bonuses are not related to cyclical variation in profit and because financial institutions do not shy away from firing thousands of employees, let alone reducing salaries, when business is not that good. The second argument is that bonuses reward individual performance and enable financial institutions to recruit and maintain the best — it is the "talent" argument all over again. The downside, and it is a big downside, is that tying bonuses to "performance", particularly on a year-to-year basis, encourages risk taking. In order to maximize bonuses, traders find it tantalizing to take risky positions. Although systems of risk control can be used to limit traders' positions, and despite the possibility of being fired in case of huge losses, traders tend to cheat by hiding their positions if they exceed what they are allowed to do. Then it becomes a matter of asking for forgiveness, not permission. Of course if they make huge profit, they will be forgiven as everyone will get a bonus.

---

[8] "Le trader livre sa version de l'affaire Société Générale", Le Monde, 29 January 2008.

A variable performance-related bonus that forms a substantial part of contractual remuneration means that the bonus recipient effectively works for a share of net profits (but not net losses) that can be attributed to them. Consider the example of a trader who earns a salary of $100,000 and a bonus of 10% of the profit generated on his portfolio, which is nominally $10 million. If the trader earns return of 10% (that is, $1,000,000) his bonus will be $100,000. If the trader loses the entire portfolio, which is not his money anyway, the worse that can happen is that he will be fired. Assume that that this trader believes that the market is so bullish that he can earn much bigger profit and hence a big bonus if he takes a position of $1 billion, which can be achieved by leveraging 100:1 (just to follow the good example of LTCM that leveraged 100:1 prior to its collapse in 1998). If the market return is 10%, the trader will generate profit after loan repayment (at 1%) of $90.1 million, which means that he receives a bonus of $9.01 million. This is much better. If, however, the market goes down 5%, a loss of $59.9 million will be incurred, charged to shareholders or to taxpayers if this institution is a TBTF or a Systematically Important Financial Institution (SIFI) creature.[9]

This is how the bonus system, coupled with greed, leads to excessive risk-taking through leverage, which may be achieved by fraudulent means. The bonus culture encourages risk taking and causes booms and busts, bubbles and crashes, happiness and misery, etc. In 2009, the UK's Treasury Select Committee issued a report on bank pay in which they slammed bonus schemes for encouraging risk taking at the expense of shareholder interests and the long-term health of the banks themselves (The Telegraph, 2009). The Committee said that "the mega-bonus pay culture among banks encouraged a lethal combination of reckless and excessive risk-taking".

In reality it is more often than never that bonuses are not related to performance as they are awarded irrespective of performance — just because bonuses are expected as an acquired right.

---

[9] The calculations are based on a borrowing cost of 1%. This is how a low interest environment encourages this kind of behavior and leads to the formation of bubbles. The effect of low interest rates and quantitative easing will be discussed in Chapter 9.

When performance is good, bonuses are paid out as a reward. When performance is bad, bonuses are paid out on the pretext of retaining "talent". When a financial institution fails and bailed out, bonuses are still paid out so that bonus recipients would repair the damage that they caused in the first place. Consider the case of the Royal Bank of Scotland (RBS), which cost British taxpayers billions of pounds worth of bailout money. Although the RBS is owned mostly by taxpayers, the management demands bonuses for losing 10 billion pounds only as opposed to losing 20 billion pounds — a spectacular achievement indeed. And guess what, they get their bonuses, because they are the only people who have the talent to put back the RBS on its feet again. The argument is that if those geniuses are not paid their bonuses they will leave the RBS, perhaps the whole of the UK to go somewhere where they can get the bonuses they deserve. Moyer (2009) reported that the board of RBS was threatening to resign if the government (the major shareholder) did not let it pay 1.5 billion pounds in bonuses, claiming that they had lost 1,000 employees to rivals (bad luck to rivals). So much for giving shareholders a say over pay! It is not obvious why the authorities have not considered closing down this losing venture and treat it as a sunk cost.

Cuomo (2009) illustrates the delink between performance and bonuses in the US financial sector. As the New York State's Attorney General, Andrew Cuomo conducted an inquiry into the financial meltdown of 2008 to examine the role played by the bonus culture in the meltdown, asking bank executives for the justification of paying bonuses. One executive claimed that it was a reward for performance, as he declared that "employees should share in the upside when overall performance is strong and they should all share in the downside when overall performance is weak". However, the truth is that they share in the upside whether or not there is an upside. This is what Cuomo says about two financial institutions that incurred huge losses in 2008, yet they distributed fat bonuses:

An analysis of the 2008 bonuses and earnings at the original nine Troubled Asset Relief Program (TARP) recipients illustrates the point. Two firms, Citigroup and Merrill Lynch, suffered massive losses of more than $27 billion at each firm. Nevertheless, Citigroup paid out $5.33 billion in bonuses and Merrill paid $3.6 billion in bonuses. Together, they lost $54 billion, paid out nearly $9 billion in bonuses and then received TARP bailouts totalling $55 billion.

Consider now the share of those bonus recipients in the downside. Figure 6.7 shows earnings, bonus payments and the bailout money received in the accordance with TARP in 2008 for nine TBTF financial institutions. The figures are outrageous, to say the least. Ironically, bonus payments are more strongly correlated with bailout money than with earnings — bonuses, it seems, are more related to the generosity of taxpayers than the performance of bonus recipients. If performance is measured in terms of the rise or fall in stock prices, the same conclusion is reached: that bonus payments are not related to performance. In Figure 6.8, we observe the bonuses paid to the top-five executives against the percentage change in the stock price of the underlying firm in 2008. In all cases, stock prices went down, but that did not prevent the top-five

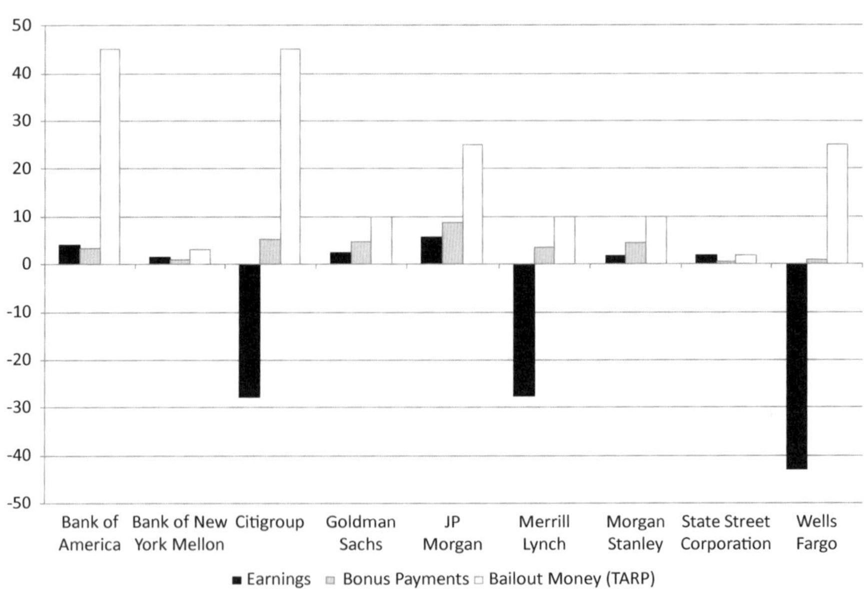

Figure 6.7:   Earnings, Bonuses and Bailout Money ($ billion, 2008)

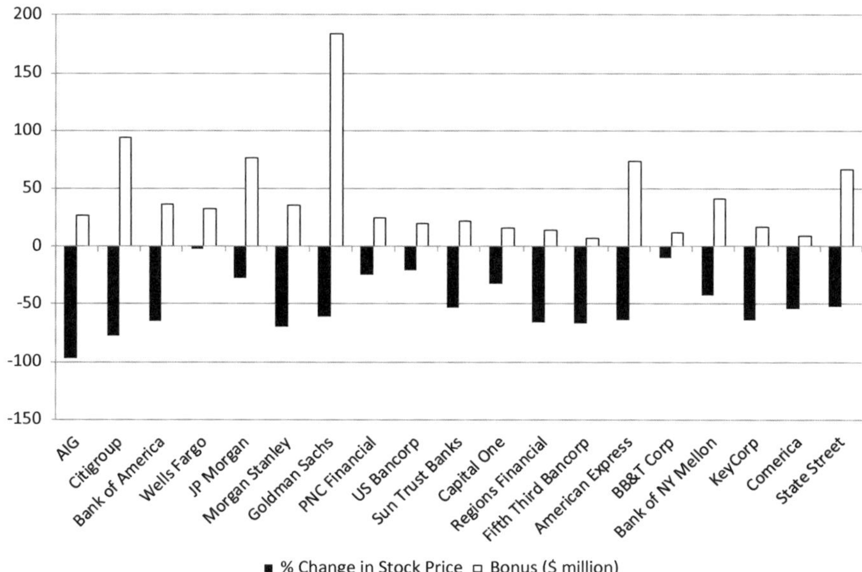

Figure 6.8:   Bonuses of Top-Five Executives and Stock Price Performance (%)

executives from rewarding themselves (for failure) with lavish bonuses. Indeed the figures show that bonus payments are negatively correlated with performance. The lack of correlation between pay and stock prices is best described by Harrington and Hjelt (2001) in a cynical manner as follows:

> You might have expected it to go like this: The stock isn't moving, so the CEO shouldn't be rewarded. But it was actually the opposite: The stock isn't moving, so we've got to find some other basis for rewarding the CEO.

Harrington and Hjelt (2001) go on to quote Michael Jensen, an enthusiastic efficient marketeer, who said the following: "I've generally worried these guys weren't getting paid enough. But now even I'm troubled". Recall that the efficient market hypothesis is used to justify exuberant pay, but what we have here is an efficient marketeer who says that the level of pay is so high that not even the almighty market cannot justify.

The conclusion of the Cuomo report is the following:

In sum, as we seek to learn lessons from this economic crisis and repair the damage it has wrought, it will be vital to develop and implement sound principles and rationales for executive compensation and bonuses that promote sustainable and rational economic growth. The repeated explanation from bank executives that bonuses are tied to performance in a manner designed to promote such growth does not appear to be accurate. Indeed, our investigation suggests a disconnect between compensation and bank performance that resulted in a "heads I win, tails you lose" bonus system. In other words, bank compensation structures lacked consistent principles and tended to result in a compensation system that was all "upside".

In Figure 6.8, we can see that the worst performance in terms of the percentage change in prices was posted by American International Group, Inc. (AIG), when the stock lost 97% of its value — yet the top-five executives gave themselves bonuses worth $26.9 million, but that is not all, because other people on the AIG payroll received bonuses as well. The AIG case triggered outrage, so we will consider the scam in some detail in a separate section.

4. The AIG Bonus Fiasco

The AIG bonus payments fiasco began when in March 2009 the company declared that it would pay millions of dollars in bonuses to the employees of the financial products unit, which is the very unit that got the company bankrupt. The people who were going to receive bonuses were the very people who created the mess. That announcement was made at a time when AIG posted a loss of $61.7 billion, the greatest ever for any company. It also came at a time when the company received billions of dollars' worth of bailout money from taxpayers who were effectively told to foot the bill for the payment of bonuses. Before proceeding to a discussion of the justification for paying those bonuses, it is worth mentioning that the damage was mostly caused by the head of the financial products unit until March 2008. When he was fired, he received an exit bonus of $35 million on top of the $280 million he made between 2000 and 2008, but that is not all — he was subsequently brought on board as a "consultant" at the modest fee of $1 million a month to clean up the mess.

Justification for the bonus payments centered on two arguments: (i) the bonus recipients were the only people capable of cleaning up the mess and (ii) these were retention payments, to make sure that those talented wizards would not leave the company. The first reason sounds like rewarding an arsonist for putting off a fire that he started deliberately. The second reason makes no sense because if those wizards were as talented as they were portrayed to be, the mess would not have arisen in the first place. The talent issue was raised by AIG's President, Edward Liddy, who told Treasury Secretary Tim Geithner that the payments were needed "to retain the best and the brightest talents" to run AIG (Mintz, 2009). An editorial in the Star Ledger (2009) reacted to this "talent propaganda" as follows:

> This band of 'best and brightest' just blew a $62 billion hole in the company. What's to retain? Heads should be rolling. Besides, is there really that much cutthroat competition for such an overpaid bunch of losers? Maybe there is — which would explain a lot about what passes for talent around lower New York City these days and, if so, is downright frightening.

It was also claimed (by the company) that the payments were made because bonuses were contractual, which would have been linked to performance or otherwise. If the bonuses were linked to performance, they should not have been paid because that was the worst performance in corporate history. If they were not linked to performance, they were not really bonuses, because bonuses are supposed to be tied to performance. We have seen that one argument for the payment of bonuses is that it gives companies flexibility because they can reduce bonuses in bad times, which cannot be done with basic salaries. If this argument was valid, then AIG should not have paid bonuses at the worst time in its history.

On the "contractual payment" argument, Rachel Maddow (of MSNBC News) had the following to say on Late Night with David Letterman (Mintz, 2009):

> Sometime in early 2008, that company signed contracts with its employees that said: 'Even if you cause the company to fail and nearly bring down the worldwide economic system, you will still get a bonus' ... I mean, who writes those contracts?

We know one thing for sure, that the person who wrote the contracts and promised bonuses no matter what is not the same person who paid the bonuses. Rick Newman of *US News & World Report* argues that the allegation that those wizards are the only people capable of cleaning up the mess is "tantamount to extortion" (Newman, 2009). MSNBC host David Shuster said the following: "The argument that these were so-called retention bonuses is undermined by the fact that 52 of the people who received them have already left the company".[10]

The declaration of the AIG bonus payments triggered outrage. President Obama said the following (*New York Times*, 2009).

> It's hard to understand how derivative traders at AIG warranted any bonuses, much less $165 million in extra pay. How do they justify this outrage to the taxpayers who are keeping the company a float? ... In the last six months, AIG has received substantial sums from the US Treasury. I've asked Secretary Geithner to use that leverage and pursue every legal avenue to block these bonuses.

The Washington Post reported the following (Dennis and Cho, 2009):

> Hired guards stood watch outside the suburban Connecticut offices of AIG Financial Products, the division whose exotic derivatives brought the insurance giant to the brink of collapse last year. Inside, death threats and angry letters flooded e-mail

---

[10]Countdown with Keith Olbermann (transcript), MSNBC, 19 March.

inboxes. Irate callers lit up the phone lines. Senior managers submitted their resignations. Some employees didn't show up at all.

Politicians on both sides of Congress reacted with outrage to the planned bonus payments. Senator Chuck Grassley made a dramatic statement by saying the following (Edwards and Oswald, 2009):

I would suggest the first thing that would make me feel a little bit better toward them if they'd follow the Japanese example and come before the American people and take that deep bow and say, I'm sorry, and then either do one of two things: resign or go commit suicide.

Senator Chuck Schumer accused AIG of "Alice in Wonderland business practices", saying that "it boggles the mind" (Kennedy, 2009). He threatened to tax the bonuses at up to 100%. Senator Jon Tester said that "this is ridiculous" and that "AIG executives need to understand that the only reason they even have a job is because of the taxpayers" This is one of the quotes collected by Mintz (2009) — some of the others are the following:

- *Senator Harry Reid*: "Recipients of these bonuses will not be able to keep all of their money".
- *Senator Chuck Schumer*: "If you (bonus recipients) don't return it (bonus) on your own, we will do it for you".
- *Representative Tim Ryan*: "It boggles my mind how these executives can be so unaware of what the American people are going through".
- *Representative Barney Frank*: "Paying the bonuses is rewarding incompetence".
- *Ben Bernanke*: "I understand why the American people are angry. It's absolutely unfair that taxpayer dollars are going to prop up a company that made these terrible bets — that was operating out of the sight of regulators, but which we have no choice but to stabilize, or else risk enormous impact, not just in the financial system, but on the whole US economy".

- *Lawrence Summers*: "The easy thing would be to just say … off with their heads, violate the contracts. But you have to think about the consequences of breaking contracts for the overall system of law, for the overall financial system".

We can see that only Bernanke and Summers qualified their condemnation by expressing their views in a "yes … but" style. Bernanke was wrong to believe that there was no alternative but to stabilize the company because the alternative course of action would have been to let AIG go the way of Lehman Brothers. The "enormous impact" would have been no more than Goldman Sachs and other allegedly TBTF institutions, as well as a large number of non-American institutions, losing a few billion dollars and the stock market dipping, perhaps substantially. Nothing would have been as apocalyptic as portrayed by Bernanke and the management of AIG. As for the "breaking contracts" argument of Summers, I wonder if the contracts for the "overall financial system" stipulate that bonus recipients will be rewarded even if the company collapses, but by the admission of AIG's top executives those were retention bonuses, paid in reward for failure. It is preposterous to suggest that bonuses can be contractual and unrelated to any measure of performance. If a company fails or makes losses, shareholders do not receive dividends, in which case it does not make sense that the employees of this company demand and receive bonuses. Even if the bonuses were contractual (and they should never be contractual), a losing or failed company cannot meet its obligations. Why is it that a failed company can default on its contractual payments to bondholders and other creditors but not on the "contractual" payments to bonus recipients? This is a case of double standards — is it not?

There were also some interesting media commentaries, of which the following are examples:

- *Charles Krauthammer*: "I would deny them the bonuses if possible. I would be for an exemplary hanging or two. Have it in

Times Square, invite Madame Defarge. You borrow a guillotine from the French and we could have a party".[11]

- *William Kristol*: "Can capitalism survive the behavior of some capitalists? It's always been an open question. But if capitalism is to survive, shouldn't the Republican party, the party that defends democratic capitalism, be particularly vehement in denouncing its excesses? Isn't this a pretty spectacular one" (Kristol, 2009).
- *Robert Lenzner*: "The $170 billion bailout of AIG and the $165 million bonus outrage are the result of reckless behavior by AIG and most especially by its egomaniacal former chairman, Maurice (Hank) Greenberg. This supposed paragon of higher finance was just plain playing Russian roulette with his shareholders' money, destroying nearly $200 billion in equity and putting an onerous cost on Uncle Sam and taxpayers" (Lenzner, 2009).

Without going into too much detail on who said what, the following is a selection of comments that have been made on the AIG bonus fiasco.[12]

- Certainly, we can screw these guys out of these bonuses the way they screwed us.
- The public is angry. They are steaming, off-with-their-heads mad at AIG and other financial companies for the greed and cheating that pushed us into a financial meltdown.
- The bonuses bring a whole new meaning to the phrase "bank robber". These bankers and brokers and investing Svengalis knew exactly how their obscene cash-grabbing orgy would look to the rest of us. They just did not care.

It is ironic that some of those who contributed to the *status quo* by defending deregulation complain about the AIG bonuses. In a

---

[11] "Special Report Panel on Outrage Over AIG Bonuses", Fox News, 17 March 2009.
[12] See the Wikipedia entry "AIG Bonus Controversy".

nationally syndicated opinion column, economist Thomas Sowell claimed that the politicians who did the most to create the situation that led to the use of taxpayer money to fund the bonuses are now the same ones who are complaining the most about the bonuses. Sowell (2009) also wrote: "If members of Congress can't be bothered to read the laws they pass, then they have no basis for whipping up lynch mob outrage against people who did read the law and acted within the law". One has to be fair and admit that those politicians and regulators, including Bernanke and Summers, did not condemn AIG outright but used qualified statements.

In a small-scale orgy of defending the indefensible, and despite the justifiable outrage triggered by the AIG fiasco, some commentators considered the payment of bonuses to be appropriate and legitimate. Former White House Press Secretary, Dana Perino, defended AIG as follows: "if they don't get it (the bonus), maybe they won't be motivated enough to try to help the company turn around" (Armbruster, 2009). The question that arises here is whether the wizards of AIG were motivated enough by causing the spectacular collapse of the company. This attitude of "if I don't get my bonus I will not clean up my mess" is indeed extortion, but extortion is nothing new to AIG. The company obtained bailout money through extortion by warning that any failure by the government to bail it out would have "catastrophic" consequences. This is the same company that, in the words of O'Rourke (2009), adopted financial practices that "displayed a shameful level of arrogance and irresponsibility" and the same management that was unable to "practice even the most basic risk management".

In an AIG (2009) document dated 26 February 2009, the company used fear mongering by warning that "the failure of AIG would have a cascading impact on a number of US life insurers", that "the government's unwillingness to support AIG could lead to a crisis of confidence over other large financial institutions", that "the loss of confidence is likely to be particularly acute in countries that have large investments in US companies and securities and whose citizens may suffer significant losses as a result of the failure of AIG's foreign insurance subsidiaries", that "this could lead directly to a decrease in the attractiveness of US government securities and a consequent increase in borrowing costs for the US government", that "the failure of AIG could create a chain reaction of enormous proportions", and that "the failure of AIG would have a devastating impact on the US and global economy" — and there is much more. The language of fear is reflected in the use of expressions like "cascading impact", "crisis of confidence", "chain reaction of enormous proportions", and "devastating impact". If these claims were true then the people who caused the problem should be tried for crimes against humanity (on the contrary, they got their bonuses out of taxpayers' money). It is not obvious whether Ms Perino truly believed the AIG propaganda or said what she said because she is driven by right-wing ideology, hence believing that the private sector does not do anything wrong and that anything that goes wrong should be blamed on the government.

Another defender of AIG was Terence Corcoran who wrote an article claiming that "AIG is innocent" and that the problem was caused by "massive government failure on the part of Barack Obama who doesn't get it" (Corcoran, 2009). This again is the kind of mentality associated with the belief that no problem is caused by the private sector and all problems are due to government intervention. It is ironic that without government intervention the AIG wizards would not have obtained bonuses. Naturally, someone from the *Wall Street Journal* had to defend AIG — and that someone was Evan Newmark who accused those "attacking" AIG of being "hysterical, bloodthirsty ravings" and "populist hurly-burly" (Newmark, 2009). Andrew Sorkin of *The New York Times* argued for the case for paying bonuses, saying that there was likely some truth to AIG's claim that it needed to retain its top talent, and that its most talented employees could find employment elsewhere. Sorkin also said that not paying the bonuses could spark problems across the business community because "if you think this economy is a mess now, imagine what it would look like if the business community started to worry that the government would start abrogating contracts left and right" (Sorkin, 2009). Joshua Zumbrun of *Forbes* argued that the outrage over bonuses distracted from a larger issue: that AIG had taken much of the bailout money and used it to settle contracts with its counterparties, Wall Street banks, hedge funds and non-US banks, at full price (Zumbrun, 2009). Of course there was the right-wing commentator Rush Limbaugh who defended AIG by saying: "we've got peasants with their pitchforks phoning in death threats at AIG" and "we have members of the United States Senate and the United States House of Representatives sounding like communist dictators". Limbaugh described the bonuses as "legal and productive", saying that "this money went to American citizens"! He defended the bonus payments by using his expertise in macroeconomics to say the following (Limbaugh, 2009):

> These people who got the bonus are going to spend it. That's called private sector stimulus … The ones who got the bonuses did so on the basis of sales success. These were reported as merit bonuses that they are contractually permitted to get. If you violate their contract, if you don't give them their bonus, you have got a lawsuit on your hands.

What this defender of the indefensible says is indeed more outrageous than the bonuses themselves. The private sector stimulus argument of the self-declared macroeconomist, Rush Limbaugh, is ridiculous because the marginal propensity to consume of bonus recipients is rather low (if not zero), while their marginal propensity to save in tax havens is very high. And what "sales success" is he talking about? The alleged success is like selling car insurance to someone, and when the insured puts in a claim following an accident the insurer says "sorry I do not have the money to meet my obligations". This can hardly be described as "success". Yes, the money went to a few American citizens (perhaps not all of them were American citizens) but that same money was stolen from thousands or millions of American citizens and even if those bonuses were contractual, the company could have obtained bankruptcy protection.

5. Golden Parachutes

A golden parachute (also known as a golden handshake) is an agreement between a company and an employee (typically an upper executive) specifying that the employee will receive significant benefits if employment is terminated. Traditionally, a golden parachute is executed only if the termination of employment is the result of a merger or takeover, and this is why a golden parachute is also known as "change-in-control benefits". Things have changed, however, as the term is now used to describe perceived excessive severance payments that are unrelated to changes in ownership — that is, golden parachutes are not necessarily associated with mergers and takeovers.

The first use of the term "golden parachute" is credited to a 1961 attempt by creditors to oust Howard Hughes from the control of Trans World Airlines. The creditors provided Charles C. Tillinghast an employment contract that included a clause whereby he would be paid in the event of losing his job.[13] The use of golden parachutes expanded greatly in the early 1980s in response to the large increase in the number of takeovers and mergers.[14] At the same time, golden parachutes prompted shareholder suits challenging the validity of the payments. Attempts have been made to limit payments through the SEC's termination agreement disclosure rules of 1986 and the provisions of the Deficit Reduction Act of 1984 aimed at limiting the size of future parachutes with a special tax on payouts that topped three times annual pay. For example, the Deficit Reduction Act disallowed "excess parachute payments" and imposed a 20% excise tax on the recipients of these payments. According to the Act, excess parachute payments arise if compensation is in excess of the employee's "base amount", which is the average gross annual income paid to the employee by

---

[13] http://content.time.com/time/specials/packages/article/0,28804,1848501_1848500_1848418,00.html.

[14] In the early 1980s, wholesale deregulation started and belief in the power of the market started to be the guiding beacon. It is not a coincidence that the golden parachute and bonus culture gained tremendous momentum in the 1980s.

the company over the preceding five year period. Golden parachute payments that exceed three times this base amount are assumed to be unreasonable compensation, which makes them subject to penalties in the form of tax (for details, see Bress, 1987).

In the 1990s, some efforts were made in the US to reduce change-in-control benefits. As of 1996, Section 280G of the Internal Revenue Code denies a corporation a deduction for any excess parachute payment made to a departing employee, while Section 4999 imposes on the recipient a non-deductible 20% excise tax, in addition to regular income and social security taxes. The 2010 Dodd–Frank Act includes in its provisions a mandate for shareholder votes on any future adoption of a golden parachute by publicly traded firms (see, for example, Bebchuk *et al.*, 2010b). In Switzerland, a referendum was put to a vote on 3 March 2013 to determine whether or not to give shareholders the power to veto executive pay plans, including golden parachutes (Revill *et al.*, 2013). Voters approved measures to curb executive pay and outlawed golden parachutes that can result in directors pocketing huge payoffs (Willsher and Inman, 2003).

While golden parachutes are not restricted to the financial sector, two observations must be made in this respect. First, in Figure 6.9, we can see that the number of golden parachutes was extraordinarily high in 2008 as bankruptcies surfaced due to the eruption of the global financial crisis. The second observation is that some of the most outrageous golden parachutes were awarded in the financial sector for CEOs who single-handedly caused the collapse of their firms. This is the ultimate example of rewarding failure or rewarding what is nothing to reward. The following are some examples of golden parachutes:

- For just five years of service at US Bankcorp, Jerry Grundhofer earned deferred compensation worth more than $111 million.
- Stan O'Neal presided over Merrill Lynch's collapse in the subprime crisis. When he retired (more accurately, forced to retire) in 2007 he forfeited pension, perks and deferred compensation worth $54 million. Still, he walked away with equity profits

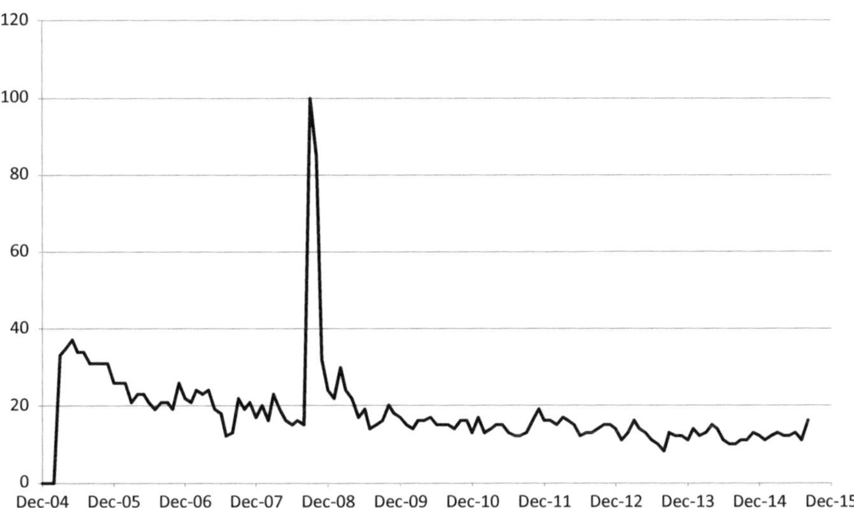

Figure 6.9:   The Number of Monthly Golden Parachutes in the US

worth over $160 million. His departure coincided with a quarterly loss of $2.3 billion (the largest in the company's 93-year history) and an $8.4 million fine from the government related to the subprime mortgage crisis.

- John Kanas stepped down from North Fork after the Long Island-based bank was bought by Capital One for $14.6 billion in 2006. In total, his equity profits and perquisites totaled $213 million (although his pension was no more than $1 million).
- When Bank of America bought the struggling Countrywide Financial Corp, Angelo Mozilo, the former CEO of Countrywide, took home about $44 million, in addition to the $140 million in Countrywide stock that he sold off in 2006–2007.
- In a 2007 emergency board meeting, Citigroup's Charles Prince announced his resignation and walked away with $99 million in vested stock holdings and a pension, on top of the $53.1 million salary and bonuses he racked up during his four year tenure.
- According to *The Economist* (2012b), Fred Goodwin (formerly, Sir Fred Godwin) led RBS into a ditch and dumped the bill on British taxpayers, but he managed to leave with a pension of over £700,000 a year.

Arguments for golden parachutes rest on the "benefits accruing to shareholders", which include the following: (i) golden parachutes make it easier to hire and retain executives, particularly in industries that are more prone to mergers; (ii) they encourage executives to remain objective about the company during the takeover process and (iii) they dissuade takeover attempts by increasing the cost of a takeover. The third argument, in particular, is flawed because golden parachute costs are a very small percentage of the cost of a takeover and do not affect the outcome. All of these arguments are related to takeovers and nothing about rewarding failure, but even if golden parachutes are associated with mergers and acquisitions, they can create moral hazard. For example, a golden parachute may cause an otherwise loyal manager to approve (or even invite) a less than optimal merger or takeover. Another example is that a parachute may, perversely, reward a manager for transforming a healthy, well-managed company into a prime takeover target.

It does not make any sense to claim that golden parachutes are beneficial to shareholders. During the global financial crisis, shareholders of big financial institutions watched helplessly their wealth evaporate — yet they had to finance the award of golden parachutes to the very people who caused their wealth to evaporate. In any case, shareholders had no say in what was paid to the likes of Stan O'Niel. This is why Bress (1987) thinks that the term "golden parachute" derives from the widespread image of a laughing executive landing softly with his reward while the company goes down in flames and so do the shareholders.

Several arguments can be presented against golden parachutes. To start with, dismissal is a risk in any occupation, and executives (unlike ordinary workers) are already well compensated. Another argument is that executives have a fiduciary responsibility to the company, and should not need additional incentives to stay objective — in other words, they should not be rewarded for what they are expected and paid to do. Critics invariably question golden parachutes as gifts, waste or the product of executive self-dealing (Bress, 1987). The central query, according to Bress (1987), is whether the executives who hold golden parachutes (the "golden parachute beneficiaries") give adequate compensation in return for their parachutes. In economic terms, the question is whether the expected cost to the firm of providing golden parachutes exceeds the expected benefits to be derived from them. Another argument centers on the effectiveness of golden parachutes. Bress (1987) suggests that "parachutes are ineffective, because they cannot possibly overcome the executive's desire to remain at the corporate helm". He cites others who argue that no level of remuneration will overcome even the most obstinate executive's entrenchment biases and those who focus their criticism on the potential moral hazard created by parachute contracts that compensate their beneficiaries too handsomely.

Campbell (1990) presents what seems to be a comprehensive list of arguments against golden parachutes, including the following: (i) golden parachutes are a waste of corporate assets, rewarding executives for performing tasks that they are legally and ethically bound to perform as part of their corporate duties; (ii) far from inducing corporate loyalty, golden parachutes enhance disloyalty by encouraging executives to seek mergers as a way of accelerating the benefits of their contracts; (iii) searching for the right trigger, executives may agree to suboptimal acquisitions; (iv) golden parachutes create both apathy and recklessness, thus harming shareholder interests and (v) the presence of ego and the absence of fear of post-merger termination encourage managers to fight takeovers ruthlessly, increasing transaction costs and reducing shareholder profits. On the other hand, *The Economist* (2012b) argues that a golden parachute can persuade the boss not to obstruct a takeover.

Golden parachutes provide yet another means whereby greedy executives rip off shareholders and in some cases taxpayers. They are unfair because they are awarded to people who are already paid excessively. They are unfair because they are not awarded to the majority who do the work (in other words, they are a privilege of the 1% only). They are unfair because it is invariably the case that shareholders have no say in the matter. And they are unfair, to say the least, because sometimes they are awarded to people who mismanage the company, burn it to the ground and deprive hundreds or thousands of employees from employment as they lose their jobs. A typical employee may get an end-of-service benefit of a one month salary for each year of service. In fact, down-to-earth employees walk away with nothing apart from a small pension. Why is it that people on top of the pyramid who spend most of their time play golf get paid multiples of big monthly salaries for each year of service? Is it because the market says so?

6. Arguments for and against the Regulation of Remuneration

The regulation of remuneration in the financial sector in particular can be justified in terms of the arguments presented so far against the exuberant level of pay, the bonus culture and golden parachutes. Hindery (2008) argues that "the cancer of excessive CEO pay is at the core of America's economic woes, and it demands government attention". He goes on to say the following:

> Confronted with the daunting array of economic failures confronting the nation, it may seem improbable for me to say that excessive executive compensation is one of the issues needing the early attention of the next President and next Congress. Yes this particular cancer — which has been growing exponentially for almost two decades — is at the core of many of our nation's economic ills.

One argument for the regulation of remuneration is that excessive pay contributed to the global financial crisis. In a letter published by the *Financial Times* on 4 September 2009, Christine Lagarde, the Managing Director of the IMF, attributed the global financial crisis to "overly-complex financial instruments, lack of risk evaluation, insufficient regulation of some players and some products, and the insatiable greed of other players, for whom enough was never enough" (Lagarde, 2009).[15] In this letter a call is made for a strict compensation policy to be put in place. The following are excerpts from the letter:

> Guaranteed bonuses for more than one year should be prohibited. Bonus payments should be spread out over a few years and paid bonuses should reflect the individuals and banks' true performances over time. Proposals have been made to go further, including capping bonuses, possibly taxing them, or imposing additional obligations to banks. It is clear that these rules are the first part of a larger set of necessary regulation in the financial sector. In addition, given the bold decisions taken by governments and central banks, which were decisive in bringing back bank profits, we expect equally bold moves in the banking sector to use these profits to the benefit of the real economy. Today, we have a unique opportunity to act decisively to protect our citizens and ensure that our economies run smoothly.

Unfortunately, regulators are always in an apologetic mood towards bankers. With respect to the regulation of remuneration, Martin Wheately, the boss of the UK Financial Conduct Authority, declares: "We can't change bank bonus culture overnight" (Wheatley, 2014). Why is that? In 2009, the UK's Treasury Select Committee urged the Financial Services Authority (FSA) to make tackling pay reform a higher priority (The Telegraph, 2009), arguing that "the FSA seems not be taking tackling this issue seriously enough". Members of Parliament urged the City watchdog "not to shy away" from using powers to sanction firms over poor pay practices and give regular updates on its progress. In a report the Committee said: "This would enhance transparency and provide reassurance to the public that changes in remuneration practices within the sector are being enforced". The Committee also pushed for genuine reform to prevent a return to the excesses of the past

---

[15] The letter was also signed by the finance ministers of Sweden, the Netherlands, Luxembourg, Spain, Germany and Italy. Is it surprising that there is no mention of the finance ministers of the UK and the US? Not at all.

and for a more widespread use of powers to clawback bonuses to align the interests of managers and shareholders. The report acknowledges resistance to reform by saying the following: "We have a suspicion that many bankers remain unconvinced by the need for change and believe that, once 'the storm dies down', it will be a case of business as usual". We should expect nothing other than resistance from the financial oligarchs, but this is not a good enough reason to maintain the *status quo*.

Some economists object to the intervention of government in the decisions of private firms in matters of executive compensation (for example, Wyplosz, 2009). However, Wyplosz points out that "macro-prudential regulation will push banks to develop incentive packages that are more encouraging of long-term behavior". So, the solution is not to force bankers to quit bad habits but rather to provide the right environment and hope (only hope) that they may (only may) quit bad habits. It does not make sense to argue that executive pay is an internal affair as far as the firm is concerned, yet the government is called upon to intervene in case of failure so that those highly-paid wizards preserve their pay, even after inflicting damage on their firms and the society. The financial oligarchs tell the government to keep away when things are going well, then shout "help" when things go bad. What makes things worse is that the oligarchs do not shout "help please" but rather "help or else" in the spirit of the TBTF bonanza. They demand — they do not beg or ask.

Some observers believe that the regulation of remuneration is a trivial issue that is distracting attention from more important issues or that it is not so important as to command the attention it is given. For example, Philip Wood, partner at Allen & Overy and a member of the International Bar Association's Task Force on the Financial Crisis, believes that bonuses are not the most important issue the G20 needs to address. "Big bonuses did not cause the financial crisis", he says (Watson, 2009). Wood, who is not an economist, is in a disagreement (about the role played by executive pay in the global financial crisis) with the Director of the International Monetary Fund, several G20 finance ministers, the FCIC, the majority of observers, the vast majority of ordinary people, and common sense. Naturally, he does not explain why it is wrong to suggest that executive pay did not play a role in the crisis. On the other hand, he may be given the benefit of the doubt, because he did not say that executive pay "did not play a role" but rather that it "did not cause the financial crisis", which is true in the narrow sense that it did not cause the crisis on its own.

Another compromising argument is put forward by Clementi *et al.* (2009) who argue that "the real issue may not require the wholesale redesign of top management compensation, but rather how to address the difficulties investors have in perceiving risks and accurately valuing the equity of financial firms. In other words, do nothing about remuneration and deal with an obscure issue such as the one they mention. How can regulators make investors better at evaluating risk? Perhaps by requiring potential investors to attend a course in risk management and pass a test, just like potential drivers are required to pass a driving test. Does this mean that financial institutions can do what they want and sell products of dubious quality but the onus is on investors to evaluate the risk embodied in transactions and products? This is like saying that building contractors can do what they want and use material of dubious quality but it is up to the potential occupants of the building to assess the probability of the building collapsing on their heads. The presence of other issues that must be dealt with does not preclude the need to deal with a pressing issue such as remuneration.

One problem with the regulation of remuneration is that it should be done on an international level, otherwise some financial centers will be at a competitive disadvantage in relation to the other financial centers. The underlying argument is that "no country is going to put itself at a competitive disadvantage by having prescriptive rules that make its banks or financial institutions unattractive from a recruitment perspective" (Watson, 2009). It is the talent argument all over again — if we do not pay the wizards exuberant amounts they will pack up and go somewhere else. The UK in particular is wary of imposing restrictive rules on executive compensation because of the fear that London as a financial center will be at a disadvantage in the so-called "the war for talent" as put by Hendrik Haag, Chair of the IBA's Legal Practice Division (Watson, 2009). The solution, according to Paul Moore (a whistleblower) is that the regulation of remuneration should be international. This is what he says (Watson, 2009):

> There's only one way to solve the regulation of pay and, for that to happen, there needs to be a political will, at least among the G8 countries.... There also needs to be an overriding set of regulatory principles that can apply not just in the UK and the US but in the other important financial centres. You can't have just one country regulating pay.

It is a misrepresentation of the truth that this whistleblower argues that it is not fair if the regulation of remuneration is undertaken in the UK and US only when the excessive remuneration in the financial sector is an Anglo-American invention. As a matter of fact, objection to the regulation of remuneration comes mostly from London and New York. The British Chancellor of the Exchequer, George Osborne, officially opposed plans proposed by the European Union to put a cap on bonus payments. If anything, it is the US and UK that need to do something about executive remuneration because they were dented by the global financial crisis and put an extraordinary burden on taxpayers who saved TBTF financial institutions run by highly-paid staff.

It is not obvious why it is problematic to deal with this issue on an international level. The global financial crisis was caused by American bonus recipients, then exported to the rest of the world. If, and this is not a big if but rather the truth, the crisis was caused (among other factors) by exuberant pay, then why is it problematical to strike an international agreement on remuneration in the financial sector? Actually there is already an international agreement on bank regulation (the Basel accords), so why not extend the accords by including provisions to regulate remuneration? If countries are in a position to agree on the capital ratio, the liquidity ratio and the leverage ratio, why can't they agree on the bonus ratio (the ratio of bonus to basic salary)? But there is no need for that — if the New York–London axis, as Wojcik (2013) calls it, took the initiative (for example, by capping bonus payments), the rest of the world would follow. The problem is that it is unlikely that the axis will take such an initiative. After all, the bonus culture and exuberant remuneration were invented by the axis, and it is where opposition to regulation comes from. It is not that London cannot do it because it will lose "talent" to other financial centers — it is that London opposes initiatives taken by others, including the European Union.

Another argument against the regulation of remuneration is that excessive pay does not boost the tendency for risk taking because when a firm collapses the wealth of executives will be wiped out if the pay consists mainly of stocks and stock options. Those dismissing both the role of remuneration structures in inducing risk taking and the potential value of regulating remuneration argue that when the likes of Bear Stearns and Lehman Brothers collapsed, the wealth of the top executives of these firms was wiped out. For example, Clementi *et al.* (2009) argue that to the extent that some of the top executives in the firms that went down have lost fortunes along with the taxpayers implies that the system actually works and that reward and punishment are to some extent aligned. Bebchuk *et al.* (2010a) argue against this proposition, as they found out that the top-five executive teams of these firms cashed out large amounts of compensation during the period 2000–2008 because remuneration was not clawed back when the firms collapsed. Their estimates show that the top executive teams of Bear Stearns and Lehman Brothers derived cash flows of about $1.4 billion and $1 billion respectively from cash bonuses and equity sales during the period 2000–2008. They conclude on the basis of their results that "the executives' pay arrangements provided them with excessive risk-taking incentives".

Naturally, we have to come back to the "talent" argument, the argument that regulation will drive away "talent". On this issue a talent enthusiast says the following (Baily, 2010):

> Even among those with similar professional qualifications, there are tangible differences in the skills of financial employees, and even a small difference in skill can have an enormous impact on the profits of a financial firm. An extra 1% return on a $10 billion investment portfolio adds $100 million to a firm's earnings. An investment banker who structures a transaction incorrectly can quickly transform a large acquisition from a brilliant idea to a $200 billion albatross.

Baily (2010) wants to discourage any regulation of the level of pay because "there has been no convincing evidence that high levels of compensation create an inherent or fundamental risk for these companies or the larger economy". In fact, he argues that "executives contribute mightily to the success of their employers" because "even a small difference in talent can translate into tremendous returns given the size and complications present in this business". It seems that doing a job properly is called "talent". Why is it that the talented people who ran Merrill Lynch, Lehman Brothers, Bear Stearns, RBS, Northern Rock, AIG, and many other TBTF institutions got it so horribly wrong? After all, those were extremely "talented" people, judged by the bonuses they received. So, if they get it right, they deserve lavish compensation because they have earned it, and if they get it wrong they have to be compensated so that they get it right next time. This is a truly "heads I win, tails you lose" situation.

Going back to an issue that we dealt with earlier, those opposing the regulation of remuneration take this stance on the grounds that the government does not have a legitimate interest in telling shareholders how to spend their money and that the choice of remuneration structures belongs to the province of private business decisions where regulators should not trespass. Bebchuk (2010) argues that this objection is not persuasive because the government does have a legitimate interest in the compensation structures of private financial firms out of concern about the safety and soundness of financial firms, let alone the possibility that those firms may ask for bailout money. Furthermore, it is not the shareholders who decide how to spend their money, but rather managers and directors decide on how to spend shareholders money on themselves, sometimes by fraudulent means. This is fraud, and the government has an obligation to combat fraud. Why is it that the government should not intrude on the "province of private business" when private business is doing well, but the government is called upon to the rescue when things go wrong?

Opponents of the regulation of remuneration also argue that regulators will be at an informational disadvantage when setting pay arrangements. Bebchuk (2010) responds to this line of reasoning by suggesting that placing limits on remuneration structures that incentivize risk taking would be no more demanding in terms of information than regulators' direct intervention in investment, lending and capital decisions. Furthermore, the setting of pay arrangements should not be left to the unconstrained choices of informed players inside financial firms because they do not have incentives to set risks at levels that are socially desirable. Then, of course, there is always the argument that regulation can be circumvented. For example, *The Economist* (2013a) argues that "where there are laws, there are bound to be loopholes". True, but this does not mean that nothing should be done to correct the conditions that led to the 2008 crisis and may lead to the next crisis. Just because some criminals avoid prosecution does not mean that they should not be prosecuted.

7. Regulatory Proposals

If remuneration in the financial sector is to be regulated, how should this proceed? A number of proposals have been put forward — these proposals are discussed in turn.

7.1. Strengthening shareholders rights

Shareholders get ripped off by directors and managers who award themselves lavish bonuses and golden parachutes. It makes sense to think that shareholders would not mind receiving dividends as opposed to executives receiving bonuses. This proposal is typically termed as giving shareholders a "say on pay", as shareholders have weak rights, particularly in the US. Bebchuk (2010) identifies the arrangements that weaken shareholders rights, including the following: (i) absence of majority voting, with a small number of "for" votes being sufficient to elect directors; (ii) staggered boards, which make board replacement more difficult; (iii) supermajority requirements that make it difficult for shareholders to amend the company's bylaws and giving boards excessive control over the company's governance arrangements; (iv) shareholders lack the power to place director candidates on the corporate ballot and (v) they lack the power to bring to a shareholder vote proposals to amend the corporate charter. Bebchuk (2010) contends that "reducing the extent to which shareholders rights are weakened in these ways would make boards more attentive to shareholder interests — both in general and with respect to the setting of pay arrangements". Likewise, Hindery (2008) makes the recommendation that shareholders be granted the right to call a meeting to vote out the current board and to render an advisory vote on executive compensation, arguing that these measures "would align shareholder and management interests as to both governance and executive compensation".

More specifically, say on pay may take the form of a non-binding vote of the general meeting to approve pay packages, with a mandatory binding vote for large amounts. A vote like this provides a signal to a board that shareholders do not wish to see salaries raised beyond reasonable levels. A complementary measure would be a requirement for more disclosure with respect to remuneration, so that shareholders know and decide whether or not they think remuneration is fair. Clementi *et al.* (2009) argue that greater disclosure and transparency of compensation practices is necessary in order to apply greater market discipline to top management pay practices.

Oddly enough, some scholars contend that shareholders intentionally pay exuberant amounts to mangers. Cheng *et al.* (2015)

argue against the proposition that managers take big risks at the expense of shareholders, suggesting instead that managers are paid by the shareholders specifically to assume more risk. According to them, "the big pay packages on Wall Street are the flip side of excessive risk-taking" (Kardashian, 2014). The underlying idea is that shareholders, not mangers, are greedy so they force the helpless managers to gamble with their money to earn higher returns. The question is how do shareholders, who could be in the thousands, convey this message to the managers? Do they vote in the annual general meeting on a risk-return combination? This argument makes no sense whatsoever, but sometimes it pays to express an extreme view that is out of line with the general consensus.

7.2. The bonus-malus system

A bonus-malus system would correct the asymmetric payoff to bonus recipients who receive bonuses for good performance but not penalized for bad performance (as a matter of fact, they may even be paid for bad performance when the payment takes the form of retention bonuses). A mild version of this system is not to pay bonus for bad performance. For example, bonus recipients may be forced to forego two-thirds of their bonus payments for up to five years if they run up losses for their banks. If the investments turn out to be loss-making, the deferred part of the bonus will be canceled.

Clementi *et al.* (2009) support the introduction of a bonus-malus system by arguing on the following lines:

> In good times, with a rising tide lifting all boats, the combination of the rising tide and leverage makes it impossible to tell good performers from bad ones, since most people generate decent to spectacular returns. It is in bad times that the wheat is separated from the chaff.

This means that compensation should have a multi-year structure, such that the bonus pool is reduced in response to bad outcomes.

In July 2014, it was announced that the Bank of England planned to force badly-performing bankers to pay back bonuses up to seven years after being awarded, even if the bonuses have been spent (BBC, 2014). As expected, the British Bankers' Association (BBA) said that the pay rules would put the UK at a competitive disadvantage. This is what Anthony Browne of the BBA said in response to the proposal:

> We now have the toughest regime in banking pay of any global financial centre. Bankers are paid less here (in London) than in New York, Singapore or Hong Kong, and ultimately this could have an impact on the competitiveness of London as a financial centre.... We have the world's largest international banking sector and we do have to make sure that we can continue to employ banking talent from around the world.

The proposal is intended to modify bonus contracts to include a clawback clause that enables the awarding institution to reclaim the cash if a deal turns sour or when the bonus recipient behaves improperly (for example, indulging in a scandal of some sort like rigging a market) in the years after it was given. Another rule is that when a banker moves jobs, any bonuses that have been awarded but not yet paid out are bought out by their new employer. Once again, I must question the concept of "banking talent" that is used to justify extravagant pay. What is needed is not banking talent but rather banking honesty.

7.3. Progressive taxation

Taxation on bonuses was considered for the first time in relation to the bonuses granted to the AIG gurus for wrecking the whole system. The underlying idea here is that bonus payments are taxed at a higher rate than regular income. The *status quo* is far away from this kind of arrangement.

Kasperkevic (2013) explains how the tax code in the US provides a subsidy to bonus recipients, arguing that "a large portion of their pay is tax deductible — which creates, effectively, a government subsidy for corporate bonuses". In 1993, Congress capped the tax deductibility of executive pay at \$1 million, while allowing companies to deduct performance-based pay (including stock options) from their federal income taxes. The companies use the tax-deductible stock options to reduce their tax bills, which means that "those rich executive bonuses turn into government subsidies". Under the CEO pay tax loophole, the bigger the bonuses given by companies to their executives, the smaller the amount paid in taxes. This means that average taxpayers have to pick up the tab.

Naturally, taxing bonuses only would not be effective as one response would be to change the structure of remuneration such that the biggest component becomes the basic salary, which is taxed at a lower rate. von Ehrlich and Radulescu (2012) provide evidence for this proposition in a study that explores the reaction of compensation components awarded to directors of UK financial institutions following the temporary adoption of the bonus payroll tax in December 2009. By using a comprehensive data set on executive compensation, they show that the introduction of the bonus tax reduced the cash bonuses awarded to directors by about 40%, accompanied by a simultaneous increase in other compensation components, leaving total compensation unaffected. Another response would be to pay the tax on behalf of the bonus recipients, hence another transfer of funds from shareholders to bonus recipients.

An interesting suggestion comes from Dietl *et al.* (2010), which is to introduce a luxury tax that is used in sport and applied to the payroll. If a club's payroll for players exceeds the luxury tax threshold, which is set above the salary cap, it has to pay tax to the league for being over the limit. They argue that "professional team sports provide a unique laboratory for deriving insights on the introduction, workings and consequences of the regulation of executive compensation". One caveat that they identify is the difference between professional team sports and the corporate sector, which sounds trivial as team sports are part of the corporate sector.

7.4. Setting an upper limit on compensation (pay caps)

There are laws for minimum wages, so why is it that there is no law for maximum wages? Hindery (2008) suggests that Congress should establish a ceiling for individual executive compensation as a reasonable multiple of average employee compensation, and penalize through the corporate income tax code and/or otherwise those companies that elect to pay in excess of that multiple. Johnson (2009) suggests that "caps on executive compensation, while redolent of populism, might help restore the political balance of power and deter the emergence of a new oligarchy". One advantage of this measure is to curtail the power of the financial sector and undermine its ability to inflict brain drain on the rest of the economy. As Johnson puts it, "Wall Street's main attraction — to the people who work there and to the government officials who were only too happy to bask in its reflected glory — has been the astounding amount of money that could be made". This is one way to deprive the financial sector of its undeserved status, as the jewel in the crown of the economy, and curb the tendency to indulge in parasitic activities. Pay caps could be applied to basic salary, bonus or both. Dietl *et al.* (2010) suggest that regulators can learn lessons from sport where pay caps are frequently used. For example, the NFL operates with a salary cap, in the sense that the league has to approve all contracts between a team and a player, which means that the cap cannot be exceeded.

In April 2013, the European Union put forward a proposal to cap bonuses at 100% of salary unless at least 65% of the firm's shareholders (75% of shareholders if there is no quorum) approve a bonus of 200% of salary (BBC, 2013). On 26 June 2013, the European Parliament and the Council of the European Union passed the "EU banker bonus cap", which took effect on 1 January 2014 (see, for example, PWC, 2013, 2014).

Naturally, the City of London opposed the EU ruling. This is what a spokesman for the British Bankers' Association said (Miller, 2014):

> We believe that shareholders should be given powers to determine staff pay — not politicians. That's why banks consult with

investors before setting staff pay and shareholders also have the power to vote on the pay of senior bankers. We believe this law runs counter to recent reforms and will make the system less robust by incentivising firms to increase fixed pay. It also puts European banks at a disadvantage when competing with firms in other parts of the world.

Of course we would expect nothing short of these comments from the BBA. Bankers know very well that if shareholders are given the power to determine bonuses, their standard of living will decline, unless of course what they mean by "shareholders" is the directors who typically collude with managers. It is not obvious what "recent reforms" refer to because bankers still expect and obtain bonuses that they do not deserve. The shareholders of the RBS (taxpayers) opposed bonus payments to the staff of a bankrupt bank, but their wishes were not fulfilled. As for "making the system less robust", the system is not robust anyway, thanks mainly to the behavior of bankers. I assume that the "rest of the world" means the US — this is the defunct talent argument once more. *The Economist* (2013a) uses the talent argument as follows:

> London just became a less attractive base for bankers used to taking home bonuses worth many multiples of their basic salary. On 5 March EU finance ministers decided that European bankers' bonuses should be capped at a maximum of one times their base salary, rising to two times if shareholders explicitly agree. In practice, the choice facing banks is either to find a way to compete with rivals that are not bound by the cap, or to risk losing star employees to competitors.

I wish that *The Economist* gave examples of "star employees". Then why London only when the rules are applicable to the entire European Union? A similar argument is used by Baily (2010) who suggests the following:

> Pay caps imposed on a subset of firms, for example, could push their most talented bankers, traders, and other key professionals

to unregulated firms. Broader limits on the compensation of financial executives may even drive parts of this highly mobile industry to more receptive countries.

The allegations about talented and star employees have become some sort of a sick joke. It is not clear what is meant by "unregulated firms". If this is meant to be shadow banking, then shadow banking should not be left unregulated. What are the "more receptive countries"? I can only say the following to those "more receptive countries": "good luck with the banking talent that will leave London".

UK and EU banking regulators have also clashed over attempts by British banks to sidestep the bonus cap by awarding banking executives "allowances", paid alongside salaries to bolster their pay. The British government thinks that there is no evidence to suggest that a bonus cap will make the banking system any safer, arguing instead that it could make matters more precarious because large fixed salaries are not as easy to cut during a downturn. The British government put forward six legal arguments to support its case against the EU ruling, but none of them were found to be valid (Miller, 2014). In particular, George Osborne, Britain's finance minister, was unable to block the measure despite arguing that it would simply drive up base salaries and add rigidity to the banking system. *The Economist* (2013a) claims that this view is "shared by many regulators, no friends of the banks". Well, the facts on the ground indicate the opposite — that most regulators are friends of the banks. The regulators who share this view are those who aspire for lucrative banking jobs in the life after regulation.

7.5. Rethinking the design of bonus of payments

Bebchuk (2010) identifies two principles for a desirable design of bonus schemes. The first principle is to avoid rewarding executives with bonuses that they may keep even if performance deteriorates. This means that bonuses should not be cashed immediately, but instead placed in a company account for several years so that they can be reduced if the justification for the bonus award is no longer valid. The second principle is that guaranteed bonuses should be avoided. Bebchuk (2010) argues that "an analysis of the effects of such guarantees shows that they create perverse incentives to take excessive risks" and that "guaranteed bonuses are worse for incentives than straight salary". Guaranteed bonuses insulate bonus recipients from the downside risk they are exposed to but leave them with the upside, which is a recipe for risk taking.

7.6. Equity compensation as a reward for long-term performance

Bebchuk (2010) suggests that to link equity compensation to performance, it is desirable to separate the time that equity-based compensation can be cashed out from the time in which it vests — otherwise it will be "pay without performance". As soon as an executive has completed an additional year at the firm, the equity incentives promised as compensation for that year's work should vest, and should belong to the executive even if he or she immediately leaves the firm. The cashing out of these vested equity incentives should be blocked for a specified period (say five years) after vesting. Furthermore, bonus recipients should be permitted to cash out no more than a specified fraction (say 20%) of the portfolio of equity incentives in any given year. This restriction would substantially limit the weight that the executive places on short-term stock prices.

Furthermore, Bebchuk (2010) recommends several additional design features to tighten the link between the value of equity compensation and long-term shareholder value and to prevent the "gaming" of such compensation. These recommendations include the following: (i) the timing of equity awards to executives (option grants, restricted stock awards, etc.) should not be discretionary but rather they should be made only on prespecified dates; (ii) the terms and amount of post-hiring equity awards should not be based on the grant-date stock price; (iii) the payoffs from the unloading of executives' restricted stock or options should be tied to the average price over a reasonably long period of time and (iv) bonus recipients should be contractually prohibited from engaging in hedging and other transactions with respect to equity-based awards granted as incentive compensation.

On the other hand, Baily (2010) argues against equity-based compensation and recommends that a significant share of total annual compensation be withheld for several years, not in the form of stock or stock options but rather as a fixed dollar amount. Under this scheme, bonus recipients should forfeit their holdbacks if the firm goes bankrupt or receives taxpayers' money. While Clementi *et al.* (2009) do not oppose the idea of equity-based compensation, they recommend longer stock holding periods and stricter forfeiture rules.

7.7. Revolving door compensation

In August 2015, US presidential candidate Hillary Clinton endorsed a proposed law (the Financial Services Conflict of Interest Act) that would prevent corporate firms paying bonuses and golden parachutes to their executives for leaving to take senior government jobs (Reuters, 2015). Writing in the *Huffington Post*, she was critical of the "so-called revolving door" between government and Wall Street firms in particular, saying that it erodes public trust "if a public servant's past and future are tied to the financial industry". A law like this will go a long way in reducing the extent of regulatory capture, although it will not prevent it completely. A well-paid banker becoming a regulator will always be loyal to his firm.

8. Conclusion

The level and structure of remuneration in the financial sector causes excessive risk-taking, hence contributing of financial instability. More often than never, remuneration involves fraud (for example, obtaining profit through fraudulent means or manipulating earnings to claim bonuses against the reported earnings). Combating fraud and reducing financial instability, which are related as we have seen, provide strong justification for the regulation of remuneration. Regulators should not be intimidated by efficient and free marketeers who argue against any kind of regulation, including this one.

At the risk of repeating myself, I must once more emphasize how ridiculous the "talent" argument is — that "talented bankers" deserve the zillions of dollars they get paid. I challenge any defender of the financial oligarchy to give me one example of a talented banker and the criteria whereby talent is measured. Surely, if profit is the criterion, and if profit is generated by fraudulent means, this is not the kind of talent that should be rewarded. Otherwise we should reward bank robbers who crack safes (this is talent) by giving them a cut of the heist when they are caught, instead of putting them behind bars.

Banking is not such a sophisticated business that requires talent — it is not the same as working for NASA. Talented people are exemplified by a Russian mathematician, Grigory Perelman, who at the age of 44, solved one of the most intractable problems in mathematics, the Poincare Conjecture. This is a problem in topology, represented by the proposition that any three-dimensional space without holes is equivalent to a stretched sphere. The puzzle was more than 100 years old when Perelman solved it. I would love to find out the equivalent of Grigory Perelman in banking. Interestingly, he was offered a "bonus" of $1 million for his "performance" but he refused to accept it. He was so humble that he said the following:

> I'm not interested in money or fame. I don't want to be on display like an animal in a zoo. I'm not a hero of mathematics. I'm not even that successful, that is why I don't want to have everybody looking at me.

These words come from a person dubbed "the world's cleverest man" (Stewart, 2010). The financial oligarchs and their allies should learn from this extremely talented and humble person. We have to feel happy that Grigory Perelman has not accepted a banking job to design a new derivative, because his talent would have created a devastating weapon of mass destruction.

Chapter 7

The Regulation of Shadow Banking

1. Introduction

The shadow banking system consists of non-bank financial institutions and entities that provide financial services as an alternative to those provided by traditional commercial banks. Interest in shadow banking can be attributed to the belief that it played a pivotal role in the advent of the global financial crisis and that it is a source of systemic risk. For example, Kordes (2013) suggests that shadow banking "symbolizes one of many failings of the financial system leading up to the global financial crisis". He emphasizes the role played by shadow banks in the "securitization chain" and identifies shadow banks as those financial institutions that indulge in four different forms of financial intermediation, including maturity transformation, liquidity transformation, leverage and credit risk transfer. Adrian and Shin (2009a) argue that "the current financial crisis has highlighted the changing role of financial institutions and the growing importance of the shadow banking system".

Traditional banks are regulated and closely monitored by central banks and other domestic regulators and their work is subject to international banking regulation such as the Basel accords. The shadow banking system is not regulated, which provides the means whereby regulated banks can circumvent regulation by conducting business through shadow banking. By doing that, the underlying transactions become inconsequential for the balance sheets of regulated banks because they are invisible to regulators (the so-called off-balance sheet items). Effectively, therefore, the shadow banking system is a loophole in the regulatory framework, which regulated banks and financial institutions utilize to their own advantage (the word "utilization" here means circumventing regulation). Like regular banks, shadow banks provide credit and boost the liquidity of financial markets but, unlike regulated banks, they have no access to central bank funding or safety nets such as deposit insurance and debt guarantees. While they provide guarantees in other ways, such as the collateral required to conduct repos, those guarantees may all of a sudden look fragile because of adverse market conditions — as a result the system collapses.

In this chapter, it is suggested that shadow banking should be regulated because it provides the opportunity for regulated banks to circumvent regulation and because it is a major source of systemic risk. The conclusion that is reached following the discussion is that it does not make sense to regulate depository institutions while giving shadow banking entities a free hand to do what they like. It is also suggested that shadow banking is no different from the underground economy, which is unregulated but illegal.

2. Definition and Identification

The term "shadow banking system" is attributed to Paul McCulley of PIMCO, who coined it at a Federal Reserve Bank of Kansas City's Economic Symposium that was held in Jackson Hole, Wyoming in 2007 (McCulley, 2007). At that meeting he defined the shadow banking system as "the whole alphabet soup of levered up non-bank investment conduits, vehicles, and structures". McCulley's boss (Bill Gross, president of PIMCO) has the following to say about shadow banking (Gross, 2007):

> Beware our shadow banking system.... What we are witnessing is essentially the breakdown of our modern-day banking system, a complex of leveraged lending so hard to understand that

Federal Reserve chairman Ben Bernanke required a face-to-face refresher course from hedge fund managers in mid-August. My Pimco colleague Paul McCulley has labeled it the "shadow banking system" because it has lain hidden for years, untouched by regulation, yet free to magically and mystically create and then package subprime loans into a host of three-letter conduits that only Wall Street wizards could explain.

In fact not even the Wall Street wizards could explain the three-letter conduits. Obviously, Gross does not have a good impression of shadow banking, which he describes as a "secret banking system built on derivatives", implying that the main function of shadow banking is securitization. According to Fein (2013), Gross's depiction of shadow banking as a mysterious unregulated force in the financial system captured the imagination of regulators, academic economists, and the media and has distorted their views of the financial crisis ever since". Fein, who is a shadow banking enthusiast, suggests that the term "shadow banking" has been used as a scapegoat by different parties to justify their failure. This is what she says:

> Banking regulators have used it to explain how the crisis arose outside the regulated banking system beyond their powers of perception. Academics whose econometric models failed to forecast the crisis have said it was invisible. Consulting firms have converted it into an "index". The media has bandied it about like "greed" as a glib explanation of what went wrong with the financial system.

Fein disputes the characterization of shadow banking adopted by banking regulators and shows that, contrary to the picture they have painted, it exists as an integral part of the regulated banking system. She goes on to demonstrate that the regulators' definition of shadow banking mistakenly includes non-bank entities — in particular money market funds — that are highly regulated, not a cause of the financial crisis, and otherwise lacking in risk features attributed to shadow banks. Accordingly, she argues that "shadow banking is a flawed concept that has distracted regulators and hindered their progress toward a rational framework for a resilient financial system going forward". The concept of shadow banking, she argues, "ignores the important benefits of non-traditional financial products and services and may lead to misguided regulatory measures that extinguish innovation, efficiency, and competition without offsetting gains in systemic safety". Fein (2013) points out that most of the definitions of shadow banking are broad and encompass a diverse range of entities other than regulated banks that provide financial products and services and that they (the definitions) identify shadow banks as unregulated or lightly regulated entities operating outside the regulated banking system. This favorable view of shadow banking means that it must be looked after and groomed rather than condemned because it is some sort of a center for innovation. We have already seen that one of the problems with modern finance is the so-called "financial innovation". This means that shadow banking should be regulated for the very reason that it is a center for financial innovation.

There is no consensus on a unique definition of shadow banking because the underlying activities vary across countries. This is why the literature provides several definitions of shadow banking, which depend on whether the focus is on the entity that performs the activity or on the activity itself. *The Economist* (2014d) acknowledges the disagreement about what counts as shadow banking. As a broad definition, *The Economist* suggests that shadow banking "would include any bank-like activity undertaken by a firm not regulated as a bank". As an example, *The Economist* refers to the mobile-payment systems offered by Vodafone and the bond trading platforms set up by technology firms or the investment products sold by BlackRock. The Financial Stability Board provides two entity-based definitions of shadow banking: a broad definition and a narrow definition (FSB, 2014a). In a broad sense, shadow banking is defined as "credit intermediation involving entities and activities outside of the regular banking system". The narrow definition pertains only to the non-bank credit intermediation that can potentially be a source of systemic risk, subtracting "entities that are not part of a credit intermediation chain and those that are prudentially consolidated into a banking group". In terms of the broad definition, shadow banking is measured as the volume of total financial assets held by other financial intermediaries (OFIs), which include all non-bank financial intermediaries (NBFIs) besides insurance companies, pension funds and public financial institutions. The narrow measure of shadow banking is obtained by subtracting from the total financial assets held by OFIs those linked to self-securitization, non-bank financial entities not involved in credit intermediation (equity investment funds and equity real estate investment trusts) as well as non-bank financial activities that are prudentially consolidated into a banking group (finance companies and broker-dealers). Figure 7.1 depicts the size of broad and narrow shadow banking in the US, UK, China and Japan, measured in trillions of dollars, as a percentage of gross domestic product (GDP), and as a percentage of the financial sector (the latest available figures). These figures give an idea about the financialization of the economy, particularly the UK economy.

In his testimony before the Financial Crisis Inquiry Commission (FCIC) on 2 September 2010, Ben Bernanke described shadow banks as follows (FCIC, 2011):

> Shadow banks are financial entities other than regulated depository institutions (commercial banks, thrifts, and credit unions) that serve as intermediaries to channel savings into investment. Securitization vehicles, Asset-backed commercial paper (ABCP) vehicles, money market funds, investment banks, mortgage companies, and a variety of other entities are part of the shadow banking system. Before the crisis, the shadow banking system had come to play a major role in global finance; with hindsight, we can see that shadow banking was also the source of some key vulnerabilities.... Critically, shadow banks were, for the most part, not subject to consistent and effective regulatory oversight.

Other definitions of shadow banking can be found in the literature. For example, Baur and Wackerbeck (2013) view shadow banking as encompassing financial intermediaries that indulge in

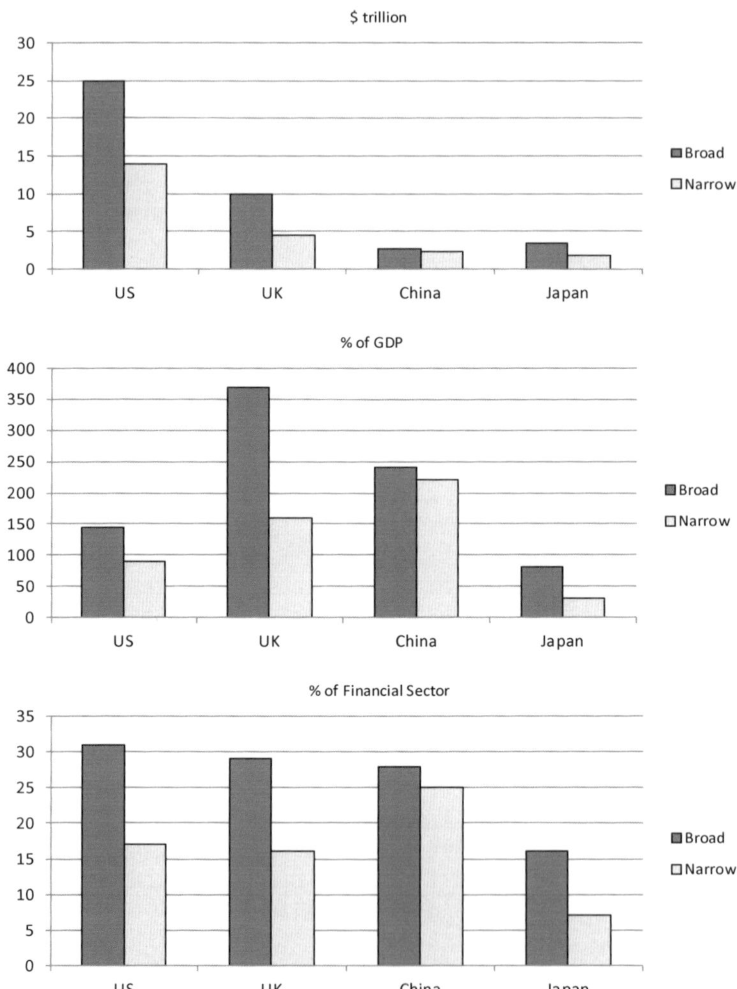

Figure 7.1:   The Size of Shadow Banking (Narrow and Broad Definitions)

liquidity transformation outside the traditional banking system without access to the liquidity of the central bank and without government deposit guarantees. Pozsar *et al.* (2010) define the shadow banking system as "the network of financial institutions that intermediate through a wide range of securitization and secured funding techniques such as ABCP, asset-backed securities (ABSs), commercial paper, collateralized debt obligations (CDOs) and repurchase agreements". Plantin (2015) defines shadow banking as "the nexus of financial institutions that perform the functions of traditional banks by financing loans with the issuance of money-like liabilities while not being subject to the prudential regulation of banks". Agirman *et al.* (2013) put forward the definition of shadow banking that it is a "wide myriad of highly leveraged non-deposit taking institutions that lend long and borrow short in liquid markets". According to Pozsar *et al.* (2010), the shadow banking sector can be defined as "financial intermediaries that conduct maturity, credit and liquidity transformation without access to central liquidity or public sector credit guarantees". The FSB (2011) defines the shadow banking system as "the system of credit intermediation that involves entities and activities outside the regular banking system".

Noeth and Sengupta (2011) point out that the meaning and scope of shadow banking is disputed in the academic literature. They view the shadow banking system as a collection of entities that include securitization vehicles, ABCP conduits, money market mutual funds, markets for repurchase agreements (repos), investment banks, mortgage companies, hedge funds, credit investment funds, exchange-traded funds (ETFs), credit hedge funds, private equity funds, securities broker dealers, and credit insurance providers. Some economists express the view that the whole financial sector is part of shadow banking. For example, Hannoun (2008) suggests that while investment banks and commercial banks conduct much of their business in the shadow banking system, most of them are not considered to be shadow banking institutions (meaning that they should be considered part of shadow banking). Shiller (2012) suggests that both Lehman Brothers and Bear Stearns were shadow banks due to the extent of their involvement in the shadow banking system. Fein (2013) argues that regulated banks, which supposedly operate outside the shadow banking system, are the "largest shadow banks". The deep involvement of traditional banks in the shadow banking system is indicated by the fact that shadow banking entities are typically sponsored by banks or are affiliated with banks through their subsidiaries or parent bank holding companies (Noeth and Sengupta, 2011).

3. The Evolution of Shadow Banking

Shadow banking is not a new phenomenon. Even in the late 1950s and early 1960s, concern emanating from the growth of NBFIs was highlighted by, among others, Thorn (1957) and Hogan (1960). Thorn (1957) advocated some degree of control over credit expansion by NBFIs as that of banks. Hogan (1960) found that, while the role of banking system in Australia was declining from the late 1930s to the 1950s, the role of other financial intermediaries was rising — as a result, he called for controlling the liquidity of the non-banking sector. Furthermore, Ghandi (2014) argues that while shadow banking is a universal phenomenon, it takes on different forms, depending on the degree of economic and financial development. In developed countries, where the financial system is mature, shadow banking takes the form of "risk transformation through securitisation". In developing countries, where financial markets are rudimentary, shadow banking activities are supplementary to those of regular banks. However, the universal characteristic is that shadow banking operates outside the regular banking system where financial intermediation activities are undertaken with less transparency and regulation as compared with conventional banking. Ghandi (2014) remarks that "shadow banks are like icebergs — more deeply spread than what they seem to be".

McCulley (2007) identifies the birth of the shadow banking system with the development of money market mutual funds in the 1970s. Chan (2014) quotes the International Monetary Fund's (IMF) financial stability report as stating that the growth of shadow banking can be attributed to a shift of traditional banking activities into the shadows, which was helped by "ultra loose monetary policies". Gorton and Metrick (2010b) attribute the rise of shadow banking to "regulatory and legal changes that gave advantages to three main institutions: money market mutual funds (MMMFs) to capture retail deposits from traditional banks, securitization to move assets of traditional banks off their balance sheets, and repurchase agreements (repos) that facilitated the use of securitized bonds as money".

Gorton and Metrick (2010b) attribute the decline of the traditional banking model to "fundamental changes in the financial system in the last 30–40 years". Commercial banks have been faced by competition from non-bank financial institutions and their products (such as junk bonds and commercial paper) on the asset side and from MMMFs on the liability side. In particular, the growing demand for securities that can be used as collateral gave impetus to the development of securitization and the use of repos as a money-like instrument — these were aided by regulatory rules that allowed securitization and repos special treatment under the bankruptcy code. As a result, traditional banks became less profitable and sought new profit opportunities by establishing presence in, and channeling some of their business to, the shadow banking system. Since the 1970s there has been a major shift in the preferred medium for deposit-like transactions from demand deposits to MMMFs — the shift came in response to the imposition of interest rate ceilings on demand deposits (Regulation Q). According to Gorton and Metrick, "one key driver of the increased use of repos is the rapid growth of money under management by institutional investors, pension funds, mutual funds, states and municipalities, and nonfinancial firms". These entities hold cash for various reasons but would like to have a safe investment that earns interest, while retaining flexibility to use the cash when needed (a demand deposit-like product). One aspect of repos that has led to the explosive growth of this activity is that a repo collateral can be rehypothecated — that is, the collateral received in a repo deposit can be reused freely in another transaction with an unrelated third party. For example, bonds received as collateral can be posted to a third party as collateral in a derivatives transaction — that party can then borrow against the same collateral, and so on.

In Figures 7.2 and 7.3, we observe the rapid growth of shadow banking according to the estimates of the Financial Stability Board.

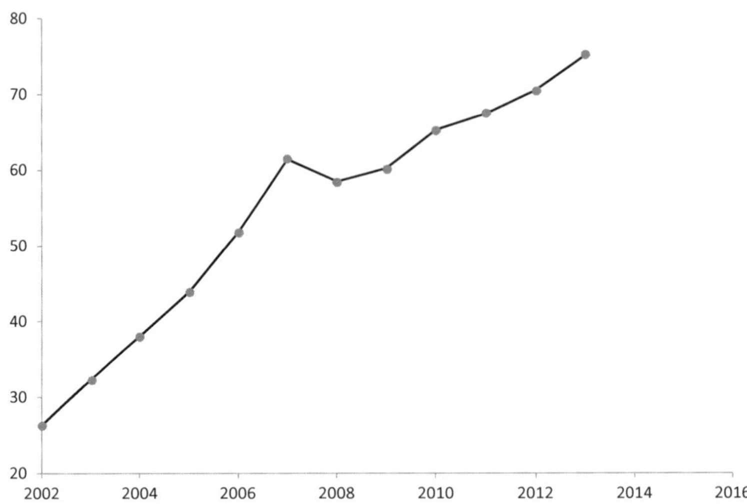

Figure 7.2: **The Global Shadow Banking System ($ trillion)**

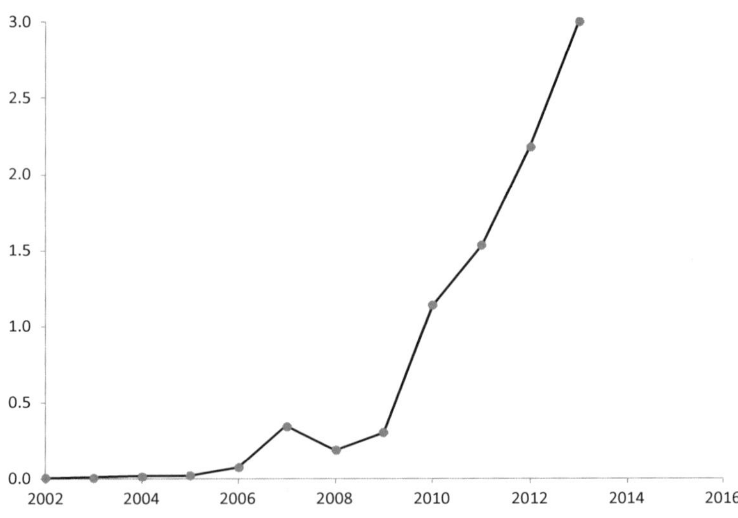

Figure 7.3: **The Chinese Shadow Banking System ($ trillion)**

In Figure 7.2, we can see that the global shadow banking system is about $80 trillion. Following the dip of 2008, the global shadow banking system surpassed the pre-crisis level in 2010. The Chinese shadow banking system is approaching the $3 trillion mark (Figure 7.3).

Unlike the global system, Chinese shadow banking is growing more rapidly than in the pre-crisis period, raising concerns about the soundness and health of Chinese banking.

4. The Functions of Shadow Banking

Shadow banking institutions perform the function of intermediation between investors and borrowers, in the process generating income from fees or from the difference in interest rates between what they pay investors and what they receive from borrowers. However, they are not subject to the same level of regulation as traditional depository institutions. Shadow banking provides off-balance sheet financing, which differs from the on-balance sheet financing of traditional banks in several important ways. In the traditional system, a depositor transfers money to the bank in return for credit on an account, from which they can withdraw at any time. The depository institution lends these funds to a borrower and holds the loan on its balance sheet to maturity. Traditional banks are exposed to the risk of runs, which can be covered through deposit insurance. Since shadow banks are not covered by deposit insurance, they use other mechanisms, such as repos, to generate the same effect. Under this arrangement, an institutional investor deposits an amount and receives some asset from the bank as collateral. The bank agrees to repurchase the same asset at some future time (perhaps the next day) for another amount that is typically higher than the amount deposited. The loans generated by the bank are moved off the balance sheet of the bank by pooling and securitizing those loans. The products of securitization (for example, CDOs) are either purchased directly by institutional investors or used as collateral for other repo transactions. In effect, the bonds created by securitization are often the main source of collateral that provides insurance for large depositors.

Fein (2013) identifies the functions of shadow banking as follows:

- Securitization vehicles such as ABCP conduits and structured investment vehicles (SIVs);
- Securities lending;

- Repurchase agreements;
- Money market mutual funds;
- Securities broker-dealers;
- Investment funds, including ETF and hedge funds that provide credit or those that are leveraged;
- Finance companies, including auto finance companies and leasing companies;
- Providers of credit insurance and financial guarantees.

According to Fein (2013), all of these entities or activities perform a useful function in the financial system and they are not inherently risky or harmful. In particular, she argues, they enhance innovation and reallocate risks away from the federal safety net. While it costs nothing to make such claims on paper, the facts on the ground show the opposite. We will find out that by performing these functions, shadow banks contributed to the advent of the global financial crisis — as a matter of fact it is believed that the crisis started in the shadow banking system by a run on money market mutual funds. Fein argues that these activities are "shadowy" in the eyes of regulators because of the perception that "they crept into the financial system largely unseen and for the purpose of evading regulatory requirements, bringing unsuspected hazards". Yet, she further argues, "the facts show that all of these activities emerged in broad daylight right under the nose of regulators". This is because, prior to the crisis, regulators approved the activities they now label as shadow banking. The true story is that regulators did approve these activities (particularly securitization) as a result of regulatory capture and that regular banks have used these activities to avoid regulation.

It seems that there is a consensus view that securitization is the most important function of shadow banking. Securitization is the process whereby loans are packaged and sold in capital markets. This process involves special purpose vehicles (SPVs), which are legal entities that issue securities linked to the loan portfolios. Loans are pooled into portfolios and sold to SPVs, which finance these purchases by selling securities in the capital markets. Securitization may take one of the two forms: pass-through securitization and tranched securitization. In a pass-through securitization, the issuer pools a set of assets and issues securities to investors backed by the cash flows. A single type of security is issued so that each investor holds a proportional claim on the underlying assets. Tranched securitization, which is more complex, involves the pooling of a set of assets to manufacture different classes of securities, or tranches, with prioritized claims on the collateral. In a tranched deal, like a CDO, some investors hold more senior claims than others. If (and when) default occurs, the losses are absorbed by the lowest priority class of investors before higher priority investors are affected.

The market for structured finance has experienced remarkable development since the inaugural issue of mortgage-backed securities (MBSs) by Bank of America in 1977. While there are many different types of structured products, the following is a brief description of the main types of a few of them:

- ABS are bonds or notes backed by pools of assets rather than a single entity. Common types of collateral for ABS are auto loan receivables and student loan receivables.
- MBS are ABS backed by the cash flows arising from mortgage loans. MBS can be divided into residential mortgage-backed securities (RMBS) and commercial mortgage-backed securities (CMBS), depending on the type of property underlying the mortgages.
- Home equity loans (HELs) securities are RMBS whose cash flows are backed by a pool of home equity loans.
- CDOs consist of structured securities that are pooled and tranched. CDOs are backed by a pool of assets, such as other structured finance securities, but classes of securities with some investors have priority over others.
- Collateralized bond obligations (CBOs) are CDOs backed primarily by high-yield corporate bonds.

- Collateralized loan obligations (CLOs) are CDOs backed primarily by leveraged high-yield bank loans.
- Collateralized mortgage obligations (CMOs) are CDOs backed by mortgage collateral (often RMBS or CMBS rather than individual mortgages).

The growth of securitization can be seen in Figures 7.4 and 7.5 in terms of the flows and stocks of ABS, according to the figures provided by the Securities Industry and Financial Markets Association (SIFMA). In Figure 7.4, we observe the flows of new issues of ABS, whereas Figure 7.5 shows the outstanding stocks of each category. The effect of the global financial crisis on both the stocks and flows of ABSs is conspicuous. Recovery from the crisis is evident in some, but not all, asset classes.

5. Shadow Banking and the Global Financial Crisis

The shadow banking system is thought to have contributed significantly to the advent of the global financial crisis (Simkovic, 2009; Harvey, 2010; Gorton, 2010). Despite the overwhelming evidence and common sense, some shadow banking enthusiasts disagree with this diagnosis. For example, Fein (2013) argues that "the shadow banking delusion has led banking regulators to adopt a misleading narrative of the financial crisis". In other words, the crisis should not be blamed on shadow banking but rather on China or the iceberg that sank the Titanic, which means that regulators should keep hands off shadow financial institutions. Another shadow banking enthusiast argues that the global financial crisis was a "one-of-a-kind event" that overwhelmed all forms of regulation, which means that a failure under these conditions implies nothing about the inherent stability of shadow banks (Wallison, 2012). Wallison, therefore, suggests that there was no difference between regular banking and shadow banking with respect to the global financial crisis. Most analysts, however, believe that the crisis started with a run on shadow banking. As any faithful free marketeer, Wallison argues that the financial crisis was caused by

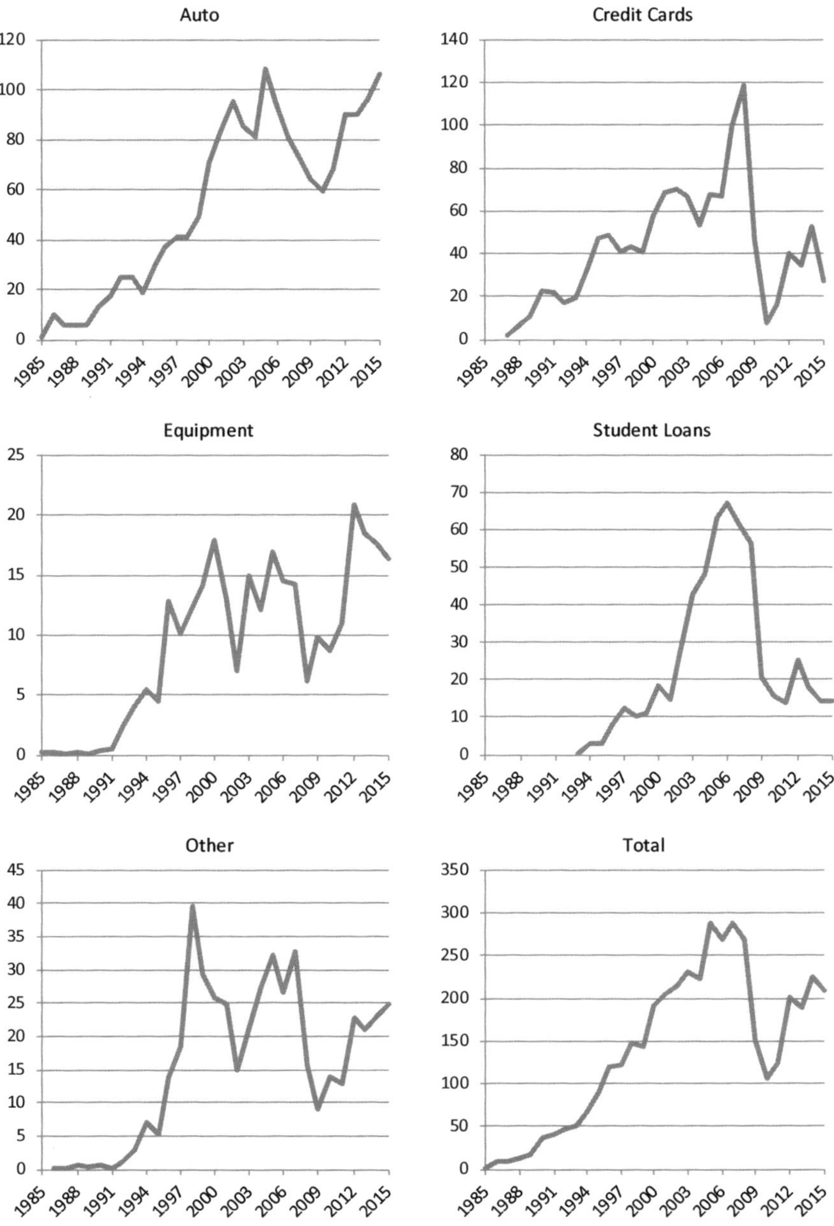

Figure 7.4:   Flows (New Issues) of ABS ($ billion)

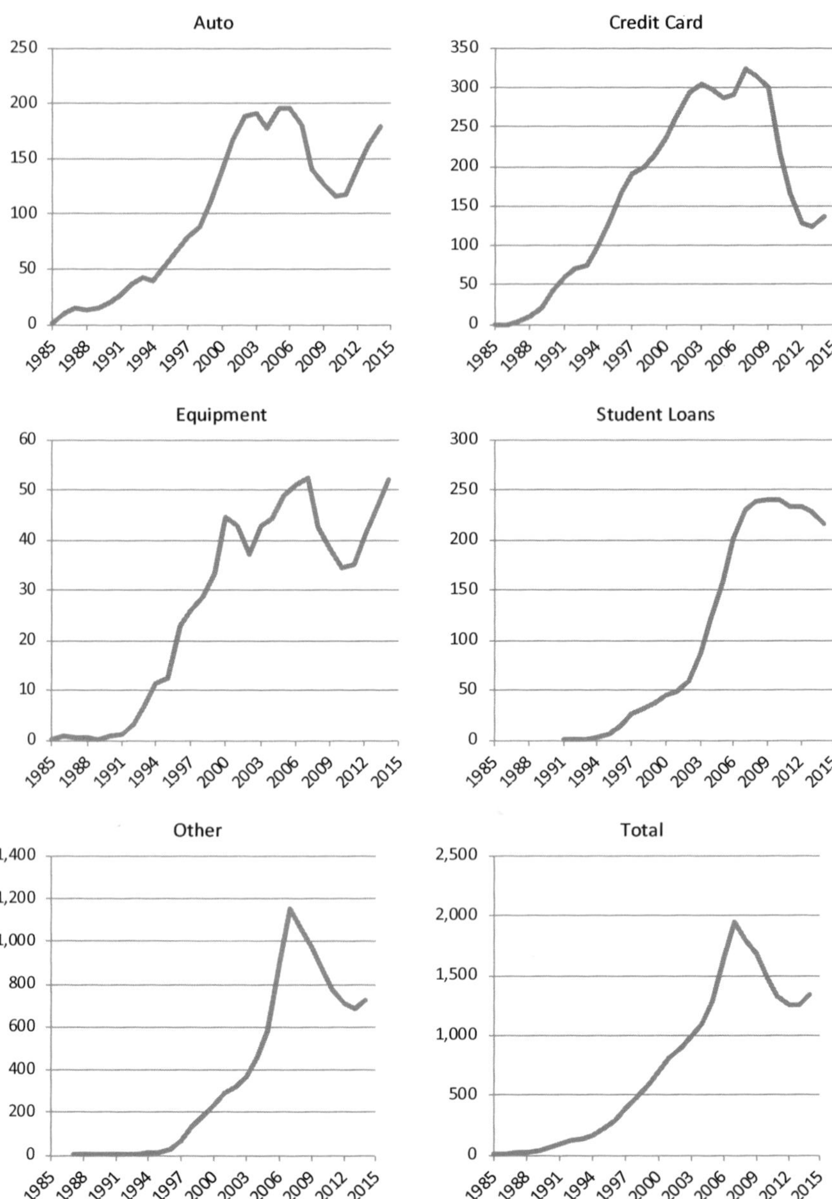

Figure 7.5:   Stocks of Outstanding ABS ($ billion)

the government's housing policy — implemented principally through the government-sponsored enterprises Fannie Mae and Freddie Mac. This policy, he argues, created financial conditions that simply overwhelmed both the regulated banking industry and the unregulated shadow banking system. It is refreshing to see that Wallison does not blame the global financial crisis on China but rather on the government, which means that the government should not interfere through regulation.

In a June 2008 speech, the former US Treasury Secretary, Timothy Geithner, placed significant blame for the freezing of credit markets on a run by the counterparties on shadow banking institutions (Geithner, 2008). Krugman (2009) describes the run on the shadow banking system as the "core of what happened" to cause the crisis, referring to the lack of controls as "malign neglect". Gorton and Metrick (2010b) argue that the panic of 2007 did not begin in the traditional system of banks and depositors, but instead was centered in the shadow banking system. Sanchez (2014) argues that the global financial crisis can be viewed as a banking crisis that originated in the shadow banking system. This is why, he argues, "we did not observe people rushing to their banks to withdraw their deposits (that is, we did not witness bank runs). Even those who believe that China caused the global financial crisis, and every other mishap, acknowledge the role played by shadow banking. For example, Volcker (2011) refers to the role of imbalances in causing the global financial crisis but he argues that "the build-up in leverage, the failure of credit discipline, and the opaqueness of new kinds of securities and derivatives such as credit default swaps helped facilitate, to a truly dangerous extent, accommodation to the underlying imbalances and to the eventual bubbles".

The best way to understand the role played by shadow banking in the global financial crisis is to examine the factors that are believed to have caused the crisis, then relate these factors to the activities of shadow financial institutions. For this purpose, we examine the factors suggested by Walter (2010) and the FCIC (2011). Walter (2010) identifies the following pre-crisis characteristics of the financial environment that led to the crisis: (i) too much leverage; (ii) inadequate capital to absorb losses; (iii) excessive credit growth based on weak underwriting standards; (iv) under pricing of liquidity risk and credit risk; (v) insufficient liquidity buffers; (vi) overly aggressive maturity transformation; (vii) inadequate risk governance and poor incentives to manage risk; (viii) inadequate cushions to mitigate the inherent procyclicality of financial markets and its participants; (ix) too much systemic risk, inter connectedness and common exposure to similar shocks and (x) inadequate oversight.

The FCIC (2011) attributes the crisis to (i) widespread failures in financial regulation and supervision; (ii) a combination of excessive borrowing, risky investments, and lack of transparency; (iii) failure of corporate governance and risk management; (iv) a systemic breakdown in accountability and ethics; (v) deteriorating mortgage lending standards; (vi) mortgage securitization pipelines and (vii) the use of over-the-counter (OTC) derivatives. According to the Commission, there was an explosion in risky subprime lending and securitization, an unsustainable rise in house prices, widespread predatory lending practices, dramatic increases in household mortgage debt, and exponential growth in financial firms' trading activities, unregulated derivatives, and short-term repo lending markets. The factors that caused the global financial crisis tie very well with the characteristics and activities of shadow financial institutions, shaped by the lack of regulation. They are highly leveraged, they hold inadequate capital, they adopt poor underwriting standards, they are illiquid, they perform aggressive maturity transformations, they have poor incentives to manage risk, they pose systemic risk, they exhibit a systemic breakdown in accountability, and they are heavily involved in securitization and OTC derivatives.

Tarullo (2013) observes similarities between the bank runs that periodically afflicted the US banking system before the creation of federal deposit insurance in 1913 and the dramatic short-term wholesale funding runs that began in 2007. These episodes are similar because both had "cascading, self-reinforcing quality, fueled by questions concerning the solvency of borrowing entities — whether deposit-taking banks or dealers seeking credit in repo markets". Some depositors in 1932 needed their money in order to meet the requirements of daily life, while many repo counterparties in 2008 needed their money to meet other short-term obligations. Tarullo (2013) believes that "the dynamics unleashed by short-term wholesale funding runs in 2007 and 2008 directly exacerbated financial stress". Many assets funded through the shadow banking system were traded assets, which is why the fire sales resulted in massive asset liquidations by some trust companies during the panic of 1907 and by some securities firms in the 1930s. In 2008, these fire sales created adverse feedback loops of mark-to-market losses and margin calls, leading to further liquidations. Tarullo concludes that "the unwinding of the risk illusion — that is, the assumption that lending to shadow banks was essentially risk-free — helped transform a dramatic correction in real estate valuations into a crisis that engulfed the entire economy".

According to Tarullo, therefore, the very nature of shadow financial institutions and their work style caused the global financial crisis. This sentiment is shared by Lenzner (2014) who blames the global financial crisis on runs and illiquidity in the shadow banking system. Specifically, he argues that "the 2008 financial crisis was triggered by a run on short-term bank debt, illiquidity in the commercial paper market and a sudden lack of confidence in the MMMF industry". These financial products belong to the shadow banking system, which cannot depend on the safety net of either a lender of last resort like the Fed or other regulatory agencies. Lenzner recognizes SIVs as the "principal culprit" in the global financial crisis — these are legal entities created by banks to sell loans repackaged as bonds. Although they were notionally independent, when these entities got into trouble they pulled in the banks that had set them up. Another source of instability was MMMFs, through which firms and individuals invested short-term funds, which had been thought of as risk-free. When it became apparent that they were not as safe as previously thought, MMMFs suffered a run.

Like Tarullo (2010), Gorton and Metrick (2010b) argue that the breakdown of shadow banking during the global financial crisis is reminiscent of previous banking panics when safe liquid assets suddenly appeared to be unsafe, leading to runs. They argue that the global financial crisis was centered in several types of short-term debt (such as repos, ABCP and MMMF shares) that were initially perceived as safe and "money-like" but later found to be imperfectly collateralized. In this way the crisis was effectively a banking panic, structurally similar to centuries of previous panics involving money-like instruments such as bank notes and demand deposits, but with the "banks" taking a new form. For example, MMMF shares, which appeared to be as safe as insured deposits to many investors, suddenly appeared vulnerable, leading to runs on those funds. Securitization, which investors had trusted for a long time, suddenly lost investor confidence. As a result, investors exited all securitizations (markets for structured products), creating a new environment where the high quality collateral necessary for repos no longer existed.

Gorton and Metrick (2010b) present a comprehensive account of the role played by shadow banking in the global financial crisis, which they view as a run on various forms of "safe" short-term debt. According to them, the chain of causation started with a shock to house prices, which had a detrimental effect on subprime mortgages, leading to a quick loss of value in ABSs linked to subprime mortgages. The shock spread quickly to other asset classes as entities based on short-term debt were unable to roll over debt or faced withdrawals. Essentially, there was a run on short-term debt, particularly in the repo market, the market for ABCP, and MMMFs. Gorton (2010) argues that the core problem in the financial crisis was a run on repos. The panic occurred when those who participated in repo transactions with shadow financial institutions expected the failure of these institutions, forcing them to sell the collateral in the market to recover their invested funds.

Shleifer (2010) disputes the proposition that the withdrawal of short-term funds was responsible for the crisis. He contends that reductions in short-term financing of long-term positions in ABSs began in the summer of 2007, as the market for ABCP dried up. It is far from clear, therefore, whether the withdrawal of short-term financing in August and September 2008 was a cause or a consequence of the collapse. Shleifer concludes that "there is no evidence that the repo market in government or agency paper malfunctioned badly during the crisis". Tarullo (2010) argues in favor of Gorton and Metrick (2010b) and against Shleifer. In the absence of a regulated traditional banking system, a run on assets in the entire repo market ensued. The resulting forced sale of assets into an illiquid market turned many illiquid institutions into insolvent ones. This is basically the argument raised by the FCIC (2011) that deregulation caused the global financial crisis.

6. Arguments for Regulation

Many calls have been put forward to regulate the shadow banking system. *The Economist* (2014d) suggests that "shadow banking certainly has the credentials to be a global bogeyman" because "it is huge, fast-growing in certain forms and little understood — a powerful tool for good but, if carelessly managed, potentially explosive". Furthermore, most observers agree that the growth of shadow banking has been largely driven by regulatory arbitrage, which refers to the creation of new ways of doing business in order to avoid regulatory restrictions (for example, Acharya *et al.*, 2013). While the global financial crisis has initiated a trend toward the imposition of restrictive capital requirements on traditional banks, regulators have been largely silent on many aspects of shadow banking. As noted by Adrian and Aschcraft (2012), Kashyap *et al.* (2010) and Stein (2010), this neglect raises the possibility that the imposition of more restrictive capital requirements on traditional banks are likely to trigger even more regulatory arbitrage than in the past, leading to further growth of shadow banking.[1] One of the adverse consequences of the growth of shadow banking is that the solvency of the traditional banking system is compromised.

---

[1] Kashyap *et al.* (2010) provide a survey of the evidence on this issue.

I would argue that shadow banking is far away from being a tool for good and that if it remains unregulated it will bring about the next financial crisis.

Some economists believe that shadow banking must be regulated because it can lead to inefficient outcomes (Adrian *et al.*, 2013; Ghandi, 2014). The first of these outcomes is regulatory arbitrage as stated above — it happens because shadow banking allows the possibility of restructuring activity to avoid capital requirements. The second is that shadow banking institutions accumulate assets that are particularly sensitive to tail events because they are tailored to take advantage of mispriced tail risk. Shadow banks are subject to funding fragilities because of the potential run on their liabilities. The fragility of shadow banking institutions can also be interpreted as the result of the leverage cycles of market-based financial institutions. The splitting up of intermediation activity across multiple institutions, as in the shadow banking system, has the potential to aggravate the underlying agency problems. Shadow banking poses challenges to the conduct of monetary policy because the opaqueness of its structure, size, operations and interlinkages with commercial banks might distort the information content of monetary policy indicators and thereby undermine the conduct of monetary policy. This means that shadow banking boosts the procyclicality of the banking industry. The FSB (2012) observed that interconnectedness of shadow banks with regular banks might aggravate the procyclical build-up of leverage and consequently heighten the risk of asset price bubbles, particularly when asset prices are correlated. In the rest of this section, we go through the arguments for regulating shadow banking.

6.1. Vulnerability

Duca (2014) argues that commercial paper and the debt instruments issued by shadow banking institutions are vulnerable to financial market shocks as reflected in the sharp post-2007 drop in shadow bank lending and as emphasized, *inter alia*, by Adrian and

Shin (2009a, 2009b, 2010). This vulnerability is transmitted to the real economy.

6.2. The lessons of history

The run on shadow banking in 2007 and 2008 reminds us that similar disorderly flights of uninsured deposits from banks lay at the heart of the financial panics of the late 19th and early 20th centuries, particularly the bank runs of the early 1930s. We have learned from financial history that what looks like safe assets may turn out to be not safe at all. Krugman (2009) contends that regulators should have realized that they were recreating the kind of financial vulnerability that made the Great Depression possible, which means that they should have responded by extending regulations and the financial safety net to cover these new institutions.

6.3. Contribution to the global financial crisis

We have seen that the shadow banking system played a pivotal role in the advent of the global financial crisis. Mark Carney, the head of the Financial Stability Board, told the World Economic Forum in January 2013 that central bankers would finally be addressing this "forgotten bit of reform" as they try to complete an overhaul of financial regulation over the next two years (Reuters, 2013). There are, however, those who believe that the global financial crisis does not provide a sound policy reason to impose greater regulation on shadow banking (for example, Wallison, 2012).

6.4. Circumvention of regulation

The Economist (2014d) suggests that "regulated shadow institutions can be used to circumvent the strictly regulated mainstream banking system and therefore avoid rules designed to prevent financial crises". The very existence of shadow banking represents a regulatory loophole, which means that a proper regulatory framework should govern both traditional and shadow banks. This is essentially the regulatory arbitrage argument.

6.5. Systemic risk

Shadow banking is a source of systemic risk that arises because (i) shadow financial institutions are closely intertwined with regular banks through loans; (ii) they are connected with the traditional banking system via credit intermediation chains and (iii) the collateralized funding of shadow institutions can lead to high levels of financial leverage.

6.6. Regulatory failure and deregulation

Failure to regulate shadow banking is likely to bring about yet another financial crisis because regulatory failure and deregulation played a major role in the advent of the global financial crisis. The FCIC refers to the "pivotal failure" of the Fed to stem the flow of toxic mortgages and to the stripping away of "key safeguards, which could have helped avoid catastrophe" (FCIC, 2011).

6.7. Shadow banking as a conduit to fraud

Bernie Madoff managed to commit fraud on a massive scale only because the shadow banking system is characterized by opaqueness, lack of transparency and inadequate disclosure. The big enablers of fraud are products of shadow banking: OTC derivatives, which are exempt from the securities rules applicable to economically similar deals, and repos which were used by Lehman Brothers to hide losses.

7. Arguments against Regulation

Those who suggest that deregulation did not cause the global financial crisis implicitly or explicitly oppose the regulation of shadow banking. Fein (2013) argues that shadow banking is a flawed concept because "the shadow banking theory provides a largely bogus explanation of what caused the financial crisis and thus lacks factual credibility as a basis for reform". She describes what she calls the "shadow banking fallacy" as "flawed to the extent it seeks to apply bank regulatory concepts to non-bank entities operating outside the regulated banking system and federal safety net". She disagrees with the proposition that "shadow banking is inherently harmful or nefarious when in fact it has important benefits". Fein also argues that "regulators have recognized the benefits of shadow banking but become schizophrenic in their attempts to repress it while preserving its positive aspects". The arguments against the regulation of shadow banking are discussed in this section.

7.1. Shadow banking as an integral part of regulated banking

According to Fein (2013), shadow banking is an integral part of the regulated banking system, implying that all of the activities classified by regulators as shadow banking are core activities of large banks. Avraham *et al.* (2012) argue that regular banks are the "drivers" of the shadow banking system, attributing the growth of shadow banking to the transformation of the largest banks since the early 1980s from traditional activities to securitization and off-balance sheet operations and from a credit-risk intensive, deposit funded, spread-based process, to a less credit-risk intensive, but more market-risk intensive, wholesale funded, fee-based process. Gorton (2007) points out that "the banking system was metamorphosing into an off-balance sheet and derivatives world — the shadow banking system". Likewise, Turner (2012) contends that "we need to understand shadow banking not as something parallel to and separate from the core banking system, but deeply intertwined with it". The problem is indeed the shift from the so-called "boring banking" to the extravaganza of "modern banking". Whether these operations are shadowy or not, the shift away from boring banking has been motivated by greed, and it is totally unnecessary. A question that arises here is the following: if we accept the proposition that shadow banking is an integral part of the banking industry, what is the implication for regulation? Suppose that we stopped describing these operations as shadowy, does this mean that they should not be regulated? On the contrary, if regular banks are regulated and the shadowy operations are conducted by regular banks, there is a very good reason for regulating these operations. What we are talking about here is the regulation of operations that enable fraud, irrespective of what they are called and who indulges in them.

7.2. Shadow banking is a by-product of regulation

Fein (2013) suggests that shadow banking is largely the creation of banking regulators who fostered and nurtured it over three decades. She goes on to say the following:

> It took hold in the banking system in the 1980s when financial markets began to evolve rapidly in response to technological innovations, volatile interest rates, and new sources of competition. Banking regulators feared that the traditional deposit-based model of banking would become unviable if banks were not empowered to seek funding and fee-based revenue from activities in the capital markets. Banking regulators allowed banks to become shadow banks in order to preserve the regulated banking system.

What actually happened in the 1980s was that banks lost big money in the international debt crisis — as a result they shifted to some gimmicks that enabled them to make more money by ripping off customers. Then came the bonus culture that fueled the drive for more profit by all means. If, as Fein claims, change was enabled by regulators, then they would have made a big mistake — massive deregulation was a big mistake. This is more of a reason to regulate these activities than turning a blind eye to them.

7.3. Securitization is part of the business of banking

We have already seen that securitization is the main function performed by shadow banking. However, Fein (2013) argues that securitization became a permissible activity for banks in 1986 when the Comptroller of the Currency determined that such activities are part of the "business of banking" under the National Bank Act and not prohibited by the Glass–Steagall Act. Cetorelli and Peristiani (2012) show, with the help of empirical evidence, that regular banks have been a "significant force in securitization all along" and that they "have in fact played a dominant role in the emergence and growth of asset-backed securitization". The implication here is that shadow banking should not be targeted by regulators, but no one is saying that shadow banks should be targeted while regular banks are set free. If regular banks are involved in shadow banking activities, these activities should be regulated. This is about the regulation of securitization and other functions, not about the regulation of who performs them.

7.4. Shadow banking is superior

Fein (2013) argues that the critics of shadow banking imply that traditional banking is a superior form of financial activity when in fact the traditional banking model has proven inefficient and unsustainable over time. Traditional banks have depended on shadow banking activities to complement their deposit-based banking activities and could not have survived without shadow banking. Yes, but this does not rule out the fact that shadow banking activities represent an unnecessary extravaganza at best and a conduit to fraud at worst. We should expect nothing less from the financial oligarchy than indulging in activities that boost their bonuses. The so-called traditional banking worked well for hundreds of years, so it is not clear why it is not sustainable, except perhaps that it does not provide the kind of profit that allows the financial oligarchs to pay themselves exuberant bonuses and golden parachutes. It is a travesty to claim that traditional banking is unsustainable because a bank can always survive by borrowing at 5% and lending at 8%. Of course, it is a different matter if "unsustainable" means unable to pay big bonuses to "talented" bankers.

7.5. Shadow banking as a natural consequence of growth

The rationale behind the argument that shadow banking is a natural consequence of growth is that economic growth gives rise to the need for a diversified set of financing modes and sources. Another growth related argument is put forward by Wallison (2012) who goes as far as saying that the regulation of shadow banking would "add costs that will impair economic growth". It is not clear why economic growth requires different forms of financing and why straight bank credit cannot do the job. Wallison's claim that the regulation of shadow banking will impair economic growth is counterfactual. It was shadow banking activity that impaired growth on a scale that has not been experienced since the Great Depression.

7.6. Shadow banking is little understood

Another argument against the regulation of shadow banking is that we do not know if the system is bad because it is little understood (for example, Reuters, 2013). Shadow banking is not understood because it is secretive, opaque and works in darkness, and this is why it should be regulated. This argument goes as follows: shadow banking lacks transparency, hence it is not understood, which provides a reason for exempting it from regulation. Serial killers are little understood, but this does not mean that they should not be "regulated". The right argument is that shadow banking should be regulated because it is not understood.

7.7. Shadow banking provides necessary and distinct functions

It is not clear why the necessary and distinct functions of shadow banking cannot be performed within the confines of financial regulation. If these are the benefits obtained from the operations of shadow financial institutions, what are the costs? The proponents of shadow banking claim that it provides important financial intermediation functions that are distinct from those performed by banks and capital markets, as confirmed by its continued growth (Claessens *et al.*, 2012), But just because something grows fast does not mean that it is benign (cancer is one example, OTC derivatives provide another).

7.8. Shadow banking helps achieve regulatory requirements

The shadow banking system plays a helpful role because it buys bad loans from commercial banks, which means that regular banks can meet the stricter capital rules and be fit for all kinds of stress tests, much to the delight of regulators. This is like a hot potato that is passed on from one party to another. The fact that shadow banks hold toxic assets on behalf of regulated banks does not mean that the risk of holding toxic assets goes away.

7.9. Regulation is knee-jerk reaction

Wallison (2012) criticizes the regulation of shadow banking because it is a "rush to judgment in light of the fact that both regulated deposit banking and the unregulated or lightly regulated securities market were overwhelmed by the financial crisis". There is no "rush" here because we witnessed the damage inflicted by the global financial crisis and the Great Recession in 2008 and 2009.

7.10. Shadow banking is not inherently unstable

The regulation of shadow banking, according to Wallison (2012), would not be a sound policy without evidence indicating that the shadow banking system is inherently unstable. He argues that shadow banking has been remarkably stable in comparison to regulated banking for at least the last 35 years and that no events in shadow banking can be classified as systemic. I suppose that the last 35 years include 2007 and 2008. This argument is contrary to the analysis presented earlier on the role played by shadow banking in the global financial crisis and its contribution to systemic risk.

7.11. Regulating shadow banking kills innovation

Wallison (2012) describes shadow banking as being "innovative", and since regulation kills innovation, the shadow banking system should not be subject to regulation. We have already come across the argument that it may be a good idea to kill financial innovation and put an end to the "great inventions" of financial engineers.

7.12. Self-discipline

While imposing discipline on traditional banking relies on costly regulation, shadow financial institutions are self-disciplined by their reputation concerns — that is by their "This is a call for self-regulation", which is a joke.

8. Regulatory Proposals

The discussion so far leads to the conclusion that the regulation of shadow banking makes sense, to say the least. Unfortunately, regulators have the attitude that shadow banking is some sort of a sacred cow that has to be treated gently. Gorton and Metrick (2010b) raise the following question: if the growth of shadow banking was central to the crisis and was facilitated by regulatory changes, then why not simply reverse all these changes? However, they cast doubt on the proposition that reversal of the regulatory changes that have led to the rise and growth of shadow banking will bring about a safer system dominated by traditional banks. They argue against such a "radical course of action" because it is not possible or desirable. Instead they wonder how the current regulatory structure could be adapted to make the system safer without driving its activity into a new "unregulated darkness". The irony is that shadow banking is already unregulated darkness. Contrary to what Gorton and Metrick believe, reversal of regulatory changes is both possible and desirable (perhaps even imperative).

In the US, the Dodd–Frank Act, passed in 2010, goes some way toward regulating the shadow banking system by stipulating that the Federal Reserve System would have the power to regulate all institutions of systemic importance, irrespective of whether they belong to the proper or shadow system. Specific provisions to regulate shadow banking include the following: (i) hedge funds must register with the Securities and Exchange Commission (SEC); (ii) much OTC derivatives trading is to be moved to organized exchanges; (iii) all systemically important institutions will be regulated by the Federal Reserve and (iv) retail lenders are to be subject to consistent federal level regulation through the Consumer Financial Protection Bureau. Naturally, the financial oligarchs oppose these provisions just like they are opposing the Volcker rule and the liquidity and leverage provisions of Basel III. This is the case despite the fact that some of these rules are inadequate. Requiring hedge funds to register with the SEC does nothing to the opaqueness and heavy leverage of these entities. What is required, as far as hedge funds are concerned, is a rule forcing them to be less secretive by enhancing disclosure. We have not seen much in terms of moving "much" OTC derivatives to organized exchanges, but then the question is why "much" instead of "all" as was suggested by Broksley Born in the 1990s? The regulation of systemically important shadow financial institutions only is inadequate, let alone the difficulty of determining which institution is systemically important (Moosa, 2010).[2] It makes no difference whether retail lenders are regulated at the federal or state level — what matters is how they will be regulated and what to do about poor underwriting standards.

Tarullo (2013) argues for providing discount window access to broker-dealers, guaranteeing certain kinds of wholesale funding, or both. However, he is wary of any such extension of the government safety net, preferring instead a regulatory approach that requires market participants using or extending short-term wholesale funding to internalize the social costs of those forms of funding.

---

[2]Typically the identification of systematically important financial institutions (SIFIs) is required to arrange a bailout or a bail-in, not to protect consumers from them.

Unlike deposit insurance, the savings of most US households are generally not directly at risk in short-term wholesale funding arrangements. Furthermore, counterparties in short-term wholesale funding should be capable of providing some market discipline in at least some of the contexts in which such funding is provided.

Tarullo suggests two kinds of policy options that can be considered, individually or together, in responding to the financial vulnerability caused by large amounts of short-term wholesale funding. The first is to impose a regulatory charge calculated by reference to reliance on securities financing transactions (SFTs), which encompass repo and reverse repo, securities lending and borrowing, securities margin lending, and other forms of short-term wholesale funding. The second option is intended to boost directly the very low charges under current and pending regulatory standards attracted by SFT matched books. There is no reason why regulators should think about different regulatory rules for shadow financial institutions as opposed to regulating them like the mainstream financial sector — by doing so, the shadow system will be "unshadowed".

Gorton and Metrick (2010b) suggest that proper regulation should be designed in such a way as to make it clear, through either insurance or collateral, which assets are truly safe and which are not. Their proposals pertain to MMMFs, securitization and repos, which they believe to be the three main functions of shadow banking. As far as MMMFs are concerned, the Gorton–Metrick proposal is similar to that of the Group of Thirty (2009), requiring MMMFs wishing to continue to offer bank-like services to reorganize themselves as narrow savings banks (NSBs), with appropriate prudential regulation and supervision, government insurance, and access to central bank lender of last resort facilities. On the other hand, institutions that wish to remain as MMMFs should only offer a conservative investment option with modest upside potential at a relatively low risk. The regulation of MMMFs is supported by Vlocker (2011) for the reason that they can be vulnerable along the lines suggested by Gorton and Merdick (2010b).

To regulate securitization, Gorton and Metrick propose the establishment of narrow funding banks (NFBs), which would be genuine banks with charters, capital requirements, periodic inspections, and access to the central bank's discount window. Under this proposal, all securitized products must be sold to NFBs and no other entity would be allowed to buy ABSs (NFBs could also buy other high-grade assets such as US Treasury securities). NFBs would be new entities located between securitizations and final investors. Instead of buying ABSs, final investors would buy the liabilities of NFBs. Regulators would have to monitor the portfolios of NFBs and take corrective action if necessary.

The repo proposals include the following: (i) banks (NFBs, NSBs and commercial banks) would be allowed to engage in repo financing; (ii) non-bank entities would also be allowed to engage in repos, but only with a license, and would face other constraints; (iii) eligible collateral for banks in repo transactions would be restricted to US Treasury securities, liabilities of NFBs and other asset classes that the regulator deems appropriate; (iv) eligible collateral for non-bank entities could be any type of security, but the transaction would be subject to minimum haircuts and position limits; (v) minimum haircuts would be required on all collateral used in repos and could be specific to the two parties and the collateral offered; (vi) position limits would be set for non-bank entities, in terms of gross notional amounts issued or held, as a function of firm size and the collateral used and (vii) rehypothecation would be limited automatically by the minimum haircuts.

Shleifer (2010) argues against the regulatory proposals of Gorton and Metrick on the grounds that allowing only narrow funding banks to purchase ABSs would deprive other potential buyers of ABSs of access to these securities and that ABS repos do not occupy the central position in the crisis to which Gorton and Metrick have elevated them. He casts doubt on the desirability of prohibiting anyone but NFBs from buying ABSs, particularly if some investors are interested in holding these assets. Undoubtedly, the financial establishment would have applauded the defense of shadow banking put forward by Shleifer and Tarullo by criticizing the proposals of Gorton and Metrick, not that those proposals are radical in any sense. As a matter of fact, Gorton and Metrick are easy on shadow banking, as they argue against the reversal of the conditions that have led us to the mess we are in now.

In response to the G20's request, the FSB has developed an overall approach to strengthen the oversight and regulation of the shadow banking system (see, for example, Annen, 2012). The FSB identifies a number of potential regulatory responses to address risks in the shadow banking system falling under four categories: (i) the regulation of banks' interaction with shadow banking entities (indirect regulation); (ii) the regulation of shadow banking entities; (iii) the regulation of shadow banking activities and (iv) macroprudential measures. The FSB makes some recommendations falling under the four categories, including the following:

1. Consolidation rules should ensure that any shadow banking entities that the bank sponsors are included on its balance sheet for prudential purposes (for example, in the calculation of risk-based capital and leverage ratios as well as liquidity ratios).
2. Limits on the size and nature of a bank's exposures to shadow banking entities should be enhanced.
3. The risk-based capital requirements for banks' exposures to shadow banking entities should be reviewed to ensure that such risks are adequately captured.
4. Restricting banks' ability to stand behind any entities that are not consolidated following the application of more rigorous consolidation rules by applying stricter regulatory treatment of "implicit support".
5. Incentives associated with securitization should be adequately addressed.
6. The regulation of secured funding markets, in particular repos and securities lending, should be assessed carefully and further enhanced from the prudential perspective as necessary.
7. The transparency and reporting of information should continue to be improved as appropriate.

8. The underwriting standards for all relevant financial institutions should be rigorous and continue to be improved as appropriate.

All of these recommendations are steps in the right direction, but whether or not they will see the light in the form intended originally is a different matter. Whenever a disaster strikes, regulatory measures are put forward but then they are either not implemented at all in the original form or get watered down as a result of pressure from the financial oligarchy.

9. Concluding Remarks

A radical solution to the problems caused by shadow banking is to reverse the conditions that led to its rise — this is not as a formidable task as what Gorton and Metrick (2010b) think. Why is it that regulated financial institutions cannot perform the functions of shadow institutions? Do we really need the extravaganza of modern finance? Do we need OTC derivatives? Do we need a financial sector that dwarfs the real sector of the economy when the financial sector is supposed to serve the real sector by providing credit and means of payment? Is financial extravaganza worthwhile in terms of costs and benefits? These are the questions that should be considered as opposed to proposing half-hearted measures.

Stiglitz (2010) believes that banks should be forced to return to the "boring" business of commercial banking. Removing systemic risk is better achieved by eliminating incentives to bear risk and killing moral hazard. Perhaps the way out is to go back to the good old days, the days of "boring banking" when J.P. Morgan ran his bank as a partnership with unlimited liability — as a result risk taking was limited and credit was extended cautiously. In those days banks were liable for their own mistakes, in which case they had every reason to be careful. In those days, the positions taken by banks were straightforward, free of toxic assets and unnecessarily complex derivatives. In those days there was no firm-wide risk management function because the risk that faced banks was no more than the risk of individual loans. In those days trading activities were limited and the bonus culture did not exist. According to Dowd *et al.* (2011a) the boring banking model worked because decision makers had to bear the consequences of their own mistakes. In those days shadow banking did not exist but the world survived (even thrived) without it.

Taleb (2009) presents a way forward in the form of "ten commandments", the most relevant of which are the following: (i) complex derivatives need to be banned because nobody understands them and few are rational enough to know it; (ii) citizens must be protected from themselves and from bankers selling them "hedging" products and (iii) citizens should not depend on financial assets or fallible "expert" advice for their retirement. He recommends a move to Capitalism 2.0 by helping what needs to be broken to break on its own, converting debt into equity, banning leveraged buyouts, putting bankers where they belong, and clawing back their bonuses. These recommendations say it all about the shadow banking system. A world without shadow banking will be a better world.

Shadow banking is the financial equivalent of the underground economy. Arguing against the regulation of shadow banking is like arguing against the regulation of the underground economy. It is not clear therefore why no one advocates the underground economy and no one claims that the underground economy performs useful functions. The case for regulating shadow banking, even purging it altogether, is very strong, indeed.

Chapter 8

The Regulation of Credit Rating Agencies

1. Introduction

Credit rating agencies (CRAs) perform the function of assigning credit ratings to the issuers of debt securities, which can be firms, state or local governments, non-profit organizations and even sovereign governments. A rating represents the creditworthiness of the issuer (borrower) as well as the quality of the issued security in terms of credit risk (the risk of default). A high rating indicates a low probability of default and the ability of the borrower to make timely payments, and vice versa. Ratings are used by investors (such as pension funds, insurance companies, hedge funds, banks and governments) to decide whether or not a particular debt security offers acceptable good risk-return trade-off. The debt securities rated by CRAs include government bonds, corporate bonds, municipal bonds, certificates of deposit (CD), preferred stock, and structured products such as mortgage-backed securities (MBSs) and collateralized debt obligations (CDOs). The ratings are important for the issuers of securities because a high rating enables the issuer to offer a lower interest rate on the underlying security than a security with a lower rating. This is why the return on Treasury bonds

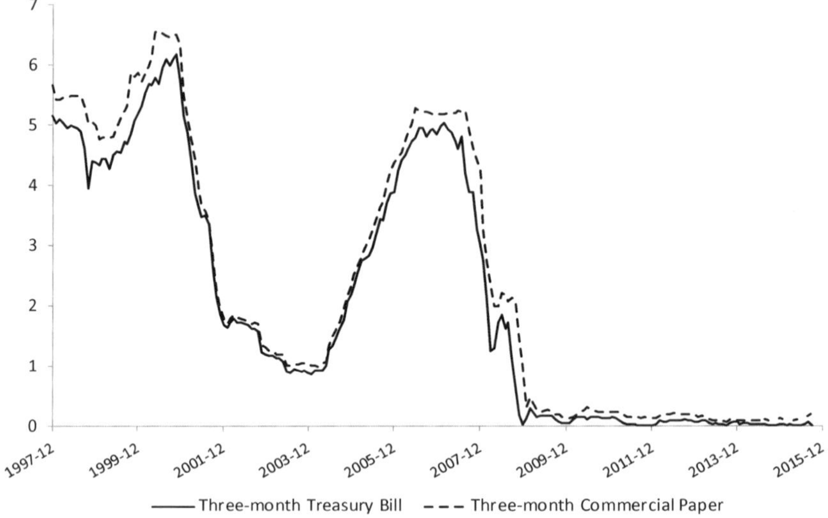

Figure 8.1:   Return on Treasury Bills and Commercial Paper

is always lower than the return on comparable corporate bonds and why the return on a corporate bond rated AAA (the top rating) is lower than a comparable corporate bond rated lower than that.[1] This can be observed very clearly in Figures 8.1–8.3. Furthermore, highly-rated securities are easier to sell and more liquid than securities with low ratings. This is why the market for Treasury bonds is more liquid than the market for corporate bonds.

---

[1] Treasuries and government bonds in general are given top rating because in theory a government is always able to pay back its debt as it has the power to generate revenue by raising taxes and printing money (monetizing the deficit). Governments may choose not to do that because raising taxes may be politically unacceptable and because money printing has inflationary consequences. Therefore, a government may choose to default on debt in its own currency, and this is why even sovereign governments are rated by the rating agencies. On 5 August 2011, Standard and Poor's (S&P) relegated the US from AAA to AA when it was thought that the US government would default because of Congressional disagreement about raising the debt ceiling. We will come back to this story later on. The credit ratings of several European countries have been lowered because of the European debt crisis.

Figure 8.2:   Return on Treasury and Corporate Bonds

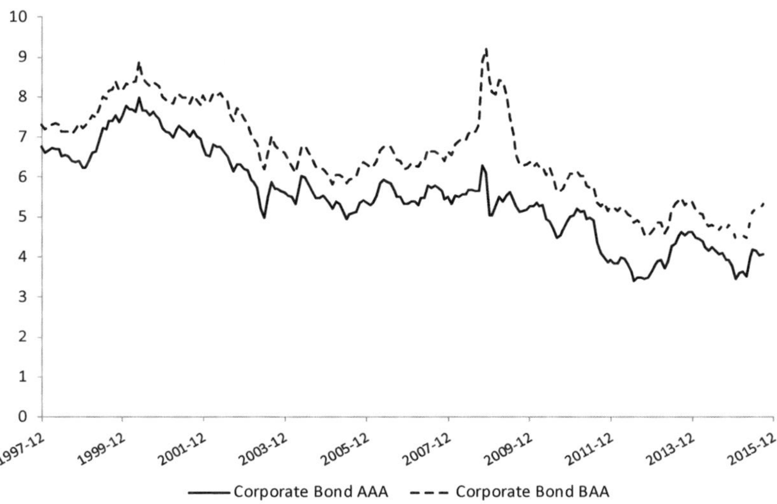

Figure 8.3:   Return on Corporate Bonds with Different Ratings

The role played by the CRAs is important because a downgrade is likely to raise the cost of capital and adversely affect profitability — it may even force a downgraded firm out of business. Utzig (2010) argues that "the growth of the international financial markets over the last 20 years would have been unthinkable without CRAs". He goes on to say the following:

> Only because of the availability of clear, internationally accepted indicators of the risk of default were investors willing to invest in international securities — whether corporate or government bonds — whose credit quality they would have been virtually unable to assess on their own. The CRAs worked for decades on designing a simple and readily understandable system that would allow any investor to invest in international securities with which they were not directly familiar.

This is a sanguine view of the CRAs. We will never know if financial markets had grown the way they did in the absence of the CRAs. And we have to remember that the use of the services of the CRAs is typically required by regulators and that it does not emanate from the desire of investors to be guided by the ratings of the CRAs. Unlike this sanguine view, we will find out that the ratings provided by the CRAs are far away from being "clear, internationally accepted indicators of the risk of default" and that the work of the CRAs, unlike what is claimed by Utzig (2010), is rather sloppy. Even if we accept at face value the proposition that international financial markets would not have grown without the CRAs, this means that they are responsible for the excessive financialization of the world economy far beyond what is required to support real economic activity.[2]

The CRAs have been under scrutiny since the advent of the global financial crisis, as they are accused of contributing massively to the turmoil. Utzig (2010) contends that the CRAs "bear some responsibility for the financial crisis", which is "acknowledged by policy makers, market participants, and by the agencies themselves". According to him, the CRAs "underestimated the credit risk associated with structured credit products and failed to adjust their ratings quickly enough to deteriorating market

---

[2] The credit rating of Greece was so good at one time that German banks rushed to accumulate Greek debt to satisfy the Basel capital requirements. These banks are now in trouble, threatened by Greek default, forcing the European Union to bailout Greece because the alternative is to bailout too big to fail (TBTF) banks.

conditions" and that "their work involves both methodological errors and unresolved conflicts of interests, with the result that market participants' confidence in the reliability of ratings was seriously shaken". Hundreds of thousands of securities that had been previously given the highest ratings were downgraded to the junk status during the crisis, causing the downfall of big names in the finance industry, most notably Lehman Brothers. The Financial Crisis Inquiry Commission (FCIC) puts a big chunk of the blame for the global financial crisis on the agencies (FCIC, 2011). European Union officials blame the agencies for contributing to the advent of the European sovereign debt crisis. As a result, several lawsuits have been filed against the agencies, most notably the 2013 lawsuit filed by the US Department of Justice against Standard and Poor's.[3]

While they are meant to provide investors with reliable information on the riskiness of debt securities, the CRAs have instead been accused of defrauding investors by offering overly favorable evaluations of insolvent financial institutions and giving their seal of approval to extremely risky MBS, just like when the Health Foundation gives its tick of approval to heart-friendly food products.[4] The debate on how to reform and regulate the CRAs centers on what to do about the business model (that is, how they get paid for their services) and how to curtail their power, which emanates from their oligopolistic status and the fact that their services are required by law.

2. History

Ekins and Calabria (2012) trace the origin of CRAs to financial publishing in the 19th century. The Mercantile Agency was founded in 1841 to collect information on operating statistics, business

---

[3] A settlement was reached in February 2015 whereby S&P's paid over $1 billion in compensation.

[4] The difference between the Heart Foundation and CRAs is that it is unlikely that the Foundation will give its seal of approval to high-fat sausages. The CRAs gave their seal of approval to some structured products that are as bad for the financial health of investors as high-fat sausages for the health of the heart.

standing, and the creditworthiness of businesses, with the objective of disseminating this information to subscribers. The present time CRAs emerged at the turn of the 20th century as publishers from the financial press, such as John Moody and Henry Poor, with the objective of collecting financial and operating statistics on the railroad bond market and selling the information to subscribers. What we would now recognize as credit ratings were first issued by Moody's Analyses Publishing Company in 1909, H.V. and H.W. Poor Company in 1916, Standard Statistics Company in 1922, and Fitch Publishing Company in 1924. The industry grew rapidly following the passage of the Glass–Steagall Act of 1933 and the separation of investment banking (hence the securities business) from commercial banking. In 1936, regulation was introduced to prohibit banks from investing in bonds deemed (by the rating agencies) to be "speculative", allowing them to hold only "investment grade" bonds. While the use of ratings by investors had been entirely voluntary, the 1936 requirement by bank regulators to make ratings mandatory meant that "these ratings acquired the force of law", giving the CRAs oligopolistic powers. With the passage of time, ratings were extended to non-bank financial institutions and, in terms of securities, to commercial paper and certificates of deposit.

In 1975, the Securities and Exchange Commission (SEC) came up with a new designation for the CRAs, that of nationally recognized statistical rating organization (NRSRO), which ushered in the dominance of the big three (Moody's, S&P's and Fitch). Subsequently the SEC erected barriers to entry, allowing only four more rating agencies to obtain the NRSRO designation. However, mergers of the new four with Fitch meant that only the original big three had the crucial NRSRO designation at the end of 2000.[5] As Altman *et al.* (2010) put it, only the big three could bless the expanding volume of mortgage bonds with their all-important

---

[5] Lubochinsky and Raingeard (2008) highlight the SEC's own role in cementing the CRA oligopoly since the 1970s, when it adopted the NRSRO designation, which dissuaded many competitors from seeking to enter the market. They identify this course of action as one of the main reasons why only three CRAs exist at present.

ratings — especially their top AAA and AA ratings — for institutional investors". This means that the NRSRO designation was (and is) effectively a barrier to entry that gave the big three oligopolistic power.[6]

In the 1980s and 1990s, a significant expansion in financial markets took place, creating more business for the rating agencies.[7] The biggest area of growth was structured finance, the products of "financial engineering" such as CDOs, CDOs squared and synthetic CDOs.[8] Since these products are highly complex, investors (and regulators) became increasingly dependent on the scores assigned by the agencies, but this is not to say that the CRAs knew what they were doing as these financial "innovations" constitute a totally different ball game from that of rating straight, down-to-earth bonds. It was mostly structured finance that brought about the downfall of CRAs although they seem to be back in action. This, however, does not mean that it took the global financial crisis and complex products to expose the poor performance of the CRAs.

---

[6] Ekins and Calabria (2012) suggest that the NRSRO designation inadvertently created a *de facto* oligopoly, which primarily propped up three firms: Moody's, S&P, and Fitch. However, they point out that the introduction of the NRSRO designation was "not intended to be an oligopolistic mechanism or to reduce investor due diligence, but rather was intended to protect consumers", in the sense that only those firms qualified as NRSROs could provide sound advice to investors.

[7] The significant expansion in financial markets was caused by deregulation, leading to the growth of business for the CRAs. Causation ran from the growth of financial markets to the growth of business for CRAs. This means that CRAs did not cause the growth in financial markets, as Utzig (2010) claims — but they certainly benefited from an ever expanding financial sector.

[8] The FCIC (2011) presents some interesting facts and figures about Moody's performance in the heyday of structured products when rating CDOs was a lucrative business. Moody's rated 220 deals in 2004, 363 in 2006, 749 in 2006, and 717 in 2007. The value of those deals rose from $90 billion in 2004 to $162 billion in 2005, $337 billion in 2006, and $326 billion in 2007. The reported revenues of Moody's from structured products grew from $199 million in 2000, or 33% of Moody's revenues, to $837 million in 2006 or 44% of overall corporate revenue. The boom years of structured finance coincided with a company-wide surge in revenue and profits. From 2000 to 2006, Moody's revenues surged from $602 million to $2 billion while its profit margin climbed from 26% to 37%.

Sicilia (2011) contends that the recognition of bad performance of the CRAs came much earlier than the Enron scandal, which is the commonly held view. He argues, for example, that the CRAs failed to anticipate the financial collapse of New York City in the mid-1970s. In the face of a decade-long rising tide of dire financial news, Moody's and S&P raised the city's ratings, then held firm. It was not until October 1974 that Moody's downgraded the New York City bond rating from A to B (marginally speculative) and then to Caa (very speculative). In the wake of New York City's debacle, a writer for the *New York Times* noted that "one of the major casualties of that debacle appears to be the rating agencies' creditability".

3. Market Structure and Business Models

The credit rating "industry" constitutes an oligopoly because it consists of three big firms only. Lawrence White notes that "a striking fact about the structure of the (rating) industry is the persistent fewness of incumbents" (White, 2002). In 2003, the SEC submitted a report to Congress detailing plans to launch an investigation into the anti-competitive practices of CRAs (Teather, 2003), which is ironic because it is the SEC and other regulatory bodies that erected barriers to prevent or impede entry to the industry and forced regulated financial institutions to pay for the services of the unregulated rating agencies. According to Frank Partnoy, "the regulation of CRAs by the SEC and Federal Reserve Bank has eliminated competition between CRAs" (Wall Street Journal, 2009). On an international level, financial institutions subject to international banking regulation (as enshrined in the Basel accords) are forced to do the same because the Basel rules depend on ratings to assign the weights required for the calculation of the risk-weighted capital ratio. According to Nicolas and Firzli (2011), the Basel rules "have unduly encouraged the use of ready-made opinions produced by oligopolistic rating agencies".

The structure of the credit rating industry is consistent with the characteristics of an oligopolistic market: (i) only a few large firms operate, which distinguishes oligopoly from monopoly where the market is dominated by one firm; (ii) the presence of high barriers to entry, which distinguishes oligopoly from perfect competition and monopolistic competition where barriers to entry are not present and (iii) oligopolistic firms may produce either differentiated or homogeneous products. Under oligopoly, any firm is big enough to affect the market but decisions on output and price are taken with reference to what the rivals want to do. This is why game theory is used to determine equilibrium in an oligopolistic market.

Under oligopoly the price is higher and output is lower than under perfect competition, resulting in the loss of both productive efficiency and allocative efficiency — in general, a loss of welfare. A monopolistic industry may be characterized by a homogenous product (for example, petrol) or differentiated products (such as up-market fashion clothes and handbags). In the credit rating industry, the output is a service that takes the form of providing a credit rating such as AAA or AA, and so on. A homogenous product in this case means that the CRAs give on average the same rating to the same security, as (for example) when they use a stringent methodology that gives top rating to a handful of high-quality securities issued by reputable firms. However, if one of the CRAs is less stringent in giving top rating, then it will have a differentiated product that issuers like and are prepared to pay for. If the product is identical, no agency would want to change its price because if one of them starts to charge a higher price, the others will not follow, causing a loss of market share for the agency initiating the price change. If, on the other hand, one of the agencies decided to reduce its price, the other two would follow, hence the price changer would not benefit. Under these conditions, there is no incentive to change the price and the agencies will be better off colluding and acting like a monopoly. If the product is differentiated, when one of the agencies uses lower standards, other agencies could do the same (that is, using lower standards) to maintain market share. Unlike the design fashion industry, CRAs cannot compete on quality, since quality can be matched by the others (if one CRA gives top rating to a security, there is no reason why others cannot do the same).[9] Thus, even with a differentiated product, the CRAs act like a monopoly. Daly (2011) describes the market structure indirectly by suggesting that the CRAs follow each other with respect to awarding inflated ratings. This is what he says:

> My guess is that by acting high and mighty, S&P is trying to make us forget how low and dirty it was back in August 2004. That was when S&P relaxed its standards to keep Wall Street happy and itself flush with fees Wall Street pays it for ratings. At the time, Wall Street was in the midst of underwriting $3.2 trillion in sub-prime mortgages. It packaged them into securities, foisting them off on "investors" as the suckers were called. To win over the suckers, the banks needed AAA ratings. Moody's was the first to declare itself willing to oblige, instantly making itself the place for Wall Street to go for ratings.

Monopolies are problematical — in fact monopoly power is a major justification for regulation in general. Monopolies cause a loss of efficiency and welfare because a monopolist produces a smaller quantity and sells at a higher price compared with a competitive firm. The comparison can be seen in Figure 8.4, where a monopolist faces a downward sloping demand curve (D), while a perfectly competitive market faces a perfectly elastic demand curve at the price P_c. The monopolist produces the level output Q_m corresponding to the profit maximization condition of the equality of marginal cost and marginal revenue ($MC = MR$), which gives a price (P_m) derived from the demand curve. A competitive firm, on the other hand, produces the quantity Q_c at the price P_c. A competitive firm, therefore, satisfies the conditions for productive efficiency, where the price is equal to the minimum average

---

[9] This is product quality if the objective of investors is to satisfy the regulatory requirement of investing in securities of certain ratings. If investors are interested in more than a three-letter rating, then product differentiation may take the form of more detailed analysis and follow up services. This is not happening because the only thing the agencies provide (and are required to provide) is a rating.

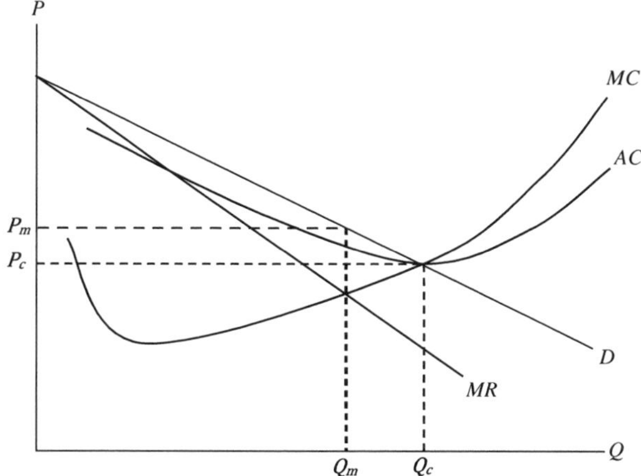

Figure 8.4:   Output and Price under Monopoly and Perfect Competition

cost (*AC*), and allocative efficiency where the price is equal to the marginal cost. In the case of monopoly the price is higher than both *MC* and *AC*.

The CRAs are described by Partnoy (2010) as "gatekeepers" (just like accounting and law firms) who benefit greatly from regulatory measures that give rise to demand for their services. Partnoy believes that by creating these rules, regulators have corrupted financial markets by giving the CRAs and other gatekeepers "pervasive power". Some literature deals with collusion and the conditions under which CRAs generate low and inflated ratings. Mahlmann (2008) examines the implications of rating publication rights and reveals the existence of equilibrium with partial non-disclosure of low ratings. Skreta and Veldkamp (2008) deal with the issue of "rating shopping" and show that when issuers can choose from several agencies, product complexity can lead to rating inflation, even if CRAs produce unbiased ratings. Bolton *et al.* (2008) find that CRAs may assign inflated ratings in the presence of many naive investors or when (exogenous) reputation costs are low. Mathis *et al.* (2008) model reputation costs endogenously and find that a CRA may assign inflated ratings when a large fraction of the agency's income stems from the rating of complex products. Stolper (2009) formulates a repeated principal-agent problem in which a regulator approves CRAs and shows that CRAs may collude to assign inflated ratings. However, he also reveals the presence of an approval scheme that induces CRAs to assign correct ratings. The problem is determining what constitutes a "correct rating".

CRAs generate revenue from a variety of activities related to the production and distribution of credit ratings. The sources of revenue are generally the issuers of securities and investors. The agencies operate under one or a combination of two business models: the subscriber-pays model and the issuer-pays model. Under the subscriber-pays model, the CRA does not make its ratings freely available to the market, in which case investors pay a subscription fee for the privilege of access to ratings. Under the issuer-pays model, agencies charge issuers a fee for providing credit rating assessments. In this case the ratings are made freely available to the broader market, typically via the internet.[10]

The subscriber-pays model prevailed until the early 1970s, when the big three switched to the issuer-pays model for several reasons, including growing investor demand for credit ratings and the widespread use of information sharing technology, which allowed investors to share the information provided by the agencies. According to the Organization for Economic Co-operation and Development (OECD) (2010) this shift may have occurred in part because the CRAs found issuers more willing to pay for their services than investors, since the issuers needed certain ratings in order to sell their bonds to regulated financial institutions.[11] Most criticism of credit raters centers on the issuer-pays model, which is

---

[10] The CRAs do not charge sovereign borrowers for rating their debt but they make the information publicly available. This is the "public relations" part of the business.

[11] The fact that issuers are more willing to pay for ratings than investors means that the ratings are rubber stamps that enable issuers to sell their securities rather than constituting a useful source of information that enables investors to make sound investment decisions. Therefore the perceived increase in the demand of investors for ratings may be a myth.

an issue that is related to product differentiation. Since issuers pay, the only thing they are interested in is top rating for which they are prepared to pay to make it easier for them to sell the securities. In fact, the last thing issuers want is a detailed analysis that may leave any shadow of doubt in investors' minds with respect to the quality of securities.

4. The Performance of CRAs

The performance of the CRAs, in the sense of providing information that is useful for investors, has been dismal, to say the least. A view has been expressed that the CRAs "do make astrologers and bone casters look extraordinarily accurate" and that they are "opportunistically inefficient".[12] The CRAs are accused of supplying inaccurate ratings — and that was not only during the global financial crisis. Critics refer to the near-defaults, defaults, and financial disasters that escaped detection by the rating agencies as well as failure to downgrade troubled firms until just before (or even after) the declaration of bankruptcy. For example, critics complain that "not a single analyst at either Moody's or S&P lost his job as a result of missing the Enron fraud" and that "management (of the agencies) stayed the same" (McLean and Nocera, 2010). Enron was exposed by the activities of short sellers who got it right by analyzing the situation thoroughly while the rating agencies thought that there was nothing to worry about.[13] Despite rising mortgage delinquencies, Moody's continued to rate Freddie Mac's preferred stock triple-A until mid-2008, when it was downgraded to one tick above the junk bond level.[14] *The Economist* (2005) casts doubt on the ability of the rating agencies to provide reliable

---

[12] https://www.youtube.com/watch?v=eErg78D6GoA.

[13] This is why it is rather strange that regulators are more interested in the regulation of short selling than the regulation of CRAs although short sellers provide much more useful and accurate information than CRAs.

[14] The downgrade was precipitated by Warren Buffett's telling CNBC that he had "passed on an opportunity to help the troubled mortgage giant" (International Herald Tribune, 2008).

estimates of the probability of default, arguing that they missed the crises of Enron, WorldCom, and Parmalat.

The findings of some empirical studies suggest that the CRAs follow the market — that is, the market alerts the CRAs of trouble, and not vice versa (Kliger and Sarig, 2002). Hawkins and Turner (2000) warn that "many would be wary of putting too much emphasis on the assessment of CRAs". To support their argument, they refer to the performance of the agencies during the Asian crisis. While they did not downgrade most Asian countries before the crisis (when imbalances were developing), their downgrades in the midst of the crisis made it even worse.[15] They conclude that "rating agencies were backward-looking rather than forward-looking in their assessments". Likewise, Rodriguez (2002) argues that the ratings tend to follow market trends rather than anticipate them.

In response to the claim that their performance has been less than satisfactory, defenders of CRAs complain about the market's "lack of appreciation". According to Robert Clow, "when a company or sovereign nation pays its debt on time, the market barely takes momentary notice … but let a country or corporation unexpectedly miss a payment or threaten default, and bondholders, lawyers and even regulators are quick to rush the field to protest the credit analyst's lapse" (Sinclair, 2005). Other advocates of CRAs point out that bonds assigned a low credit rating by rating agencies have been shown to default more frequently than bonds that receive a high credit rating, suggesting that ratings still serve as a useful indicator of credit risk (Madura, 2011). It is not clear what appreciation is for because CRAs are paid well to do their job (it sounds as if the CRAs should receive tips or bonuses on top of the regular fees paid for their services).

The proposition that CRAs get it right most of the time is not consistent with the record. During the global financial crisis, hundreds of billions of dollars' worth of triple-A-rated MBSs were

---

[15] The performance of CRAs with respect to the rating of sovereign debt (of countries) has been as bad as performance with respect to the rating of private debt (of companies).

abruptly downgraded from triple-A to "junk" within two years of the issue of the original ratings. About 73% (over $800 billion worth) of all MBSs that one CRAs (Moody's) had rated triple-A in 2006 were downgraded to the junk status two years later.[16] It is inconceivable that a vast number of MBSs turn rotten so quickly and decline from the top to the bottom of the quality ladder. One would tend to think that those securities were not top quality, which means that they did not deserve the AAA designation to start with. Critics, therefore, are justified in characterizing the work of the agencies as "catastrophically misleading" and in believing that the CRAs "provided little or no value" (Casey, 2009; Lippert, 2010).

The aggregate (for the big three agencies) figures of downgrading are startling, showing indeed that the CRAs follow the market than anticipate events. In Figure 8.5, we observe the number of downgrades in structured products and corporate bonds. We can readily see the explosion in the number of downgraded structured products in 2007 and 2008, which brought havoc on the financial institutions and other investors holding those products. On the other hand, the number of downgraded corporate bonds does not reflect the advent of the global financial crisis as there is no jump in downgrades in 2007 or 2008. The same can be observed in Figure 8.6, which shows the downgrades of structured products classified under asset-backed securities (ABSs), CDOs, commercial mortgage-backed securities (CMBS) and RMBS. These figures tell us two things: (i) the CRAs do follow the market in the sense that downgrades come after the event (ex post) and (ii) it was structured products in particular that exposed the weakness of the CRAs.

---

[16] As of February 2008, Moody's had downgraded at least one tranche of 94.2% of the subprime residential mortgage-backed securities (RMBS) issues the agency rated in 2006 and 76.9% of the issues rated in 2007. As of March 2008, S&P had downgraded 44.3% of the subprime tranches it rated between the first quarter of 2005 and the third quarter of 2007. As of December 2007, Fitch had downgraded approximately 34% of the subprime tranches it rated in 2006 and in the first quarter of 2007. In February 2008, Fitch placed on "Ratings Watch Negative" all of the RMBSs backed by subprime first-lien mortgages that Fitch rated in 2006 and the first quarter of 2007 (Hill, 2010).

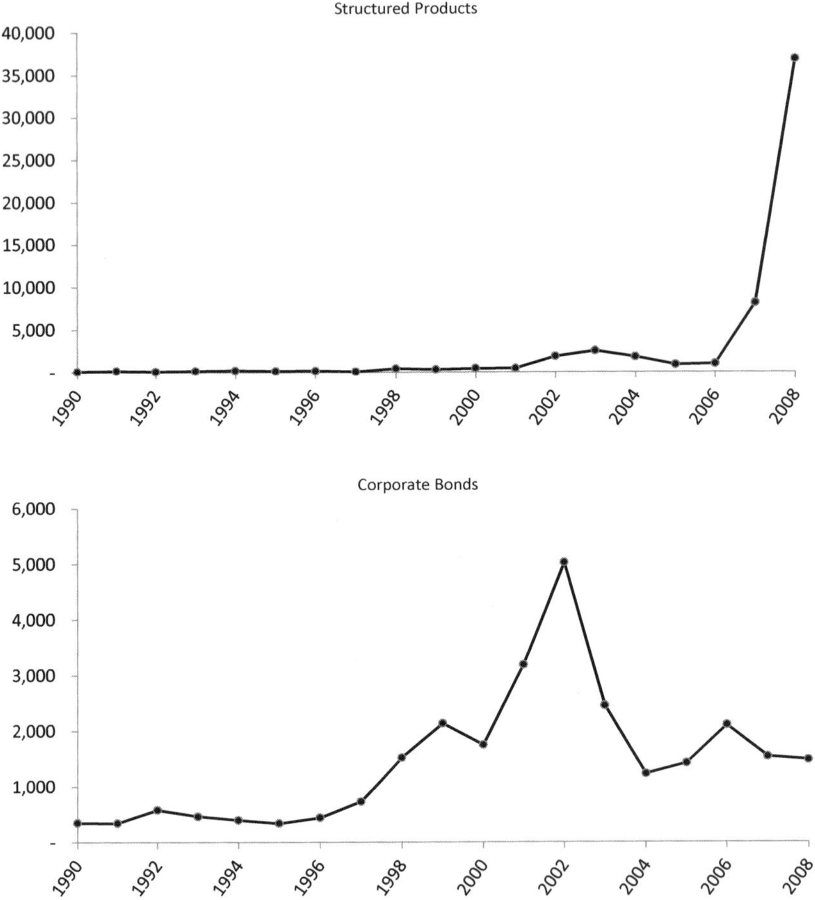

Figure 8.5:   Downgrades of Structured Products and Corporate Bonds

With limited staff, it is not possible that the CRAs would have been able to deal with a vast number of complex products — so they failed.

The CRAs maintain that their ratings are simply opinions about credit risk, not guarantees (Jones, 2009; *The Economist*, 2013b). They argue that their ratings are designed to measure the probability of default, not to recommend the purchase of individual securities or to predict market prices. Cliff Griep, the chief credit officer of S&P, argues that ratings pertain to creditworthiness, not market risk,

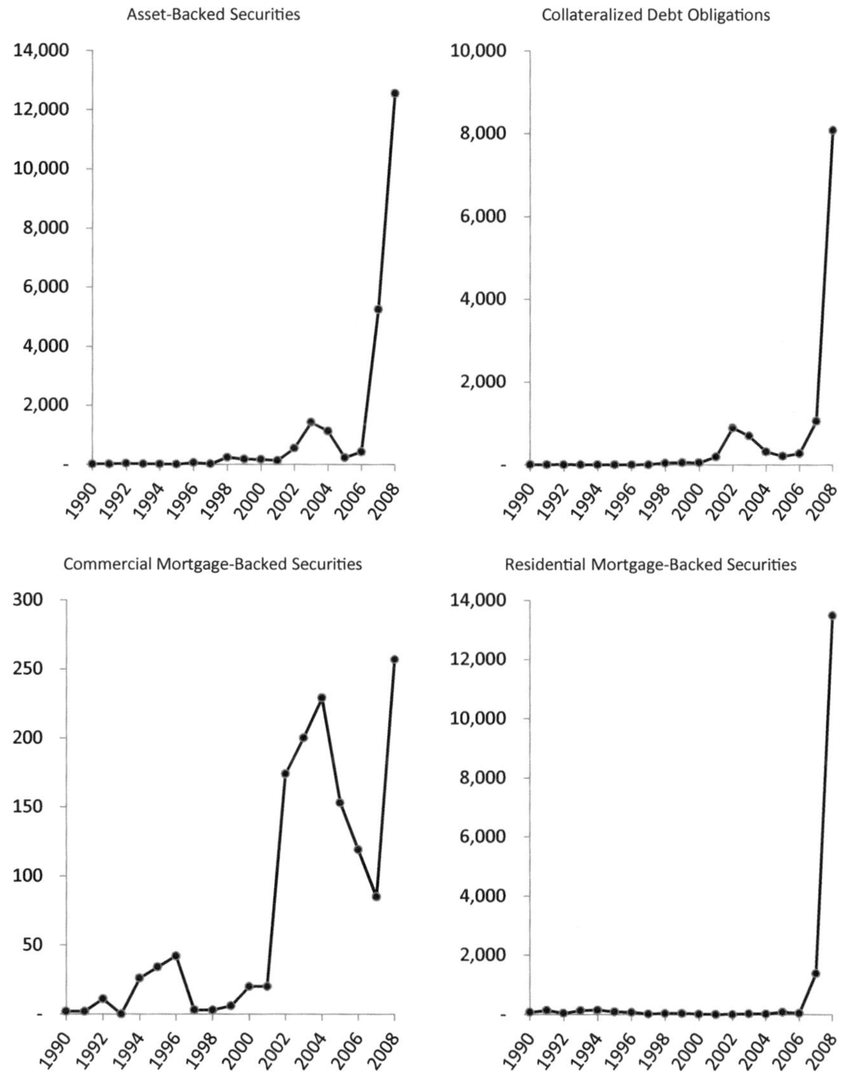

Figure 8.6:   Downgrades of Structured Products by Type

and are driven by fundamentals, not fluctuating prices (*The Economist*, 2007a). These propositions make no sense, to say the least. The "opinions, not guarantees" claim is nonsense because investors buy securities on the basis of risk-adjusted return, where (credit) risk is measured by the scores granted by the rating agencies. True, the agencies do not tell investors to buy this or that product, but they tell investors that if they bought a product rated AAA, it was very unlikely that they would suffer credit losses resulting from default. The triple A designation implies that the issuer is in a sound financial position to the extent that investors should rest assured that they will get back every cent of their invested money plus the accrued return. Thus, a good rating constitutes a recommendation to buy. Griep's argument is flawed because creditworthiness and market risk are closely related: a perceived drop in creditworthiness (measured by a high probability of default, hence a low credit rating) results in market losses. This is why the statement "driven by fundamentals not market prices" makes no sense whatsoever (after all, fundamentals affect prices). It is either that Griep does not know or pretends not to know the meaning of "market risk" and "fundamentals".

Then there is the claim that the CRAs should not be held responsible for faulty ratings (and the implicit advice based on them) on the grounds that they should be able to express their constitutional right to free speech. The free speech argument holds only if the agencies did not get paid for the ratings, but because they get paid they should be held liable for selling faulty products. In October 2015, it was announced that Volkswagen had to recall 8.5 million cars (and that is just in Europe) as a result of the fallout from the alleged installation of illegal emission software that makes it possible to cheat emission tests. That was the worst business crisis in the company's 78-year history, which wiped more than a third off its market value. The cost to VW is estimated to be $10.4 billion and, perhaps more importantly, the irreparable damage to its reputation. This is what happens when a firm sells a faulty product, which makes one wonder why this universal law does not apply to the CRAs. Even after the failure of the CRAs, they are back in business as usual and their profits are soaring once more. A very important difference between VW and Moody's (or the other two) is that customers are not forced to by the products of VW, but the customers of Moody's (and the other two) are required by law to buy their products.

5. The Failure of CRAs as an Operational Loss Event

Utzig (2010) attributes the failure of CRAs to the following factors: (i) overreliance on mathematical and statistical methodologies based on inadequate data, (ii) insufficient consideration of market and macroeconomic developments as factors influencing ratings, (iii) failure to take account of interdependencies, (iv) disregard of conflicts of interests, and (v) inadequate disclosure practices with regard to models and model assumptions. The failure of the CRAs can be viewed as an operational loss event.

Operational losses result from the failure of people, processes, systems and from external events. The failure of people can be attributed to incompetence, negligence and fraud. Before a consideration of the possible causes of the failure of the CRAs, we must first consider the issue of how they failed. Surely they have not failed in the same sense as Lehman Brothers and Bear Stearns, because they are still in business although they have incurred some legal losses. They have failed in the sense that they have not done their job properly by providing inferior products (ratings), thus contributing significantly to the advent of the global financial crisis. Like any operational loss event, the failure of CRAs can be explained in terms of the failure of people, processes, systems and from external events. There is a certain degree of overlap in this classification of the sources of operational failure, which are discussed in turn, starting with external events and ending up with the failure of people.

5.1. External events

The external event that caused the failure of the CRAs is the same event that caused the failure of all firms that failed during the global financial crisis — that is, the failure of the housing market in the US. Other external events may include some of the typical explanations for the global financial crisis, such as monetary policy and foreign surpluses. The underlying idea here is that no one predicted the collapse of the housing market, which means that the

CRAs failed because of factors beyond their control. This implies that the CRAs did a thorough job, using state-of-the-art models and made available the required resources to execute the underlying tasks but, like everyone else's models, their models failed because they could not predict 20-sigma events that are supposed to happen once every few billion years. In this sense, the performance of the rating agencies was not worse than the performance of others.

The Economist (2013b) seems to support this view by suggesting that "no other entity — including America's federal regulators — did any better". Take, for example, American International Group, Inc. (AIG) whose model predicted that the housing market could not collapse country-wide, but it did. And take Long-Term Capital Management (LTCM) whose model predicted the impossibility of divergence between the yields issued by countries like Russia and the US. According to *The Economist* (2012a), "financial firms quickly found themselves racking up daily losses that the computer said should occur once in millions of years. We must bear in mind that there is a considerable tendency in the business world to claim credit for success and attribute failure to external factors (see, for example, Ramiah *et al.*, 2014).

5.2. The failure of systems

What is meant by "systems" here is the models and methodologies used by the CRAs to calculate the probability of default and consequently to assign ratings. For example, Utzig (2010) argues that the methodologies employed by the agencies to rate and monitor securities may be inherently flawed, which brought about operational failure. Benmelech and Dlugosz (2010) refer to model error, in particular underestimation of default correlation across firms and households. Partnoy (2006) has argued that the statistical models were essentially flawed in that they provided the markets with an opportunity to arbitrage the CRAs' mistakes, rather than the risk profiles of the underlying assets.

In its report on enhancing market and institutional resilience, the Financial Stability Forum (2008) concludes that the CRAs' substantial underestimation of the risk inherent in structured products was partly due to methodological shortcomings. Singled out for criticism were the inadequate historical data, which lead to a significant increase in model risk, and the fact that CRAs had not taken sufficient account of deteriorating lending standards. The report also calls for a distinction to be made between the ratings of structured products and other corporate bonds in order to highlight the differences in the methodologies used and the significantly different risk characteristics involved. Likewise, the De Larosière Group (2009) argues that flaws in rating methodologies were the major reason for underestimating the credit default risks of instruments collateralized by subprime mortgages. The Group is particularly critical of the lack of sufficient historical data on the US subprime market, the underestimation of correlations in the defaults that would occur during a downturn, and the inability to take into account the severe weakening of underwriting standards by certain originators.

5.3. The failure of processes

McLean and Nocera (2010) attribute the failure of the CRAs partly to staff shortage, pointing out that they may have been significantly understaffed during the subprime boom, which made them unable to assess properly every debt instrument. In this case, the underlying process constitutes a proper response to the increasing work load. In Figure 8.7, we observe the number of structured products provided by the issuers to go through the rating process. It is very unlikely that the CRAs had in place a process to accommodate the explosion and exponential growth in the new issues of structured products. This might have been a human resources or (more precisely) a recruitment issue.

A related human resources issue is that the analysts working for the CRAs may be underpaid relative to similar positions with financial institutions, resulting in a migration of credit rating analysts to higher-paying jobs with the issuers of securities. Brian Clarkson, who oversaw the structured finance group before

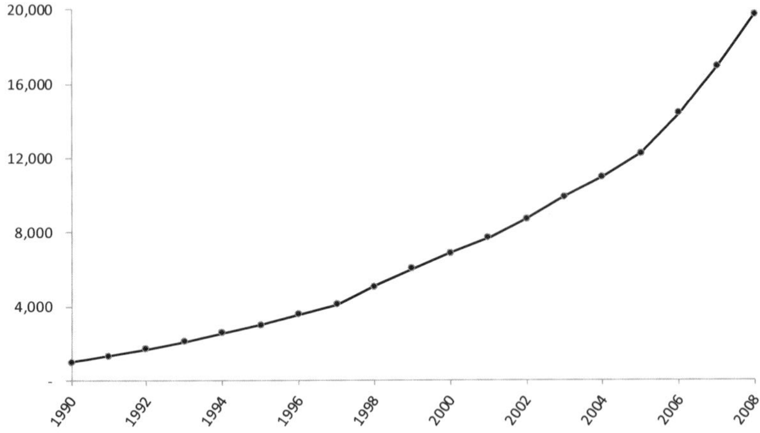

Figure 8.7:   Number of Structured Products Requiring Ratings

becoming the president of Moody's, told the FCIC (2011) that retaining employees was always a challenge, for the simple reason that banks paid more. Such a state of affairs (i) aggravated the understaffing problem at the CRAs and (ii) made it possible for the issuers to manipulate the ratings by acquiring insider information on the mechanics of ratings (Lewis, 2010).

The FCIC (2011) discusses this problem with respect to Moody's. The increase in the CDO group's workload and revenue was not paralleled by a staffing increase. In his testimony, Gary Witt (formerly of Moody's CDO unit) said the following:

> Moody's penny-pinching and stingy management was reluctant to pay up for experienced employees. "The problem of recruiting and retaining good staff was insoluble. Investment banks often hired away our best people. As far as I can remember, we were never allocated funds to make counter offers. We had almost no ability to do meaningful research.

Eric Kolchinsky, a former team managing director at Moody's, told the FCIC that "from 2004 to 2006, the increase in the number of deals rated was huge ... but our personnel did not go up accordingly". By 2006, Kolchinsky recalled, "my role as a team leader was crisis management" because "each deal was a crisis".

5.4. The failure of people: negligence

There is every indication that the CRAs did not do a good job in the spirit of "why bother about product quality if customers are willing to buy it" — even worse if they are forced to buy it. Rating agencies have come under fire for sacrificing quality ratings to win a bigger share of the booming structured products business. By 2006, Moody's had earned more revenue from structured finance ($881 million) than all its business revenues combined for 2001 (Council on Foreign Relations, 2015). In defense of their position and performance, the CRAs argue that rating decisions are made by rating committees, not individual analysts, and that analysts were not compensated based on their ratings. This makes no difference because committees can also be accused of negligence, collective negligence in this case.

Negligence means that the rating agencies were in a position to make sound judgement but they did not make the effort to do a thorough job, particularly that they could sell any product. Under these conditions, and given the bullishness prevailing at that time, the agencies might have felt that it was a safe bet to give so many securities the AAA designation and boost their revenue in the process. The FCIC points out in its report on the global financial crisis that from 2000 to 2007, Moody's rated nearly 45,000 mortgage-related securities as triple-A. This compares with six private-sector companies in the US that carried this rating in early 2010. In 2006, Moody's put its triple-A stamp of approval on 30 mortgage-related securities every working day (FCIC, 2011). How on earth did they have time to do that, given the complexity of the underlying products, and given that the agencies were understaffed? The CRAs were essentially exposed to fiduciary risk (a form of operational risk) aiding the issuers to sell products that were inferior to what had been advertised.

5.5. The failure of people: incompetence

Incompetence as a reason for the failure of CRAs implies that the agencies did not have the expertise to do the job they were entrusted to do, particularly when it came to the evaluation of risk embedded in structured products. Hill (2010) notes that search on Google for "rating agency incompetence" yields 2,010 hits" and that "the same search performed without the quotation marks yields approximately 180,000 hits". There is some overlap here with the failure of systems, in the sense that incompetence produces faulty models and methodologies.

The FCIC (2011) discusses in detail the failure of analysts at Moody's to assign ratings to CDOs. According to the FCIC, Moody's analysts faced two key challenges: (i) estimating the probability of default, and (ii) measuring correlation between defaults — that is, the likelihood that securities would default at the same time. To estimate the probability of default, Moody's relied almost exclusively on its own ratings of the MBS constituting the CDOs. At no time did the analysts look through the securities to the underlying subprime mortgages. To determine the likelihood that any given security in the CDO would default, the analysts plugged in assumptions based on those original ratings. The problem is that if the initial ratings turned out to reflect poorly the quality of the mortgages in the bonds, the error would be compounded when MBS were packaged into CDOs. Even more difficult was the estimation of default correlation between the securities in the portfolio. Moody's analysts, therefore, relied explicitly on their judgment.

In his testimony in front of the FCIC, Gary Witt (formerly of Moody's CDO unit) said that "Moody's didn't have a good model on which to estimate correlations between MBS — so they made them up". He added: "they went to the analyst in each of the groups and they said, 'Well, you know, how related do you think these types of MBS are?'" According to the FCIC, the analysts assumed that securitizers could create safer financial products by diversifying among many MBS, when in fact these securities were not that different to begin with.

Jones (2008) examines the process whereby the CRAs handled a particular product, the constant proportion debt obligation (CPDO), which was designed by a team of credit analysts at the Dutch bank ABN AMRO and called the "Holy Grail of structured finance" by analysts at Bear Stearns.[17] The product was designed with a view to achieving triple-A ratings, while paying investors a substantial return. CPDOs were not mortgage-backed, but rather collections of bets on the creditworthiness of hundreds of European and US companies. Both Moody's and S&P rated the first cohort of CPDOs in August 2006 as triple-A. About two weeks after those first ratings came out, Fitch (which was not hired to rate any CPDOs) said that its own models put CPDOs barely above junk grade, but this revelation (echoed by a few other researchers) did not change anything as the product was bestseller.[18] On this occasion it turned out that Moody's analysts had made a mistake: a small error in the computer coding that Moody's used to run its CPDO performance simulation had thrown the results way off. When the error was corrected, the likelihood of CPDO default went up significantly. CPDOs, it turned out, were not triple-A products at all. The error was not disclosed to investors or clients — it was corrected and the same model was then used to rate new CPDOs that still achieved triple-A ratings. This action involves some kind of fraud, which is considered next.

5.6. The failure of people: fraud

The Economist (2013b) suggests that "it is beyond argument that ratings agencies did a horrendous job evaluating mortgage-tied securities before the financial crisis hit", but "whether that failure was a crime has long been a matter of debate". In this sense, fraud

---

[17]It is noteworthy that both Bear Stearns and ABN AMRO failed during the global financial crisis.

[18]One may safely assume that had Fitch been invited to rate CPDOs, it would have come up with a triple-A rating. As one observer put it, "the Triple-A ratings were handed out like Kleenex" (http://www.foxbusiness.com/markets/2008/10/23/credit-rating-agencies-moment-shame/).

means that the CRAs sold an inferior product knowing that it was an inferior product, that they deliberately and knowingly rated securities above where they should have been and that they put their AAA stamp on securities without doing the necessary work to determine the rating. Under the fraud scenario, the CRAs knew that the risk was great or that the securities were not really AAA, yet they passed them as AAA. As Daly (2011) puts it, "the business was so important that S&P and Moody's kept issuing AAA, investment-grade ratings even as it became increasingly clear they were certifying garbage as gold". In particular reference to S&P, Daly says the following:

> You stand in front of S&P's bustling headquarters on Water St. and wonder why anybody listens to it, why it was never held accountable, why it is even still in business. The front of the building should be taped off like a crime scene or boarded over like some foreclosed home.

Selling junk securities as AAA assets is like knowingly selling horse meat while claiming that it is beef, selling fake aircraft parts as genuine ones, and selling food products knowing exactly that they are past their "use by" date. In a confidential memorandum tendered in evidence to the US House of Representatives Committee on Oversight and Government Reform, Moody's Chief Executive Officer (CEO) indicated that the agencies may have suffered from an overconfidence syndrome, and that they often acted under considerable pressure from institutional investors not to downgrade the ratings. His comments are particularly significant as they indicate awareness, in the sense that the CRAs persisted in doing something although they knew it was wrong, just to boost the bottom line. On this issue, Bunjevac (2009) has the following to say:

> It turns out that ratings quality has surprisingly few friends: issuers want high ratings; investors don't want rating downgrades; short-sighted bankers labor short-sightedly to game the rating agencies for a few extra basis points on execution.

Bunjevac (2009) argues that while the CRAs may be perceived as "willing victims" of investment bankers and investors, there is also evidence to suggest that the transparency, quality and integrity of the CRAs' other practices and processes was substantially lowered in order to support the extraordinary growth of their structured finance operations. Likewise, Hill (2010) argues that "there is evidence that rating agencies were cutting corners", a practice that "may have been prompted by more than just huge deal volume". In effect, Hill argues that the agencies deliberately overlooked the possibility that their ratings may have been unwarrantedly high. Jones (2008) refers to one analyst at Moody's who recalled rating a $1 billion structured deal in 90 minutes. Waxman (2008) tells an amazing story about the rating of a CDO called "Pinstripe", which Moody's was asked to rate. When Mr. Raiter, who was in charge of the task, asked for the "collateral tapes" so that he could assess the creditworthiness of the home loans backing the CDO, he got the following response from the managing director:

> Any request for loan level tapes is TOTALLY UNREASONABLE!!! Most investors don't have it and can't provide it. Nevertheless we MUST produce a credit estimate…. It is your responsibility to provide those credit estimates and your responsibility to devise some method for doing so.

Mr. Raiter was ordered by his boss to rate Pinstripe without access to essential credit data. The malpractices of the CRAs did not escape the attention of Transparency International, an international agency that deals with corruption. Herman (2009) quotes the organization as saying the following:

> The ratings agencies, in particular, had a conflict of interest and turned a blind eye towards high levels of risk. They were paid and trusted to give honest advice on financial products and we now have sufficient evidence to see that many did not. This is a form of corruption.

According to Herman (2009), Mr. Poortman (global programs director at Transparency International) accepts that some rating errors were the result of oversight or misunderstanding, but insisted that others were deliberate, saying that he knows of "at least one instance where incorrect ratings were given for financial gain".

When rating agencies are willing to overlook facts and figures to come up with high ratings for financial gain, they encourage the issuers of securities to indulge in "rating shopping", which occurs when an issuer chooses the rating agency that assigns the highest rating or that has the most lax criteria for achieving a desired rating. Unless investors demand multiple ratings on deals, issuers will tend to use only rating from the agency with the most lenient standards. Benmelech and Dlugosz (2010) argue that while rating shopping has been suggested as one of the explanations for the poor performance of structured finance products, little empirical research is available on the effect of rating shopping on rating quality and performance. The fact of the matter is that fraud is enabled by rating shopping.

The US government has launched investigations into possible criminal behavior and took legal action against rating agencies. In 1996, the Department of Justice (DOJ) initiated an investigation into possible improper pressuring of issuers by Moody's in order to win business (in the process of "how much will you pay for AAA?)" On 5 February 2013, the DOJ filed a complaint against S&P's in a Los Angeles federal court, claiming that the agency "limited, adjusted and delayed updates to the rating criteria and analytical models" needed to evaluate risk, and (based on information from an unnamed executive) "did so deliberately to protect its business". In this sense the DOJ accused the rating agency of misrepresentation. In response S&P claimed that its performance during the crisis was consistent with that of others trying to determine the validity of the troubled credits, and that it operated in "good faith". The rating agency claimed that the decision-making process was "inherently subjective" rather than "intentionally fraudulent". Implicit in this defense is the notion that the decision to invest is ultimately the responsibility of the buyer — particularly if the buyer is large, established and operating under the scrutiny of federal regulators. The rating agency went as far as accusing the DOJ of acting against it in retaliation for the downgrading of US sovereign debt in 2011. In announcing the case, Eric Holder, the former US attorney general, said that S&P had misrepresented the credit risk of the securities it rated and pretended to act objectively. Holder asserted that "S&P's desire for increased revenue and market share led it to favor the interests of investment banks issuing securities over those of investors" (*The Economist*, 2013b; Department of Justice, 2013).

6. Contribution to Financial Crises

A widespread and justifiable belief is that, through malpractice, the rating agencies played a major role in the advent of the subprime crisis, the global financial crisis, and the European sovereign debt crisis. Altman *et al.* (2010) describe "the three large global CRAs" as "central players in the subprime residential mortgage debacle of 2007–2008", describing what happened as follows:

> Their initial overly optimistic ratings on mortgage-related securities encouraged the housing boom and bubble of 1998–2006. When house prices ceased rising and began to fall, mortgage default rates rose sharply, and the prices of the mortgage bonds cratered (as did their ratings), wreaking havoc throughout the US financial system.

In its final report on the causes of the global financial crisis, the FCIC found the CRAs to be "guilty as charged", going as far as suggesting that the crisis could not have happened without the help of the agencies. This is what the Committee says in its report (FCIC, 2011):

> The failures of credit rating agencies were essential cogs in the wheel of financial destruction. The three credit rating agencies were key enablers of the financial meltdown. The mortgage-related securities at the heart of the crisis could not have been marketed and sold without their seal of approval. Investors relied on them,

often blindly. In some cases, they were obligated to use them, or regulatory capital standards were hinged on them. This crisis could not have happened without the rating agencies. Their ratings helped the market soar and their downgrades through 2007 and 2008 wreaked havoc across markets and firms.

The FCIC (2011) also makes the comment that "the machine churning out CDOs would not have worked without the stamp of approval given to these deals by the three leading rating agencies".[19] Moreover, a big player in the crisis, AIG, was aided by the CRAs to cause the damage it inflicted on the financial system, which would have caused many more corporate failures if it was not for the generosity of the US Treasury with the taxpayers' money. The CRAs granted AIG the AAA status, which made it possible for the insurance giant to sell credit default swaps (CDSs) without having adequate funds to cover potential losses from default. AIG earned billions of dollars in commissions by selling CDSs — effectively insurance against default by the issuers of structured products acting on the assumption of the impossibility of the collapse of the housing market nationwide. When the collapse came, AIG did not have adequate funds to pay the holders of CDSs, which prompted the US government to intervene by bailing out yet another "TBTF" institution. Lewis (2009) presents an interesting account of the role played by AIG in the crisis, correctly arguing that one man (the head of the financial products unit of AIG) single-handedly brought the company, the US economy and the global financial system down to their knees. It would be unfair to blame the mishap on the CRAs alone: AIG should not have been

---

[19]It is not clear why the demise of Lehman Brothers and other financial institutions was blamed mostly on short sellers, which cannot be further away from the truth. The failure of those institutions was caused by the strategic error of accumulating billions of dollars worth of structured products, believing in the wisdom of the CRAs, only to become insolvent as a result of abrupt downgrading. Merrill Lynch suffered a similar fate for the same strategic error, having fired anyone with a dissenting voice who dared oppose the "strategic vision" of senior management (typically one person who happens to be the "king of the mountain").

allowed (by regulators) to go into uncharted territory without having adequate funds to pay out if things turned sour. It was like allowing a nurse to perform heart or brain surgery (do you see why regulation is important?). Just because it had the AAA status, AIG should not have been allowed to sell "insurance policies" to the holders of CDOs without having adequate funds to cover potential claims. This is the free market ideology gone wrong.

The CRAs, together with the faulty Basel regulation, have contributed significantly to the advent of the European sovereign debt crisis. At one time the bonds issued by OECD countries (including Greece) were ranked highly and more or less equally (that is, Germany and Greece were judged to have the same degree of sovereign risk). Everyone was happy — the CRAs were getting paid handsomely, banks were happy to buy Greek bonds to satisfy the Basel requirements, and the Greeks were happy to borrow as much as they wanted.[20] The rest of the story is similar to what happened with structured products — when trouble surfaced, Greece and other countries were downgraded, making it more difficult and more expensive for them to borrow funds from the capital market. In early 2011, and in response to the belief that the CRAs did contribute to the advent and aggravation of the European crisis, the EU established an independent authority, known as the European Securities and Markets Authority (ESMA), tasked with regulating the activities of rating agencies relative to EU standards. In 2014, the European Commission adopted regulatory technical standards that specify the disclosure and reporting requirements for CRAs (European Commission, 2014).

7. The Regulatory Debate

For free marketeers, the regulation of anything, including CRAs, is a bad idea because the market takes care of them (and everything else), in the sense that it forces good behavior. The

---

[20]It is not meant here that the CRAs were paid for rating sovereign nations. However, this is a profitable public relations exercise that caused some damage.

argument goes as follows: CRAs should not be regulated because if they get it wrong they will lose their customers, but this does not happen in an oligopolistic market where customers are forced (required by law) to buy the products of the dominant players. Who cares about reputation if it does not affect business, which is exactly the case of the CRAs who are back in business as usual?

Most scholars believe that the CRAs cannot be controlled by the threat of losing business if they do a bad job. Bunjevac (2009) concludes that "the recent events have discredited the so-called 'reputational capital' theory, which claims that the reputation of a business operates as a market-based mechanism for ensuring the highest standards of quality". However, Schwarcz (2002) contends that "under certain conditions, reputation alone could act as a sufficient substitute for regulation because it has the disciplining effect of driving accountability". He points out that "the lack of regulatory scrutiny has not significantly affected ratings accuracy of the traditional debt instruments over several decades", but what about the ratings accuracy of complex structured products? Schwarcz's "reputational capital" argument cannot be supported by any empirical evidence or even by casual observation — that is, there is not even anecdotal evidence to support the proposition that the CRAs can be disciplined by the threat of losing their reputation. The existing evidence and casual observation lead to the conclusion that significant qualitative differences exist between the historical performance with respect to the ratings of traditional debt instruments (such as corporate bonds) and that of structured finance products, as we saw earlier.[21] Hunt (2009) presents a historical analysis of the recent crisis, which suggests that there were far more multi-notch downgrades among the structured finance ratings than there were among the traditional debt ratings. Based on these observations, Hunt concludes that the CRAs' reputation for ratings of traditional bonds did not pose a sufficient deterrent against low-quality ratings of structured products. Hunt also

---

[21]It is fair to assume that a large number of ex post downgrades implies that the original ratings were wrong.

argues that "straightforward market mechanisms clearly haven't helped discipline the agencies, as investors seem to rely on them even after they've performed exceedingly badly".

There are indeed good reasons for advocating the regulation of CRAs. *The Economist* (2007b) argues that their business is built upon a rather shaky tripod: (i) regulatory requirements have made ratings a formal part of the financial system; (ii) the claim that they are acting as independent assessors of credit risk, and thus are immune to legal challenge on the basis of their "free speech" rights and (iii) they have a conflict of interest, since they are paid by the issuers whose securities they rate. This is a rather strange business ecology because, as *The Economist* puts it, it is untenable to have a situation where patients are forced to use doctors whose incomes depend on the pharmaceutical companies, but who are immune from lawsuits if they prescribe a toxic drug. The fact of the matter is that the CRAs cannot (and should not) claim that their ratings represent an opinion that is protected by freedom of speech while they get paid for expressing these "opinions". In this case "opinions" are actually business products that other suppliers (issuers of securities) are required to acquire in order to sell their products to customers (investors). Thus, *The Economist* argues, if the views expressed by the CRAs are given a regulatory imprimatur, they should be subject to legal challenge, but if ratings represent independent expressions of opinion, then either investors (not issuers) should pay them, or they should be divorced from the regulatory system.

It follows that something ought to be done about an untenable situation — CRAs must be regulated. The following question is raised by Altman *et al.* (2010): how should public policy with respect to the rating agencies proceed? The conventional view is that the way to proceed is to plug the loopholes in the system. Like the case with shadow banking, a more radical piece of regulation is required.

8. Regulatory Proposals

In this section, we deal with the proposals that have been put forward to regulate the CRAs. These proposals are discussed in turn.

8.1. Reducing the power of CRAs

In a 2003 hearing before the German parliament's finance committee, the president of the Federal Financial Supervisory Authority (BaFin) expressed the view that "CRAs are the biggest uncontrolled power in the global financial system, and thus in the national financial system too" (Deutscher Bundestag, 2003). As we have seen, the power of CRAs is reflected in (i) the oligopolistic nature of the industry and (ii) regulatory reliance on ratings. Eliminating the power resulting from the oligopolistic nature of the industry is simple: make the CRAs more competitive by removing the barriers to entry erected by regulators.[22] Perhaps the CRAs are "too big to be held accountable", so the same remedy used with TBTF banks can be applied here: break them up and make them smaller. Hill (2010) is skeptical about the soundness of this course of action, arguing that "if regulatory reforms succeeded in appreciably increasing the number of rating agencies, companies then might be able to play the rating agencies off one another, as they were able to do with their accounting firms". This is essentially the shopping around argument, but shopping around would not be a problem if ratings were not mandatory and if the agencies were paid by investors. It can happen, and it did happen, in the present oligopolistic market for ratings. Unlike Hill (2010), Ekins and Calabria (2012) suggest that financial markets would have been better served if the CRA industry had been more competitive.

Ratings should not be an integral part of the regulatory process — that is, regulators should not force regulated firms to hold only the securities that have the CRAs seal of approval on them. As Altman *et al.* (2010) put it:

> The disastrous consequences of the three large raters' errors were greatly magnified because seven decades of financial regulation had thrust these three into the center of the bond markets and had forced the major players in those markets to heed their ratings. Without such forced reliance, bond market investors — primarily financial institutions — would be able to access a wider array of opinions as to bonds' creditworthiness.

---

[22]Those barriers represent yet another example of bad regulation.

It is a good idea to require regulated financial institutions to hold securities of certain quality in terms of credit risk, but quality should not be determined by the CRAs as if they and they only have the expertise to do this job. Altman *et al.* (2010) suggest that if regulated financial institutions are to hold securities with low default risk, the judgment of CRAs should be replaced with a "more direct system of scrutinizing the bond portfolios of their institutions". They also suggest that "the boards and senior managements of financial institutions should not be able to abrogate their fiduciary responsibilities by uncritically accepting information from any source". Once regulatory reliance on ratings has been eliminated, the need for the NRSRO designation disappears, which means that barriers to entry are eliminated.

According to *The Economist* (2011a), the power of CRAs can be curtailed by severing the link to regulation and boosting competition. Regulators are thinking along those lines but progress seems to be very slow. For example, the Financial Stability Board, which co-ordinates the G20's financial policies, has asked regulators to find ways of taking ratings out of the rules governing bank capital (the Basel rules), fund holdings, margin agreements and so on. The Dodd–Frank Act requires the removal of ratings-related regulatory requirements or replacement by appropriate alternatives. The SEC has proposed numerous changes, covering securities registration, money market funds and capital standards for brokers. Interestingly, S&P's boss argues that his firm's analysis would still find takers without a regulatory stamp of approval" (*The Economist*, 2011a). If anything, one can only say "that is the spirit", but we will have to wait and see if he is vindicated. Oligopolists hate to lose their oligopoly power because it means a lower level of profit and the possibility of going out of business.

8.2. Replacing the simple letter score

A letter score or grade does not mean much except that the probability of default is lower for a security designated AAA than another security designated ZZZ. Even a numerical value for the probability of default, which is invariably estimated with a high standard error, does not convey an adequate amount of information that can be relied upon to make sound investment decisions. Altman *et al.* (2010) suggest the provision of information pertaining to the degree of certainty associated with the estimated probability of default, or even better, a set of alternative estimates for "what if" scenarios. This objective can be achieved more easily in a competitive market where producers compete on product quality (and hopefully not on prices). This will be bad for issuers who are only interested in obtaining top rating without exposing the details and without having to justify why a particular security has a top rating. Furthermore, this measure will convert an oligopolistic market without product differentiation into an oligopolistic market with product differentiation. However, it will not solve the problem associated with faulty models — a faulty model can be used to produce a letter rating, a numerical value for the probability of default or detailed analysis.

8.3. Reducing conflict of interest

A search on Google for "rating agency conflict of interest" yielded 274,000 hits (Hill, 2010). A survey of fund managers and institutional investors conducted in 2008 revealed a view held by many participants that significant conflicts of interest exist between rating agencies and the entities they deal with (Roland, 2008). Of the 1,956 investment professionals surveyed by the CFA Institute, 11% said that they had seen a CRA change a bond grade in response to pressure from an issuer, underwriter or investor. Of the 211 respondents who said they had witnessed an agency change its rating in response to pressure, 51% said the pressure took the form of a threat "to take future ratings business to other rating agencies". The CFA survey went further to reveal that many respondents felt that the most harmful conflict of interest results from the issuer-pays model. The results of this survey support two of the propositions put forward earlier (i) that shopping around for ratings occurs even in an oligopolistic market and (ii) that there is an element of fraud in ratings — it can only be fraud when a rating agency gives a rating to a security while knowing that it does not deserve that rating.

Bunjevac (2009) identifies several aspects of conflict of interest. First, he argues that the analytical side of the business must be separated from the trading side in order to prevent considerations of business and staff remuneration from affecting the objectivity of the analytical criteria. For example, rating analysts were aware of the specific business agendas in securing the rating deals, including fee schedules and actual negotiated fees. In addition, the evidence suggests that analysts were also aware of the market share considerations and competitors' rating practices, including the credit support levels required for competition on the rating deals. Second he suggests that whilst the conflicts were inherent in the issuer-pays model in general, they appeared "particularly inherent" in the structured finance ratings process. Third, he raises concern about how the management of conflicts of interest relates to the CRAs' provision of ancillary services and the practice of issuing rating downgrades as a disciplining mechanism. These include free pre-rating assessments, unsolicited assessments and corporate consulting services, which have the potential to be in conflict with rating objectivity. One particularly problematic practice is the CRAs' provision of free rating previews, which allows the issuers to engage in rating shopping. In addition, CRAs often provide ancillary and consulting services to assist businesses in achieving high post-transaction ratings.

Conflict of interest arises primarily from the issuer-pays business model. One argument for this model is that the information is disseminated instantaneously to the market. Cole and Cooley (2014) do not like the subscriber-pays model on the grounds that the subscriber "might choose not to release the ratings they pay for". They even argue that "much of the regulatory obsession with the conflict created by issuers paying for ratings is a distraction" and that "regulatory reliance on ratings and the increasing importance of risk-weighted capital in prudential regulation have more likely contributed to distorted ratings than the matter of who pays for them". This is a truly strange argument, given that the products of the rating agencies are not public goods. Why would the subscriber release the information, and so what? Actually, it is a good thing not to disseminate the information because this may create panic, as what happened during the global and European crises. Concern about the problems associated with the issuer-pays model is not an "obsession" but rather a justifiable reaction to an unsatisfactory state of affairs. Blaming "distorted ratings" on the "increasing importance of risk-weighted capital in prudential regulation" is finding a scapegoat for the same unsatisfactory state of affairs.

Proponents of the investor-pays model argue that the model is conceptually superior to the issuer-pays model and that it may be more effective in protecting the interests of investors (Bunjevac, 2009). As a matter of fact, the investor-pays model worked well after it was initially devised by John Moody and utilized by the three main CRAs until the 1970s. In support of the investor-pays model, Sean Egan refers to a number of examples suggesting that his agency, Egan–Jones Ratings, which is funded exclusively by investors, has had a superior track record to that of the main three CRAs during the recent crises.[23] However, Jerome Fons (2008) is not persuaded that a CRA market based on the investor-pays model would be superior, for a number of reasons. First, he points to the free rider problem, which initially emerged with the advent of the photocopier, allowing non-paying investors to benefit from easy access to the rating lists. Second, the investor base per bond is simply too small to support adequate technical analysis, which was one of the main reasons why the CRAs began charging the issuers in the first place. Third, the investor-pays model arguably involves conflicts of interest because the paying investors would prefer to have lower ratings on the bonds they purchase. The fourth reason is that an investor-funded model would possibly restrict access to a selective group of investors and undermine the current status of credit ratings as "public goods". These reasons are so trivial that they cannot be used to advocate the

---

[23]See Transcript of Proceedings, Committee on Oversight and Government Reform, US House of Representatives, Washington DC, 22 October 2008, http://www.gpo. gov/fdsys/pkg/CHRG-110hhrg51103/html/CHRG-110hhrg51103.htm.

issuer-pays model. It is never the case that the seller of a house pays a surveyor to assess the state of the house.

Altman *et al.* (2010) suggest that one way to preserve the information advantages of the issuer-pays model while eliminating conflict of interest is to establish a clearing house of qualified rating firms. When an issuer requests a rating, the clearing house could assign a rating firm randomly from among the qualified group, which would eliminate the ability of the issuer to "shop around". The success of this approach would depend crucially on the quality control of the clearing house. A similar idea is suggested by Richardson and White (2009) who argue that the SEC should create a department that houses a centralized clearing platform for rating agencies. This model, they argue, has the advantage of solving simultaneously (i) the free rider problem because the issuer still pays; (ii) the conflict of interest problem because the agency is chosen by the regulating body and (iii) the competition problem because the regulator's choice can be based on some degree of excellence, thereby providing the rating agency with incentives to invest resources, innovate, and perform high quality work. It does, however, put tremendous faith in the ability of the regulator to monitor and evaluate the rating agencies' performance.

A 2009 World Bank report proposed a "hybrid" approach in which issuers who pay for ratings are required to seek additional scores from subscriber-based third parties (Katz *et al.*, 2009). Other proposed alternatives include a public-sector model in which national governments fund the rating costs, and an exchange-pays model, in which stock and bond exchanges pay for the ratings (Securities and Exchange Board of India, 2009; Fennell and Medvedev, 2011). Crowd-sourced collaborative models, such as Wikirating, have also been suggested as an alternative to both the subscriber-pays and issuer-pays models (Greenwood, 2012).[24]

---

[24] It has been suggested that there is a real independent and transparent alternative to the common rating agencies, which is Wikirating, https://www.youtube.com/watch?v=eErg78D6GoA.

8.4. The need for more transparency

Bunjevac (2009) suggests that there are "significant concerns about the integrity and transparency of CRAs' internal governance procedures, surveillance, as well as staff independence". *The Economist* (2007b) quotes Joshua Rosner of Graham Fisher (an investment firm) as saying that the agencies should be more transparent and improve their monitoring. Following bonds once they are traded in the secondary market is much less lucrative for the agencies, he argues, and they devote far fewer resources to it. Although the agencies make it clear what rating they will give a bond on issue, it is less clear what will cause them to downgrade it later on. However, transparency is not only about monitoring and surveillance after the initial rating — it is also about the initial rating itself. As we saw earlier, the report of the FCIC revealed that the CRAs made up some numbers (FCIC, 2011). They would certainly not be transparent about this practice.

The fundamental problem with respect to transparency is that the rating agencies provide little information about the process whereby they determine the ratings of a borrower. Under the Basel rules, regulators are required to approve the internal models that banks use to determine economic (hence, regulatory) capital, but no such requirement is applicable to CRAs. Even if it were applicable, such a requirement is problematical for two reasons: (i) regulators may not have the expertise to evaluate and validate the models and (ii) putting regulators in a position like this is tantamount to regulatory capture because they would feel that failure of the models would be their own failure. Reason (i) does not pose a big problem if the models used by the CRAs are not complex, but reason (ii) poses a big problem.

8.5. Making the agencies liable for their views

If the CRAs are to be paid for their views, they should be made legally liable for what they say. In this case, a court will establish whether they got it wrong because of factors beyond their control or because of a deliberate misrepresentation. But the potential damage claim for making a an erroneous rating could be so large that agencies might either be driven out of business or made excessively cautious by the threat of legal action. This will make the business unviable. It is, however, only fair to say that if credit ratings are no longer a formal part of regulation, then the "opinion only" argument will make sense. *The Economist* (2011a) argues that by removing ratings from the regulatory requirements "it might also become easier to defend the industry's much-pilloried line against those who bring liability lawsuits: that ratings are mere opinions, protected by free speech".

8.6. Reducing reliance on client-provided data

Sicilia (2011) argues that, judged by the Enron fiasco, the CRAs tend to rely exclusively on client-provided data and that they fail to investigate in the face of persistent and profound questions about the veracity of that data. As long as CRAs claim no responsibility for verifying the accuracy of borrower-supplied information on which they base ratings, regulators need to ensure that independent auditors perform their work diligently and in ways that support the ratings function. If the auditing function fails, so will the rating function, but this brings us back to the problem of regulatory capture when regulators are in charge of model validation.

8.7. A more radical solution

If we accept the proposition that the rating agencies are here to stay, in the sense that their ratings remain mandatory and an integral part of the regulatory framework, then we can only tweak around the edges, dealing with them according to the proposals presented earlier. However, it is imperative that the power of the CRAs is curtailed by boosting competition and depriving them of the privilege of considering their opinions as a regulatory requirement. The rating agencies may remain as information providers and compete with other information providers on the basis of "consumer sovereignty", where consumers are investors, not the issuers of securities. Those who think that the rating agencies provide useful information and are willing to pay for it are welcome to do so. The market for ratings becomes a market for investment advice similar to the market for forecasts where no mandatory requirement exists to determine which forecaster is chosen by the customer.

This is what Richardson and White (2009) call a "180-degree turn", which "would be to withdraw the financial regulations that thrust the rating agencies into the centre of the bond markets". The regulatory goal would still be for financial institutions to have safe bond portfolios, but those institutions would have more latitude and flexibility with respect to where they could seek advice. Therefore, regulated financial institutions would be free to seek advice from sources that they consider to be most reliable. The decision would be based on the track record of the advisor, the business model of the advisor (including the possibility of conflicts of interest), the other activities of the advisor (which might pose potential conflicts), and anything else that is considered to be relevant. Again, the institution would have to justify its choice of advisor to its regulator. But, subject to that constraint, the bond advisory information market would be opened to new ideas (about business models, methodologies, and technologies) and new entry in a way that has not been witnessed since the 1930s.

Some may wonder how, without the rating agencies, we can make sure that banks and pension funds invest in "investment grade" securities only. To start with, we have already seen that a security designated AAA by a rating agency may not be investment grade, as demonstrated over and over again. We have seen how two rating agencies rated a security as AAA when in fact it was not far away from the realm of junk securities. In general we have seen that the rating agencies convinced investors — or "suckers" as Daly (2011) calls them — to hold junk assets thinking that they were high-quality assets. More importantly, we should not consider the regulation of CRAs in isolation of other regulatory measures, including the separation between commercial banking and investment banking, abandoning the myth of TBTF (and the new myth of systemically important financial institutions), and the regulation of remuneration away from the bonus culture that has corrupted the finance industry. Also important is the regulation of over-the-counter (OTC) derivatives — even better to outlaw OTC derivatives altogether, so that regulators do not have to worry about bank failure caused by excessive exposure to betting devices whose degrees of risk are unknown. If these regulatory reforms were introduced, then investment banks could do whatever they wanted with their money without anticipating to be bailed out (or bailed in).

How do we know that commercial banks do not gamble with depositors' money by holding risky assets? By killing the bonus culture we can remove moral hazard, and the incentive to take on excessive risk. Furthermore regulators can inspect bank's securities and loan portfolios just like they inspect capital requirements, leverage ratios and liquidity ratios. We do not need a rating agency to tell us that Apple and Microsoft are AAA companies and that German bonds are better than Greek bonds. An important function of regulators will be to inspect the concentration of banks' assets because one of the most important principles of finance is that diversification reduces risk. If these regulatory measures are introduced, the need for CRAs' input as a regulatory requirement will disappear. They can then operate as information providers in a competitive market — and good luck to them. We cannot argue for free trade and against the protection of local industry while protecting the CRAs from competition by imposing improper regulatory requirements.

We must not forget an important historical fact. Remarkable financial tranquility was experienced between the introduction of the Glass–Steagal Act in the 1930s and the initiation of wholesale financial deregulation in the 1980s. One may possibly suggest that the rating agencies provided the right advice that allowed banks to hold high-quality assets, and this is why bank failure was rather rare during that period. However, the truth is that the period of tranquility is attributed to regulation, not the role of the CRAs. When regulation was dismantled collapse came initially despite the role played by the CRAs and subsequently because of the advice provided by the CRAs. Sound and comprehensive regulation is what we need — not oligopolistic rent-seeking firms (CRAs) advising banks what to do with depositors' money.

9. Why are CRAs Still in Business?

A widespread and justifiable belief is that the CRAs have contributed to the advent and aggravation of the global financial crisis and the European sovereign debt crisis. The CRAs have not done a good job that is commensurate with the oligopoly power that they have been enjoying since the 1930s. Their "unsatisfactory" performance can be attributed to factors beyond their control, incompetence, negligence, fraud or a combination thereof. The need for regulation is warranted — after all, the notion of self-regulation is preposterous.

A question that remains unanswered is why the CRAs are back in business as usual. This is what Gillen (2009) says about this observation:

> The words sound almost quaint in this post-subprime age: "Credit. Man's Confidence in Man." But there they are, inscribed on a gilded frieze on the 20th floor of the Moody's Corporation-the same Moody's that, along with its peers, stamped gilt-edged credit ratings on many mortgage securities that are now nearly worthless. Few have any confidence in those investments now. So it might come as a surprise that many investors still seem to have a lot of confidence in Moody's. Despite talk of a big shake-up for the tainted credit ratings establishment, things seem to be looking up, not down, for the likes of Moody's. The granddaddy of the industry, Moody's has become something of a stock market darling in this, its 100th year. Its share price is up nearly 44% this year. At nearly $29 on Thursday, the stock was hovering near its highest level since the dark days of last September.

It is particularly amazing that the CRAs are still believed to be capable of rating structured products, as securitization comes back from the dead. As far back as September 2009, while the destruction inflicted by the global financial crisis was still fresh in our minds, four firms (Bank of America, Nissan, Discovery and American Express) issued structured products worth more than $6 billion, and paid Moody's to rate them. Gillen (2009) points out that the CRAs "are now earning fees from a new source: re-Remics, an acronym for resecuritization of real estate mortgage investment conduits".[25] Hill (2010) explains this observation by describing the use of the CRAs as "quite sticky" because "the individuals making the day-to-day investment decisions have guidelines, practices, and form documents, all providing for purchase of debt instruments rated by S&P's and Moody's, from which they don't have reason to deviate".

Bunjevac (2009) argues that the main reason for the survival of the CRAs, despite recent mishaps, is that ratings are required by law. Another reason is the absence of any opportunity for independent evaluation of credit risk. This is exactly why more competition is needed, as a competitive market provides other means of assessing credit risk and other suppliers of services. Yet another reason, according to Bunjevac, is the complexity of the risk modeling processes employed by the issuers and the CRAs, which require sophisticated quantitative risk models, sufficient human resources and technical expertise to assess the risks. The problem here is that it is doubtful if the CRAs and the issuers themselves realized the extent of risk in the Frankenstein products created by the so-called "financial engineers". Blinder (2007) describes CDOs as being "probably too complex for anyone's good" — yet "investors placed too much faith in the rating agencies which, to put it mildly, failed to get it right". The fourth reason suggested by Bunjevac is that the CRAs have built a strong market reputation for being competent, honest and diligent arbiters of risk. I am not sure if this is true: the reputation of the CRAs has been tarnished not only by the global financial crisis but, before that, by the Enron

---

[25]These are transactions that take downgraded mortgage securities and separate the riskiest assets from the strongest, making the strongest easier to sell.

scandal, the Asian financial crisis and by the financial collapse of New York City in the mid-1970s. The CRAs have lost any credibility that they might have had at one time. Tweaking around the edges will not work and the only pragmatic solution to this state of affairs is to deprive the CRAs of their legal oligopoly power.

Blinder (2007) argues that "it is tempting to take the rating agencies out for a public whipping", but "it is more constructive to ask how the rating system might be improved". While it is true that looking forward is the way to go, an attitude of "forget and forgive" may not prevent the recurrence of abuse. Does Blinder mean that it was wrong to bring charges against the CRAs and fine them? Does he mean that we overlook fraud, if fraud is proven to have been involved in the operations of the CRAs? I hope, for the sake of killing moral hazard in the financial sector, that this is not the case. Then if a brave decision is taken to deprive the CRAs from their power and elevated status, this would be tantamount to "public whipping", in which case there is nothing wrong with "public whipping".

Chapter 9

The Regulatory Implications of Quantitative Easing

1. Introduction

The objective of financial regulation in the post-crisis era is to make the recurrence of a similar crisis less likely, based on the lessons learned from the experience of 2007–2008. We have learned from the crisis that something must be done about leverage, liquidity, underwriting standards, moral hazard and several other factors that caused the crisis and determined its severity. It seems, however, that we have not learned anything about the role of macroeconomic policy in initiating the crisis — that is, the hazard of keeping interest rates so low for so long. The low interest rate environment that prevailed for a long time in the run-up to the crisis led to bubbles in asset markets, particularly the housing market. Motivated by greed, the financial oligarchs capitalized on the low interest environment and asset market bubbles and indulged in a kind of behavior that eventually inflicted enormous damage on the economy and society. If low interest rates played a pivotal role in the initiation and intensification of the crisis, it does not make any sense to pursue an ultra-low interest policy in its aftermath. Furthermore, the effectiveness of regulation in preventing future crises will be undermined by a monetary and financial environment that is conducive to the occurrence of crises.

The environment of ultra-low interest rates prevailing world-wide at the present time is the result of quantitative easing (QE), a policy whereby the central bank produces new money that is used to buy securities (of various kinds and maturities) from financial institutions. In the process, security prices rise and yields decline — in other words, the objective of QE is to keep interest rates at a low level across a spectrum of maturities. The declared objective is to boost the real sector of the economy as lower interest rates provide an incentive for households and firms to spend more than they would otherwise, boosting economic activity. QE is used to push down the cost of borrowing to a lower level than what can be achieved by using conventional interest rate policy, which typically targets a particular short-term rate (such as the federal funds rate).

A debate has ensued about whether or not quantitative easing has worked and whether or not it has been worthwhile in terms of benefits relative to the unintended adverse consequences. Supporters of QE argue that the policy has kept interest rates low for households and firms, stimulated job creation and saved the US economy from a much more severe downturn. However, this is only a counterfactual observation as we do not know whether or not a more severe downturn would have happened in the absence of QE. Critics, on the other hand, contend that QE could lead to a new financial crisis and raging inflation, and that it has punished responsible savers (not to mention the insurance industry). One observer believes that "the jury is still out — and will be for a long time — on whether it (QE) has worked" (Walker, 2014). Some opponents of the policy suggest that by indulging in QE, central banks are sowing the seeds of the next crisis, a proposition that can be rationalized on the basis of recent experience as follows: low interest rates caused the asset price bubble that eventually burst, bringing about the global financial crisis. Therefore, one of the issues that are discussed in this chapter is whether or not low interest rates indeed caused, or contributed to the advent of, the crisis. The second issue is that the anticipated inflation resulting from rapid monetary expansion has not materialized, which requires an explanation, unless QE is non-inflationary.

The argument put forward in this chapter is that QE is inflationary but so far inflation has only appeared in asset prices. This means that QE is causing yet another asset price bubble that will eventually burst, leading to another crisis. It is in this sense that by indulging in QE, central banks are sowing the seeds of the next crisis. We start by examining the inflationary consequences of QE, resulting from the effect of monetary expansion on the prices of goods and service. Then we move on to an examination of the financial effects of QE, particularly the effect on interest rates and asset prices. It will be demonstrated that low interest rates caused the crisis of 2007–2008 and that QE has produced the ultra-low interest rate environment of the present time. It follows that QE will cause the next crisis and undermine the effectiveness of regulatory measures aimed at averting, or at least reducing the severity of, the next crisis. We start with a brief history of QE in the US, UK and the Eurozone, then concentrate on examining the facts and figures from a US perspective.

2. A Brief History of QE

The consensus view is that the Japanese invented quantitative easing in an attempt to get the Japanese economy out of the deflationary spiral that started in the early 1990s. However, some economists argue that the Federal Reserve used a form of quantitative easing in the 1930s and 1940s in response to the Great Depression (for example, Bordo, 2014; Fowler, 2013). QE as we know it today was initiated by the Federal Reserve in November 2008, in response to the global financial crisis and the Great Recession, and put to an end in October 2014, in response to observed improvement in the labor market and the economy at large. Since the advent of the global financial crisis, QE has been used by the Federal Reserve in the US, the Bank of England in the UK, and the European Central Bank (ECB) in the Eurozone.

In late November 2008, the Federal Reserve initiated the first round of quantitative easing (QE1) by buying $600 billion worth of mortgage-backed securities (MBSs) and by March 2009, the Fed held

$1.75 trillion of bank debt, MBS, and Treasury notes — this amount reached a peak of $2.1 trillion in June 2010. Purchases were put to an end as the economy started showing signs of improvement, but the operation resumed in August 2010 when the Fed decided that the economy was still weak. In November 2010, the Fed announced a second round of quantitative easing (QE2), buying $600 billion of Treasury securities by the end of the second quarter of 2011. QE3 was announced on 13 September 2012 when the Federal Reserve decided to launch $40 billion per month purchases of MBS. On 12 December 2012, the Fed announced an increase in the amount of purchases from $40 billion to $85 billion per month. Purchases were halted on 29 October 2014, by which time the Fed had accumulated $4.5 trillion in assets. That was when QE in the US came to an end officially. There is no reason why the Fed will not initiate QE4 if it believes that the economy is still weak, which is what happened in 2010. It could be just a lull rather than an outright abandonment of the operation.

The Bank of England indulged in QE by buying gilts (government bonds) from financial institutions, along with a smaller amount of relatively high-quality debt issued by private companies. Beginning in March 2009, the Bank of England had purchased around £165 billion in assets as of September 2009 and around £175 billion worth by the end of October 2009. At its meeting in November 2009, the monetary policy committee of the Bank of England voted to raise total asset purchases to £200 billion. In October 2011, the Bank of England announced that it would undertake another round of QE, creating an additional £75 billion, and in February 2012 it announced an additional £50 billion. In July 2012, the Bank announced another purchase of £50 billion, bringing the total amount to £375 billion. Since then there have been no further purchases. Again, this could be no more than a lull as central banks have become addicted to QE.

On 22 January 2015, Mario Draghi, President of the ECB, announced an expanded asset purchase program whereby the ECB would buy €60 billion per month worth of euro-area bonds from central governments, agencies and European institutions.

Beginning in March 2015, the stimulus was planned to last until September 2016 at the earliest with a total of at least €1.1 trillion. Draghi announced that the program would continue "until we see a continued adjustment in the path of inflation", referring to the ECB's need to combat the growing threat of deflation across the Eurozone (ECB, 2015; BBC, 2015). This European "initiative" may provide encouragement for the Fed and Bank of England to resume the cancerous growth of their balance sheets to the detriment of everything else that has been done to prevent a recurrence of 2007–2008.

3. Monetary Expansion as a Consequence of QE: The US Experience

Figures 9.1 and 9.2 show the growth of monetary aggregates as well as output growth and inflation in the US. In Figure 9.1, we can see the big jump in the monetary base at the end of 2008, when QE was initiated, and the two big jumps that followed in November 2010 and November 2012.[1] This behavior is not reflected in the monetary aggregates, M1 and M2, but it is clearly reflected in reserves whose behavior mirrors that of the monetary base. This observation simply means that expansion in the monetary base has been translated mostly into an accumulation of reserves, not into growth in deposits that corresponds to growth in bank lending (which is the scenario envisaged by the engineers of QE). Between the two monetary aggregates, M1 has been more responsive to changes in the monetary base than M2.[2]

In Figure 9.2, we observe the behavior of prices (measured by the consumer price index, CPI) and output (measured by industrial production). The behavior of the CPI shows that inflation is stable

---

[1] The monetary base, also called M0, is currency in circulation plus the reserves of commercial banks held with the central bank.

[2] M1 is the narrow money supply, comprising currency in circulation and deposits that can be converted easily into cash. M2 is M1 plus short-term deposits in banks, including savings and time deposits.

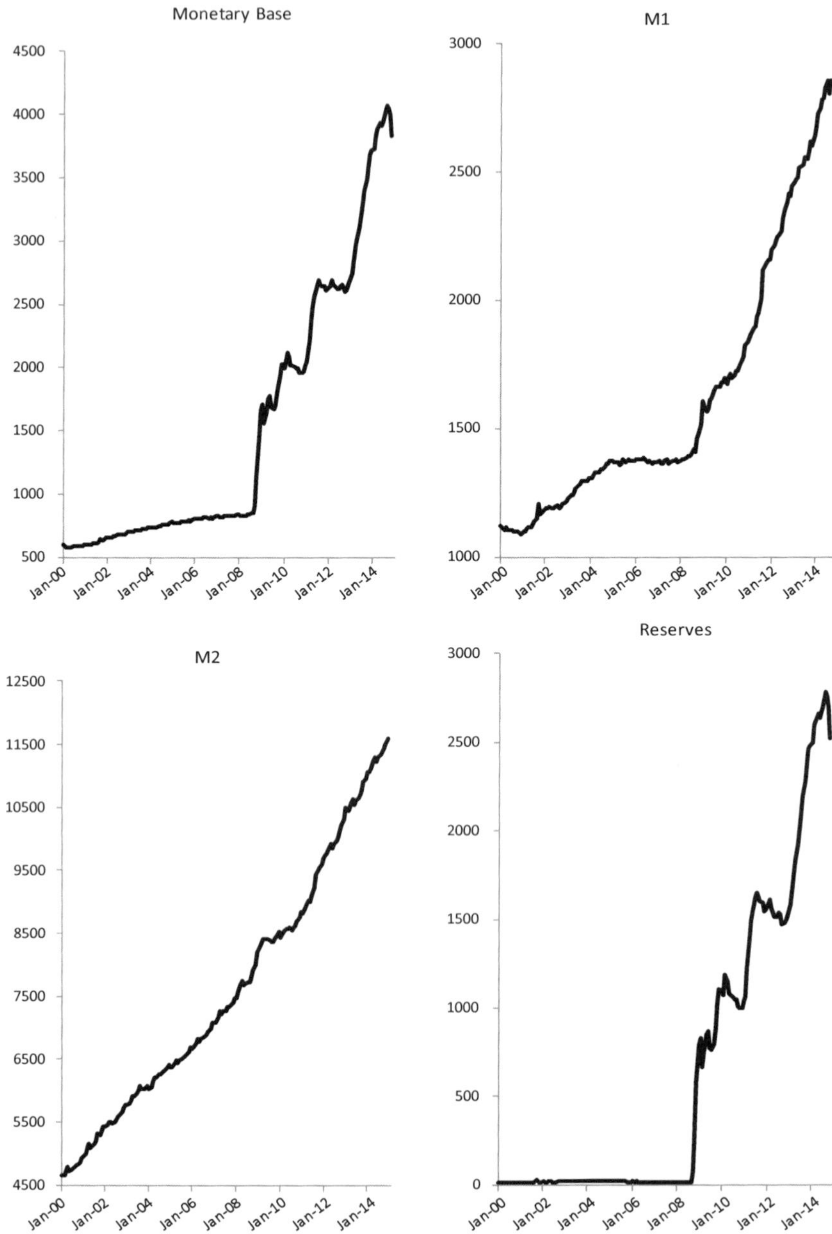

Figure 9.1:   US Monetary Aggregates and Reserves

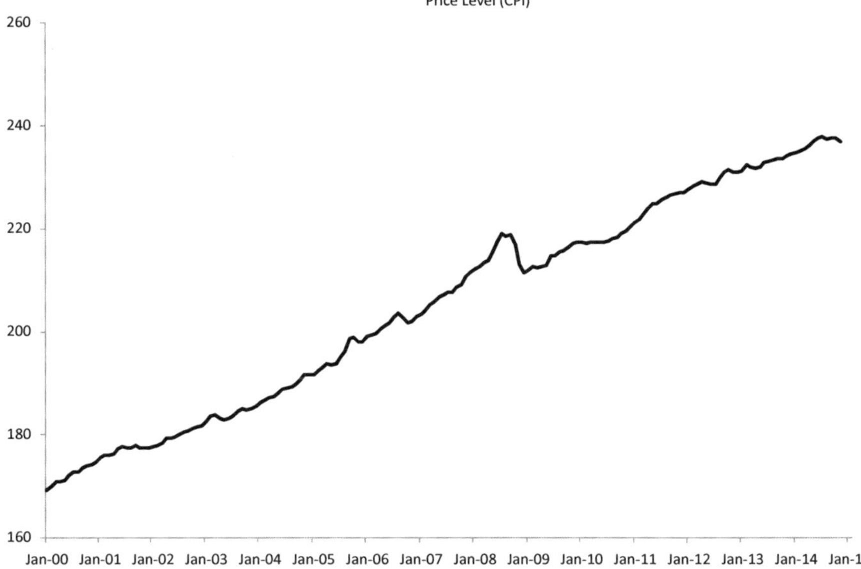

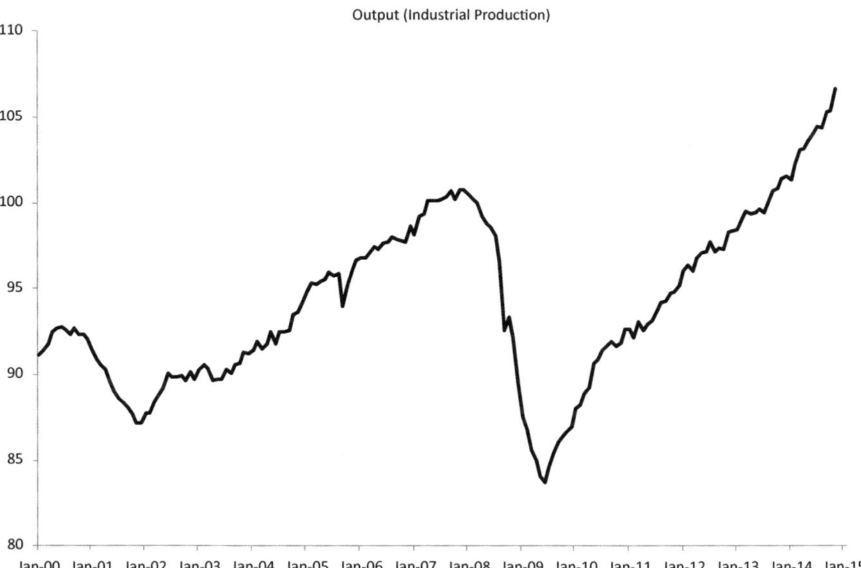

Figure 9.2:   US Inflation and Growth

and subdued with a deflationary period in the fourth quarter of 2008. This behavior is not consistent with the predictions of the quantity theory of money, as it does not resemble (even remotely) the behavior of monetary aggregates, let alone the behavior of the monetary base. The time plot of industrial production shows very clearly the Great Recession, as well as the recovery since the trough of June 2009. The recovery has implications for monetary growth because it signifies an increase in the demand for credit. If banks are willing to extend credit (and they are certainly capable of doing so) that will reduce the reserve ratio and lead to acceleration in monetary growth.

In Figure 9.3, we observe two measures of growth of monetary aggregates, as well as prices and output. The first of these measures is the annualized compound growth rate over the period September 2008–November 2014. We can see that the monetary base grew at an average rate of 23.54% while bank reserves grew at a rate of 58.46% because reserves started from a very low level. As a result of the increase in reserves, the monetary aggregates (M1 and M2) grew more slowly. However, liquid deposits (those included in M1) grew at a rate of 14.68%. The annualized monthly inflation rate has averaged 1.29%, below the growth rate of output. The second measure is the ratio of the peak value of an item to the value in September 2008. By this measure, reserves rose over 37 times, compared 4.48 times for the monetary base. M1 and M2 rose 1.09 times and 1.49 times, respectively, much less than the rate of growth of the monetary base.

Expansion in the monetary base has not led to a corresponding expansion in monetary aggregates because of reserve buildup. Since inflation is related to growth in monetary aggregates (because they represent purchasing power), no inflationary consequences have materialized. One explanation for this observation is that, irrespective of monetary growth, the US economy is still operating under capacity, a condition under which inflation does not emerge. Just because inflation has not emerged yet does not mean that it will not emerge in the future and, as we will see later, inflation may surge at low levels of capacity utilization. There is also the possibility that monetary growth is inflationary but at this stage it is shown in

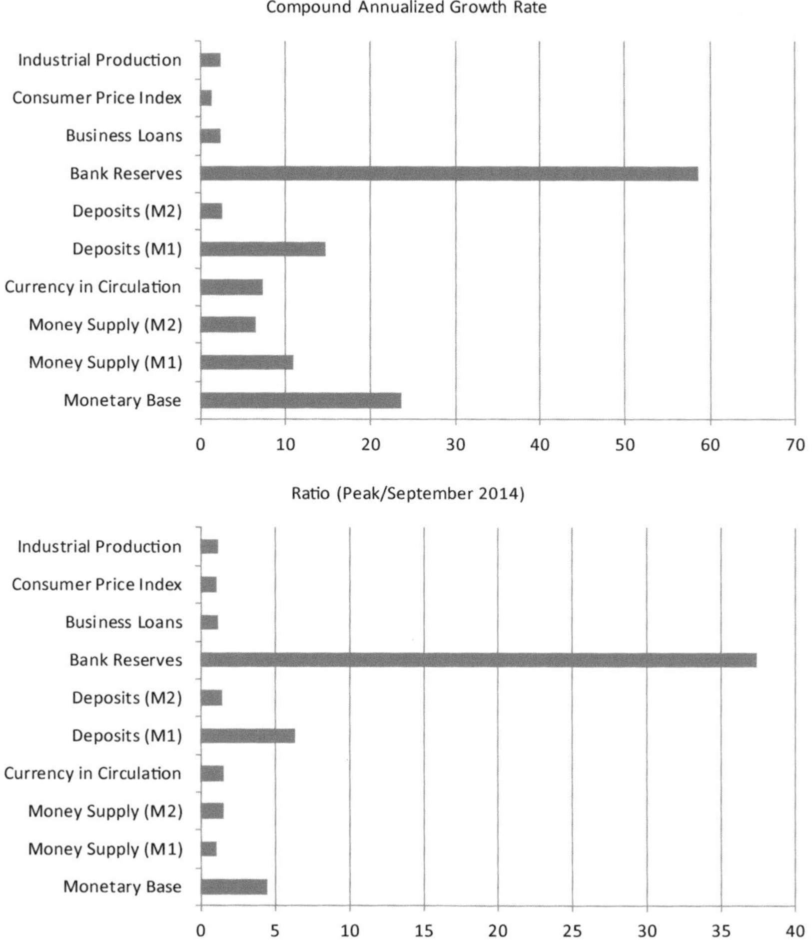

Figure 9.3:   **Measures of Growth in the QE Period (September 2008–November 2014)**

asset prices, not in the prices of goods and services. We will come back to this point later on.

4. The Inflationary Consequences of QE: Some Theoretical Considerations

QE is inflationary, as its opponents believe, if (i) it leads to monetary expansion and (ii) monetary expansion leads to inflation.

For example, Martin Feldstein is quoted by Walker (2014) as saying that "the risk is that banks might in the future use their reserves to expand lending to firms and households, which would increase the money supply and add to inflationary pressure". Walker also quotes a Fed economist as warning of "serious inflation risk". As far as the first point is concerned, QE leads to monetary expansion if banks do not accumulate reserves and extend credit instead. This is a prediction of the money multiplier model, which will be described later to explain why inflation has not emerged yet. In this section, a monetarist model of inflation is used to deal with point (ii) and illustrate the cause and effect relation between money and prices. The reason why a monetarist model of inflation is presented here is that we are dealing with a monetary phenomenon, rapid monetary expansion, if and when it materializes.

In the monetarist model of inflation the demand for money function is given by

$$m_d = py^\beta, \tag{9.1}$$

where m_d is the nominal demand for money, p is the price level, y is real output and β is the output elasticity of the demand for money. If the money supply (m) is exogenous, then equilibrium in the money market means $m_d = m$, which gives

$$m = py^\beta. \tag{9.2}$$

By differentiating Equation (9.2) with respect to time, we obtain

$$\frac{dm}{dt} = \frac{\partial m}{\partial p}\frac{dp}{dt} + \frac{\partial m}{\partial y}\frac{dy}{dt}, \tag{9.3}$$

or

$$\frac{dm}{dt} = y^\beta \frac{dp}{dt} + \beta py^{\beta-1}\frac{dy}{dt}. \tag{9.4}$$

Dividing each side of Equation (9.4) by m, we obtain

$$\frac{1}{m}\frac{dm}{dt} = \frac{1}{p}\frac{dp}{dt} + \beta\frac{1}{y}\frac{dy}{dt}. \tag{9.5}$$

By using the dot notation, Equation (9.5) can be written as

$$\frac{\dot{p}}{p} = \frac{\dot{m}}{m} - \beta \frac{\dot{y}}{y}. \qquad (9.6)$$

In continuous time, $\dot{p}/p$ is the inflation rate, $\dot{m}/m$ is the rate of monetary growth and $\dot{y}/y$ is the growth rate of real output. This equation takes us to a very basic definition of inflation that it is too much money chasing too few goods, which can happen at any level of capacity utilization.

The relation between money and prices is not contemporaneous, as economists who believe that inflation is caused by monetary growth also believe that there is a lag between the cause and effect. One reason for the lag is believed to be price stickiness. Friedman (1972) updated his previous work (Freidman, 1961) and concluded that "monetary changes take much longer to affect prices than to affect output". He estimated the lag between M1 and CPI to be 20 months whereas the M2 lag was put at 23 months.

Since then, new evidence has emerged in support of Friedman's estimates, which is why Batini and Nelson (2001) argue that "it is now something of an international rule of thumb for countries that have experienced moderate inflation". They update and extend Friedman's (1972) evidence, reaffirming his finding that it takes over a year before monetary policy actions have their peak effect on inflation. Bernanke *et al.* (1999) describe a two-year lag between policy actions and inflation as a "common estimate". They observe that this estimate has been embodied in the forecasting and decision-making of several inflation targeting central banks. Gerlach and Svensson (2001) document an approximate 18-month lag between money growth and inflation in the euro area. Carlson (1980) points out that economists generally agree that money affects prices with a lag. Research conducted at the Federal Reserve Bank of St Louis suggests that a change in the growth rate of money is fully reflected in the inflation rate in about five years.

In a more recent study, Mandler and Scharnagl (2014) use the wavelet transform to estimate local correlation as a measure of the extent of comovements between the growth rate of the broad monetary aggregate M3 and inflation at different frequencies and different points in time.[3] Their results indicate strong comovements close to a one-to-one relationship between the very long-run fluctuations (24–32 years) in M3 money growth and inflation, with money growth leading inflation by about two to three years. They also find evidence for a weakening at medium to long-run fluctuations (8–16 years) after the mid-1990s, which is in contrast to the results obtained by using more conventional techniques in the frequency domain. Various modifications to the analysis (such as correcting the money growth series for real gross domestic product (GDP) growth or replacing the broad monetary aggregate M3 with the narrow monetary aggregate M1) lead to similar results.

The fact that inflation has not arisen yet, which can be explained easily, does not mean that it will not necessarily arise in the future. Some economists even entertain the possibility of hyperinflation. According to Bourque (2012), the US is engaging in excessive amounts of quantitative easing and is threatening hyperinflation. In an open Letter to Ben Bernanke, several leading economists warned that the planned asset purchases by the Fed "risk currency debasement and inflation" (Asness *et al.*, 2010). Wade and Bilson (2012) express "legitimate concerns" over the impact of the huge expansion in the monetary base. Although the view that QE is inflationary is not universally accepted, those who express this view have on their side theory, empirical evidence, practical experience and history (not about QE as such but about the money-inflation nexus).

5. The Opposite View: QE is not Inflationary

Roche (2013) quotes Larry Kudlow as declaring that the deficit hawks (the inflationistas) are the losers of the long raging inflation

---

[3] M3 is M2 plus long-term, less liquid deposits. Since 2006, the Federal Reserve no longer reports M3 for the US, but the ECB reports this monetary aggregate for the Eurozone.

debate.[4] Kudlow thinks that "the debate appears to have been convincingly won by the inflation doves (those who think that inflation will be low despite QE)". Roche believes that one reason why inflation has not arisen is that "QE doesn't have a transmission mechanism to substantially increase aggregate demand". In reality, however, the debate is not over yet as inflation may accelerate in the future. The point raised by Roche, that QE is not inflationary because it does not have a transmission mechanism to boost aggregate demand, is flawed. It is not quantitative easing as such but rather the effect of money on inflation, which is highlighted by episodes of hyperinflation and in theory in the aggregate supply and demand model. The liquidity effect may be the mechanism. If, as Roche claims, QE has no transmission mechanism then this is the antithesis of QE, which is a deliberate policy action taken to influence aggregate demand (or this is at least what we are told by central banks).

Matthews (2013) questions the proposition that quantitative easing is inflationary, arguing that the fears of runaway inflation are unfounded. He further writes the following:

> If the government literally began printing money and started mailing out new $100 bills to citizens, that would lead to price inflation. But quantitative easing isn't the equivalent of mailing out $100 bills — it's merely the managing of long-term interest rates much in the same way the Fed always has managed short-term interest rates.

The argument put forward by Matthews shows misunderstanding of the concept of the money supply. He does understand how part of the monetary base is converted into currency in circulation, which is a component of the money supply, but in a modern economy it is a very small part. In the case of QE the central bank creates a $100 bill electronically to buy a bond from a commercial bank. If the reserve ratio is 0.1, this bank can give a customer a

---

[4]http://www.pragcap.com/scott-sumner-vs-peter-schiff.

$1,000 loan by crediting the customer's account with this amount. The customer now has some purchasing power which (when exercised) generates pressure on the general price level and creates inflation. Typically, people pay for things not by using $100 bills but by using credit and debit cards in a process that involves the transfer (sooner or later) of funds from one deposit to another.

An opposite view is expressed by Barron (2013) who is highly critical of the Fed for believing that quantitative easing is benign (as far as inflation is concerned). He argues that "there is no miracle or mystery as to why prices have not gone significantly higher" and that "our monetary authorities have not found the magic formula that allows the government to engage in non-inflationary spending sprees, funded neither by an increase in taxes nor an increase in interest rates". He further writes the following:

Our monetary masters remind me of the story of the man who jumps off the Empire State Building. As he is passing a floor on the way down, an office worker leans out a window and asks him how he's doing. He replies: so far, so good!

It seems that Barron believes in the confidence model of hyperinflation as he argues that "no one can predict when people will begin to lose confidence in the purchasing power of the dollar" and that "each new dollar that the Fed creates is like one more strand of straw laid on a mountain of straw". The real question, as far as he is concerned, is if the next strand of straw is going to be the one that breaks the camel's back. With respect to the emergence of inflation, it is "so far so good", but only in the sense of jumping off the Empire State Building before hitting the ground. While *The Economist* (2014e) understates the possibility of inflation, it is also stated that "these fears will be difficult to judge until more time has passed".

Paul Krugman argues against the inflation (or hyperinflation) scenario from a Keynesian perspective as he suggests that "Keynesian theories predicted that QE would have little effect" whereas "a whole bunch of alternative schools predicted that there would be high inflation" (Smith, 2014). According to Krugman, the failure of inflation to materialize means that Keynesians prevailed, which (as he puts it) makes sense, suggesting that "the theories that predicted inflation seem to be due for a reexamination, especially in light of Japan's very similar experience in previous decades". This point is similar to the point raised by Larry Kudlow to which the response is simple: the debate is not over yet. On the other hand, Krugman (2012) sounds as if he thinks that QE is inflationary as he suggests that higher inflation in the US would be beneficial in alleviating private debt and encouraging consumption and thus recovery. According to Krugman, higher inflation would "erode the real value of this debt, deter the private sector from hoarding its current cash reserves and therefore promote consumption, investment and economic recovery". It is not clear whether Krugman defends QE because it is non-inflationary or because it is inflationary but inflation is good under the present circumstances.

Some economists reach the same conclusion that QE will not cause inflation by using rational expectations analysis. Anderson *et al.* (2010) examine the experience of selected central banks that have used large-scale "balance sheet expansion" (that is, quantitative easing) as a monetary policy instrument. The case studies they examine focus on central banks responding to the global financial crisis and Nordic central banks during the banking crises of the 1990s. They conclude that large-scale balance sheet increases are a viable monetary policy tool, provided that the public believes that the process will be reversed appropriately. They summarize their findings as follows: (i) a large increase in a central bank's balance sheet can be stimulative in the short run; (ii) the reason(s) for the action should be communicated because inflationary expectations do not change if households and firms understand the reason(s) for policy actions; (iii) the type of assets purchased matters less than the balance sheet expansion and (iv) when the crisis has passed, the balance sheet should be unwound promptly. This is a valid point but it will be demonstrated later that the Fed will have a hell of a job unwinding its balance sheet.

Anderson *et al.* (2010) argue that the breakdown in the money-inflation nexus arises in a variety of macroeconomic models. The main reason for the breakdown is that inflationary expectations are little affected by QE if growth in the central bank's balance sheet is perceived as temporary. Goodfriend and King (1981) demonstrate this result in the context of Barro's (1976) rational expectations model by introducing a central bank that is credibly committed to a long-run path for the money supply while indulging in short-term money supply expansion. Recently, Berentsen and Waller (2013) showed the same result in a search-theoretic real business cycle model in which monetary policy is assumed to have short-run and long-run components focusing on stabilizing real activity (in the presence of shocks) and the long-run inflation trend, respectively.

Similar results arise in the classical long-run equilibria of New Keynesian models that contain incomplete information and adjustment costs, although there may be interim increases in economic activity (Woodford, 2004; Clarida *et al.*, 1999). Among the differences in these papers, as noted by Berntsen and Waller (2013), is that New Keynesian models rely on "nominal rigidities, such as price or wage stickiness, that allows monetary policy to have real effects" and that the models "are 'cashless' in the sense that there are no monetary trading frictions". In their general equilibrium real business cycle model, all prices are flexible but money overcomes trading frictions. Hence, in New Keynesian models, *ad hoc* stickiness may allow real effects of monetary shocks even under complete information.

Some of those who reject the eventuality of inflation dispute the proposition that money does matter, arguing that money is irrelevant to inflation, provided that the economy does not "overheat". This view is a reflection of the role of the output gap, where inflation appears only if the gap is positive — that is, when the economy is producing over capacity (or above the natural level of output). If this view is valid then there is no reason to believe that the monetary expansion caused by quantitative easing has inflationary consequences. Stiglitz (2012) argues that QE3 will not cause "serious" inflation because of the economy's underutilized productive capacity. Likewise, Levine-Weinberg (2012) points out that quantitative easing will not cause inflation because of a high unemployment rate in the US.[5] Harvey (2011) suggests that there is no reason why quantitative easing will not lead to a rise in production and employment as opposed to prices, as long as excess money balances are invested in productive activities to meet the new demand, but only a small part of business loans is invested in productive capacity (most of the loans are used to finance speculative activity). The excess money balances we are talking about here are of hyperinflationary proportions, not the small amounts associated with moderate demand-pull inflation.

The view that "money doesn't matter" flies in the face of what is arguably one of the strongest empirical relations in macroeconomics. While some economists emphasize the importance of the output gap in the determination of inflation, the empirical evidence supporting the relation between the output gap and inflation is weak and statistically tenuous. Orphanides and van Norden (2004) reach the conclusion that their results "call into question the practical usefulness of the output gap concept for forecasting inflation". Mehra (2004) summarizes the results of studies of the output gap as indicating that the gap is irrelevant and that inflationary expectations constitute the major determinant of inflation. Kasriel (2004) describes the relation between the output gap and inflation as being "well known — but unsupported by statistics and history". He even shows that the two variables are related negatively and proceeds to demonstrate a positive relation between monetary growth and inflation. Biggs and Mayer (2010) suggest that "past experience has shown that estimates of the output gap are highly uncertain and that reliance on such estimates for the conduct of economic policy (or for investment decisions) can lead to serious errors". Not even casual empiricism supports the importance of the

---

[5] Obviously, things have changed since Levine-Weinberg put forward his proposition. Unemployment in the US is no longer high, at least as things stand in mid-2016.

output gap. A record level of US capacity utilization was reached in January 1967 (89.4) when inflation was subdued, but it was at less than 75 at the height of the 1970s inflation.

There are those who believe that money causes inflation, yet they argue that monetary expansion is not inflationary under the present conditions because of declining velocity.[6] Wade and Bilson (2012) suggest that hyperinflation is not currently a threat in the US because the increase in the monetary base via quantitative easing has been matched by huge reductions in the velocity of circulation. Wen and Arias (2014) argue that "the issue has to do with the velocity of money", suggesting that "if for some reason the money velocity declines rapidly during an expansionary monetary policy period, it can offset the increase in money supply and even lead to deflation instead of inflation". In Figure 9.4, we can see that velocity has been declining, but the pattern of behavior does not reflect the quantity theory of money in a strict sense (Figure 9.5). During the period between the fourth quarter of 2008 and the fourth quarter of 2014, the price level rose by 9.2% while M1 and M2 rose 77.9% and 12.2%, respectively. During the same period, the velocity of M1 declined by 15.4% and the velocity of M2 declined by 35.2% while output rose by 14.3%. These figures do not support the proposition that disparity between monetary growth and inflation can be explained by variations in the velocity of circulation.

Since independent measures of velocity are not available (as it is calculated as a residual item), disparity between inflation and monetary growth cannot be explained plausibly by variations in velocity. If we try to do that, we will end up with mere tautology saying that the inflation rate is equal to the inflation rate. Moosa (2012) presents other explanations such as the significant portion of the US money supply, particularly currency, held abroad. According to the estimates of Federal Reserve Bank of St Louis, approximately 50% of all US currency in circulation is held in other countries

---

[6]The velocity of circulation is a measure of how fast a monetary unit changes hands on average. For the whole economy, it is measured as the ratio of nominal output to the money supply.

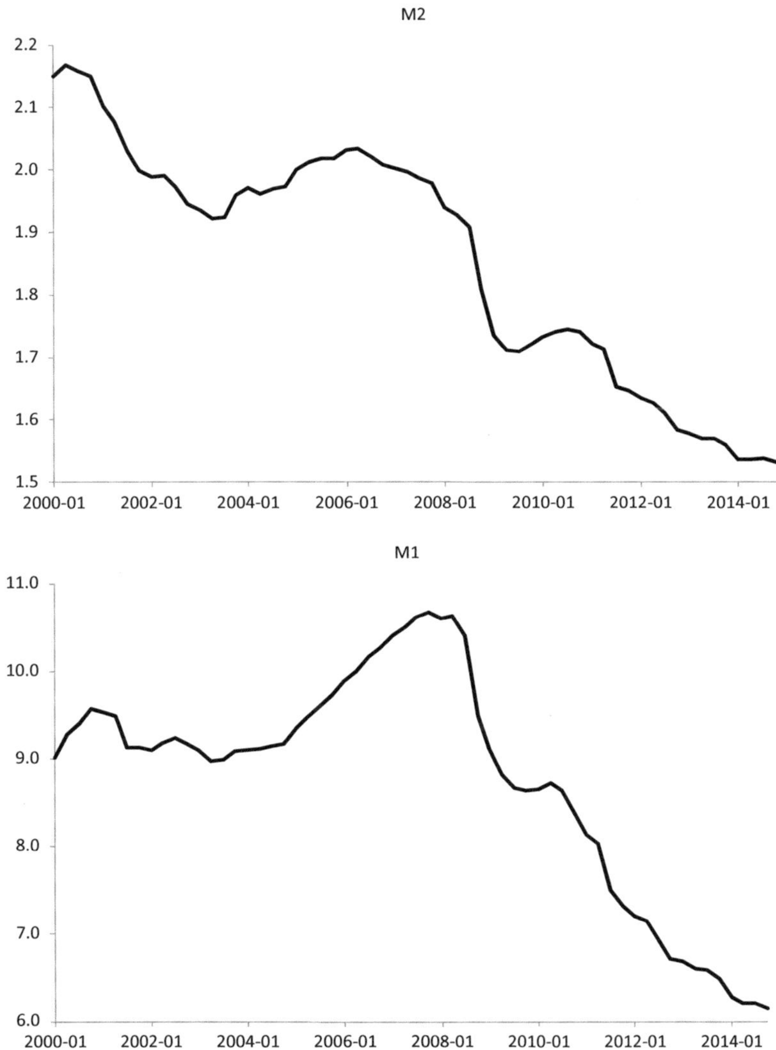

Figure 9.4:   Velocity of Circulation in the US

(Anderson and Williams, 2007). A more plausible explanation is that monetary growth has been reflected mostly on asset prices. This explanation is used to rationalize the proposition that indulging in QE is effectively sowing the seeds of the next crisis. We will come back to this point later on.

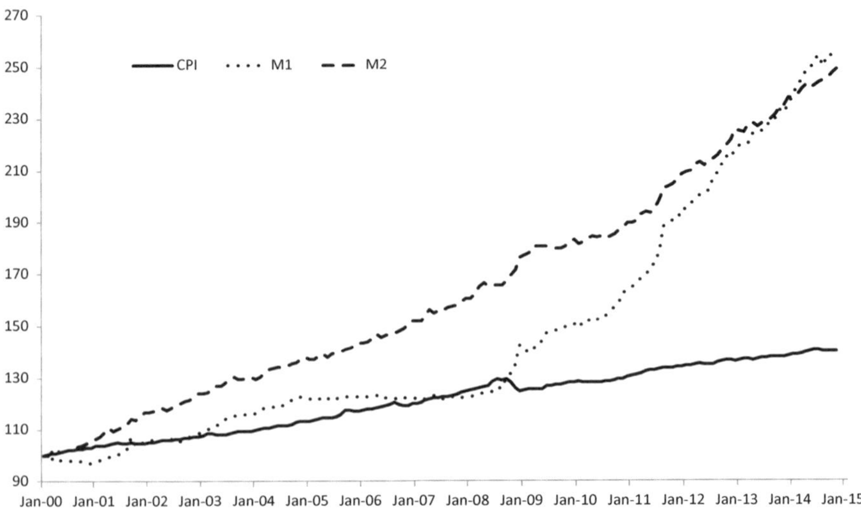

Figure 9.5: US CPI and Monetary Aggregates (Indices, Jan 2000 = 100)

6. Another View: QE is Deflationary

While it is only natural to think that a monetary expansion caused by quantitative easing will eventually lead to inflation, some economists believe that deflation is the most likely outcome. They think that both outcomes are possible, depending on current and future policy actions. Duncan (2012), for example, concludes that the price level could either collapse or surge higher, depending on whether governments cease or, by attempting to prevent deflation, maintain quantitative easing, thus generating hyperinflation. Likewise Bourque (2012) argues that "whether we have inflation or deflation depends on just how much governments are willing to do to prevent deflation". Since the Fed has put an end to QE, it follows from this line of reasoning that deflation should be underway but this has not happened yet.

Arguments for deflation are based on the proposition that the US economy is already pushing towards a debt deflationary depression as a result of an extended credit bubble. According to the theory of debt deflation of Fisher (1933), an economic depression is the result of the credit cycle, as a reduction in debt results in an economic downturn. Fisher postulated that the end of a debt bubble leads to a liquidation of assets and distress selling. As loans are paid off, the velocity of circulation declines, causing a fall in prices and subsequently shrinking output and employment. Deflation is a characteristic of severe economic downturn where high unemployment means that the government finds it difficult to control debt in the face of falling prices and wages, and hence tax revenue. This is probably what happened in the 1930s, but there is a big difference between the 1930s and the present time. In the 1930s, the US money supply contracted by about one-third, but this episode is characterized by rapid monetary growth. Moreover, the US economy has been recovering since 2009. The scenario envisaged by Fisher is not apparent in the current state of affairs.

Support for a deflationary outcome comes from the proposition that by reducing returns on government bonds, quantitative easing reduces the consumption of those receiving interest income such as annuities. For example, Stiglitz (2012) argues that quantitative easing will punish consumers invested in government bonds and curtail their consumption. Reduced consumption and hoarding of cash by these sectors of the economy will produce deflation, a situation that is exacerbated by an ageing population. It is also argued that quantitative easing can impact consumer and producer sentiment negatively, which promotes a deflationary environment. McTeer (2010), for example, argues that the use of the term "quantitative easing" has a significant impact on consumer confidence that drives down stock prices, giving rise to an adverse wealth effect. However, two reasons can be suggested to explain why low interest rates are unlikely to have an adverse effect on consumption. The first is that low interest rates provide a boost for financial markets, creating a positive wealth effect. The second is that the income derived from interest payments represents a small fraction of the total economy. In this sense, QE has a distributional effect, not a depressive effect. The facts and figures show that QE has provided a significant boost for stock prices. This is why it is plausible to suggest that QE is designed to propel economic activity by creating a positive wealth effect resulting from rising asset prices. We will come back to this point later on.

Some observers contend that the US economy is already in a deflationary phase. Chapman (2010) cites evidence indicating that the US has been in a deflationary state since 2002 and that quantitative easing is merely postponing a deflationary depression. The indicators for this state of affairs include depressed consumption, close to zero interest rates, a high unemployment rate and a weak dollar. Bourque (2012) argues that the world is already in a deflationary economic period as a result of "too much government and personal debt, hyper-speculation and aging baby boomers moving beyond their peak spending years". He points out that the contraction of the world economy is being fended off by governments that are trying to secure their positions by quantitative easing measures that are intended to "shake the world out of its deflationary mood". In the US at least, conditions have changed substantially since Bourque wrote these words — unemployment is low and declining, the economy is growing and the dollar is strong.

Several economists put forward the argument that as soon as large amounts of government debt make quantitative easing no longer viable, deflation and economic downturn will follow. Chapman (2010) argues that the continued creation of government debt and monetization of the deficit by the Fed means that "a deflationary collapse, one way or another, is inevitable". Duncan (2012) points out that current economic conditions are similar to those that resulted in the Great Depression (caused by large fiat-money denominated credit bubbles) which were described by Fisher (1933) as debt-deflation dynamics. Duncan goes on to say that as soon as the government withdraws stimulus or "the government's capacity to provide any more stimulus is exhausted … the deflationary death spiral will resume". At the risk of repetition, one has to stress the big difference between the Great Depression and the current situation (monetary contraction versus expansion).

It is inconceivable to believe that policy makers in a heavily indebted country like the US would choose to pursue a deflationary policy, knowing very well that what is needed to reduce the real value of debt is inflation. Japan has been experiencing deflation not because of, but despite, QE. Unless there is a valid conspiracy theory, policy makers must believe that QE is inflationary.

7. Money Creation versus Money Printing

One of those rejecting the proposition that quantitative easing will lead to inflation is Kerkhoff (2013) who argues on the basis of the distinction between "money printing" and "money creation", citing Bernanke as saying that "the Fed is not printing money". Central bankers tend to claim that quantitative easing is not about printing money just to give the impression that it is not inflationary (because money printing is inflationary but money creation is not!). For example, the Bank of England describes quantitative easing as follows: "The Bank of England electronically creates new money and uses it to purchase gilts from private investors such as pension funds and insurance companies".[7] The word "electronically" is used to emphasize the claim that QE does not involve money printing.

Kerkhoff (2013) suggests that it is more accurate to say that the Fed is "creating", not "printing" money on the grounds that money is created when the Fed credits the balances of the reserve accounts of its member banks in return for the purchased securities (which is not the same as using a printing press to produce banknotes). This, the argument goes, is not the same as "printing" as in the episode of the German hyperinflation of the 1920s. In the case of "creation", the Fed provides reserves to its member banks while removing an equivalent amount of assets (bonds) from the balance sheets of those same banks. The result, the argument goes, is that "no new net financial assets enter the economy". This process is not a one way flow of money into the economy, but rather it is more like a "liquidity swap". Carney (2013) suggests that "QE

---

[7] http://www.bankofengland.co.uk/monetarypolicy/Pages/qe/default.aspx.

makes a lot more sense when it is viewed as a swap that reduces the supply of long-duration assets (Treasury bonds and MBS), which means that "QE isn't inflationary or deflationary". Likewise, Matthews (2013) disputes what he describes as the "myth" that quantitative easing is printing money, arguing that it is misleading to call this process "money printing" because "it doesn't actually do anything to increase the amount of money in circulation", given that "in our monetary system, most money is created by private banks and not the Federal Reserve". However, Matthews seems to overlook the fact that private banks cannot create money unless they have excess reserves, which come from the base money created by the central bank. QE provides the raw material used by banks to "manufacture" money.

Some observers go as far as accusing Bernanke (and his successor) of pursuing policies that are identical to those adopted by Rudolf Havenstein, the governor of the Reichsbak during the German hyperinflation. Turk (2009) thinks so, suggesting that "Mr Bernanke is creating more currency by creating more debt, which is the singular underlying cause of hyperinflation". Jericho (2012) puts it succinctly as follows:

> Quantitative easing is the rather weasel-word phrase given to when the central bank buys a stack of bonds, which has the effect of increasing the money supply in the economy — essentially printing more money (but doing it electronically).

Whether money is produced by a printing press or a computer makes no difference for the inflationary consequences of monetary growth. It is absurd to suggest that the printing press is inflationary but the computer is not.

8. QE as a Monetization of the Budget Deficit

Alan Meltzer (quoted by Walker, 2014) is worried about the inflationary consequences of buying government debt to finance what he calls "outsize deficits". The point raised by Meltzer, that he is troubled by the consequences of buying government debt to finance the budget deficit, is rejected by the proponents of QE on the grounds that it does not involve a monetization of the deficit. Under quantitative easing, they argue, the central bank does not buy securities from the Treasury but rather from private-sector financial institutions.

Central banks that indulge in quantitative easing stress the distinction between creating (not printing) money to buy financial assets and to buy goods and services — the latter representing a monetization of the deficit. The underlying idea is that buying bonds from banks is different from buying bonds directly from the government — only the latter constitutes a monetization of the deficit. Ben Bernanke, for example, remarked once that the government would not print money and distribute it "willy nilly" but would rather focus its efforts in certain areas (for example, buying federal agency debt securities and MBS) (Wolf, 2008b). However, Richard Fisher, president of the Federal Reserve Bank of Dallas, warns of "the risk of being perceived as embarking on the slippery slope of debt monetization", suggesting that "once a central bank is perceived as targeting government debt yields at a time of persistent budget deficits, concern about debt monetization quickly arises" (Fisher, 2010). He reaches the conclusion that the Fed is monetizing government debt when he suggests the following:

> The math of this new exercise is readily transparent: The Federal Reserve will buy $110 billion a month in Treasuries, an amount that, annualized, represents the projected deficit of the federal government for next year. For the next eight months, the nation's central bank will be monetizing the federal debt.

Adam Fergusson, the author of an influential book on the German hyperinflation, thinks that quantitative easing is not different from what the German central bank did in the 1920s. This is what he thinks of quantitative easing (Fergusson, 2010):

> Money may no longer be physically printed and distributed in the voluminous quantities of 1923. However, 'quantitative easing', that modern euphemism for surreptitious deficit financing

in an electronic era, can no less become an assault on monetary discipline. Whatever the reason for a country's deficit — necessity or profligacy, unwillingness to tax or blindness to expenditure — it is beguiling to suppose that if the day of reckoning is postponed economic theory will come in time to prevent higher unemployment or deeper recession.

He also writes:

It is alarming that some respected bankers and economists today, in the US as in Britain, are still able to command 'the printing press' (in so many words!) as a fail-safe, a last resort. A country's budget can indeed be balanced in that way, but at the cost, to whatever degree, of its citizens' savings and pensions, their confidence and trust, their morals and their morale.

Economists who believe that QE amounts to a monetization of the deficit envisage the possibility of hyperinflation. Dowd *et al.* (2011b) portray a picture of how hyperinflation will hit the US, arguing that "if the Fed persists along its declared path, the prognosis is accelerating inflation leading ultimately to hyperinflation and economic meltdown". They predict that the Fed will be forced to monetize the whole of the federal debt, which requires a rapid expansion of the monetary base. The fact that QE involves the purchase of securities from financial institutions, not directly from the Treasury, makes no difference whatsoever. In both cases the subsequent increase in purchasing power is bound to have inflationary consequences.

9. Where is the QE-Triggered Inflation?

In this section, the money multiplier model is used to demonstrate why inflation has not emerged yet. Changes in the money supply, defined as currency in circulation and deposits, occur under a fractional reserve system as follows. The central bank issues currency, which is the monetary base or "high-powered money". Some of the issued currency is held by the public, which they use to buy goods and services (settling typically small transactions). This part of the monetary base, currency in circulation, is a component of the money supply. The other part is held by banks as reserves. Against these reserves, banks extend loans and create deposits in the process. Under a fractional reserve system banks can extend loans (and create deposits) while holding a much smaller amount of reserves than under a full reserve system. Thus, for every unit increase in bank reserves, resulting from an increase in the monetary base, deposits and the money supply increase multiple times. However, this happens only if banks extend loans instead of holding reserves.

Let us see how this process works formally. Define the monetary base, B, as the sum of currency held by the public, C, and banks' reserves, R. Hence

$$B = C + R. \tag{9.7}$$

The money supply is defined as the sum of currency and bank deposits, which gives

$$M = C + D. \tag{9.8}$$

By dividing Equation (9.8) by Equation (9.7), we obtain

$$\frac{M}{B} = \frac{C+D}{C+R}. \tag{9.9}$$

By dividing the right-hand side of Equation (9.9) by D, we obtain

$$\frac{M}{B} = \frac{\dfrac{C}{D}+1}{\dfrac{C}{D}+\dfrac{R}{D}}, \tag{9.10}$$

or

$$M = \left[\frac{c+1}{c+r}\right]B, \tag{9.11}$$

where c is the currency to deposits ratio as determined by public preferences and r is the banks' reserve to deposits ratio, which is determined by their preferences as well as the reserve requirements imposed on banks by the central bank. Equation (9.11) can be simplified to

$$M = mB, \tag{9.12}$$

where m is the money multiplier. Under a factional reserve system $r < 1$, which means that $m > 1$. For each dollar increase in the monetary base, the money supply increases by a factor or multiple determined by the two ratios, c and r. If banks decide to lend more, r will decline in the same way as when the central bank decides to reduce r through a policy action (expansionary monetary policy). As r declines the value of the multiplier rises, thus a greater amount of money can be created for a given increase in the monetary base. The money supply is inversely related to the reserve ratio because

$$\frac{\partial M}{\partial r} = -\frac{(c+1)B}{(c+r)^2} < 0. \tag{9.13}$$

In the extreme case, when banks decide to stop lending and keep full reserves against deposits, $r = 1$ and $m = 1$, which means that an increase in the monetary base will translate into an equivalent increase in the money supply. The money supply expands when banks lend — this is the connection between credit and money. This simple relation may be the key to answering the question as to why quantitative easing has not produced inflation.

Figure 9.6 shows why expansion in the monetary base is not reflected in the two monetary aggregates (M1 and M2) — this can be explained in terms of the fall in the value of the money multiplier as a result of a rising reserve ratio. We can also observe the fall in the currency ratio corresponding to M1 (the ratio of currency to the deposits included in M1). This is due to a more rapid increase in the demand for liquid deposits as a result of flight to quality, the move away from securities to deposits (liquidity preference as a behavior towards risk). This is why we can see faster growth in M1 than in M2 (Figure 9.5).

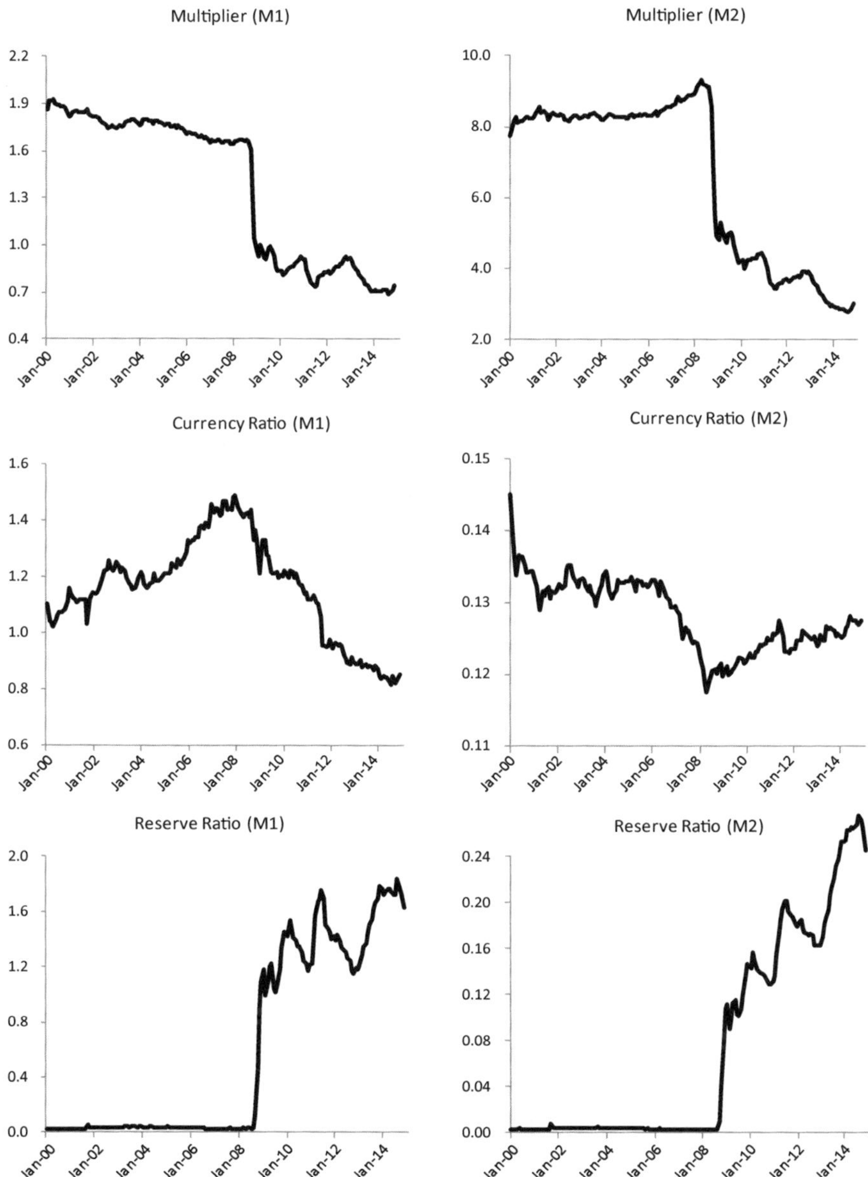

Figure 9.6:   US Multipliers and Ratios

Inflation has not emerged yet because of the accumulation of reserves, which is recognized by economists and observers. Wheelock (2010) wonders why the increase in the money stock is so small when the increase in the monetary base is so large, an observation that he explains in terms of the willingness of depository institutions (banks) to lend and the perceived creditworthiness of potential borrowers. McTeer (2010) contends that the large expansion of the Fed's balance sheet remains as excess reserves, which are not used for money-creating lending and investing. He concedes that excess bank reserves (while potentially inflationary) are currently not. Ben Bernanke is quoted as saying that "scarred banks curtail their lending to companies after financial crises even if they have sufficient funds, inhibiting economic growth" (*The Economist*, 2015c).

Two factors have led to the accumulation of reserves: (i) fear about the creditworthiness of borrowers in the aftermath of the global financial crisis and the Great Recession and (ii) the fact that reserves no longer represent a non-interest bearing asset. While the first reason is straightforward, the second requires some elaboration. Since October 2008, the Fed has been paying interest on the reserves of commercial banks held with it.[8] According to Garbade (2011), "paying interest on reserves can immobilize reserves in a way not contemplated by the traditional pre-2008 money multiplier model". As long as the interest paid on reserve accounts is high enough to deter banks from converting their new reserves to

---

[8] The Federal Reserve has been paying interest on bank reserve deposits since October 2008 under authority granted by the Emergency Stabilization Act of 2008 (Anderson, 2008). Paying interest on reserve balances was designed to broaden the scope of the Fed's lending program to address conditions in credit markets while maintaining the federal funds rate close to the target established by the Federal Open Market Committee (FOMC), the Fed's monetary policy decision makers. A number of central banks have the authority to pay interest on the reserves held against deposits. For example, the Bank of England has been paying interest on reserves since 2009, and the European Central Bank has had this authority from its inception in 1999 (Federal Reserve Bank of San Francisco, http://www.frbsf.org/education/publications/doctor-econ/2013/march/federal-reserve-interest-balances-reserves#_ftn2).

interest-earning assets by extending loans to households and firms, expansion of the monetary base will not translate into expansion in the money supply. This is what has been happening so far.

Although this line of reasoning makes sense, a recent study by the Bank of England shows that even in the period 2009–2013 QE produced some inflationary consequences. Weale and Weiladek (2014) examine the impact of QE on the CPI in the UK and US by using a Bayesian vector autoregression (VAR) and obtain results indicating that an asset purchase of 1% of GDP leads to a 0.38% rise in the CPI for the US and 0.3% in the UK. If this is the case while banks were accumulating reserves, the effect will be more pronounced when banks start offloading their reserves. Although monetary growth has been slower than what it would have been in the absence of reserve buildup, this growth has produced (moderate) inflation.

10. Is Inflation Likely to Emerge in the Future?

Many economists worry that bank lending and monetary growth will eventually surge and, ultimately, cause inflation. Martin Feldstein believes that if banks start lending on a big scale then this will boost the money supply and ignite inflation (Walker, 2014). This view reflects belief in the money multiplier model and the quantity theory of money. The question here is under what conditions will banks start converting their reserves into loans, bringing down the reserves ratio and raising the value of the multiplier? This will happen when banks feel that it is more attractive, in terms of risk-adjusted return, to lend than to earn interest on reserves. Such a trend is already in motion as we can see in Figure 9.7, which shows that business loans are growing at the pre-crisis pace.

The proponents of QE argue that if inflationary pressures emerge, the Fed can respond in two different ways. One option is to sell securities outright or under repurchase agreements, which will cause the monetary base to shrink. Another option is to raise the interest rate paid to banks on their reserve balances, which

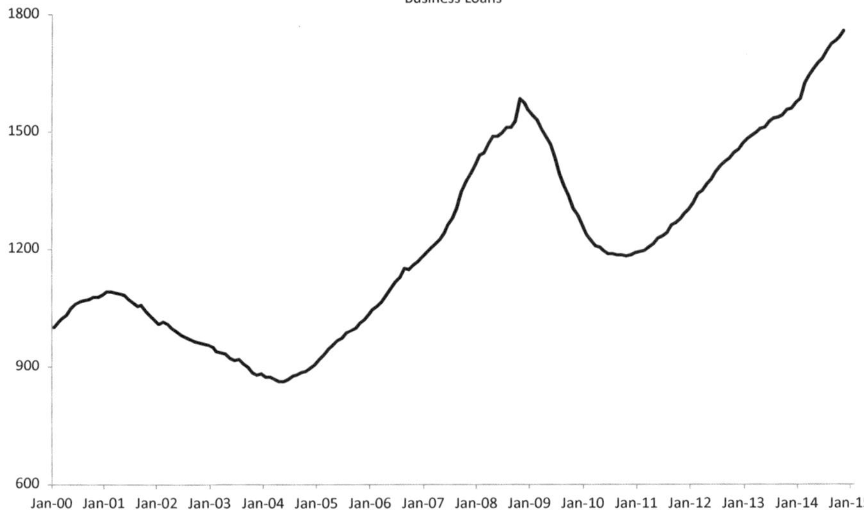

Figure 9.7: US Business Loans

would lead to a higher opportunity cost of lending, upward pressure on market rates generally, and slower growth of credit (and hence the money supply). However, because the Fed has little experience with paying interest on reserves, it is difficult to predict how much bank loans would change in response to an increase in the interest rate paid on reserve deposits. Furthermore, the Fed will not find willing buyers for the trillions of dollars worth of existing securities, given that new securities will add to the glut as the budget deficit persists and securitization comes back with vengeance. Selling securities through repurchase agreements will not achieve the objective of reducing the size of the balance sheet. *The Economist* (2011b) makes it clear that "it is easy to start quantitative easing but difficult to get out of it". If the Fed cannot sell the Treasury bonds it has acquired from banks, that will be effectively a monetization of the deficit. Now we are not sure what the deal is. The stated objective of QE is to boost the ability of banks to grant credit. If this is the case, why would the

Fed take action to reduce the ability and willingness of banks to grant credit when they start to do so?

QE is hard to reverse, not only because it is difficult for the Fed to reduce its balance sheet. Huberts (2013) argues that it is even difficult to stop the program and resist the temptation to start again. One reason suggested by Huberts is national politics because QE is perceived as providing a solution to a crisis, the alternative to which is austerity. The second reason he puts forward is that QE amounts to currency devaluation that boosts the competitiveness of exports. Hence, Huberts presents global competition as another reason why the reversal of QE is not that easy. If QE cannot be reversed appropriately then the process envisaged by Anderson *et al.* (2010) will not materialize and QE will have inflationary consequences. Even if QE in the US has come to an end for now, the belief that the policy works may bring about QE4, particularly that the strength of the US dollar dents exports.

As *The Economist* (2014e) points out, "history suggests that leaving QE behind is never simple" and that "a premature exit from QE3 is a good way to make sure there is QE4". Huberts (2013) believes that the tipping point towards inflation is determined by the cumulative QE as well as public and private debt. Hence, he argues, if a country overshoots its tipping point, inflationary expectations become unanchored, which could happen first in financial markets through such channels as currency depreciation. He further argues that policy makers obtaining comfort from the stabilization of inflation in recent years should pay more attention to the Lucas critique, which postulates that functional economic relations can change drastically when policies are altered. Huberts believes that while hyperinflation is possible, it is not yet probable, but "economic stagnation over an extended period of time combined with QE would certainly increase the odds of elevated inflation".

We have already argued that it is implausible to suggest that QE is not inflationary because of declining velocity and a low level of capacity utilization. Even if the velocity argument is valid, the expectation is that velocity will rise because it tends to fall in recessions and rise in recovery, albeit after a while. A private-sector report shows that velocity went up in every recovery of the post-war era although it does not begin to rise right at the start of the recovery (Wells Capital Management, 2013). The report predicts that velocity is poised to rise on the basis of a composite indicator comprising consumer confidence, monetary growth, the bond yield credit spread and the slope of the yield curve. As for the argument based on the output gap, it suffices to say that US capacity utilization was at 80 in November 2014, up from a low of 66.9 in 2009 (it was 88.8 in the mining sector), compared with a high of 85 in 1994–1995. Inflation is known to pick up at much lower levels of capacity utilization. Our contention is that inflation is already in place, taking the form of asset price inflation rather than goods price inflation.

11. The Financial Effects of QE: Interest Rates and Asset Prices

The argument put forward in this section is straightforward: low interest rates, coupled with some malpractices and poor risk management, caused the global financial crisis. It is therefore plausible to suggest that since QE has kept interest rates near zero for a long time in the aftermath of the crisis (until now), it is likely that QE will cause the next crisis. Asset price inflation triggered by QE is already underway, which means that the next crisis will be a typical bubble followed by a crash.

Low interest rates contributed to the advent of the global financial crisis by creating an incentive for investors (institutional and otherwise) to seek assets with better risk-return profiles than, for example, bank deposits. In the run-up to the crisis, there was a stampede to accumulate asset-backed securities (ABSs) and the CDOs based on those securities, which were portrayed to be almost risk-free with a yield of several hundred basis points higher than what was offered by US Treasury securities. Furthermore, low interest rates made it attractive for financial institutions to indulge in leveraged buyouts and for investors in general to accumulate assets financed by leverage. While any bubble eventually bursts and causes problems, a bubble financed by leverage can be devastating when it bursts (what is worse than a bubble is a bubble financed by leverage). The stability of interest rates at low levels and the illusion of the so-called "Great Moderation" made it tantalizing to accumulate leverage. In a nutshell, low and stable interest rates created an asset price bubble and a boom that was followed by a crash — and there is no reason why this would not happen again.

The role of low and stable interest rates in the global financial crisis has been established beyond reasonable doubt. Taylor (2009) argues in general terms that "the classic explanation of financial crises is that they are caused by excesses — frequently monetary excesses — which lead to a boom and an inevitable bust". The global financial crisis, he argues, was no different as "a housing boom followed by a bust led to defaults, the implosion of mortgages and mortgage-related securities at financial institutions, and resulting financial turmoil". Taylor describes "monetary excesses", as implied by persistently low interest rates, as "the main cause of the boom", pointing out that the Fed held its target interest rate, particularly during the period 2003–2005, well below known monetary guidelines for good policy as prescribed by historical experience. The empirical research conducted by Taylor shows that the Federal Reserve held interest rates excessively low for a long time before the crisis, which was "a big deviation from the kind of policy that had worked well for more than 20 years in the 1980s, 1990s until this time". He suggests that "keeping interest rates on the track that worked well in the past two decades, rather than keeping rates so low, would have prevented the boom and the bust". He cites corroborating evidence for several countries as provided by the Organisation for Economic Co-operation and Development (OECD) — this evidence shows that monetary excesses cause housing booms. Taylor points out that "there is also evidence that excessive risk-taking was encouraged by the excessively low interest rates".[9]

Holt (2009) identifies four primary causes of the housing bubble that preceded the global financial crisis — low mortgage

---

[9] Taylor (2013) makes similar arguments.

interest rates, low short-term interest rates, relaxed standards for mortgage loans and irrational exuberance. Likewise, Gwartney *et al.* (2008) identify four factors leading to the housing bubble and credit crisis: (i) relaxed mortgage lending standards, (ii) low short-term interest rate policy of the Fed, (iii) increased leveraging by investment banks and (iv) increased debt-to-income ratio for households. Holt (2009) argues that low mortgage rates were maintained by capital inflows as foreign investors sought good deals (in terms of risk and return) in MBS. Initially, foreign investors focused on the MBS issued by Fannie Mae and Freddie Mac, but eventually they started investing in the MBS issued by Wall Street firms. Low mortgage interest rates contributed to the housing bubble by keeping monthly mortgage payments affordable for more buyers. Low short-term interest rates contributed to the housing bubble by encouraging the use of adjustable-rate mortgages (ARMs) and leveraging (investing with borrowed money). Low short-term interest rates make it attractive to boost return through leverage by investing in high-yield, presumably low-risk, assets such as MBS. When the housing bubble eventually burst and house prices fell, the impact of the crash of the housing market was aggravated by the degree of leverage in the economy.

In its 84th annual report, the Bank for International Settlements (BIS) warned that record low interest rates are generating conditions for another global financial crisis that may be worse than the first (BIS, 2014; Janda, 2014). In particular, the BIS expressed serious concern that global stock markets had reached new highs and that the interest rate premium for many risky loans had fallen. According to the BIS, "financial markets have been exuberant over the past year, at least in advanced economies, dancing mainly to the tune of central bank decisions" — this has led to "another run up in global debt, with private debt outside the banking sector now 30% bigger than it was before the financial crisis". Of more concern than the total size of the debt, the BIS argues, is where debt has gone as signs are emerging that risk is underpriced and finances being misdirected to speculative asset booms, which was exactly what happened in the run up to the global financial crisis.

The BIS argues against policies aimed at maintaining low interest rates, suggesting that a recent upturn in the global economy is "a precious window of opportunity that should not be wasted to start returning interest rates to more normal levels, while also putting other measures in place to temper booms".

It is plausible to suggest that QE may be intentionally designed to boost asset prices on the grounds that the resulting wealth effect will boost the economy. The underlying idea is that when the stock market goes up, people and businesses feel wealthier and consequently more inclined to spend, invest and take risks (in theory). Furthermore, the idea is that as balance sheets become more attractive in terms of the ratio of assets to liabilities, the underlying entities will be in a better position to borrow, invest and consume. Even indirectly, QE boosts asset prices because low interest rates push investors to seek higher returns in assets such as stocks and property, even junk bonds — in general, risky assets. Stock markets flourish as a result of low interest rates, which allow companies to borrow cheaply to buy back their shares and eventually raise dividends. Low rates also allow speculators to indulge in margin trading and leverage, betting on rising financial asset prices.

Let us now look at the facts and figures on interest rates, house prices and stock prices. In Figure 9.8, we observe US short-term and long-term interest rates over a long period of time. The rates include the federal funds rate, one-month Eurodollar rate, one-month Treasury bill rate and the 10-year Treasury bond yield. We can see very clearly that short-term and long-term interest rates are at historical lows and very stable. These conditions encourage the accumulation of leverage and the assumption of risk. In Figure 9.9, we observe US interest rates since January 2000, just to demonstrate that low interest rates led to the 2007–2008 crisis and that they are likely to lead to the next crisis.

From 2002 to 2004 the Federal Reserve pushed the federal funds rate down to historically low levels in an attempt to strengthen the recovery following the 2001 recession. The US economy plunged into a recession in March 2001, to which the Fed reacted by reducing the federal funds rate 11 times, from 6.50% to 1.75%. When the economic

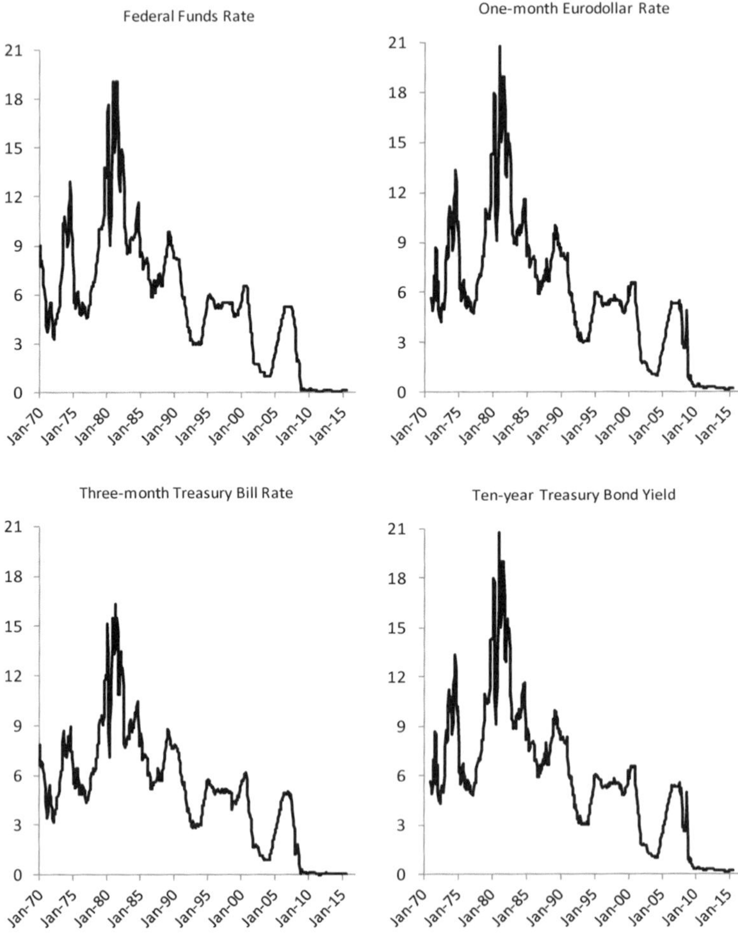

Figure 9.8:   US Interest Rates Since 1970

recovery proved sluggish and no sign of significant inflation appeared, the Fed continued its low interest rate policy, reducing the federal funds rate further to 1.25% in November 2002 and to 1% in June 2003. The Fed began to push the rate upward in June 2004, but it remained at 2% or lower for more than three years. Between 2004 and 2006, the Fed raised the federal funds rate 17 times, and by 2006 the rate had moved up to 5.25%, which reduced the demand for housing and raised the level of monthly payments for ARMs.

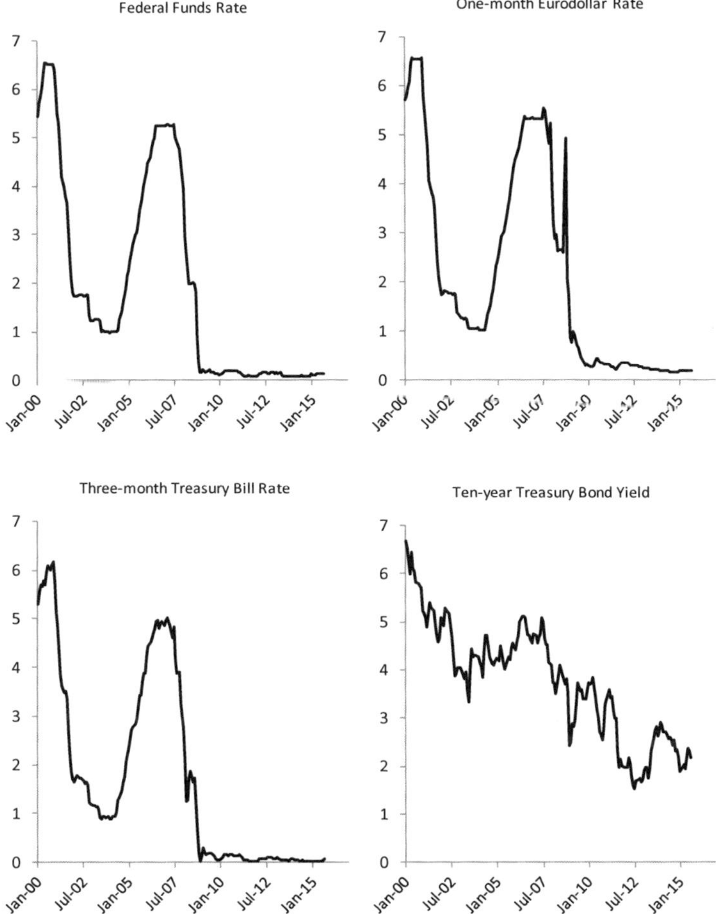

Figure 9.9:   US Interest Rates Since 2000

Rising interest rates and monthly mortgage payments caused massive defaults. The resulting foreclosures led to an increase in supply, and consequently to lower house prices. In Figure 9.10, we observe the rise and fall in house prices prior to and following the global financial crisis. In both nominal and real terms, house prices reached a historical high prior to the advent of the crisis then collapsed. In Figure 9.11, we observe house prices during the period January 2000 to September 2015, with a trend superimposed

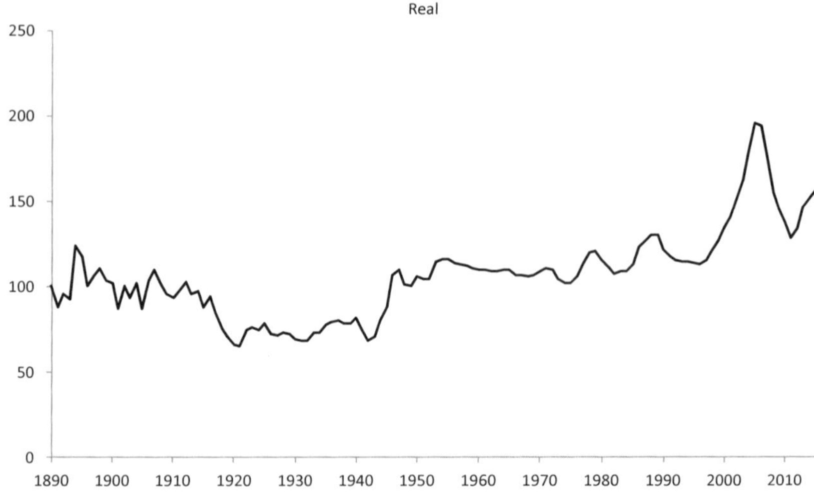

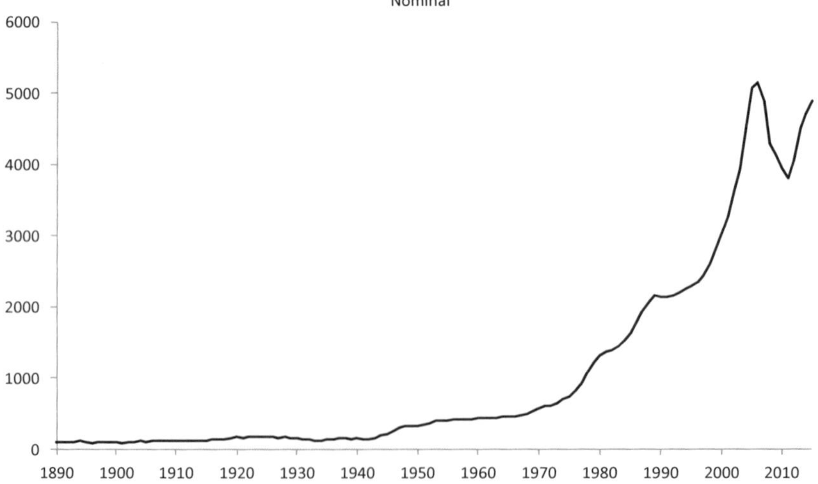

Figure 9.10:   Historical US House Prices (1890–2015)

on the graph. The rebound in house prices coincides with quantitative easing and low interest rates. The trend indicates that house prices are heading toward the pre-crisis peak — it is not that far away, anyway.

The same story can be told about stock prices as we can see in Figure 9.12, which shows that the increase in stock prices coincided

Figure 9.11: Monthly US House Prices (January 2000–April 2015)

with quantitative easing and that stock prices started to decline when QE came to an end toward the end of 2014. While this observation cannot be a mere coincidence, the decline in stock prices in 2015 cannot be attributed only to the end of QE. Negative sentiment emerged as a result of bad economic news out of China, which played a central role in the extraordinarily poor performance of companies like Apple that relies to a significant extent on Chinese customers for growth. Since bottoming out in the spring of 2009, the US stock market has enjoyed an excellent run (propelled by QE), dented by some hiccups centered mainly on sporadic political crises. But interest rates are still very low, which will provide support for the stock market because they make it possible for companies to borrow money cheaply in order to spend on share-boosting strategies like higher dividends or companies buying their own stock.

There is also the possibility that the Fed may resume QE by initiating stage four, or QE4, if it is felt that the economy is still not

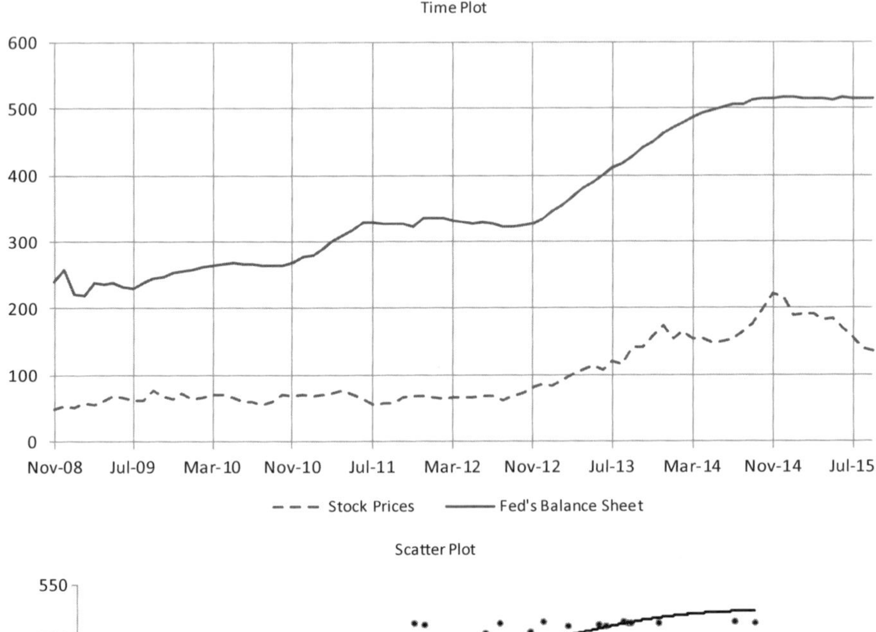

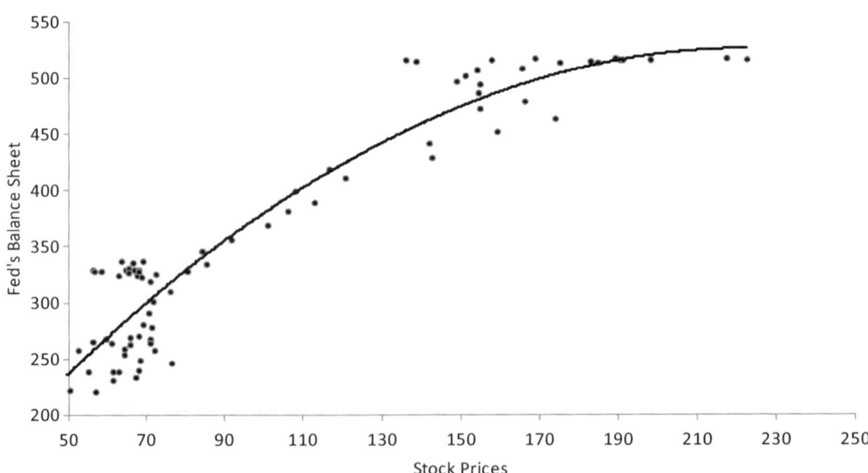

Figure 9.12: US Stock Prices and the Fed's Balance Sheet (July 2007 = 100)

strong enough and that there is a possibility of dipping into recession again. For example, Cox (2015) quotes Peter Schiff, head of Euro Pacific Capital and a well-known Fed critic, as saying that "the Fed is not going to raise rates", that "the Fed is not done with QE, they're just getting started", and that "the Fed is doing QE4,

QE5", which is a "never-ending process". El-Erian (2015) entertains the possibility of the Fed embarking on QE4 by considering why the previous episodes of QE came into being. This is what he says about QE1, QE2 and QE3:

> The first round, QE1, during the global financial crisis, was aimed at repairing a highly dysfunctional financial intermediation system. QE2, in 2010, was intended to stimulate economic activity. The Fed resorted to additional stimulus, including its QE3 program, as the economy then languished in a low growth, "new normal" equilibrium.

He then contends that the effect of QE has been reflected mostly on asset prices, from which he contemplates the possibility of QE4. This is what he says:

> Despite a few hiccups and disappointing economic growth, this string of so-called unconventional monetary measures succeeded in lifting asset prices and kept market volatility in check, turning central banks into close allies of the markets. It was to be expected that the recent vertiginous plunge in equities and other risky assets, along with a spike in volatility, would lead to predictions that a new set of measures was in the offing.

Despite these propositions, El-Erian presents four reasons why the Fed will not resume QE any time soon: (i) the Fed now wants to normalize monetary policy, and not venture even deeper into uncharted territory; (ii) QE has not proved as effective as expected in stimulating high and sustainable growth; (iii) the origin of the financial market dislocation is outside the US this time (mainly China) and (iv) having exited QE3 in a relatively orderly fashion, the Fed would be hesitant to place itself in the same position again. He concludes that "it's premature to expect the Fed to come to the rescue of the markets via a QE4".

Peter Schiff disagrees with the view that China caused the plunge in US stock prices, attributing it to declarations that the Fed intended to raise interest rates (McGuire, 2015). He predicts that "not only won't the central bank officials raise rates, they will actually launch a fourth round of quantitative easing to re-inflate the stock market bubble". This is what he says about the course of action that is likely to be followed by the Fed:

> The Fed's going to call off the rate hike. In fact, I don't think they ever planned on raising rates. The whole thing was a bluff. The markets just haven't figured that out yet … And in fact, the Fed plans something even more sinister, and dangerous…. The Fed is going to come back with QE4. It's going to hurt the real economy just like QE3, 2 and 1 did but it is going to blow some air back into the stock market bubble.

Most observers believe that the Fed will resume QE sooner or later. To the surprise of these observes the Fed decided to raise interest rates in December 2015 and declared that a gradual rise would follow with four more hikes in 2016. Financial markets reacted positively because this action indicated that the US economy was improving. However, the level of interest rates is and will be extremely low by historical standards. It is expected the federal funds rate will be at about 1.375% by the end of 2016, up from its current range of 0.25–0.50%, but then recall that the last crisis was caused by a decision to raise interest rates following a long period of low rates.

12. Conclusion

Quantitative easing was initiated by the Fed and other central banks in an attempt to revive the economy in the aftermath of the global financial crisis. Central bankers seem to forget that "you can take the horse to the water but you cannot force it to drink". Low interest rates do not necessarily lead to more borrowing and more spending. Furthermore, there is every indication now that people with money in banks are willing to earn nothing or even negative (nominal) returns on their deposits because the alternative is unclear and less appealing. Then it does not make any sense to initiate a policy with the objective of making banks more willing and able to grant credit while at the same time providing a disincentive for banks to do so by paying them interest on reserves. It is for this reason that the rebound in economic activity may be unrelated to QE. In fact the economy should have done much better given the amount of money that has been created by QE.

While the inflationary effect of QE has not materialized yet in terms of the prices of goods and services, some observers believe that inflation is already manifested in asset prices. Indeed it could be that QE is intended to boost economic activity not through the effect of low interest rates on consumption and investment, but rather through the wealth effect emanating from rising asset prices. Thus, it could be that an asset price bubble is what the Fed aims for, although this does not make much sense. The wealth effect will be limited to asset holders who typically have a low marginal propensity to consume, in which case the effect on economic activity will not materialize. On the other hand, an asset price bubble is bound to burst and a crash will ensue. If low interest rates caused the crisis of 2007–2008, the current ultra-low interest rates will cause the next crisis. It seems therefore that the regulatory measures that have been taken since 2008 to prevent the recurrence of a crisis on the same scale as the last one will be undermined by QE. It does not make any sense to legislate regulation to avoid financial crises while at the same time creating an environment that is bound to lead to a crisis.

Chapter 10

Financial Reform in Iceland

1. Introduction

Relative to the size of its economy (with a population of just 300,000) the financial collapse of Iceland, which was caused by a switch from fishing to finance, was more significant than any other similar experience. As it is typically the case, the financial crisis led to a severe economic downturn in the period 2008–2011 as well as political unrest. The crisis was the result of excessive financialization and the adoption of free market policies, which created the right environment for bankers to pursue greed-driven self-interest. In general, it is recognized that three main factors caused the crisis: (i) appreciating currency and high interest rate differentials against other countries, which brought about foreign capital attracted by carry trade; (ii) heavy borrowing (by both commercial banks and non-financial companies) from international markets, further boosting capital flows into Iceland and (iii) expansion of the off-shore balance sheets of Icelandic commercial banks. In particular, the three largest banks managed to inflate their balance sheets with ease, given the high rating awarded to them by the credit rating agencies (CRAs). It was a bubble that eventually burst. On this occasion, like any similar occasion, pursuing self-interest (by bankers) did not produce benefits for the public at large — on the contrary, everyone was slapped by Adam Smith's "invisible hand".

On the bright side, the Icelandic bitter experience has produced useful lessons for all. The first lesson is that financial *laissez faire* leads to hubristic behavior that produces disastrous outcomes, which means that bankers should be kept on a short leash. When Icelandic bankers were allowed to do as they pleased, in the name of the free market, Iceland's three largest banks, (Kaupthing, Landsbanki and Glitnir) expanded exponentially. At the end of the second quarter of 2008, the total assets of the three banks stood at 14.437 trillion Icelandic kronas (ISK), about 11 times the country's gross domestic product (GDP). The second lesson is that government intervention and regulation do work, as the economy and financial system have been stabilized by extreme and painful policy measures. Iceland has learned this lesson the hard way, and this is why the Icelandic government is embarking on a financial reform program that aims at depriving bankers from the ability to create money. The third lesson is that no matter how big a financial institution, it can be allowed to fail, thus busting the myth of too big to fail (TBTF). Unlike most of the countries that are effectively run by the financial elite, the Icelandic government has shown courage by prosecuting those who contributed to the creation of the crisis (in other countries, the culprits were rewarded with fat bonuses and extravagant golden parachutes). Thus, the fourth lesson is that the financial oligarchs should not be rewarded for failure and prosecuted if necessary.

2. Causes and Consequences of the Icelandic Crisis

In 2001, the government of Iceland declared war on regulation, thereby sowing the seeds of the crisis. From then on it was all about financial hubris — everyone was dancing while the music was playing, as Chuck Prince (a former CEO of Citigroup) said once.[1] As a result, and given that Iceland has a small domestic market, banks started to accumulate debt, financing their expansion by

---

[1] http://dealbook.nytimes.com/2007/07/10/citi-chief-on-buyout-loans-were-still-dancing/?_r=0.

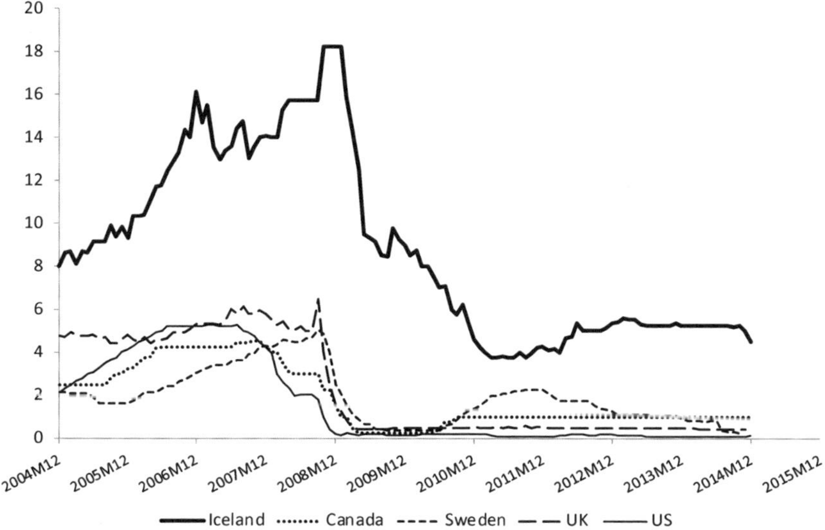

Figure 10.1:   Money Market Interest Rates

borrowing from the interbank market and by attracting deposits from outside Iceland. Households also took on large amounts of debt, equivalent to 213% of disposable income. The situation was exacerbated by the central bank, which provided liquidity to banks on the basis of newly issued, uncovered bonds, which effectively boils down to printing money on demand. Furthermore, the Central Bank of Iceland kept interest rates high, encouraging foreign investors to hold deposits in ISK with banks located in Iceland and their foreign branches in Europe. In Figure 10.1, we can see that the money market rate in Iceland was much higher than in other countries, which caused capital flows into the ISK, as investors rushed to take advantage of the interest rate differential. A bubble was created as investors overestimated the true value of the krona. At one time the three major banks held foreign debt in excess of €50 billion, or about €160,000 per Icelandic resident, compared with Iceland's gross domestic product of €8.5 billion.

When the global financial crisis erupted, Icelandic banks (like banks around the world) found it increasingly difficult or impossible to roll over their loans in the interbank market as their creditors insisted on payment while other banks were not willing to provide fresh loans. Investors started to perceive Icelandic banks to be risky, and as trust in banks faded gradually, the ISK depreciated sharply in 2008, further weakening the ability of banks to roll over short-term debt. In Figure 10.2, we observe the depreciation of the

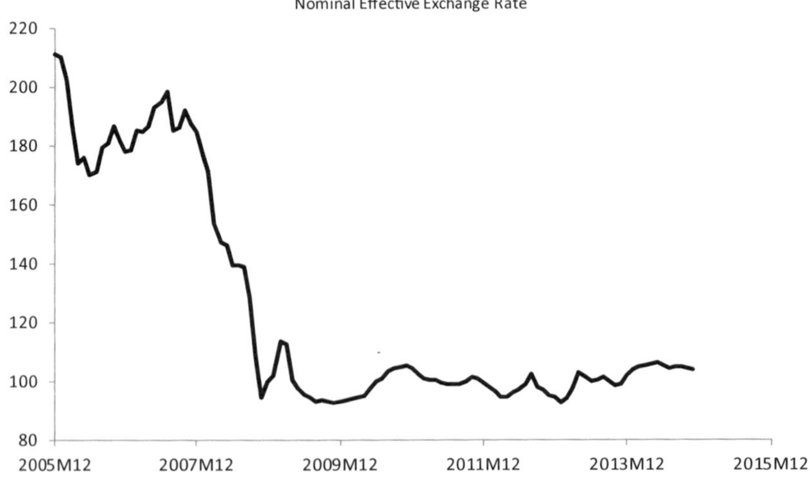

Figure 10.2: The Rise and Fall of the Icelandic Krona

krona, both against the US dollar and in effective terms. In such a situation, a bank would normally request a loan from the central bank as the lender of last resort. However, because Icelandic banks were so much larger than the national economy, the Central Bank of Iceland and the Icelandic government could not guarantee the payment of banks' debt, leading to a banking collapse. Mistrust in the banking system was further aggravated by the inability of the Central Bank of Iceland to act as a lender of last resort. The stock market collapsed as we can see in Figure 10.3.

Efforts to restore faith in the banking system failed. On 6 October 2008, a number of private interbank credit facilities to Icelandic banks were shut down. Prime Minister Geir Haarde addressed the nation, and announced a package of new regulatory measures that were to be put to the Althing (Iceland's parliament) immediately, with the co-operation of the opposition parties. These measures allowed the Financial Supervisory Authority (FSA) to take over the running of Icelandic banks without nationalizing them. At the same time, retail deposits in Icelandic branches of Icelandic banks were guaranteed in full. In Figure 10.4, we can see the collapse of the Icelandic financial sector and economy in terms

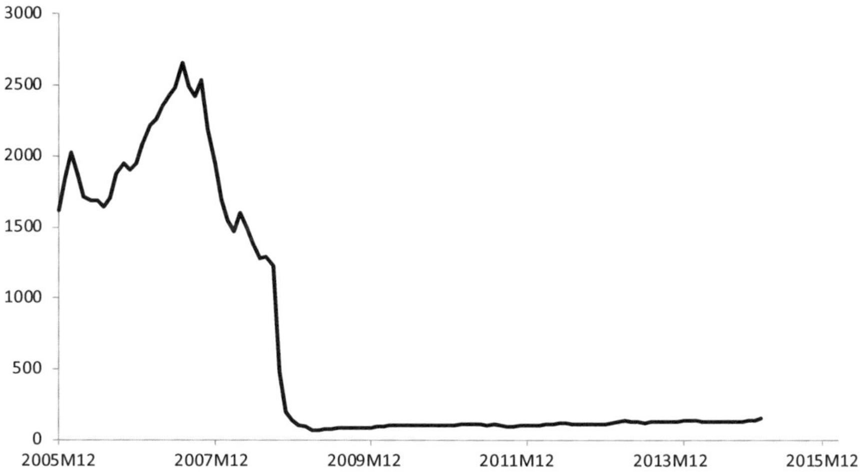

Figure 10.3:   The Collapse of Icelandic Stock Prices

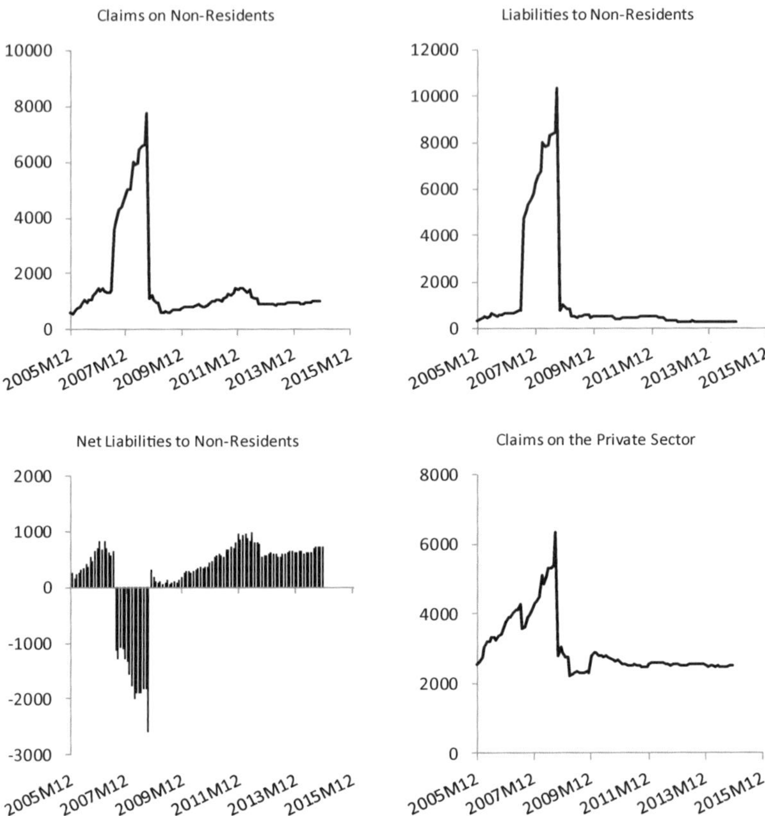

Figure 10.4:   The Collapse of Icelandic Depository Institutions

of claims on non-residents, liabilities to non-residents, net liabilities to non-residents and claims on the private sector.

As part of the regulatory response to the financial crisis, new banks were founded to take over the domestic operations of the big three, Kaupthing, Landsbanki and Glitni. As they were put into receivership and liquidation, shareholders and foreign creditors endured huge losses. Outside Iceland, more than half a million depositors lost access to their accounts in the foreign branches of Icelandic banks. In an effort to stabilize the situation, the Icelandic government stated that all domestic deposits in Icelandic banks would be guaranteed, imposed strict capital controls to stabilize the value of the Icelandic currency and secured a sovereign debt package from the International Monetary Fund (IMF) and Nordic countries consisting of an IMF loan of $2.1 billion as well as $2.5 billion of loans and currency swaps from Norway, Sweden, Finland and Denmark (the deal was agreed upon on 19 November).

The FSA placed Landsbanki into receivership on 7 October 2008. On 9 October, Kaupthing was placed into receivership, following the resignation of the entire board of directors. The bank said that it was in technical default on its loan agreements after its UK subsidiary had been placed into administration. Kaupthing's Luxembourg subsidiary asked for, and obtained, a suspension of payments (similar to Chapter 11 protection) in the Luxembourg District Court. Kaupthing's Geneva office, which was a branch of its Luxembourg subsidiary, was prevented from making any payments of more than 5,000 Swiss francs by the Swiss Federal Banking Commission. The directors of Kaupthing's subsidiary on the Isle of Man decided to wind up the company. The Finnish Financial Supervision Authority took control of Kaupthing's Helsinki branch to prevent money from being sent back to Iceland.

The financial crisis had a serious negative impact on the Icelandic economy, which experienced severe economic downturn. The national currency depreciated sharply and the capitalization of the Icelandic stock exchange fell by more than 90%. Trading in the stocks of six financial companies on the OMX Nordic Iceland Exchange was suspended on 6 October 2008 by order of the FSA. On 9 October, trading was frozen for two days to prevent further panic spreading throughout the country's financial markets. The market reopened on 14 October with the main index, the OMX Iceland 15, at 678.4, which corresponds to a plunge of about 77% compared with 3,004.6 before the closure. This reflects the fact that the value of the three big banks, which form 73.2% of the value of the OMX Iceland 15, had been set to zero.

Over £840 million in cash from more than 100 UK local authorities was invested in Icelandic banks (BBC, 2008). Of all the local authorities, Kent County Council had the most money invested in Icelandic banks, about £50 million. Transport for London, the organization that operates and coordinates transport services in London, had an investment of £40 million. Local authorities had been working under government advice to invest their money across many national and international banks as a way of spreading risk. Other UK entities that invested heavily in Icelandic currency deposits include police services and fire authorities, and even the Audit Commission. On 11 October 2008, an agreement was reached between the Icelandic and Dutch governments on the savings of about 120,000 Dutch citizens. According to the agreement, the Icelandic government covered the first €20,887 on the savings accounts of Dutch citizens held by a subsidiary of Landsbanki, Icesave, using money lent by the Dutch government. The total value of Icesave deposits in the Netherlands was €1.7 billion. At the same time, Iceland and the UK reached an agreement on the general contours of a solution regarding the Icesave deposits in the UK amounting to £4 billion in 300,000 accounts.[2]

Conditions deteriorated to the extent that on 27 February 2009, the *Wall Street Journal* reported that Iceland's new government was trying to raise $25 million by selling its ambassadorial residences in Washington, New York, London and Oslo (Lewis, 2009). On 28 August 2009 Iceland's parliament voted 34-15 (with 14 abstentions) to approve a bill (commonly referred to as the Icesave bill) to pay the UK and the Netherlands more than $5 billion lost in Icelandic deposit accounts. Initially opposed in June, the bill was passed after amendments were added to set a ceiling on the payment based on the country's gross domestic product. Opponents of the bill argued that Icelanders, already reeling from the crisis, should not have to pay for mistakes made by private banks under the watch of other governments. However, the government argued that if the bill failed to pass, the UK and the Netherlands might

---

[2] On 9 October 2008, the British Chancellor of the Exchequer, Alistair Darling, took an unprecedented measure by invoking anti-terrorism laws to freeze the British assets of the collapsed Icelandic bank, Landsbanki Islands. This action was taken to protect the deposit savings of UK residents who had invested in the bank's online savings branch, Icesave. This is yet another example of how the words "terrorist" and "terrorism" can be stretched to serve certain purposes.

retaliate by blocking a planned aid package for Iceland from the International Monetary Fund. Under the deal, up to 4% of Iceland's GDP would be paid to the UK from 2017–2023 while the Netherlands would receive up to 2% of Iceland's GDP over the same period (Valdimarsson, 2009). Talks between Icelandic, Dutch and UK ministers in January 2010 did not result in any agreement on specific actions (Nicholson, 2010).

On 23 January 2009, Prime Minister Geir Haarde announced that he would be stepping down as leader of the Independence Party for health reasons. Björgvin Sigurðsson, Iceland's Commerce Minister, resigned on 25 January 2009, citing the pressures of the economic collapse, as political leaders failed to agree on how to lead the country out of its financial crisis. One of his last acts as minister was to dismiss the director of the FSA. He acknowledged that "Icelanders have lost faith in their government and political system" and declared that he wanted to shoulder his part of the responsibility for that (Stringer, 2010).

Iceland elected a new government in April 2013, which wanted, as a top priority, to negotiate a debt haircut toward foreign creditors of the three failed Icelandic banks as part of a deal to lift the capital controls that were put in place in November 2008 (Financial Times, 2013). The current capital controls ban a swap/exchange of ISK denominated assets to foreign currency, effectively trapping repayment of ISK denominated assets to creditors — this in theory means that they (creditors) should be willing to accept a haircut in return for getting the capital controls lifted (Valdimarsson, 2013). The Icelandic government wanted to route the saved money from the negotiated debt haircut for creditors into a national household debt relief fund, enabling a 20% debt relief for all household mortgages.

3. Official Investigation into Fraud and Corruption

On 12 December 2008, the Icelandic parliament established a Special Investigation Commission (SIC) to look into the causes and lessons of the crisis. The Office of the Special Prosecutor was founded with the passage of a bill in parliament on 10 December 2008.[3] The aim was to investigate suspected criminal conduct pertaining to the banking crisis and to follow up these investigations by bringing charges in court against those concerned. In April 2009, Iceland's state prosecutor hired Eva Joly, the Norwegian-French investigator to investigate suspicions of criminal actions in the period preceding the collapse of the Icelandic banks (Hauksson, 2009). By September 2013, the top managers of all three Icelandic banks that collapsed during the financial crisis had been charged.

The investigation focused on a number of questionable financial practices that Icelandic banks engage in. For example, almost half of the loans made by Icelandic banks were granted to holding companies, many of which were connected with the same banks. Money was allegedly lent by the banks to their employees and associates so that they could buy shares in the same banks while using those same shares as collateral for the loans. Borrowers were then allowed to defer paying interest on the loans until the end of the period, when the whole amount plus the interest accrued was due. The same loans were then allegedly written off days before the banks collapsed. Kaupthing allowed a Qatari investor to purchase 5% of its shares. It was later revealed that the Qatari investor bought those shares using a loan from Kaupthing itself and a holding company associated with one of its employees (in effect, the bank was buying its own shares) (Mason, 2009; Faris, 2013).

Those who were prosecuted (and some of whom were acquitted) include Aron Karlsson (a businessman), Baldur Guðlaugsson (permanent secretary of the Ministry of Finance), Bjarni Ármannsson (President of Glitnir), Friðfinnur Ragnar Sigurðsson (Managing Director of Markets of Glitnir), Guðmundur Hjaltason (Managing Director of Corporate Banking of Glitnir), Hannes Smárason (Chairman and President of FL Group), Hreiðar Már Sigurðsson (President of Kaupthing Bank), Jón Þorsteinn Jónsson (Chairman of Byr Savings Bank), Lárus Welding, (CEO of Glitnir), Lýður Guðmundsson (Chairman of Exista), Magnús Guðmundsson,

---

[3] http://www.serstakursaksoknari.is/english/special-prosecutor/.

(President of Kaupthing Bank in Luxembourg), Ólafur Ólafsson (Shareholder of Kaupthing Bank), Ragnar Zophonías Guðjónsson (President of Byr Savings Bank), Sigurður Einarsson, (Chairman of Kaupthing Bank), Sigurjón Árnason (President of Landsbanki), Steinþór Gunnarsson (Managing Director of Brokerage of Landsbanki), and Styrmir Bragason (President of MP Bank).[4] In London and New York, the counterparts of these people got rewarded for a "job well done under conditions beyond anyone's control". The Icelandic authorities have shown extraordinary bravery by putting offending financial and business oligarchs where they belong: behind bars.

Apart from the prosecutions, those who were once regarded as heroes became villains. The financial gurus once credited for developing Iceland's economy were exposed to intense public scrutiny for their roles in causing the financial crisis. This is how Mason (2009) describes the situation:

> Iceland's super-rich were once heroes — entrepreneurs who gave the small country a sense of pride as they embarked on raiding missions buying up businesses in the UK and across continental Europe. But the collapse of Iceland's banking system and currency has rocked the small country. Thousands of Icelanders have lost their life savings, unemployment has hit 9% and interest rates have risen as high as 18%. Demonstrations have toppled the government and central bank chief. Six months after the country's three largest banks — Glitnir, Landsbanki and Kaupthing — were seized by the government, the entire Icelandic financial community is now under official scrutiny and its former heroes are facing tough questions.

The heroes-turned-villians include Jón Ásgeir Jóhannesson and Jóhannes Jónsson, the owners of the Baugur Group retail empire, which includes Hamleys, House of Fraser, the Oasis Centre and a large portion of Iceland's media. Jón Ásgeir, who had been known as the "popstar businessman" due to his shaggy golden mullet, has become the subject of a satirical video on YouTube set to the theme

---

[4] https://en.wikipedia.org/wiki/2008%E2%80%9311_Icelandic_financial_crisis.

of the movie The Godfather. In addition, a former mistress later revealed details of his "playboy lifestyle" during a trial that found him guilty of false accounting (which prompted the Baugur Group to relocate to the UK).

4. Crisis Resolution and Recovery

Several factors played a role in the recovery from the crisis. The emergency legislation passed by the Icelandic parliament in October 2008 served to minimize the impact of the financial crisis on the domestic economy. Another factor is painful austerity measures and significant tax hikes that resulted in the stabilization of central government debt at around 80–90% of GDP. Yet another factor is the resurrection of a viable but sharply downsized domestic banking system on the ruins of the banking system that the government was unable to bailout.[5] The enactment of capital controls also played a role. According to the IMF (2015), the capital controls introduced in 2008 were critical for avoiding a more severe collapse of the Icelandic economy. While capital inflows have been liberalized, most outflows remain restricted. What might also have helped was the decision to apply for membership in the EU in July 2009, which might have enhanced the credibility of the country on international financial markets.

One sign of the success of the measures taken by the Icelandic government to stabilize the economy is that the government was successfully able to raise $1 billion with a bond issue launched on 9 June 2011. This development indicates that international investors have given the government and the new banking system a clean bill of health (Institutional Investor, 2011; Jonsson, 2011). By mid-2012 Iceland was regarded as a recovery success story as the economy experienced two years of growth. Unemployment was down to 6.3% as the country was attracting immigrants to fill jobs. Currency

---

[5] This observation provides evidence for the proposition that a large banking sector (or a large financial sector in general) can be detrimental to economic stability. Excessive financialization of the economy is another form of the Dutch Disease.

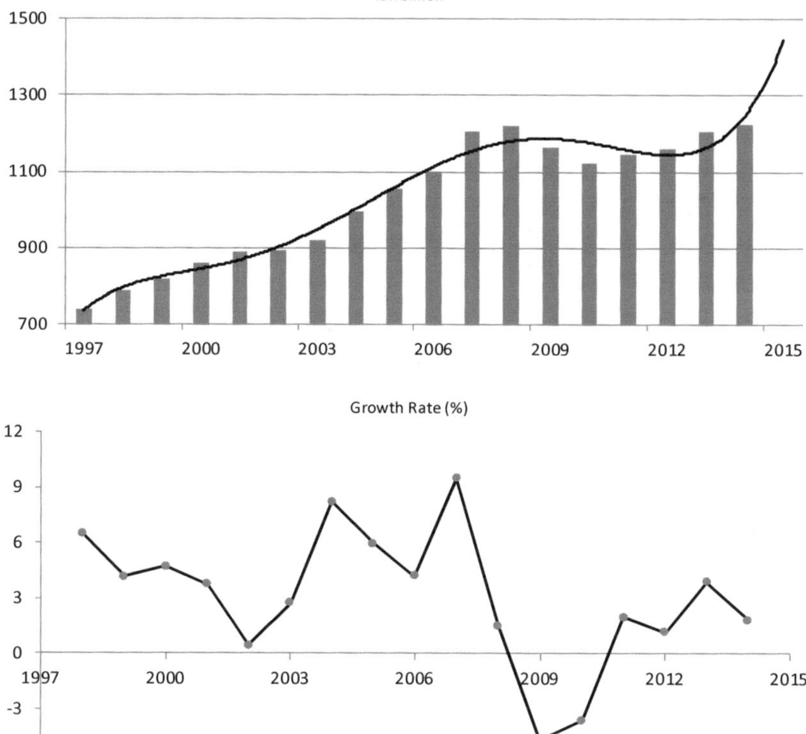

Figure 10.5:   Iceland's GDP (Chain Volume Measure, Seasonally Adjusted)

depreciation effectively reduced wages by 50%, making exports more competitive and imports more expensive. 10-year government bonds were issued below 6%, lower than some of the PIIGS countries (Portugal, Italy, Ireland, Greece and Spain).

The real economy has certainly recovered. Following negative growth in 2009 and 2010, the Icelandic economy grew at an average annual compound rate of 2.2% during the period 2011–2014, exceeding growth in the euro area crisis economies and the Organisation for Economic Co-operation and Development (OECD) average. Figure 10.5 shows the level and growth rate of real GDP in terms of the chain volume measure where the upward trend is conspicuous. The IMF (2015) expects economic activity to be on the way to surpass

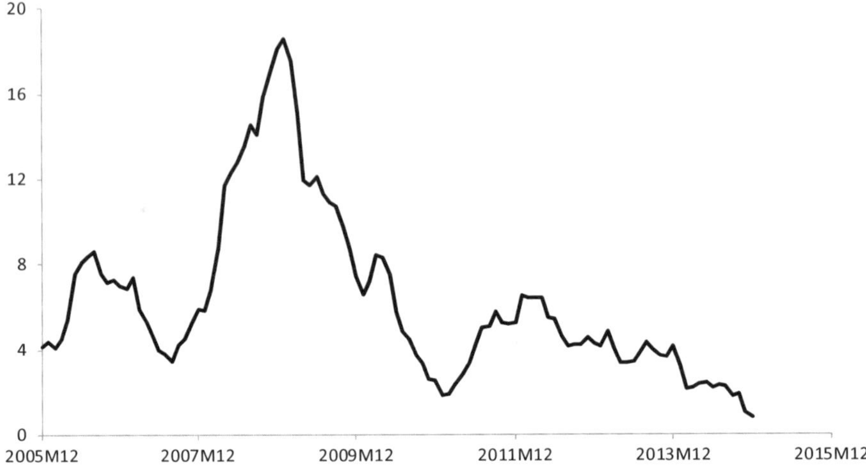

Figure 10.6:   Iceland's CPI Annual Inflation Rate (%)

pre-crisis levels in 2015. However, the recovery has not been costless. Despite recent growth, private consumption remains subdued. Credit growth to businesses is weak and business investment has just started to show signs of revival. Public investment has suffered amid ongoing fiscal consolidation and, with debt reduction a medium-term objective, it is unlikely to recover soon. All in all, domestic demand remains below its historical average (IMF, 2015). The inflation rate has fallen to a level within the target range of the Central Bank of Iceland, helped by an appreciating currency. Inflation started to accelerate toward the end of 2007, reaching a peak of 18.6% in January 2009, as a result of excessive credit (and therefore monetary) expansion, given the ability of banks to create money under a fractional reserve banking system. In Figure 10.6, we observe the annual inflation rate measured as the percentage change in the consumer price index (CPI) over the same month of the previous year. In Figure 10.7, we observe the expansion in credit to households, which peaked in the third quarter of 2008. However, household indebtedness remains at a high level.

The external balance is showing some improvement, both in terms of the current account, which has already shifted into surplus, and the net international investment position (NIIP), as

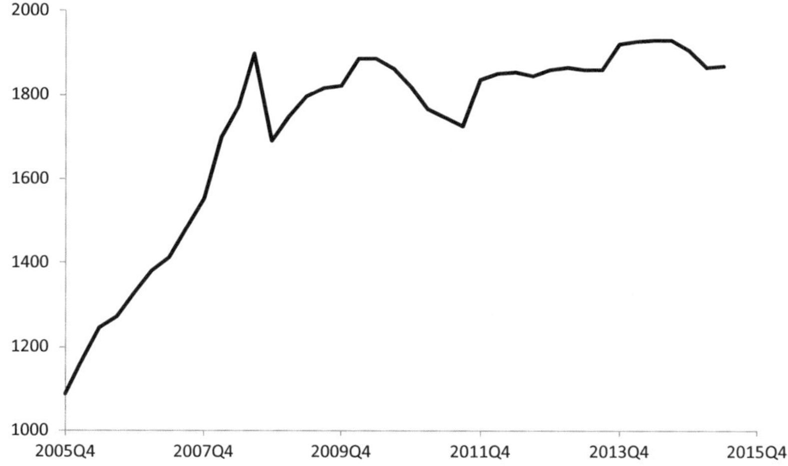

Figure 10.7:   Credit to Households (ISK billion)

shown in Figure 10.8. Improvement in the current account is attributed by the IMF (2015) "not only to cyclical factors but also to an improvement in price competitiveness and a structural growth in tourism". It is also due to improvement in the saving-investment balance as saving has recovered.[6] The crisis has brought significant adjustments in external assets and liabilities not explained by the current account. This is attributed by the IMF (2015) to valuation changes and debt restructuring resulting from extensive bankruptcies. As a result, Iceland's overall NIIP has improved significantly. According to the IMF (2015), Iceland's NIIP as a percentage of GDP is currently lower than that of its Nordic peers and most other OECD economies, but in line with some advanced economies such as the Czech Republic. However, external vulnerabilities remain significant as external debt is still high while external reserve buffers are low.

A rapid improvement in the fiscal balance (Figure 10.9) has contributed to a reduction in public debt. The general government

---

[6] According to the IMF (2015), the saving rate dropped to its lowest level in 2008 but started rising the following year, reaching 20% of GDP in 2013.

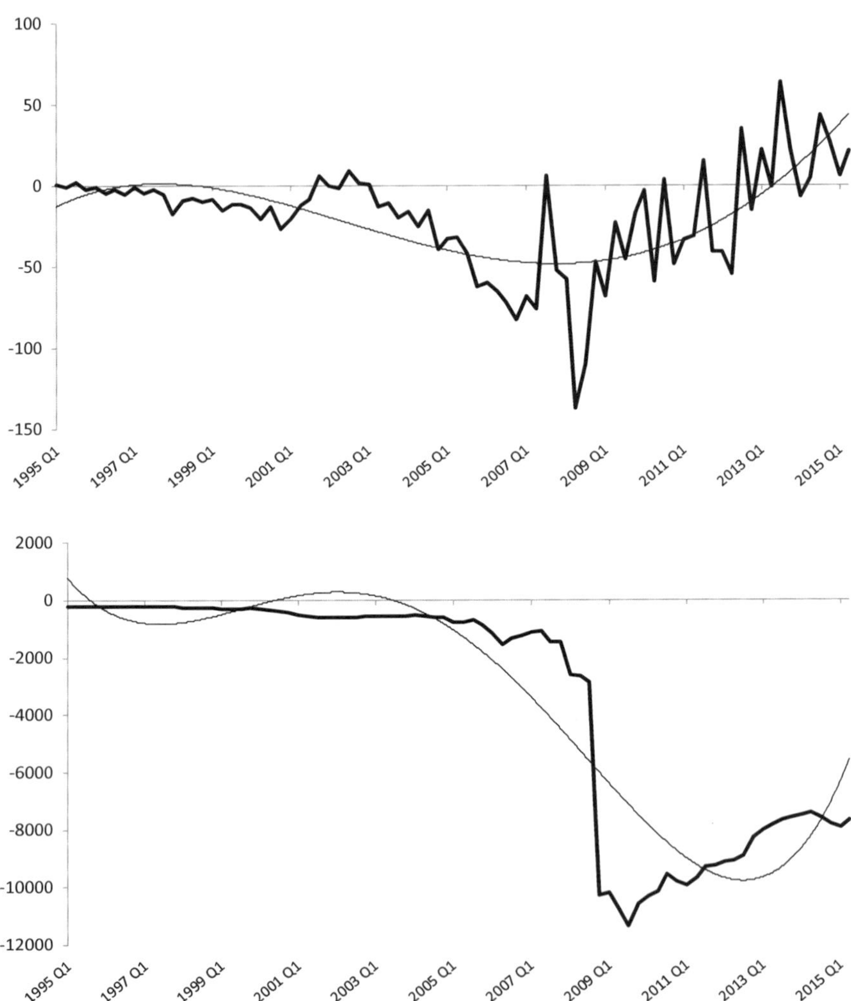

Figure 10.8:   Iceland's Current Account and NIIP (ISK billion)

deficit has approached zero from a post-crisis high of about 10% of GDP. As a result, debt was down to 86% of GDP at the end of 2013 from its peak of 95% of GDP. The composition of debt is relatively good: less than a third of total debt is denominated in foreign currency, less than 20% is linked to inflation, the average duration is over four years, and only 15% involves floating interest rates.

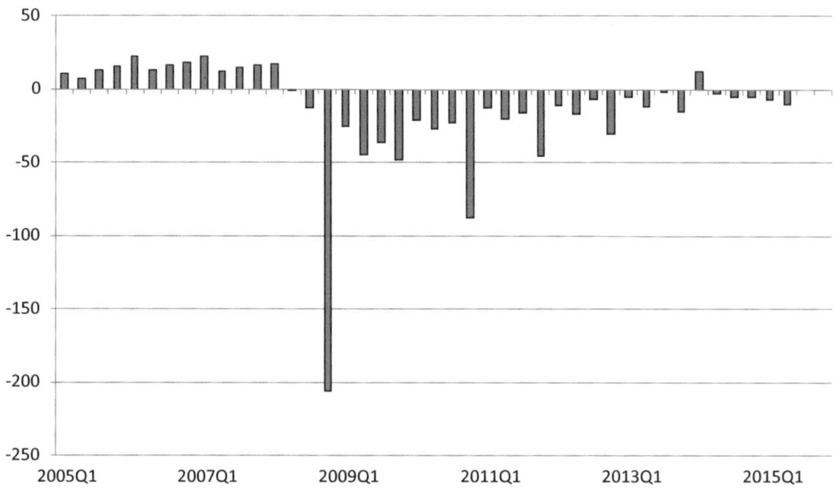

Figure 10.9: Iceland's Fiscal Deficit (ISK billion)

Net debt fell to around 63% of GDP by the end of 2013, the difference from gross debt largely reflecting borrowing for reserve purposes deposited at the central bank. Yet, according to the IMF (2015), "fiscal vulnerabilities remain elevated in comparison to Iceland's recent past and to peers" because the government is starting with less fiscal space than before the crisis (total debt stood at 27% of GDP in 2007 compared to 86% in 2013).

Improvements are also witnessed on the financial side of the economy as deleveraging has led to improvement in household and corporate balance sheets. According to the IMF (2015) several rounds of debt restructuring have led to a decline in household debt to 101% of GDP at the end of 2013 from 122% at the end of 2009. Corporate balance sheets have also improved, as total debt dropped from 290% of GDP at the end of 2009 to 131% at the end of 2013. However, the IMF (2015) warns that debt remains high, raising the potential impact of negative income and wealth shocks on domestic demand. Currently, corporate and household debt levels are comparable to those of other Nordic countries but they are high relative to other European countries, including the crisis countries (such as Greece). Banks' balance sheets are stronger as the capital adequacy and Tier 1 ratios have risen to reach 26% and 24%, respectively, at the end of 2013, compared to 16% and 15%, respectively, in 2009. Improvement is also observed in loan defaults, net foreign exchange positions and liquidity ratios. Yet, the IMF (2015) warns, "vulnerabilities to both sides of the balance sheet are high", as asset quality can deteriorate rapidly in the event of a shock to unemployment and inflation while, on the liabilities side, funding relies highly on short-term deposits.

On 8 June 2015, the Icelandic government announced that it would lift capital controls, with "one big caveat" (*The Economist*, 2015d). Investors holding Icelandic assets will be free to move in and out of these assets and Icelanders will be free to buy foreign currencies, but those who are owed money by the estates of the failed banks must agree to haircuts and maturity extensions. In August 2015, the Icelandic Ministry of Finance and Economic Affairs announced a "comprehensive strategy for capital account liberalisation". The government has agreed to present before parliament two bills of legislation to lay the foundation for a comprehensive strategy for capital account liberalization. This is what the announcement said (Ministry of Finance and Economic Affairs, 2015):

> The public interest demands that the capital controls be lifted without jeopardising economic and financial stability. The objectives of the current liberalization strategy are based on the fundamental principal [*sic*] that the controls must be lifted in stages without upsetting the balance in the economy and without imposing additional financial burdens on the Treasury or the Icelandic people.

Capital controls were introduced via the "Rules on Foreign Exchange Act" on 28 November 2008 to regain domestic economic and financial stability following the collapse of the banking sector. The restrictions on capital account transactions have been modified several times since 2008. The prohibition on two-way capital flows related to trade in goods and services was lifted almost immediately in November 2008. In October 2009, controls on foreign capital inflows were lifted, allowing foreign and domestic investors to import foreign capital to invest in Iceland, with full freedom to repatriate capital and earnings. Capital account liberalization is likely to proceed in three stages: (i) reducing and extending the maturity of non-resident net claims on domestic assets, (ii) dealing with the principal and interest associated with non-resident-owned, ISK-denominated bonds that matured after the imposition of capital controls and whose proceeds could not be repatriated and (iii) a gradual release of capital controls on Icelandic residents.

The remarkable recovery of the Icelandic economy from the 2008 crisis is seen by many observers as a success story. In an interview with the *IMF Survey*, Peter Dohlman, IMF Mission Chief for Iceland, explained what sets Iceland apart from other countries having experienced the financial crisis (Hammar, 2015). According to Dohlman, "macroeconomic conditions in Iceland are now at their best since the 2008/2009 crisis" and "Iceland has been one of the top economic performers in Europe over the past several years in terms of economic growth". Dohlman attributes the recovery in part to sound policies, including the quick restoration of the domestic banking system and the measures taken to facilitate domestic debt restructuring. Furthermore, steady fiscal adjustment was put in place, while central bank policies helped steer inflation close to target as capital controls provided breathing room to address the remaining vulnerabilities. Other factors were rapid external adjustment through depreciation and limited government absorption of private financial sector debt (meaning that no bank was saved because it was TBTF). What also helped was that Iceland had a low debt ratio going into the crisis.

5. Financial Reform

The financial (or monetary) reform plans in Iceland are contained in a report commissioned by the prime minister and published in 2015 (Sigurjonsson, 2015). The report recaps Iceland's history of money and banking disasters and attributes the 2008 collapse to fractional reserve banking, which caused an out-of-control increase in the money supply. The report recommends the abolition of fractional reserve banking, a separation of deposit and loan banking and putting an end to deposit insurance. In a forward to the report, Adair Turner, the former head of the UK's Financial Services Authority, explains why the proposed reform takes matters further than in any other country. He writes the following:

> In the aftermath of the 2008 financial crisis, financial regulators and central banks across the world have put great efforts into making the existing financial system more stable, increasing bank capital and liquidity requirements, developing bank resolution plans, and requiring derivatives trading to go through central clearing houses. Those efforts, in which I was deeply involved from 2008 to 2013, have been valuable, reducing the probability of another financial crisis in the short term. But they have still failed to address the fundamental issue — the ability of banks to create credit, money and purchasing power, and the instability which inevitably follows. As a result, the reforms agreed to date still leave the world dangerously vulnerable to future financial and economic instability.

Mervyn King, who was the governor of the Bank of England during the period 2003–2011, had brought attention to this matter by saying the following (King, 2010):

> Of all the many ways of organising banking, the worst is the one we have today. … Change is, I believe, inevitable. The question is only whether we can think our way through to a better outcome before the next generation is damaged by a future and bigger crisis. This crisis has already left a legacy of debt to the next generation. We must not leave them the legacy of a fragile banking system too.

The report starts with the argument that the fractional reserve banking system may have limited the central bank's ability to control the money supply while giving commercial banks both the power and incentive to create too much money. There is also the recognition that the fractional reserve system may have been a long-term contributing factor to various monetary problems in Iceland, including inflation and currency depreciation. More specifically, the following problems are attributed to the fractional reserve system: (i) inability of the central bank to control the money supply, (ii) amplification of the economic cycle by bank lending, (iii) inflation and depreciation resulting from excessive monetary expansion, (iv) forgone income as a result of delegating the responsibility of creating money to commercial banks, (v) risky lending resulting from state guarantees that are made necessary by the system (the moral hazard problem) and (vi) other problems associated with state guarantees such as unfair advantage to guaranteed (TBTF) banks and the problems associated with deposit insurance. In Kotlikoff's (2010) view, the main problem with the fractional reserve system is that "banks use state guaranteed deposits to fund their 'gambling' at the taxpayers' expense".

In short, the report argues, the present fractional reserve system is unstable and encourages risk taking because banks have an incentive to create money while the central bank finds itself unable to constrain them. Under this system the central bank must resort to credit controls and the imposition of limits on the growth rate of bank lending and lending to the financial sector. One way to remove the root-cause of these problems is the adoption of the sovereign money system in which the amount of money in the economy is controlled directly by the central bank. It is envisaged that under this system, the risk of sudden bank runs is greatly reduced and a deposit guarantee scheme becomes unnecessary. The sovereign money system prevents commercial banks from creating new demand deposits in the process of lending but they continue to act as intermediaries between savers and investors and provide payment and transaction services.[7] The central bank creates money to

---

[7] Under the alternative system, banks offer two types of accounts to customers, transaction accounts (used for storing funds that are available on demand to make payments and transactions) and investment accounts that have a predetermined maturity or notice period and earn interest. The funds in transaction accounts are kept with the central bank. Investment accounts cannot be used as a means of payment, but on maturity the funds are transferred back to transaction accounts (unless the customer decides to rollover and extend their investment).

keep the growth of the money supply in line with the needs of the economy. After all, this is what the financial system is supposed to do: supporting economic activity in the real sector. The report warns of confusion between the nationalization of money and the nationalization of the banking system. A sovereign money system is effectively the nationalization of money by making the central bank the sole creator of money. However, the ownership of banks remains unchanged and they continue to provide banking services, particularly the means of payment. This is an extreme case of killing the so-called "financial innovation", which can only be good for the economy at large.

Opposition to the system of sovereign money comes mainly from free marketeers who argue that the government cannot be trusted with the money creation process. Barron (2015) argues on the grounds suggested by Hayek's theory of public choice. This is what he says in reference to the author of the report:

> It is obvious that either he's never heard of public choice theory or does not subscribe to its conclusions. Really, who today believes that government, which after all is manned by some of the most fallible humans in society, can (1) be completely altruistic in its spending decisions and (2) would know what is best anyway? (I refer Sigurjonsson to F.A. Hayek's wonderful Nobel Speech in which he clearly articulates his theory of the pretence of knowledge).

This is obviously right-wing rhetoric, saying that the good guys work for the private sector and contribute to human welfare through Adam Smith's invisible hand (it is invisible because it does not exist). Just like Barron refers Sigurjonsson to Hayek's Nobel speech, I would like to refer Barron to the brilliant piece of Thompson *et al.* (2006) "Nobels for Nonsense". The fact of the matter is that we have tried a system in which bankers are in charge and it failed miserably, so why cannot we try an alternative — perhaps it will work. Let us have a look at what some enlightened people have said about the fractional reserve banking system that gives bankers the power to create money. In 1939, Robert H. Hemphill, credit manager of the Federal Reserve in Atlanta, said the following (Hodgson-Brown, 2012):

> We are completely dependent on the commercial banks. Someone has to borrow every dollar we have in circulation, cash or credit. If the banks create ample synthetic money we are prosperous; if not, we starve. We are absolutely without a permanent money system. When one gets a complete grasp of the picture, the tragic absurdity of our hopeless position is almost incredible, but there it is. It is the most important subject intelligent persons can investigate and reflect upon.

In February 2005 financial commentator Hans Schicht wrote (Hodgson-Brown, 2012):

> The fact that the Banker is allowed to extend credit several times his own capital base and that the Banking Cartels, the Central Banks, are licensed to issue fresh paper money in exchange for treasury paper, (has) provided them with free lunch for eternity…. Through a network of anonymous financial spider webbing only a handful of global King Bankers own and control it all…. Everybody, people, enterprise, State and foreign countries, all have become slaves chained to the Banker's credit ropes.

Sir Josiah Stamp, director of the Bank of England and the second richest man in Britain in the 1920s said the following in a speech at the University of Texas in 1927 (Hodgson-Brown, 2012):

> The modern banking system manufactures money out of nothing. The process is perhaps the most astounding piece of sleight of hand that was ever invented. Banking was conceived in inequity and born in sin…. Bankers own the earth. Take it away from them but leave them the power to create money, and, with a flick of a pen, they will create enough money to buy it back again…. Take this great power away from them and all great fortunes like mine will disappear, for then this would be a better and happier world to live in…. But, if you want to continue to be the slaves of

bankers and pay the cost of your own slavery, then let bankers continue to create money and control credit.

The present fractional reserve banking system has been described as "money in the land of Oz", as described by Hodgson-Brown (2012):

> If governments everywhere are in debt, who are they in debt to? The answer is that they are in debt to *private banks*. The "cruel hoax" is that governments are in debt for money created on a computer screen, money they could have created themselves. The vast power acquired through this sleight of hand by a small clique of men pulling the strings of government behind the scenes evokes images from The Wizard of Oz, a classic American fairytale that has become a rich source of imagery for financial commentators.

Here is some more as quoted by Hodgson-Brown (2012). President Andrew Jackson called the banking cartel a "hydra-headed monster eating the flesh of the common man". Writing in the 1920s, New York Mayor, John Hylan, called it a "giant octopus" that "seizes in its long and powerful tentacles our executive officers, our legislative bodies, our schools, our courts, our newspapers, and every agency created for the public protection". Yet, the system is still in operation and die-hard free marketeers prefer it to the proposed Icelandic plan. It may not be a bad idea, after all, to bless the Icelandic move to experiment with a new system. Under the proposed system, we can rest assured that members of the "monetary creation committee" will not have the power to pay themselves bonuses and golden parachutes as a compensation for failure. If the system does not work, then I agree with Barron that the alternative may be to abandon fiat money, tie the money supply to gold or silver and, if it has no role to play, abolish the central bank.

Not everyone agrees with Barron (except fellow free marketeers, of course). For example, the Telegraph (2015) describes the proposed system as "revolutionary" and "turnaround in the history of modern finance".[8] Aquinas (2015) argues that "there may be a glimmer of hope coming from the tiny Nordic island of Iceland" because "instead of following in the global insanity of massive money creation, artificial suppression of interest rates, and all other sorts of tricks and gimmicks, Iceland is considering the prohibition of banks from artificially increasing the money supply through the fraudulent and evil practice of fractional reserve banking". Other positive comments include the following: "it's a proposal that merits serious consideration"; "Iceland's proposal is worth exploring"; "money creation is too important to be left to bankers alone"; "by bringing the axe down on fractional reserve banking the Icelanders might just regain some control over their economic destiny"; "if successful, Iceland's experience could serve as an important case study for global monetary reform"; "it would dramatically improve the ability of central bankers to stabilize nominal spending without distorting the composition of economic activity"; "Iceland's proposal is worth exploring"; and "Sigurjonsson plan is a plausible blueprint for better banking and Iceland is a good place to start". Needless, to say, something like this will never happen in London and New York where bankers call the shots.

6. Conclusion

The Icelandic authorities made a big mistake by following the right-wing ideology of financial *laissez faire* and deregulating the financial system at the beginning of this century. They made a big mistake by abandoning fishing in favor of finance. As a result, people suffered from the ramifications of a colossal financial collapse

---

[8] An enlightened reader commented on the article by saying: "it must be noted that unlike some 'central banks', I won't mention names here, Iceland's Central Bank is owned by the state (the people)". Needless to say, we all know that the 'central banks' this reader refers to is the Federal Reserve, which is a private company owned by the banks themselves (that is, the regulated firms own the regulator). I suppose that in this case Barron should be happy with the system of sovereign money because if the Fed is in charge, this means that private banks are in charge.

that led to a severe economic downturn. After all, some fishermen left fishing to be carry traders. But even those who had nothing to do with finance suffered because every financial crisis brings about economic downturn.

Most of the rest of the world followed the lead of the Federal Reserve by indulging in an orgy of quantitative easing and ultra low interest rates, thus hurting small savers (the majority of the population, including the middle class). The Icelanders, on the other hand, have decided to pursue what they thought to be more appropriate policies that, albeit painful, have produced results. More importantly perhaps, the Icelanders have shown exceptional courage by putting bankers behind bars, instead of giving them bonuses and golden parachutes as in New York and London. The Icelanders have chosen not to go down the slippery slopes of TBTF, bailouts, bail-ins and quantitative easing. While legislators in many countries are planning the next move to reward bankers by confiscating people's deposits in the case of bank failure, the Icelanders are planning to deprive them from the power to make money and destroy the economy in the process. This is because the attitude in Iceland is to let banks go down, like any other business since they do not believe that banks are the holy churches of the economy. The attitude in Iceland is to bailout people, not banks. One feels obliged to salute the small island state at the middle of no-where, hoping that those in charge of the big financial centers in New York and London will learn from the Icelandic experience (although this is doubtful, as it does not suit bankers).

The Icelanders have let three banks, which at one time were more than 10 times the size of the economy, go out of business — yet the country survived. This proves that TBTF is a myth — it is propaganda spread by the banks themselves and supported by their captors, the regulators, some politicians and some academics who act like hired guns. Iceland has survived, which makes one wonder why is it that some people, including regulators, believe that systemically important financial institutions must be bailed out or bailed in to avert a catastrophe. We should all learn from Iceland.

Chapter 11

The Way Forward

1. Triumph of the Financial Oligarchs

In September 2015, I attended a conference on banking law that was held in Queen Mary College, London. The participants were predominantly lawyers, but there were some economists, including academics and regulators as well as representatives of policy making bodies and international organizations, including the International Monetary Fund (IMF). The tone of the conference, judged by the presentations, was very reconciliatory, sometimes apologetic to bankers. While the objective was to discuss the way forward with respect to banking regulation, most of what was proposed amounted to no more than tweaking around the edges. The London Interbank Offered Rates (LIBOR) scandal represented "misconduct" and no-one (apart from this author) used the word "fraud" to describe fraud. There was even some praise of shadow banking and how essential it is for economic progress. When one of the participants was asked about what he thought of the Icelandic reform, he refused to comment. There was a lot of talk about measures such as "ring-fencing" and "total loss absorbing capacity" (TLAC), but nothing of the kind of the radical regulatory measures that are required to change the status quo. I concluded by listening to the speeches that the financial oligarchs are still calling the shots.

It is amazing that the financial oligarchs have managed to maintain their power in the aftermath of the global financial crisis and the widely resented bailouts. Elizabeth Warren, the head of the Congressional Oversight Panel, once remarked that "big banks always get what they want" because "they have all the money, all the lobbyists" whereas "there's just not a lobby on the other side" (Wee, 2009). Even when regulatory measures are put in place, they are subsequently watered down as pressure mounts from the financial oligarchs and their lobbyists. They (the oligarchs) hold carrots in front of individual regulators, with the prospect of much better future jobs, while wielding big sticks, as they have powerful friends and significant legal firepower. As a result, a cozy relationship has developed, involving the finance industry, the regulatory system and the government. Key players move back and forth between all three.

We repeatedly witness events that demonstrate the triumph of the financial oligarchs. For example, on 12 January 2014 the Basel Committee released new rules whereby big European banks were allowed off the hook of having to raise $96 billion in capital. Although they still have to meet a leverage ratio of at least 3%, the formula used for the calculation of the ratio has been softened. In April 2014, it was announced that the Federal Reserve would give banks two more years to divest collateralized loan obligations (CLOs) that fall under the Volcker rule, implying that banks will have until 21 July 2017 to shed these funds, which pool together risky loans. Does it make any sense to establish a regulatory agency such as the Commodity Futures Trading Commission (CFTC) to protect financial market participants from fraud involving derivatives, then arguing that over-the-counter (OTC) derivatives should be exempt from scrutiny by this agency? The return of securitization with vengeance is yet another victory for banks and the loss of an opportunity for regulators to redeem themselves. Banks have managed to block legislation to allow judges to modify residential mortgages in bankruptcy cases. In 2008 and 2009 the consensus view was that it was hazardous to impose restrictions on banks while the financial system was vulnerable. Now that things have improved, the attention of regulators has shifted to less urgent issues such as short selling and high-frequency trading (HFT).[1] For big banks, it seems, ring-fencing and TLAC will do the job! This is what we consider next.

2. Regulating by Tweaking Around the Edges

On 15 October 2015, the Bank of England published two consultation papers, one on ring-fencing and one on operational continuity. The objective of the ring-fencing proposal is to ensure that "ring-fenced banks are protected from shocks originating in other parts of their groups, as well as the broader financial system, and can be easily separated from their groups in the event of failure" (Bank of England, 2015). The underlying idea is simply separating investment banking and commercial banking, which was achieved under the Glass–Steagall Act until its repeal in 1999. The Bank of England suggests that "the proposed rules also mean that a ring-fenced bank can be more easily detached from the wider group by ensuring intragroup arrangements operate on an arm's length basis — helping ensure important services remain available in the event of a failure of other parts of the group". The proposal is supposed to be put in place from 1 January 2019. Andrew Bailey, deputy governor of the Bank of England and chief executive of the Prudential Regulation Authority (PRA), justified the intention to use ring-fencing by saying the following (Bank of England, 2015):

> Making our firms more resilient has been at the forefront of our post-crisis reform agenda. Today represents an important step forward in achieving this aim. We have provided clarity for affected banks on how we will implement ring-fencing and this will enable firms to take substantial steps forward in their preparations for structural reform.

If the plan goes as intended then from 1 January 2019, banks with core deposits greater than £25 billion will be required to

---

[1] This is like the police spending their time hiding and operating speed cameras to collect fines rather than going after armed robbers, arsonists and rapists.

ring-fence their core retail activities. The detailed objective of the proposal are to ensure that: (i) a ring-fenced bank has sufficient financial resources and liquidity; (ii) intragroup exposures and arrangements between the ring-fenced bank and the rest of the group are managed in a prudent manner, at arm's length; (iii) the ring-fenced bank is clear on the PRA's expectations on the use of financial market infrastructures and (iv) the ring-fenced bank can demonstrate the ability to continue to provide critical economic functions during resolution. The banks covered are HSBC, Barclays, Royal Bank of Scotland, Lloyds Banking Group, Santander UK and the Co-operative Bank. The proposals of the Bank of England resonate in the US where calls are made in the presidential election season to bring back the Glass-Steagall Act whereby investment banking was separated from commercial banking before it was repealed in 1999.

Needless to say, the ring-fencing proposal has not gone down well with large banks, which have lobbied hard against it, using the typical argument that any measure like this is a threat to the status of London as an international financial center (Knowledge@ Wharton, 2015). The ruling conservative party is calling measures like these "reregulation", which should be avoided to preserve the status of London (as the epicenter of the LIBOR scandal!). William Black, a former US regulator, believes that this is "because they (banks) want to go back to the competitive race to the bottom on financial regulation, with the idea of preserving the City of London as a top financial center". The big British banks find the ring-fencing exercise too demanding on their resources. According to Wallace (2015a), the operational separation of the banking units is expected to cost roughly £200 million per bank as a one-off cost plus around £120 million per year. But Wallace (2015b) had earlier reported that HSBC faced costs of around £2 billion to split its retail and investment banking activities.[2] Jonathan Symonds, independent

---

[2] It is not obvious why the cost of implementing ring-fencing is £200 million per bank and £2 billion or HSBC. Banks complain about costs but they pass them on to customers.

non-executive director of HSBC, explained his opposition to the House of Lords Economic Affairs Committee in a June 2015 hearing by saying the following (Wallace, 2015b):

> I have 350 IT systems to separate…. It is consuming a very substantial amount of the productive capacity of the bank to implement this, when I really would rather be improving culture and customer service. This is a pragmatic issue.

Wharton professor of legal studies and business ethics, Peter Conti-Brown advocates the ring-fencing proposal, suggesting that he is "pleasantly surprised" that the Bank of England "has stuck to its guns this far". He further said the following (Knowledge@ Wharton, 2015):

> The usual story of the political economy of bank regulation is that you get a crisis, you get a lot of populist enthusiasm for reforming the system, and then it will go quiet as major industry players start chipping away over time.

According to William Black, the Bank of England's ring-fencing proposal has "enormous weaknesses" because "its central premise is that the two branches of the bank — the investment bank and the retail bank — will treat each other as if they have no affiliation", which is never going to happen. Perhaps, but this is not why ring-fencing is under assault by the Tories, which is likely to lead to enormous exceptions to carve out of ring-fencing or kill it entirely. Conti-Brown is skeptical about the implementation of ring-fencing in 2019 in its current form — as a matter of fact, the proposal has already been watered down.

According to Binham and Dunkley (2015), the City "won the second clear signal in 24 hours of a political shift in its favor when financial regulators granted a key concession on the ring fencing rule for the UK's largest banks". For example, banks will be allowed to transfer capital from their retail arms to other parts of their businesses in the form of dividends. They contend that "the concession is a boon to the UK's largest lenders, which have complained that ring-fencing, due to be in place by 2019, puts them at a competitive disadvantage to their overseas rivals".

Bankers also won concessions from the UK Treasury. In October 2015, the Treasury announced that it was scrapping the most contentious part of a tough new accountability regime, designed to hold the most senior executives to account. Binham and Dunkley (2015) describe the U-turn as "the latest in a series of emollient moves to banks since the Tories' victory in May's general election and since HSBC and Standard Chartered threatened to move their headquarters overseas in response to proposals to stiffen regulation". Mark Garnier, a Conservative MP on the Treasury select committee and a member of the banking commission that had recommended the principle, said that "we may have gone a bit too far with reverse burden of proof".

It is always a "bit too far" when it comes to financial regulation. There is nothing new about ring-fencing to warrant a new proposal and public consultation because the history of the Glass–Steagall Act tells us that separation of investment banking from commercial banking does work, and because it does work in the sense of enhancing financial stability, it should not be justified in an apologetic manner. And because it does work, its implementation should not be delayed until 2019, by which time the original proposal would have been watered down or, on pressure from the financial oligarchy, put on the back burner indefinitely.

On the international level, the last "gimmick" from Basel is the so-called "TLAC", which is yet another attempt to determine the amount of regulatory capital that protects a bank from insolvency (with a confidence level of 99.9%, of course). On 10 November 2014, the Financial Stability Board (FSB) issued a consultative document that defined a global standard for the TLAC to be held by Global Systemically Important Banks (G-SIBs) — in other words, internationally recognized too big to fail (TBTF) institutions (FSB, 2014b). TLAC is meant to ensure that G-SIBs have the loss absorbing and recapitalization capacity so that, in and immediately following resolution, critical functions can continue without requiring taxpayer support or threatening financial stability.[3] True, under these conditions a G-SIB may not need support from taxpayers but they will need support from depositors — this seems to be just an exercise whereby bailouts are replaced by bail-ins, and needless to say, it is the FSB that has been the driving force behind the bail-in scheme.

The FSB's document (FSB, 2014b) requires a G-SIB to hold a minimum amount of regulatory capital (Tier 1 and Tier 2) plus long-term unsecured debt that together are at least 16–20% of its risk weighted assets (that is, at least twice the minimum Basel III total regulatory capital ratio of 8%). In addition, the amount of a firm's regulatory capital and unsecured long-term debt cannot be less than 6% of its leverage exposure — that is, at least twice the Basel III leverage ratio. In addition to this "Pillar 1" requirement, TLAC would also include a subjective component (called "Pillar 2") to be assessed for each bank individually, based on qualitative firm-specific risks that take into account the firm's recovery and resolution plans, systemic footprint, risk profile and other factors.

The declared objective of the TLAC proposal is to put an end to the TBTF fiasco. However, even if a regulatory measure like this is effective in protecting taxpayers from the TBTF bonanza, that will be achieved at the expense of depositors who will foot the bill for a bail-in. De Lis *et al.* (2014) make it clear that the TLAC proposal will make "bail-in feasible and credible instead of bailout". Levine (2015) has the following to say:

> The way to avoid financial crises is to clearly define the classes of people whom it is socially and politically acceptable not to pay back, and that's what TLAC is. The idea is to make a big bank's failure tidier, by clearly specifying in advance who is in line to

---

[3] As of November 2014, the FSB (2014c) identified some 30 G-SIB, including HSBC, JP Morgan Chase, Barclays, BNP Paribas, Bank of America, Credit Suisse, Goldman Sachs, Royal Bank of Scotland, UBS and Wells Fargo. On 3 November 2015, another update was published, comprising 30 banks by adding China Construction Bank and removing BBVA (FSB, 2015). The domestic counterpart of G-SIB is D-SIB.

lose money and in what order. Holders of bank capital lose first, but holders of TLAC debt — basically unsecured debt issued by the bank holding company — are on the hook next. The implication is surely that if you own something senior to TLAC debt — insured deposits, say, or derivatives liabilities — you should really expect to get paid back even if the bank fails. But, with luck, you'll get paid back out of a TLAC bail-in, not a taxpayer bail-out.

TLAC is not a solution to the TBTF problem — on the contrary it will boost moral hazard, as bankers will know that they will still get their bonuses from the confiscated depositors' money. The TBTF problem can be put to an end by reducing bank size, separating investment banking from commercial banking, killing moral hazard and, if necessary, allowing TBTF banks to fail. Why is it that regulators have not learned from the Icelandic experience?

3. Nobel Prize in Economics, Free Market Ideology and Deregulation

In Chapter 10, we saw that the system of sovereign money under consideration in Iceland is opposed by free marketeers. One such free marketeer is Barron (2015) who argues against the system of sovereign money on the basis of F.A. Hayek's theory of public choice, referring the author of the Icelandic report to Hayek's "wonderful Nobel Speech in which he clearly articulates his theory of the pretense of knowledge". So perhaps we should spend some time talking about Nobel Prize in economics and how it was motivated by the free market ideology.

The Nobel Prize in economics is not really a Nobel Prize, in the sense that the man (Nobel) himself did not envisage such a prize. This prize was created by Sweden's central bank in 1969 and given the name the "Sveriges Riksbank Prize in Economic Sciences in Memory of Alfred Nobel". Levine (2012) quotes one of the Federal Reserve banks as saying that the prize was a "marketing ploy". He also quotes one of the decedents of Nobel as saying that "it's most often awarded to stock market speculators" and that "there is nothing to indicate that [Alfred Nobel] would have wanted such a prize". Members of the Nobel family are among the harshest, most persistent critics of the economics prize, and they have repeatedly called for the prize to be abolished or renamed. In 2001, on the 100th anniversary of the Nobel Prize, four family members published a letter in the Swedish paper *Svenska Dagbladet*, arguing that "the economics prize degrades and cheapens the real Nobel Prizes".

Levine uses a conspiracy theory to explain the origin of Nobel Prize in economics. Toward the end of the 1960s, Sweden's banking and business interests were trying to introduce "free market economic reforms", with the main objective of loosening political oversight and control over the central bank. The typical argument was "efficiency gains" but the real motive was to transfer control over the central bank from the elected government to the financial oligarchy. To give the central bank some scientific credibility, the prize was created in 1969 on the 300th anniversary of the central bank. Levine believes that the intention right from the beginning was to award the prize to free-marketeers and to make sure that would happen, the bank managed to install a right-wing Swedish economist who had ties to the University of Chicago (the land of *laissez faire*), to oversee the awards committee and keep him there for more than three decades.

In 1974, five years after the prize was first created, it was awarded to Friedrich Hayek, one of the leading *laissez faire* economists of the 20th century, then in 1976 it was awarded to Milton Friedman, both of whom are enthusiastic supporters of the political independence of central banks. Hayek developed a theory that blamed government and government-controlled banking systems for all economic mishaps and argued that government intervention leads to totalitarianism. Friedman established the uses of a monetary rule, meaning that no control over banking is necessary. Levine believes that the Nobel Prize made neoclassical economics, hence deregulation, more acceptable.

Apart from Freidman and Hayek, economists won Nobel for the derivative risk models used to run a hedge fund that went belly-up nine months after the award of the prize, nearly causing a systemic collapse. Another economist won the prize for constructing experiments that show the desirability of privatization. Yet another economist won it for effectively arguing that the natural rate of unemployment is an "act of God" that should not be tampered with — therefore, if 10 million people are out of work, nothing can or should be done about it. It is these ideas that were used to justify deregulation. If Nobel Prize winners say that deregulation is a good idea, then it becomes easier to sell. Unfortunately, economists have become hired guns, used to justify policies dictated by the financial and business oligarchy on the government. The Nobel Prize in economics has made this legitimate, which is why one of the "ten commandments" of Taleb (2009) is "shutting down the Nobel in economics".

Even some economists argue for the abolition of the economics Nobel Prize. We have already come across Thompson *et al.* (2006) who argue that the Nobel Prize has been awarded for nonsense, referring in particular to the Nobel Prize winning work in finance. Bergmann (1999) suggests that "we economists ought to open our eyes and see that having a Nobel Prize for economics is making the economics profession look ridiculous". She further argues that "the prize often occasions embarrassment, since we have to explain to the public what achievement of the newest laureate is". As examples, she mentions the prize won by economists telling us that "politicians and bureaucrats act in their own interest", that "people do the best they can in doping out what to do" and that "people save and spend their savings at different times in their lives". The Nobel Prize was even awarded to an economist who came up with the unethical conclusion that slavery was a good business, at least for those with a whip. We must not forget that another Nobel Prize was awarded for the invention of that weapon of mass destruction, the efficient market hypothesis and other theories that are used to justify deregulation. Although the title of her article is "Abolish the Nobel for Economics", Bergmann suggests, as an alternative to abolishing the economics Nobel Prize, that the prize should not be awards every year but rather only when work that advances economics as an empirical science appears. As long as neoclassical economics represents the mainstream, this is unlikely to happen because the research output will be about distilling complicated phenomena into simplistic representations of cheeringly optimal processes by using the available tools of econometric testing (Bergmann, 1999).

4. Concluding Thoughts: Radical Regulatory Action

Financial Regulation is intended to deal with the abusive behavior of the financial oligarchy. To put things into perspective, let us see what we are dealing with here. Take, for example, how Jeff Scachs described the financial oligarchs while speaking at a conference at the Philadelphia Fed in April 2013 (Sachs, 2013):

> I meet a lot of these people on Wall Street on a regular basis right now. I'm going to put it very bluntly. I regard the moral environment as pathological. And I'm talking about the human interactions that I have. I've not seen anything like this, not felt it so palpably. These people are out to make billions of dollars and (believe that) nothing should stop them from that. They have no responsibility to pay taxes. They have no responsibility to their clients. They have no responsibility to people, counterparties in transactions. They are tough, greedy, aggressive, and feel absolutely out of control, you know, in a quite literal sense. And they have gamed the system to a remarkable extent, and they have a docile president, a docile White House, and a docile regulatory system that absolutely can't find its voice. It's terrified of these companies…. I have waited for four years, five years now, to see one figure on Wall Street speak in a moral language, and I've not seen it once. And that is shocking to me. And if they won't, I've waited for a judge, for our president, for somebody, and it hasn't happened. And by the way it's not going to happen anytime soon it seems.

This characterization of the financial oligarchs is by no means exaggerated, neither is the description of the failure to do anything about them. So, let us recap on incidents of fraud in the financial sector by a selective items of fraud that big banks have been indulged in.[4] These include money laundering; fraud against local governments; shaving money off of pension transactions; committing massive and pervasive fraud both when they initiated mortgage loans and when they foreclosed on them; pledging the same mortgage multiple times to different buyers; cheating homeowners by gaming laws meant to protect people from unfair foreclosure; indulging in insider trading; pushing investments that they knew were terrible, and then betting against the same investments to make money for themselves; engaging in unlawful front running to manipulate markets; engaging in unlawful "wash trades" to manipulate asset prices; participating in various Ponzi schemes; cooking the books; bribing and bullying rating agencies to inflate ratings of risky investments and much more.

The real problem is that governments have done nothing about this fraud. In the absence of prosecutions, the behavior of the financial oligarchs is unlikely to change and fraud will remain widespread. Radical measures are needed to deal with the situation. The following are just examples:

- The TBTF problem must be fixed. Systemically dangerous institutions should not be told that they are systemically important. They should be reduced in size and allowed to fail if necessary.
- Fraudulent accounting rules must be prohibited so that financial institutions recognize their losses rather than announcing profits so that they can claim bonuses.
- Exuberant remuneration drives fraud. The culture of bonuses and golden parachutes must be killed.
- Regulators should be regulators, not defenders of the institutions they are supposed to regulate. Regulators who dislike regulation and defend deregulation must be fired. Bring in as regulators Joe Stiglitz, Brooksley Born, Simon Johnson, Max

---

[4]For the full collection and related stories, see http://www.ritholtz.com/blog/2012/07/are-big-banks-criminal-enterprises/.

Keiser, Tracy Herbert and William Black. For the Mayor of London, vote in George Galloway and for the British Prime Minister vote in Jeremy Corbyn. Once London and New York, as financial centers, have been fixed, the rest of the financial world will come down to earth.

- The perpetrators of fraud must be prosecuted. It will be appropriate to have some financial oligarchs to be part of the US prison population, which comprises 25% of the total world prison population. Jack Bauer should pursue those indulging in the production and distribution of financial weapons of mass destruction.
- The so-called financial innovation must be killed and financial engineers should be sent to factories and labs where they can do a better job.

Most importantly, however, the financial sector should be reduced in terms of scale and scope. Financialization must be put to an end. Returning to "boring banking" could be the salvation that we are seeking and the only way to overcome the tyranny of the financial oligarchy. Boring banking is not really boring — it is more like what is described by Adair Turner in a speech at Mansion House Banquet in September 2009. This is what he said (Turner, 2009):

> Banks need to refocus their energies, not on those over complex products of no real use to humanity … but on their core functions of providing savings and credit and payment products to their customers … Not all financial innovation is valuable, not all trading activity plays a useful role, and a bigger financial system is not necessarily a better one.

I hope that John Bogle (2014b) is correct in predicting a much smaller financial sector, a marked decline in speculation, a growing distrust of active managers, and the rise of corporate governance. I also hope that he is right in saying that "when there is a gap between perception and reality, it is only a matter of time until reality takes over".

References

Abelson, R. (1996). Gary Lynch, Defender of Companies, Has His Critics, *New York Times*, 3 September.

ACFE. (2014). Report to the Nations on Occupational Fraud and Abuse. http://www.acfe.com/rttn/docs/2014-report-to-nations.pdf. 25 August 2015.

Acharya, V., Schnabl, P. and Suarez, G. (2013). Securitization without Risk Transfer, *Journal of Financial Economics*, 107, 515–536.

Adrian, T. and Ashcraft, A. (2012). Shadow Banking Regulation, *Federal Reserve Bank of New York Staff Report*, No. 559.

Adrian, T. and Shin, H.S. (2009a). The Shadow Banking System: Implications for Financial Regulation, *Banque de France Financial Stability Review*, 13, 1–10.

Adrian, T. and Shin, H.S. (2009b). Money, Liquidity, and Monetary Policy, *American Economic Review*, 99, 600–609.

Adrian, T. and Shin, H.S. (2010). Liquidity and Leverage, *Journal of Financial Intermediation*, 19, 418–437.

Adrian, T., Ashcraft, A. and Cetorelli, N. (2013). Shadow Bank Monitoring, *Federal Reserve Bank of New York Staff Report*, No. 638.

Agirman, E., Sercemeli, M. and Ozcan, M. (2013). Shadow Banking: An Overview, Working Paper. http://www3.eeg.uminho.pt/economia/nipe/iibc2013/6.3.pdf. 18 October 2015.

AIG. (2009). AIG: Is the Risk Systemic? 26 February. http://www.aig.com/aigweb/internet/en/files/AIG%20Systemic%20Risk2_tcm385-152209.pdf. 14 March 2015.

Aldridge, J. (2009). I am Doing God's Work- Meet Mr Goldman Sachs, *Sunday Times*, 8 November.

Altman, E.I., Oncu, S., Schmeits, A. and White, L.J. (2010). What Should be Done about the Credit Rating Agencies? 6 April. http://w4.stern.nyu.edu/blogs/regulatingwallstreet/2010/04/what-should-be-done-about-the.html. 17 October 2015.

Ambler, T. (2011). How Basel III Threatens Small Business, Briefing Paper, Adam Smith Institute. http://www.adamsmith.org/research/reports/how-basel-iii-threatens-small-businesses. 28 July 2015.

Anderson, H. (2006). Directors' Liability to Creditors — What are the Alternatives? *Bond Law Review*, 18(1). http://epublications.bond.edu.au/blr/vol18/iss2/1. 2 March 2015.

Anderson, R.G. (2008). Paying Interest on Deposits at Federal Reserve Banks, *Federal Reserve Bank of St. Louis Economic Synopses*, No. 30.

Anderson, R.G. and Williams, M.M. (2007). U.S. Currency at Home and Abroad, *Monetary Trends*, Federal Reserve Bank of St Louis, March. http://research.stlouisfed.org/publications/mt/20070301/cover.pdf. 16 June 2015.

Anderson, R.G., Gascon, C.S. and Liu, Y. (2010). Doubling Your Monetary Base and Surviving: Some International Experience, *Federal Reserve Bank of St. Louis Review*, November/December, Nos. 481–505.

Anderson, S. (2015). Off the Deep End: the Wall Street Bonus Pool and Low-Wage Workers, Institute for Policy Studies, 11 March. http://www.ips-dc.org/deep-end-wall-street/. 10 April 2015.

Annen, L. (2012). Regulatory Pressure on the Shadow Banking System, KPMG, June.

Appelbaum, B. (2015). Liar Loans: How Mortgage Fraud Helped Trigger the GFC, *Sunday Morning Herald*, 13 February. http://www.smh.com.au/business/world-business/liar-loans-how-mortgage-fraud-helped-trigger-the-gfc-20150213-13dshn.html. 3 June 2015.

Aquinas, A. (2015). Monetary Reform in Iceland: Maybe There is Still Hope? *Western Journalism*, 2 June. http://www.westernjournalism.com/monetary-reform-in-iceland-maybe-there-is-still-hope/. 20 June 2015.

Armbruster, B. (2009). Perino Defends AIG Bonuses: They are 'Middle Class People' Who 'are Expecting to Get This Bonus', 17 March. http://thinkprogress.org/politics/2009/03/17/36843/perino-defends-aig/. 10 May 2015.

Asness, C., Boskin, M., Bove, R., Calomiris, C., Chanos, J., Cogan, J., Ferguson, N., Geina, N., Grant, J., Hassett, K., Hertog, R., Hess, G.,

Holtz-Eaking, D., Klarman, S., Kristol, W., Malpass, D., McKinnon, R., Senor, D., Shlaes, A., Singer, P., Taylor, J., Wallison, P. and Wood, G. (2010). Open Letter to Ben Bernanke, *Wall Street Journal*, 15 November.

Avraham, D., Selvaggi, P. and Vickery, J. (2012). A Structural View of U.S. Bank Holding Companies, *Federal Reserve Bank of New York Economic Policy Review*, July, Nos. 65–81.

Baily, M.N. (2010). Executive Compensation Oversight after the Dodd–Frank Wall Street Reform and Consumer Protection Act, Testimony to the House Committee on Financial Services, 24 September. http://www.brookings.edu/research/testimony/2010/09/24-executive-compensation-baily. 24 September 2015.

Ball, R. (2009). The Global Financial Crisis and the Efficient Market Hypothesis: What Have we Learned, *Journal of Applied Corporate Finance*, 21, 8–16.

Bank for International Settlements. (2014). 84th Annual Report, Basel. http://www.bis.org/publ/arpdf/ar2014e.pdf. 13 July 2015.

Bank of England. (2015). News Release — Bank of England Announces Further Proposals to Strengthen the Financial System Through Structural Reform, 15 October. http://www.bankofengland.co.uk/publications/Pages/news/2015/075.aspx. 28 October 2015.

Banks, G. (2003). The Good, the Bad and the Ugly: Economic Perspectives on Regulation in Australia. http://www.pc.gov.au/news-media/speeches/cs20031002/cs20031002.pdf. 18 May 2015.

Barr, C. (2009). The $4 Trillion Housing Headache, 27 May. http://archive.fortune.com/2009/05/27/news/mortgage.overhang.fortune/index.htm. 22 April 2015.

Barro, R.J. (1976). Rational Expectations and the Role of Monetary Policy, *Journal of Monetary Economics*, 2, 1–32.

Barron, P. (2013). Why isn't QE Causing Inflation? *Mises Canada*, 13 December. http://mises.ca/posts/articles/why-isnt-qe-causing-inflation/. 9 July 2015.

Barron, P. (2015). A Half-Right Monetary Reform for Iceland, *Mises Daily*, 28 April. https://mises.org/library/half-right-monetary-reform-iceland. 22 May 2015.

Batini, N. and Nelson, E. (2001). The Lag from Monetary Policy Actions to Inflation: Friedman Revisited, Bank of England, External MPC Unit, Discussion Paper No. 6.

Batra, R. (2011). Weapons of Mass Exploitation, 8 May. http://www.truth-out.org/news/item/952:weapons-of-mass-exploitation. 25 July 2015.

Bauder, D. (2011). Gary Aguirre Major Source in Taibbi Blockbuster, 17 February. http://www.sandiegoreader.com/weblogs/financial-crime-politics/2011/feb/17/gary-aguirre-major-source-in-taibbi-blockbuster/#. 19 July 2015.

Baur, B. and Wackerbeck, P. (2013). Into the Shadows: How Regulation Fuels the Growth of the Shadow Banking Sector and How Banks Need to React, *European Financial Review*, June–July, 28–30.

Baxter, L.G. (2011). Capture in Financial Regulation: Can we Channel it Toward the Common Good? *Cornell Journal of Law and Public Policy*, 21, 175–200.

Bazot, G. (2014). Financial Consumption and the Cost of Finance: Measuring Financial Efficiency in Europe (1950–2007), Working Paper, Paris School of Economics.

BBC. (2008). Councils 'Not Reckless with Cash', 10 October. 5 August 2015.

BBC. (2013). Q&A: EU Banker Bonus Cap Plan, 28 February. http://www.bbc.com/news/business-21615513. 2 June 2015.

BBC. (2014). New Banker Rules Could Hurt London as a Financial Centre, 30 July. http://www.bbc.com/news/business-28556906. 11 October 2015.

BBC. (2015). ECB unveils massive QE boost for eurozone, Business News, 22 January. http://www.bbc.com/news/business-30933515. 25 March 2015.

Bebchuk, L.A. (2010). Compensation in the Financial Industry, *Law School Forum on Corporate Governance and Financial Regulation*, 22 January. http://blogs.law.harvard.edu/corpgov/2010/01/22/compensation-in-the-financial-industry/. 23 August 2015.

Bebchuk, L. and Bar-Gill, O. (2002). Misreporting Corporate Performance, Working Paper, Harvard University.

Bebchuk, L.A., Cohen, A. and Spamann, H. (2010a). The Wages of Failure: Executive Compensation at Bear Stearns and Lehman 2000–2008, *Yale Journal on Regulation*, 27, 257–282.

Bebchuk, L.A., Cohen, A. and Wang, C.C.Y. (2010b). Golden Parachutes and the Wealth of Shareholders, Harvard Law and Economics, Discussion Paper No. 683.

Benmelech, E. and Dlugosz, J. (2010). The Credit Rating Crisis, *NBER Macroeconomic Annual*, 24, 161–207.

Berentsen, A. and Waller, C. (2013). Price Level Targeting and Stabilization Policy, *Federal Reserve Bank of St. Louis Review*, March/April, 145–163.

Bergmann, B. (1999). Abolish the Nobel Prize for Economics, *Challenge*, 42, 52–67.

Bernanke, B.S. (2004). The Great Moderation. http://www.federalreserve. gov/BOARDDOCS/SPEECHES/2004/20040220/default.htm. 26 June 2015.

Bernanke, B.S., Laubach, T., Mishkin, F.S. and Posen, A. (1999). *Inflation Targeting: Lessons from the International Experience*, Princeton: Princeton University Press.

Bhagwati, J. (2009). Feeble Critiques: Capitalism's Petty Detractors, *World Affairs*, 172(2), 35–45. www.worldaffairsjournal.org/articles/2009-Fall/full-Bhagwati-Fall-2009.html. 27 March 2015.

Biggs, M. and Mayer, T. (2010). The Output Gap Conundrum. http://www.ceps.eu/system/files/article/2010/02/forum_Biggs_Mayer_0.pdf. 30 April 2015.

Binham, C. and Dunkley, E. (2015). Banks with Frsesh Concessions on Ring Fencing Rules, *Financial Times*, 15 October.

Bitner, R. (2008). *Greed, Fraud and Ignorance: A Subprime Insider's Look at the Mortgage Collapse*, Colleyville (TX): LTV Media.

Black, W.K. (2005). *The Best Way to Rob a Bank is to Own One: How Corporate Executives and Politicians Looted the S&L Industry*, Austin (TX): University of Texas Press.

Black, W.K. (2009). The Two Documents Everyone Should Read to Better Understand the Crisis, *Huffington Post*, 25 February. huffingtonpost.com/william-k-black/the-two-documents-everyon_b_169813.html. 27 June 2015.

Black, W.K. (2010). Statement Before the Committee on Financial Services, United States House of Representatives Regarding Public Policy Issues Raised by the Report of the Lehman Bankruptcy Examiner, 20 April. static1.firedoglake.com/30/files/2010/04/black_4.20.10.pdf. 1 May 2015.

Blanchard, O.J. and Simon, J. (2001). The Long and Large Decline in US Output Volatility, *Brookings Papers on Economic Activity*, 1, 135–174.

Blanchard, O.J. and Watson, M.W. (1982). Bubbles, Rational Expectations and Financial Markets, NBER Working Paper No. 945.

Blinder, A. (2007). Six Fingers of Blame in the Mortgage Mess, *New York Times*, 30 September.

Boehm, F. (2007). Regulatory Capture Revisited — Lessons from Economics of Corruption, Working Paper, Research Center in Political Economy (CIEP, Universidad Externado de Colombia).

Bogdanich, W. and Morgenson, G. (2006). S.E.C. Inquiry on Hedge Fund Draws Scrutiny, *New York Times*, 22 October.

Bogle, J.C. (2005a). *The Battle for the Soul of Capitalism*, New Haven: Yale University Press.

Bogle, J.C. (2005b). The Executive Compensation System is Broken. http://ssrn.com/abstract=868508. 4 October 2015.

Bogle, J.C. (2009). A Crisis of Ethic Proportions, *Wall Street Journal*, 21 April.

Bogle, J.C. (2013). Vanguard's Bogle Responds to 'Parasite' Tag, *Financial Times*, 25 August.

Bogle, J.C. (2014a). The Arithmetic of "All-In" Investment Expenses, *Financial Analysts Journal*, 70, 1–9.

Bogle, J.C. (2014b). John Bogle on the Future of Investing: The Rise of the Shareholders, *Wall Street Journal*, 7 July.

Bolton, P., Freixas, X. and Shapiro, J. (2008). The Credit Ratings Game, Working Paper, Columbia Business School and Universitat Pompeu Fabra.

Bonner, B. (2007). Goldman Sachs Was Wrong and 2 Million Families May Lose Their Homes, 14 November. http://www.dailyreckoning.com. au/goldman-sachs-3/2007/11/14/. 2 March 2015.

Bordo, M.D. (2014). Exiting from Low Interest Rates to Normality: An Historical Perspective, Economics Working Paper 14110, Hoover Institution.

Bourque, G. (2012). Fire or Ice? Inflation or Deflation? *Four Minute Finance*, 26 September.

Bress, R.P. (1987). Golden Parachutes: Untangling the Ripcords, *Stanford Law Review*, 39, 955–979.

Brock, W.A. and Hommes, C.H. (1997). A Rational Route to Randomness, *Econometrica*, 65, 1059–1095.

Brockes, E. (2009). He Told Us So, *The Guardian*, 24 January.

Brooks, D. (2008). The Behavioral Revolution, *New York Times*, 28 October.

Bunjevac, T.A. (2009). Credit Rating Agencies: A Regulatory Challenge for Australia, *Melbourne University Law Review*, 33, 39–67.

Cable, V. (2012). Banking Scandal: The Rot was Widespread, the Corruption Endemic, *The Guardian*, 1 July.

Calavita, K., Pontell, H. and Tillman, R. (1997). *Big Money Crime: Fraud and Politics in the Savings and Loan Crisis*, Berkeley (CA): University of California Press.

Campbell, D. and Griffin, S. (2006). Enron and the End of Corporate Governance, in S. MacLeod (ed.) *Global Governance and the Quest for Justice*, Oxford: Hart Publishing.

Campbell, D.H. (1990). Golden Parachutes: Common Sense from the Common Law, *Ohio State Law Journal*, 51, 279–306.

Carlson, K.M. (1980). The Lag From Money To Prices, *Federal Reserve Bank of St. Louis Economic Review*, October, 3–10.

Carney, J. (2013). Quantitative Easing Doesn't Cause Inflation or Deflation, CNBC, 9 December. http://www.cnbc.com/id/10125-4010#. 28 April 2015.

Cartapanis, A. (1996). L'Heterogeneite des Anticipations dans les Modeles de Change, *Economie Appliquee*, 49, 173–205.

Casey, K.L. (2009). In Search of Transparency, Accountability, and Competition: the Regulation of Credit Rating Agencies, Speech by SEC Commissioner, Washington, D.C., 6 February.

Cassidy, J. (2010). After the Blowup: Laissez-Faire Economists Do Some Soul-Searching — and Finger-Pointing, *The New Yorker*, 11 January.

Cecchetti, S.G., Flores-Lagunes, A.F. and Krause, S. (2006). Assessing the Sources of Changes in the Volatility of Real Growth, NBER Working Paper No. 11946.

Cetorelli, N. and Peristiani, S. (2012). The Role of Banks in Asset Securitization, *Federal Reserve Bank of New York Economic Policy Review*, July, 47–63.

Chakrabarty, K.C. (2013). Fraud in the Banking Sector — Causes, Concerns and Cures, National Conference on Financial Fraud Organised by ASSOCHAM, New Delhi, 26 July. http://www.bis.org/review/r130730a.pdf. 24 June 2015.

Chan, S.P. (2014). IMF: Shadow Banking Poses Threat to Financial Stability, *The Telegraph*, 8 November.

Chang, H.J. (2011). *23 Things They Don't Tell You About Capitalism*, New York: Bloomesbury Press.

Chapman, B. (2010). Quantitative Easing, Inflation, Hyperinflation and Global Deflationary Depression, *Global Research*, 17 October.

Chavas, J.P. (1999). On the Economic Rationality of Market Participants: the Case of Expectations in the U.S. Pork Market, *Journal of Agricultural and Resource Economics*, 24, 19–37.

Cheng, I.H., Hong, H. and Scheinkman, J.A. (2015). Yesterday's Heroes: Compensation and Creative Risk-Taking, *Journal of Finance*, 70, 839–879.

Chrispin, S. (2015). Forex Scandal: How to Rig the Market, BBC News, 20 May. http://www.bbc.com/news/business-26526905. 21 September 2015.

Claessens, S., Pozsar, Z., Ratnovski, L. and Singh, M. (2012). Shadow Banking: Economics and Policy Priorities. http://www.voxeu.org/article/shadow-banking-economics-and-policy-priorities. 12 May 2015.

Clarida, R., Galí, J. and Gertler, M. (1999). The Science of Monetary Policy: A New Keynesian Perspective, *Journal of Economic Literature*, 37, 1661–1707.

Clementi, G.L., Cooley, T.F., Richardson, M. and Walter, I. (2009). Rethinking Compensation in Financial Firms, *Financial Markets, Institutions and Instruments*, 18, 160–162.

Cochrane, J. (2013). Stopping Bank Crises Before They Start, 23 June. http://johnhcochrane.blogspot.com.au/2013/06/stopping-bank-crises-before-they-start.html. 6 August 2015.

Cohen, N. (2012). Efficient Markets Hypothesis Inefficient, *Financial Times*, 24 January.

Cole, H.L. and Cooley, T.F. (2014). Rating Agencies, NBER Working Paper No. 19972.

Colombo, J. (2014). This New Libor 'Scandal' will Cause a Terrifying Financial Crisis, *Forbes*, 4 June. http://www.forbes.com/sites/jessecolombo/2014/06/03/this-new-libor-scandal-will-cause-a-terrifying-financial-crisis/. 24 August 2015.

Cooper, H. and Savage, C. (2008). A Bit of 'I Told You So' Outside World Bank Talks, *New York Times*, 10 October.

Corbin, K. (2014). Vanguard's Bogle: We Need Less Trading, Higher Fiduciary Bar, *OnwallStreet*, 10 September. http://www.onwallstreet.com/news/practice/vanguard-founder-bogle-calls-for-less-trading-higher-fiduciary-bar-2690405-1.html. 5 July 2015.

Corcoran, T. (2009). AIG Bonuses Should be Paid, *National Post*, 17 March.

Council on Foreign Relations. (2015). The Credit Rating Controversy. http://www.cfr.org/financial-crises/credit-rating-controversy/p22328. 4 October 2015.

Cox, E.W. (1857). *New Law and Practice of Joint Stock Companies* (4th edition), London: Law Times Office.

Cox, J. (2015). Market Talk Suddenly Turns to Specter of QE4, CNBC News, 24 August. http://www.cnbc.com/2015/08/24/market-talk-suddenly-turns-to-specter-of-qe4.html. 8 October 2015.

Crotty, J. (2008). Structural Causes of the Global Financial Crisis: A Critical Assessment of the 'New Financial Architecture', Working Paper 2008–2014, Department of Economics, University of Massachusetts, Amherst.

Cuomo A. (2009). No Rhyme or Reason: The Heads I Win, Tails You Lose Bonus Culture. http://workplacebullying.org/multi/pdf/Cuomo.pdf. 16 May 2015.

D'Arcy, B.J. (2004). What is Good Regulation? Concepts and Case Studies for Control of Point and Diffuse Source Pollution, Proceedings of the 2004 WISA Biennial Conference, 2–6 May, Cape Town.

Dabla-Norris, E., Kochhar, K., Suphaphiphat, N., Ricka, F. and Tsounta, E. (2015). Causes and Consequences of Income Inequality: A Global Perspective, *IMF Staff Discussion Note*, June.

Daly, M. (2011). Standard & Poor's Acts High and Mighty to Hide low and Dirty Dealings with Wall Street, *Daily News*, 9 August.

Das, S. (2006). *Traders, Guns and Money*, London: Prentice Hall.

Davidson, P. (1982). Rational Expectations: A Fallacious Foundation for Studying Crucial Decision Making Processes, *Journal of Post Keynesian Economics*, 5, 182–198.

De Grauwe, P. and Grimaldi, M. (2006). *The Exchange Rate in a Behavioral Finance Framework*, Princeton (NJ): Princeton University Press.

De Larosière Group. (2009). Report of the High-Level Group on Financial Supervision in the EU, 25 February. http://ec.europa.eu/internal_market/finances/docs/de_larosiere_report_en.pdf. 4 June 2015.

De Lis, S.F., Pardo, J.C. and Santillana, V. (2014). Total Loss-Absorbing Capacity (TLAC): Making Bail-in Feasible and Credible Instead of Bail-out, *Global Regulation Watch*, BBVA Research, 11 November.

De Long, J.B., Shleifer, A., Summers, L.H. and Waldman, R.J. (1990). Noise Trader Risk in Financial Markets, *Journal of Political Economy*, 98, 703–738.

Dehnad, K. (2009). Efficient Market Hypothesis: Another Victim of the Great Recession, *Journal of Financial Transformation*, 27, 35–36.

Dennis, B. and Cho, D. (2009). Rage at AIG Swells As Bonuses Go Out, *Washington Post*, 17 March.

Department of Justice. (2013). Department of Justice Sues Standard & Poor's for Fraud in Rating Mortgage-Backed Securities in the Years Leading Up to the Financial Crisis, News Release, 5 February. http://www.justice.gov/opa/pr/department-justice-sues-standard-poor-s-fraud-rating-mortgage-backed-securities-years-leading. 8 October 2015.

Deutscher Bundestag. (2003). Transcript of a public hearing of the German Parliament's Finance Committee on 4 June 2003. http://webarchiv.bundestag.de/archive/2005/0825/parlament/gremien15/a07/protokolle/Protokoll_020.pdf. 29 July 2015.

Dewatripont, M. and Freixas, X. (2012). *The Crisis Aftermath: New Regulatory Paradigms*, London: Centre for Economic Policy Research.

Diamond, D.W. and Dybvig, P.H. (1983). Bank Runs, Deposit Insurance, and Liquidity, *Journal of Political Economy*, 91, 401–419.

Dietl, H., Duschl, T. and Lang, M. (2010). Executive Pay Regulation: What Regulators, Shareholders, and Managers Can Learn from Major Sports Leagues, Institute for Strategy and Business Economics, University of Zurich Working, Working Paper No. 12. 11 April 2015.

Dimitrakopoulos, K. (2011). Examining the Financial Crisis with Professor Eugene Fama. http://www.chicagobooth.edu/news/2011-10-28_fama.aspx. 11 April 2015.

Dowd, K. (2009a). Moral Hazard and the Financial Crisis, *Cato Journal*, 29, 141–166.

Dowd, K. (2009b). The Failure of Capital Adequacy Regulation, in P. Booth (ed.). *Verdict on the Crash Causes and Policy Implications*, London: Institute of Economic Affairs.

Dowd, K. (2014). Math Gone Mad: Regulatory Risk Modeling by the Federal Reserve, The Cato Institute, *Policy Analysis*, Number 754.

Dowd, K., Cotter, J., Humphrey, C.G. and Woods, M. (2008). How Unlucky is 25-Sigma? *Journal of Portfolio Management*, 34, 76–80.

Dowd, K., Hutchinson, M., Ashby, S. and Hinchcliffe, J.M. (2011a). Capital Inadequacies: the Dismal Failure of the Basel Regime of Capital Regulation, *Policy Analysis*, No 681, July.

Dowd, K., Hutchinson, M. and Kerr, G. (2011b). The Coming Fiat Money Cataclysm — and After. Paper prepared at the 29th Cato Institute Annual Monetary Conference on Monetary Reform in the Wake of Crisis, Washington DC, 16 November.

Drum, K. (2009). Big Banks, Big Banking Industry, 26 March. http://motherjones.com/kevin-drum/2009/03/big-banks-big-banking-industry. 27 August 2015.

Drum, K. (2012). Corruption and Fraud in the Financial Industry Get Worse and Worse, 19 December. http://www.motherjones.com/kevin-drum/2012/12/corruption-and-fraud-financial-industry-get-worse-and-worse. 18 September 2015.

Duca, J.V. (2014). What Drives the Shadow Banking System in the Short and Long Run? Federal Reserve Bank of Dallas, Research Department Working Paper 1401.

Dufey, G. and Kazemi, H.B. (1991). Demand and Supply of Forward Exchange Contracts Under Incomplete Information, *Journal of Economics and Business*, 43, 339–352.

Duncan, R. (2012). *The New Depression: the Breakdown of the Paper Money Economy*, New York: Wiley.

Edwards, D. and Oswald, R. (2009). GOP Senator to AIG Execs: 'Resign or Commit Suicide', 17 March. http://rawstory.com/news/2008/Grassley_to_AIG_execs_Resign_or_0317.html. 1 August 2015.

Eisinger, J. and Bernstein, J. (2010). The Magnetar Trade: How One Hedge Fund Helped Keep the Bubble Going, *ProPublica*, 9 April. https://www.propublica.org/article/all-the-magnetar-trade-how-one-hedge-fund-helped-keep-the-housing-bubble. 9 May 2015.

Ekins, E.M.C and Calabria, M.A. (2012). Regulation, Market Structure, and Role of the Credit Rating Agencies, *Policy Analysis*, No. 704.

El-Erian, M. (2015). Why QE4 Isn't in the Cards, *Bloomberg View*, 27 August. http://www.bloombergview.com/articles/2015-08-27/mohamed-el-erian-the-fed-won-t-do-a-qe4. 1 September 2015.

Enrich, D. and Martin, K. (2013). Currency Probe Widens as Major Banks Suspend Traders, *Wall Street Journal*, 1 November.

Epstein, G. (2001). Financialization, Rentier Interests, and Central Bank Policy, Working Paper, Department of Economics, University of Massachusetts, Amherst (MA).

European Central Bank. (2015). ECB Announces Expanded Asset Purchase Programme, Press Release, 22 January. https://www.ecb.europa.eu/press/pr/date/2015/html/pr150122_1.en.html. 13 May 2015.

European Commission. (2014). Credit Rating Agencies: Commission Adopts Regulatory Technical Standards to Implement Stricter New Rules, Press Release, 30 September. http://europa.eu/rapid/press-release_IP-14-1060_en.htm. 22 June 2015.

Faber, D. (2009). *And Then the Roof Caved in: How Wall Street's Greed and Stupidity Brought Capitalism to its Knees*, Hoboken (NJ): Wiley.

Fama, E. (1965). Random Walks in Stock Market Prices, *Financial Analysts Journal*, September–October, 55–59.

Fama, E. and French, K. (1993). Common Risk Factors in the Returns on Stocks and Bonds, *Journal of Financial Economics*, 33, 3–56.

Fama, E. and French, K. (1996). Multifactor Explanations of Asset Pricing Anomalies, *Journal of Finance*, 51, 55–84.

Fama, E. and French, K. (2014). A Five-Factor Asset Pricing Model, *Journal of Financial Economics*, 116, 1–22.

Faris, S. (2013). Iceland Prosecutor Investigates Convicts, Bankers for Financial Crimes, *Bloomberg Business*, 12 September.

Faunce, T.A., Neville, W. and Wasson, A. (2009). Non Violation Nullification of Benefit Claims: Opportunities and Dilemmas in a

Rule-Based WTO Dispute Settlement System, in M. Bray (ed.). *Ten Years of WTO Dispute Settlement: Australian Perspectives*, Canberra: Office of Trade Negotiations of the Department of Foreign Affairs and Trade.

FCIC. (2011). *The Financial Crisis Inquiry Report*, Washington, DC: U.S. Government Printing Office.

Fein, M. (2013). The Shadow Banking Charade. https://www.sec.gov/comments/s7-04-09/s70409-95.pdf. 25 May 2015.

Fennell, D. and Medvedev, A. (2011). An Economic Analysis of Credit Rating Agency Business Models and Ratings Accuracy, Financial Services Authority.

Fergusson, A. (2010). *When Money Dies* (revised edition), New York: Public Affairs.

Financial Stability Forum. (2008). Report of the Financial Stability Forum on Enhancing Market and Institutional Resilience. http://www.financialstabilityboard.org/publications/r_0804.pdf. 29 September 2015.

Financial Times. (2009). Japan's Lessons, 17 February.

Financial Times. (2013). Iceland's Creditors Braced for Losses, 2 May.

Finch, G. and Vaughan, L. (2015). Former Libor 'Ringmaster' Hayes Gets 14 Years for Libor Rigging, Bloomberg Business, 3 August.

Fischer, S. (1977). Long-Term Contracts, Rational Expectations, and the Optimal Money Supply Rule, *Journal of Political Economy*, 85, 191–205.

Fisher, I. (1933). The Debt Deflation Theory of the Great Depression, *Econometrica*, 1, 337–357.

Fisher, R.W. (2010). Speeches by Richard W. Fisher, Federal Reserve Bank of Dallas. http://dallasfed.org/news/speeches/fisher/2010/fs101108.cfm. 5 July 2015.

Fitch Rating Agency. (2007). The Impact of Poor Underwriting Practices and Fraud in Subprime RMBS Performance, *US Residential Mortgage Special Report*, 28 November. http://big.assets.huffingtonpost.com/FraudReport8Nov07Fitch.pdf.

Fons, J.S. (2008). Rating Competition and Structured Finance, *Journal of Structured Finance*, 7, 11.

Fowler, G. (2013). The Federal Reserve and Money Printing — Lessons of the 1930s and 1940s, *Glenmede Quarterly Market Review*, May.

Fox, J. (2009). *The Myth of Rational Market*, New York: Harper Collins.

Francis, L. (2010). Banking on Robbery: The Role of Fraud in the Financial Crisis, *Casualty Actuarial Society E-Forum*, 2, 1–54.

Frechette, D.L. and Weaver, R.D. (2001). Heterogenous Expectations of Traders in Speculative Futures Markets, *Journal of Futures Markets*, 21, 429–446.

Frieden, T. (2004). FBI Warns of Mortgage Fraud 'Epidemic', 17 September. edition.cnn.com/2004/LAW/09/17/mortgage.fraud/. 1 September 2015.

Friedman, M. (1961). The Lag in Effect of Monetary Policy, *Journal of Political Economy*, 69, 447–466.

Friedman, M. (1972). Have Monetary Policies Failed? *American Economic Review* (Papers and Proceedings), 62, 11–18.

Friedman, M. and Schwartz, A. (1963). *A Monetary History of the United States: 1867–1960*, Princeton: Princeton University Press.

FSB. (2011). Shadow Banking: Scoping the Issues, A Background Note of the Financial Stability Board. http://www.financialstabilityboard. org/wp-content/uploads/r_110412a.pdf. 5 July 2015.

FSB. (2012). Global Shadow Banking Monitoring Report 2012. http:// www.financialstabilityboard.org/wp-content/uploads/r_121128. pdf?page_moved=1. 12 September 2015.

FSB. (2014a). Global Shadow Banking Monitoring Report 2014. http:// www.financialstabilityboard.org/wp-content/uploads/r_141030. pdf. 13 August 2015.

FSB. (2014b). Adequacy of Loss-Absorbing Capacity of Global System-ically Important Banks in Resolution, Consultative Document, 10 November.

FSB. (2014c). 2014 Update of List of Global Systemically Important Banks (G-SIBs), 6 November. http://www.financialstabilityboard.org/wp-content/uploads/r_141106b.pdf. 7 May 2015.

FSB. (2015). FSB Publishes the 2015 Update of the G-SIB List, 3 November. http://www.financialstabilityboard.org/wp-content/uploads/FSB-announces-2015-update-of-group-of-global-systemically-important-banks-G-SIBs.pdf. 8 May 2015.

Furchtgott-Roth, H.W. (2000). The Art of Writing Good Regulations, *Federal Communications Law Journal*, 53(2). http://www.repository. law.indiana.edu/fclj/vol53/iss1/2. 26 August 2015.

Galbraith, J.K. (1982). Recession Economics, *New York Review of Books*, 4 February.

Galbraith, J.K. (2009). *The Great Crash 1929* (8th edition), New York: Houghton Mifflin.

Garbade, K. (2011). Will "Quantitative Easing" Trigger Inflation? *Liberty Street Economics*, 8 June. http://libertystreeteconomics.newyorkfed. org/2011/06/will-quantitative-easing-trigger-inflation.html#. VKz6CCuUeQA. 12 July 2015.

Gardiner, J. (2002). Defining Corruption, in A.J. Heidenheimer and M. Johnston (eds.). *Political Corruption: Concepts and Contexts* (3rd edition), New Brunswick: Transaction Publishers.

Geithner, T. (2008). Reducing Systemic Risk in a Dynamic Financial System, Speech Delivered at The Economic Club of New York, New York City, 9 June.

Gerlach, S. and Svensson, L.E.O. (2001). Money and Inflation in the Euro Area: A Case for Monetary Indicators? BIS Working Paper No. 98.

Ghandi, S.R. (2014). Danger Posed by Shadow Banking Systems to the Global Financial System — The Indian Case, *Presentation at the ICRIER's International Conference 21 August 21, 2014*. https://www.rbi. org.in/scripts/BS_ViewBulletin.aspx?Id=15119. 2 August 2015.

Giangreco, D.M. and Moore, K. (1999). *Dear Harry: Truman's Mailroom, 1945–1953*, Mechanicsburg (PA): Stackpole Books.

Gillen, D. (2009). In Rating Agencies, Investors Still Trust, *New York Times*, 4 June.

Goldman, E. and Slezak, S. (2006). An Equilibrium Model of Incentive Contracts in the Presence of Information Manipulation, *Journal of Financial Economics*, 80, 603–626.

Goldstein, M. (2008). The Subprime and Credit Crisis, Paper Based on Transcript of Speech Presented at the Global Economic Prospects Meeting, Peterson Institute for International Economics, 3 April.

Gongloff, M. (2013). Banker, CEO Pay Largely Responsible For Rising Inequality: Study, *Huffington Post*, 22 June.

Goodfriend, M.S. and King, R.G. (1981). A Note on the Neutrality of Temporary Monetary Disturbances, *Journal of Monetary Economics*, 7, 371–385.

Gorton, G. (2007). The Panic of 2007, NBER Working Paper No. 14358.

Gorton, G. (2010). *Slapped by the Invisible Hand: The Panic of 2007*, Oxford: Oxford University Press.

Gorton, G.B. and Metrick, A. (2010a). Securitized Banking and the Run on Repo, Yale ICF Working Papers, No. 09–14.

Gorton, G.B. and Metrick, A. (2010b). Regulating the Shadow Banking System, *Brookings Papers on Economic Activity*, Fall, 261–297.

Green, M. and Nader, R. (1973). Economic Regulation versus Competition: Uncle Sam the Monopoly Man, *Yale Law Journal*, 82, 876.

Greenwood, J. (2012). Wiki Joins Rating Game, *Financial Post*, 28 January.

Greider, W. (1981). The Education of David Stockman, *The Atlantic*, December.

Greider, W. (1982). *The Education of David Stockman and other Americans*, New York: Penguine.

Gross, B. (2007). Beware Our Shadow Banking System, *Fortune*, http://money.cnn.com/2007/11/27/news/newsmakers/gross_banking.fortune. 6 August 2015.

Grossman, S. and Stiglitz, J. (1980). On the Impossibility of Informationally Efficient Markets, *American Economic Review*, 70, 393–408.

Group of Thirty. (2009). Financial Reform: A Framework for Financial Stability. www.group30.org/pubs/recommendations.pdf. 16 March 2015.

Gwartney, J., Macpherson, D., Sobel, R and Stroup, R. (2008). The Crash of 2008: Cause and Aftermath. http://www.cengage.com/economics/book_content/0324580185_gwartney/content.html. 3 September 2015.

Hammar, K. (2015). Iceland Makes Strong Recovery from 2008 Financial Crisis, *IMF Survey*, 13 March.

Hannoun, H. (2008). Financial Deepening without Financial Excesses, 43rd SEACEN Governors' Conference, Jakarta, 21 March.

Harper, I. and Thomas, M. (2009). Making Sense of the GFC: Where Did it Come From and What Do we Do Now, *Economic Papers*, 28, 196–205.

Harrington, A. and Hjelt, P. (2001). The Great CEO Pay Heist, *Fortune*, 25 June. http://archive.fortune.com/magazines/fortune. 19 April 2015.

Harris, M. and Raviv, A. (1993). Differences of Opinion Makes a Horse Race, *Review of Financial Studies*, 6, 473–506.

Harrison, J.M. and Kreps, D.M. (1978). Speculative Investor Behavior in a Stock Market with Heterogeneous Expectations, *Quarterly Journal of Economics*, 93, 323–336.

Harvey, C.R. and Liu, Y. (2014). Evaluating Trading Strategies, *Journal of Portfolio Management*, 40, 108–118.

Harvey, D. (2010). *The Enigma of Capital and the Crises of Capitalism*, Oxford: Oxford University Press.

Harvey, J.T. (2011). Money Growth Does Not Cause Inflation! *Forbes*, 15 May.

Hauksson, M. (2009). Eva Joly Hired as a Special Consultant to the Icelandic Government, *Ice News*, 28 March.

Hawkins, J. and Turner, P. (2000). International Financial Reform: Regulatory and other Issues, Paper Presented at a Conference on International Financial Contagion, Washington DC, 3–4 February.

He, X. (2012). Recent Developments on Heterogeneous Beliefs and Adaptive Behaviour of Financial Markets, University of Technology Sydney, Quantitative Finance Research Centre Research Papers, No. 316, October.

Heckman, J. (2001). Micro Data, Heterogeneity, and Evaluation of Public Policy: Nobel Lecture, *Journal of Political Economy*, 109, 673–748.

Herald Scotland. (2015). RBS Says Sorry as it Amasses £830 Million in Penalties over Forex Rigging Scandal, 21 May. http://www.heraldscotland. com/news/13214681.RBS_says_sorry_as_it_amasses___830_million_ in_penalties_over_forex_rigging_scandal/. 15 September 2015.

Herman, M. (2009). Corruption Helped Cause Financial Crisis, *The Times*, 23 September.

Hill, C. (2010). Why Did Rating Agencies Do Such a Bad Job Rating Subprime Securities? *Pitt Law Review*, 71, 585–608.

Hilsenrath, J.E. (2004). Stock Characters: As Two Economists Debate Markets, the Tide Shifts, *Wall Street Journal*, 18 October.

Hilzenrath, D.S. (2010). Commodity Futures Trading Commission Judge Says Colleague Biased Against Complainants, *Washington Post*, 19 October.

Hindery, L. (2008). Why We Need to Limit Executive Compensation, *Business Week*, 4 November.

Hodgson, G. (2013). Banking, Finance and Income Inequality, October. http://positivemoney.org/wp-content/uploads/2013/10/Banking-Finance-and-Income-Inequality.pdf. 12 September 2015.

Hodgson-Brown, E. (2012). *Web of Debt: The Shocking Truth about our Money System and How we can Break Free* (fifth edition), Baton Rouge, Louisiana: Third Millennium Press.

Hogan, W.P. (1960). Monetary Policy and Financial Intermediaries, *Economic Record*, 36, 517–529.

Holt, J. (2009). A Summary of the Primary Causes of the Housing Bubble and the Resulting Credit Crisis: A Non-Technical Paper, *Journal of Business Inquiry*, 8, 120–129.

House Committee on Government Operations. (1988). Combating Fraud, Abuse and Misconduct on the Nation's Financial Institutions: Current Federal Efforts are Inadequate, H. R. 100–1088.

Huberts, A.C. (2013). How Exactly Could Quantitative Easing Cause 'Unbalanced' Inflation Expectations, *Investment Perspective*, May. http://www.mcm.com/assets/publications/unanchored_expectations.pdf. 19 June 2015.

Huffington, A. (2008). Laissez-Faire Capitalism Should Be as Dead as Soviet Communism, 22 December. http://www.huffingtonpost.com/arianna-huffington/laissez-faire-capitalism_b_152900.html. 11 July 2015.

Hunt, J.P. (2008). Credit Rating Agencies and the 'Worldwide Credit Crisis': the Limits of Reputation, the Insufficiency of Reform, and a Proposal for Improvement, *Columbia Business Law Review*, 1, 109–209.

Hutchinson, M. (2008). Scrap Heap for Financial Models, *Bear's Lair*, 11 February. www.prudentbear.com.

Hutton, W. (2010). Now we Know the Truth: The Financial Meltdown wasn't a Mistake — It was a Con, *The Guardian*, 19 April.

IMF. (2015). Iceland: Selected Issues, IMF Country Report No. 15/73.

Institutional Investor. (2011). Iceland to Raise $1B in Bond Sale, 9 June.

International Herald Tribune. (2008). Freddie Mac Courts Investors, Buffett Passes, 22 August.

Janda, M. (2014). Bank for International Settlements Warns Low Interest Rate Policies may Generate Next Global Financial Crisis, ABC News. http://www.abc.net.au/news/2014-06-29/bis-warns-low-rate-policies-may-generate-next-financial-crisis/5558292. 24 May 2015.

Jensen, M. (1978). Some Anomalous Evidence Regarding Market Efficiency, *Journal of Financial Economics*, 6, 95–101.

Jericho, G. (2012). US Quantitative Easing a Point of Interest for RBA, *The Drum Opinion*, 19 September. http://www.abc.net.au/unleashed/4268022.html. 5 July 2015.

Jerusalem Post. (2009). Has 'Guiding Model' for Global Markets Gone Haywire? 11 June.

Johnson, K. (2014). Federal Reserve Covers up Bankers Crimes, *American Free Press*, 2 November. http://americanfreepress.net/federal-reserve-covers-up-banker-crimes/. 25 May 2015.

Johnson, S. (2009). The Quite Coup, *The Atlantic*, May.

Johnson, S. and Boone, P. (2010). The Doomsday Cycle, *Vox*, 22 February.

Jones, A. (2009). A First Amendment Defense for the Rating Agencies? *Wall Street Journal*, 21 April. http://blogs.wsj.com/law/2009/04/21/a-first-amendment-defense-for-the-rating-agencies/. 13 July 2015.

Jones, E. (2015). The Australian Banking Sector: Predatory and Unaccountable, 31 March. https://independentaustralia.net/business/business-display/the-australian-banking-sector-predatory-and-untouchable,7539. 11 June 2015.

Jones, S. (2008). When Junk Was Gold, *Financial Times*, 17 October.

Jonsson, A. (2011). Iceland's Banks Come in From the Cold, *Wall Street Journal*, 16 June.

Kardashian, K. (2014). Did Excessive Pay Contribute to the Financial Crisis? 8 December. https://www.tuck.dartmouth.edu/newsroom/articles/did-excessive-pay-contribute-to-the-financial-crisis. 5 March 2015.

Kashyap, A., Stein, J. and Hanson, S. (2010). An Analysis of the Impact of Substantially Heightened Capital Requirements on Large Financial Institutions, Working Paper.

Kasperkevic, J. (2013). Tax Breaks for CEOs Pay for Million-Dollar Salaries, *The Guardian*, 4 December.

Kasriel, P. (2004). The Well-Known Relationship Between the Output Gap and Inflation. http://www.northerntrust.com/library/econ_research/weekly/us/pc041604.pdf. 13 September 2015.

Katz, J., Salinas, E. and Stephanou, C. (2009). Credit Rating Agencies: No Easy Regulatory Solutions, The World Bank Group, October.

Kaufman, D. (2009). Corruption and the Global Financial Crisis, *Forbes*, 27 January.

Kennedy, H. (2009). AIG bonus checks may be taxed at up to 100%, says Sen. Chuck Schumer, *Daily News*. http://www.nydailynews.com/news/money/aig-bonus-checks-taxed-100-sen-chuck-schumer-article–1.205774. 7 June 2015.

Kerkhoff, M. (2013). Why QE Isn't "Printing Money" and Hasn't Led to Inflation ... Yet, *Financial Sense*, 19 November. http://www.financialsense.com/contributors/matthew-kerkhoff/qe-printing-money-inflation. 8 May 2015.

Khatiwada, S. (2010). Did the Financial Corporate Sector Profit at the Expense of the Rest of the Economy? Evidence from the United States, International Institute for Labour Studies, Discussion Paper DP/206/2010.

King, M. (2010). Banking: From Bagehot to Basel, and Back Again, the Second Bagehot Lecture, Buttonwood Gathering, New York City.

Kliger, D. and Sarig. O. (2002). The Information Value of Bond Ratings, *Journal of Finance*, 55, 2879–2902.

Knowledge@Wahrton. (2010). Executive Compensation: More Regulation, or Just More Transparency? 17 February. http://knowledge.wharton.

upenn.edu/article/executive-compensation-more-regulation-or-just-more-transparency/. 19 July 2015.

Knowledge@Wharton. (2015). Can the Bank of England's New 'Ring-fencing' Rules Work? 20 October. http://knowledge.wharton.upenn.edu/article/can-the-bank-of-englands-new-ring-fencing-rules-work/. 30 October 2015.

Kordes, L.E. (2013). What is Shadow Banking? *Finance and Development*, June, 42–43.

Kotlikoff, L. (2010). *Jimmy Stewart is Dead*, Hoboken (NJ): Wiley.

Kourlas, J. (2012). Lessons Not Learned From the Housing Crisis, The Atlas Society, 12 April.

Kowalik, M. (2013). Basel Liquidity Regulation: Was it Improved with the 2013 Revisions, *Federal Reserve Bank of Kansas City Economic Review*, Second Quarter, 65–87.

Kristol, W. (2009). AIG Bonus Babies, *Washington Post*, 16 March.

Krugman, P. (2007). *The Conscious of a Liberal*, New York: Norton.

Krugman, P. (2009). *The Return of Depression Economics and the Crisis of 2008*, New York: Norton.

Krugman, P. (2012). Not Enough Inflation, *New York Times*, 5 April.

Kuczynski, P.P. and Williamson, J. (2003). *After the Washington Consensus: Restarting Growth and Reform in Latin America*, Washington DC: Peterson Institute for International Economics.

Kurdas, C. (2009). Goldman Critics vs. Little Goldmans, *ThinkMarkets*, 20 October (with comments). www.thinkmarkets.wordpress.com/2009/10/10/goldman-critics-vs-little-goldmans/. 13 August 2015.

Kuttner, R. (2011). A Real Pecora Commission, 25 May. http://www.huffingtonpost.com/robert-kuttner/a-real-pecora-commission_b_209572.html. 22 March 2015.

Lagarde, C. (2009). G20 Must Bring Banks' Bonus Culture to an End, *Financial Times*, 4 September.

Larsen, P.T. (2007). Goldman Pays the Price of Being Big, *Financial Times*, 13 August.

Lawson, D. (2009). Fool's Gold: How an Ingenious Tribe of Bankers Rewrote the Rules of Finance, Made a Fortune and Survived a Catastrophe by Gillian Tett, *Sunday Times*, 3 May.

Lenzner, R. (2009). Hank Greenberg Shares the Blame for AIG's Pain, *Forbes*, 17 March.

Lenzner, R. (2014). You Better Read This if You Don't Know Anything About the Shadow Banking System, *Forbes*, 30 June. http://www.forbes.com/

sites/robertlenzner/2014/06/30/the-unregulated-shadow-banking-system-triggered-the-2008-financial-crisis/. 29 September 2015.

Levin, C. (2010). Statement to Senate Permanent Committee on Investigations Hearing on Wall Street and the Financial Crisis: the Role of High Risk Home Loans, 13 April. http://www.hsgac.senate.gov/subcommittees/investigations/hearings/wall-street-and-the-financial-crisis-the-role-of-high-risk-home-loans. 17 May 2015.

Levine, M. (2015). Bonuses, Bail-Ins and Down Rounds, *Bloomberg View*, 9 November. http://www.bloombergview.com/articles/2015-11-09/bonuses-bail-ins-and-down-rounds. 25 June 2015.

Levine, Y. (2012). There is no Nobel Prize in Economics, *AlterNet*, 12 October. http://www.alternet.org/economy/there-no-nobel-prize-economics. 24 May 2015.

Levine-Weinberg, A. (2012). Why I'm Not Afraid of QE3, *Seeking Alpha*, 13 September.

Levy, F. and Temin, P. (2007). Inequality and Institutions in 20th Century America, NBER Working Paper No. 13106.

Lewis, C. (2009). Strapped Iceland Lists Homes in D.C., New York, London, *Wall Street Journal*, 27 February.

Lewis, M. (2009). The Man who Crashed the World, *Vanity Fair*, August.

Lewis, M. (2010). *The Big Short: Inside the Doomsday Machine*, New York: Norton.

Limbaugh, R. (2009). The Last Man Standing Speaks in Defense of AIG Bailout Bonuses, 16 March. http://www.rushlimbaugh.com/daily/2009/03/16/the_last_man_standing_speaks_in_defense_of_aig_bailout_bonuses. 6 March 2015.

Lippert, J. (2010). Credit Ratings Can't Claim Free Speech in Law Giving New Risks, *Bloomberg Markets Magazine*, 7 December.

Lo, A. and MacKinlay, A.C. (1999). *A Non-Random Walk Down Wall Street*, Princeton: Princeton University Press.

Lubochinsky, C. and Raingeard, O. (2008). Comments on the Proposal for a Directive/Regulation of the European Parliament and of the Council on Credit Rating Agencies, Submission to the European Commission, Consultation on Policy Proposals Regarding Credit Rating Agencies, 5 September.

Lucas, R.E. and Sargent, T.J. (1981). *Rational Expectations and Econometric Practice*, London: Allen and Unwin.

Lucas, R.E. and Stokey, N.L. (2011). Understanding Sources and Limiting Consequences: A Theoretical Framework, Federal Reserve Bank of Minneapolis, 17 May. http://www.minneapolisfed.org/publications_papers/pub_display.cfm?id=4661&. 25 July 2015.

Madura, J. (2011). *Financial Markets and Institutions*, Mason (OH): South-Western Cengage Learning.

Mahlmann, T. (2008). Rating Agencies and the Role of Rating Publication Rights, *Journal of Banking and Finance*, 32, 2414–2422.

Malkiel, B. (1973). *A Random Walk Down Wall Street*, New York: Norton.

Mandler, M. and Scharnagl, M. (2014). Money Growth and Consumer Price Inflation in the Euro Area: A Wavelet Analysis, Deutsche Bundesbank, Discussion Paper No. 33/2014.

Martens, P. and Martens, R. (2015). Brooksley Born Still Telling the Uncomfortable Truths about Wall Street, *Wall Street on Parade*, 7 May. http://wallstreetonparade.com/2015/05/brooksley-born-still-telling-the-uncomfortable-truths-about-wall-street/. 14 September 2015.

Martin, K. and Enrich, D. (2013). Forex Traders Said to Have Colluded in Effort to Profit, *Wall Street Journal*, 19 December.

Mason, R. (2009). Iceland Banking Inquiry Finds Murky Geysers Run Deep, *The Telegraph*, 13 April.

Mathis, J., Mcandrews, J. and Rochet, J.C. (2008). Rating The Raters: Are Reputation Concerns Powerful Enough to Discipline Rating Agencies? Working Paper, Toulouse School of Economics and Federal Reserve Bank of New York.

Matthews, C. (2013). Taper Tantrums: 3 Myths About Quantitative Easing, *Time*, 18 September. http://business.time.com/2013/09/18/taper-tantrums-3-myths-about-quantitative-easing/. 1 August 2015.

McCulley, P. (2007). Teton Reflections, *PIMCO Global Central Bank Focus* (August/September).

McDonald, I.M. (2009). The Global Financial Crisis and Behavioural Economics, *Economic Papers*, 28, 249–254.

McGuire, F.J. (2015). Peter Schiff: The Fed Is Spooking the Markets — Not China, *Newsmax Finance*, 24 August. http://www.newsmax.com/Finance/StreetTalk/Peter-Schiff-Federal-Reserve-Market-Crash-QE4/2015/08/24/id/671689/. 9 August 2015.

McLaughlin, D., Schoenberg, T. and Finch, G. (2015). Six Banks Pay $5.8 Billion, Five Guilty of Market Rigging, *Bloomberg News*, 21 May.

McLean, B. and Nocera, J. (2011). *All the Devils are Here*, New York: Penguin Publishing Group.

McTeer, R. (2010). Monetary Policy, Deflation and Quantitative Easing, *Forbes*, 30 July.

Mehra, Y.P. (2004). The Output Gap, Expected Future Inflation and Inflation Dynamics: Another Look, Federal Reserve Bank of Richmond, Working Paper No. 04–06.

Metais, E. (2009). The Failure of Mergers-Acquisitions, Myth or Reality? EDHEC Business School. www.edhec-mba.com/jsp/fiche_pagelibre. jsp?CODE=0337090&LANGUE=1. 25 March 2015.

Mihm, S. (2008). Dr Doom, *New York Times Magazine*, 15 August.

Miller, J. (2014). Osborne Abandons Challenge to EU Cap on Bankers' Bonuses, BBC News, 20 November. http://www.bbc.com/news/business-30125780. 18 August 2015.

Ministry of Finance and Economic Affairs (2015). Comprehensive Strategy for Capital Account Liberalisation Announced, 6 August. http://eng.fjarmalaraduneyti.is/news/nr/19594. 6 July 2015.

Mintz, P. (2009). Off With Their Heads: Samples of AIG Outrage, *Business Week*, 17 March.

Moosa, I.A. (2007). *Operational Risk Management*, London: Palgrave.

Moosa, I.A. (2010). *The Myth of Too Big to Fail*, London: Palgrave.

Moosa, I.A. (2012). *Quantitative Easing as a Highway to Hyperinflation*, Singapore: World Scientific.

Moosa, I.A. (2013a). The Capital Asset Pricing Model (CAPM): the History of a Failed Revolutionary Idea in Finance? Comments and Extensions, *Abacus*, 49, 62–68.

Moosa, I.A. (2013b). The Failure of Financial Econometrics: Confirmation and Publication Biases, *Journal of Financial Transformation*, 36, 45–50.

Moosa, I.A. (2015a). *Good Regulation, Bad Regulation: The Anatomy of Financial Regulation*, London: Palgrave.

Moosa, I.A. (2015b). The Regulation of Shadow Banking, *Journal of Banking Regulation*, (Published online, 12 August), doi:10.1057/jbr.2015.8.

Morck, R. (2005). A History of Corporate Governance around the World, Conference Report, Washington DC: NBER.

Morgenson, G. (2008). Was There a Loan It Didn't Like? *New York Times*, 1 November.

Morris, C.R. (2009). *The Two Trillion Dollar Meltdown*, New York: Public Affairs.

Moyer, K. (2009). Executive Compensation in Financial Services, 7 December. http://blogs.gartner.com/kristin_moyer/2009/12/07/executive-compensation-in-financial-services/. 6 August 2015.

Muth, J.F. (1961). Rational Expectations and the Theory of Price Movements, *Econometrica*, 29, 315–335.

Naím, M. (1999). Fads and Fashion in Economic Reforms: Washington Consensus or Washington Confusion? *Foreign Policy Magazine*, 26 October.

Narayana, N. (2010). G20 Focus on Currency Row may Leave behind Development Goals, Say NGOs, *Times*, 11 November.

New York Times. (2001). Deutsche Bank Hires Former S.E.C. Official, 2 October.

New York Times. (2009). Obama's Statement on AIG, 16 March.

Newman, R. (2009). What's Good, What's Bad About the AIG Bailout, *US News and World Report*, 17 March.

Newmark, E. (2009). Mean Street: AIG — The Revolution Will Devour Congress, *Wall Street Journal*, 18 March.

Nicholson, C.V. (2010). Icesave Talks Break Down and Referendum Looms, *New York Times*, 26 February.

Nicolas, M. and Firzli, J. (2011). A Critique of the Basel Committee on Banking Supervision, *Revue Analyse Financière*, Nov. 10 2011/Q1 2012.

Nocera, J. (2009). Poking Holes in a Theory on Markets, *New York Times*, 5 June.

Noe, T. (2003). Tunnel-Proofing the Executive Suite: Transparency, Temptation, and the Design of Executive Compensation, Working Paper, Tulane University.

Noeth, B. and Sengupta, R. (2011). Is Shadow Banking Really Banking? *Regional Economist*, Federal Reserve Bank of St. Louis, October, 8–13.

Norris, F. (2008). News Analysis: Another Crisis, Another Guarantee, *New York Times*, 24 November.

O'Rourke, M. (2009). Too Big to Fail? *Risk Management*, May, 61.

OECD. (2010). Competition and Credit Rating Agencies. http://www.oecd.org/regreform/sectors/46825342.pdf. 26 March 2015.

Office for National Statistics. (2015). Average Weekly Earnings — Bonus Payments in Great Britain, 2014–2015. http://www.ons.gov.uk/ons/dcp171766_414566.pdf. 22 October 2015.

Orphanides, A. and van Norden, S. (2004). The Reliability of Inflation Forecasts Based on Output Gap Estimates in Real Time, Federal Reserve Board, Finance and Economics Discussion Series No. 2004–68.

Osler, S. (2010). How the Roof Fell in on Countrywide, *Fortune*, 23 December.

Painter, A. (2009). The Washington Consensus is Dead, *The Guardian*, 4 October.

Painter, R. (2006). Ethics and Corruption in Business and Government: Interdependence and Adverse Consequences, University of Chicago Law School, Fulton Lectures.

Palley, T.I. (2007). What it is and Why it Matters, The Levy Economics Institute and Economics for Democratic and Open Societies, Working Paper No. 525.

Partnoy, F. (2006). How and Why Credit Rating Agencies are Not Like Other Gatekeepers, San Diego Legal Studies Paper No. 07–46.

Partnoy, F. (2010). *Infectious Greed: How Deceit and Risk Corrupted the Financial Markets*, London: Profile Books.

Pasour, E.C. (1989). The Efficient-Market Hypothesis and Entrepreneurship, *Review of Austrian Economics*, 3, 95–107.

Peston, R. (2008). We Lose in Greed Game, 28 March. http://www.bbc.co.uk/blogs/legacy/thereporters/robertpeston/2008/03/we_lose_in_greed_game.html. 27 June 2015.

Phelps, E. and Taylor, J.B. (1977). Stabilizing Powers of Monetary Policy under Rational Expectations, *Journal of Political Economy*, 85, 163–190.

Philippon, T. (2013). Finance versus Wal-Mart: Why are Financial Services so Expensive? http://www.russellsage.org/sites/all/files/Rethinking-Finance/Philippon_v3.pdf. 4 May 2015.

Plantin, G. (2015). Shadow Banking and Bank Capital Regulation, *Review of Financial Studies*, 28, 146–175.

Povel, P., Singh, R. and Winton, A. (2007). Booms, Busts, and Fraud, *Review of Financial Studies*, 20, 1219–1254.

Pozsar, Z., Adrian, T., Ashcraft, A. and H. Boesky. (2010). Shadow Banking, *Federal Reserve Bank of New York Staff Report*, No. 458, 1–38.

PWC. (2013). EU Bonus Cap Update — Cap to Apply More Broadly, May. http://www.pwc.com/us/en/financial-services/regulatory-services/publications/eu-bonus-cap-update.html. 17 September 2015.

PWC. (2014). EU Bonus Cap: Restrictions Nearly Final for Asset Managers, Regulatory Brief, March. http://www.pwc.com/us/en/financial-services/regulatory-services/publications/assets/fs-reg-brief-eu-bonus-cap-ucits-v.pdf. 17 September 2015.

Quiggin, J. (2009). Six Refuted Doctrines, *Economic Papers*, 28, 239–248.

Quinn, J. (2010). US Bank Accounting 'Masks True Debt Levels', *The Telegraph*, 10 April.

Rakoff, J.S. (2014). The Financial Crisis: Why Have No High-Level Executives Been Prosecuted? *The New York Review of Books*, 9 January. http://www.nybooks.com/articles/archives/2014/jan/09/financial-crisis-why-no-executive-prosecutions/. 3 October 2015.

Ramiah, V., Zhao, Y., Moosa, I.A. and Graham, M. (2014). A Behavioural Finance Approach to Working Capital Management, *European Journal of Finance* (Published online).

Reid, S. (2015). A Recipe for the 2008 Financial Crisis, *Turning Finance*. http://www.turingfinance.com/recipe-for-the-financial-crisis/. 8 August 2015.

Reuters. (2007). Spending Boosted by Home Equity Loans, 23 April. http://www.reuters.com/article/us-usa-greenspan-equity-idUSN2330071920070423. 29 June 2015.

Reuters. (2013). Shadow Banking Facing Tougher Regulations, 26 January. http://www.cnbc.com/id/100410132. 18 April 2015.

Reuters. (2015). Hillary Clinton Supports Ban on "Revolving Door" Corporate Bonuses, 31 August. http://www.reuters.com/article/2015/08/31/us-usa-election-clinton-bonus-idUSKCN0R01KZ20150831. 25 October 2015.

Revill, J., Walen, J. and Morse, A. (2013). Furor Ends $78 Million Pay Deal, *Wall Street Journal*, 20 February.

Richardson, M. and White, L. (2009). The Rating Agencies: Is Regulation the Answer? *Financial Markets, Institutions & Instruments*, 18, 146–148.

Roberts, P.C. and Kranzler, D. (2015). Supply and Demand in the Gold and Silver Futures Markets, LewRockwell.com, 30 July. https://www.lewrockwell.com/2015/07/paul-craig-roberts/manipulating-the-price-of-gold-and-silver/. 25 October 2015.

Roche, C. (2013). Why Didn't QE Cause High Inflation? *Pragmatic Capitalism*, 31 July. http://pragcap.com/why-didnt-qe-cause-high-inflation. 16 March 2015.

Rodriguez, L.J. (2002). International Banking Regulation: Where's the Market Discipline in Basel II? *Policy Analysis*, No. 455, October.

Rodrik, D. (2006). Goodbye Washington Consensus, Hello Washington Confusion? A Review of the World Bank's *Economic Growth in the 1990s: Learning from a Decade of Reform*, Journal of Economic Literature, 44, 973–987.

Roig-Franzia, M. (2009). Credit Crisis Cassandra: Brooksley Born's Unheeded Warning is a Refuel 10 Years on, *Washington Post*, 26 May.

Roland, N. (2008). Investors Cite Rating Agencies' Conflict of Interest, *Financial Week*, 8 July.

Roubini, N. (2007). Current Market Turmoil: Non-Priceable Knightian 'Uncertainty' Rather than Priceable Market 'Risk', *Nouriel Roubini's Global EconoMonitor*, 15 August.

Sachs, J. (2013). Fixing the Banking System for Good, Philadelphia Federal Reserve, 17 April. http://www.nakedcapitalism.com/2013/04/jeffrey-sachscalls-out-wall-street-criminality-and-pathological-greed.html#Gi77xWO2eYLE1jTD.99. 8 July 2015.

Samuelson, R.J. (2011). Reckless Optimism, *Claremont Review of Books*. http://www.claremont.org/crb/article/reckless-optimism/. 10 April 2015.

Sanchez, D. (2014). Shadow Banking and the Crisis of 2007–2008, *Federal Reserve Bank of Philadelphia Review*, Quarter 2, 7–14.

Sargent, T.J. and Wallace, N. (1976). Rational Expectations and the Theory of Economic Policy, *Journal of Monetary Economics*, 2, 169–183.

Schechter, D. (2010). Financial Fraud and the Economic Crisis, Global Research, 2 April. http://www.globalresearch.ca/financial-fraud-and-the-economic-crisis/18444. 10 July 2015.

Schwarcz, S.L. (2002). Private Ordering of Public Markets: The Rating Agency Paradox, *University of Illinois Law Review*, 1, 15.

SEC. (2009). Robert Khuzami Named SEC Director of Enforcement, Press Release, 19 February.

Securities and Exchange Board of India. (2009). Report of the Committee on Comprehensive Regulation for Credit Rating Agencies, December.

Seeking Alpha. (2007). Equity Extraction-Charts, 25 April.

Shiller, R.J. (1984). Stock Prices and Social Dynamics, *Brookings Papers on Economic Activity*, 2, 457–510.

Shiller, R.J. (2007). Bubble Trouble, Project Syndicate, 7 July.

Shiller, R.J. (2012). *Finance and the Good Society*, Princeton: Princeton University Press.

Shleifer, A. (2010). Comment on Gorton and Metrick, *Brookings Papers on Economic Activity*, Fall, 298–303.

Shojai, S. and Feiger, G. (2010). Economists' Hubris: The Case of Risk Management. http://ssrn.com/abstratct=1550622. 23 June 2015.

Shostak, F. (1997). In Defense of Fundamental Analysis: A Critique of the Efficient Market Hypothesis, *Review of Austrian Economics*, 10, 27–45.

Sicilia, D. (2011). Roots of Credit Rating Agency Shortcomings, University of Maryland, 24 May. http://blogs.rhsmith.umd.edu/financial-policy/commentary/roots-of-credit-rating-agency-shortcomings/. 24 July 2015.

Siegel, J.J. (2010). The Efficient Market Theory and the Recent Financial Crisis, The Inagural Conference of the Institute of New Economic Thinking, King's College, Cambridge, 9 April.

Sigurjonsson, F. (2015). Monetary Reform: A Better Monetary System for Iceland, 10 March. http://www.forsaetisraduneyti.is/media/Skyrslur/monetary-reform.pdf. 10 September 2015.

Simkovic, M. (2009). Secret Liens and the Financial Crisis of 2008, *American Bankruptcy Law Journal* 83, 253–296.

Simkovic, M. (2013). Competition and Crisis in Mortgage Securitization, *Indiana Law Journal*, 88, 213–271.

Sims, A. and Boyle, D. (2009). *The New Economics: A Bigger Picture*, London: Earthscan.

Sinclair, T.J. (2005). *The New Masters of Capital: American Bond Rating Agencies and the Politics of Creditworthiness*, Ithaca, New York: Cornell University Press.

Skidelsky, R. (2009). *Keynes: The Return of the Master*, London: Allen Lane.

Skreta, V. and Veldkamp, L. (2008). Ratings Shopping and Asset Complexity: A Theory of Ratings Inflation, Working Paper, Stern School of Business.

Sky News. (2009). Prime Minister Gordon Brown: G20 Will Pump Trillion Dollars into World Economy, 2 April.

Smith, A. (1776). *The Wealth of Nations* (Reprint), Oxford: Oxford University Press.

Smith, N. (2014). Here's More to QE than Krugman Thinks, 11 November. http://www.bloombergview.com/articles/2014-11-11/theres-more-to-qe-than-krugman-thinks. 9 July 2015.

Smith, Y. (2010). *Econned: How Unenlightened Self Interest Undermined Democracy and Corrupted Capitalism*, New York: Palgrave Macmillan.

Snyder, M. (2010). 11 Examples of How Insanely Corrupt the U.S. Financial System has Become, 13 April. http://endoftheamericandream.com/archives/11-examples-of-how-insanely-corrupt-the-usfinancial-system-has-become. 18 August 2015.

Sorkin, A.R. (2009). The Case for Paying Out Bonuses at A.I.G, *New York Times*, 17 March.

Soros, G. (2008). The Worst Market Crisis in 60 Years, *Financial Times*, 22 January.

Sowell, T. (2009). Cheap Political Theater, 24 March. http://www.jewish-worldreview.com/cols/sowell032409.php3. 22 May 2015.

Spaventa, L. (2009). Economist, Economics and the Crisis, *Vox*, 12 August.

Sprague, I.H. (1986). *Bailout: An Insider's Account of Bank Failures and Rescues*, New York: Basic Books.

Star Ledger. (2009). AIG's Arrogance is Stunning, 17 March.

Stein, J. (2010). Securitization, Shadow Banking, and Financial Fragility, *Daedalus*, 139, 41–51.

Stempel, J. (2014). Investors Seek over $40 billion from Madoff Victim Fund, *Reuters*, 13 May.

Stewart, H. (2012). Wealth Doesn't Trickle Down — It just Floods Offshore, *The Guardian*, 22 July.

Stewart, H. (2015). OECD: Large Banking Sectors Widen Inequality and Slow Growth, *The Guardian*, 18 June.

Stewart, W. (2010). World's Cleverest Man Turns Down $1million Prize after Solving one of Mathematics' Greatest Puzzles, *Mail Online*, 23 March.

Stigler, G. (1971). The Theory of Economic Regulation, *Bell Journal of Economics and Management Science*, 2, 3–21.

Stiglitz, J.E. (2010). *Free Fall: America, Free Markets, and the Sinking of the World Economy*, New York: Norton.

Stiglitz, J.E. (2012). Quantitative Easing Won't Cause Inflation, But That's Not Good News, *Slate Magazine*, 7 October.

Stolper, A. (2009). Regulation of Credit Rating Agencies, *Journal of Banking and Finance*, 33, 1266–1273.

Story, L., Thomas, L. and Schwartz, N. (2010). Wall Street Helped Debt Fueling Europe's Crisis, *New York Times*, 14 February.

Stringer, D. (2010). Iceland's Commerce Minister Quits, Citing Meltdown, *San Disgo Union Tribune*, 25 January.

Strubel, B. (2014). The Financial Sector is the Greatest Parasite in Human History, *New Economic Perspectives*, 31 March. http://neweconomicperspectives.org/2014/03/financial-sector-greatest-parasite-human-history.html. 18 September 2015.

Subrahmanyam, A. (2005). A Cognitive Theory of Corporate Disclosures, *Financial Management*, 34, 5–33.

Summers, L., Greenspan, A., Levitt, A. and Rainer, W. (1999). Over the Counter Derivatives Markets and the Commodity Exchange Act: Report of the President's Working Group on Financial Markets. www. ustreas.gov/press/releases/reports/otcact.pdf. 19 July 2015.

Summers, P.M. (2005). What Caused The Great Moderation? Some Cross-Country Evidence, *Federal Reserve Bank of Kansas City Economic Review*, Third Quarter, 5–32.

Sutherland, E.H. (1949). *White Collar Crime*, New York: Holt, Rinehart & Winston.

Syll, L.R. (2010). Rational Expectations — A Fallacious Foundation for Macroeconomics in a Non-ergodic World, *Real-World Economics Review*, 62, 34–50.

Taibbi, M. (2009). The Great American Bubble Machine, *Rolling Stone*, 9 July.

Taibbi, M. (2011). Why Isn't Wall Street in Jail? *Rolling Stone*, 16 February.

Taleb, N.N. (2009). Ten Principles for a Black Swan Proof World, *Financial Times*, 7 April. http://www.ft.com/cms/s/0/5d5aa24e-23a4-11de-996a-00144feabdc0.html#axzz360kcijDN. 30 September 2015.

Talley, E.L. (2013). Financial Regulation and the World's Most Important Number: LIBOR Reporting Behavior During the Credit Crisis, Working Paper, UC Berkeley School of Law, September.

Tarullo, D.K. (2010). Comment on Gorton and Metrick, *Brookings Papers on Economic Activity*, Fall, 304–310.

Tarullo, D.K. (2013). Shadow Banking and Systemic Risk Regulation, Speech given at the Americans for Financial Reform and Economic Policy Institute Conference, Washington, D.C., 22 November. http://www.federalreserve.gov/newsevents/speech/tarullo20131122a.htm. 2 September 2015.

Taylor, J.B. (2009). How Government Created the Financial Crisis, *Wall Street Journal*, 9 February.

Taylor, J.B. (2013). Causes of the Financial Crisis and the Slow Recovery: A 10-Year Perspective, Stanford Institute For Economic Policy Research Discussion Paper No. 13-026.

Teather, D. (2003). SEC Seeks Rating Sector Clean-up, *The Guardian*, 28 January.

Teather, D. (2008). The Woman Who Built a Financial "Weapon of Mass Destruction", *The Guardian*, 20 September.

The Economist. (2005). Who Rates the Raters? 26 May.

The Economist. (2007a). Debt Ratings: AAAsking for Trouble, 12 July.

The Economist. (2007b). Credit and Blame: The Rating Agencies Operate on Shaky Foundations, 6 September.

The Economist. (2009a). Too Big for its Gucci Boots, 10 September.

The Economist. (2009b). How Efficient Market Theory has been Proved both Wrong and Right, 7 March.

The Economist. (2011a). Making Financial Markets Less Reliant on Ratings will not be Straightforward, 13 August.

The Economist. (2011b). Stopping Quantitative Easing May be Harder than Starting it, 19 March.

The Economist. (2012a). The Mathematics of Markets, 14 January.

The Economist. (2012b). Pay-offs for the Boss Need to be Better Designed, 14 January.

The Economist. (2013a). Bankers Bonuses: Tilting the Playing Field, 9 March.

The Economist. (2013b). Free Speech or Knowing Misrepresentation? 5 February.

The Economist. (2014a). Back from the Dead, 11 January.

The Economist. (2014b). Leverage Ratios: Leavened, 18 January.

The Economist. (2014c). Counting the Cost of Finance, 21 June.

The Economist. (2014d). The Lure of Shadow Banking, 10 May.

The Economist. (2014e). Early Retirement, 1 November.

The Economist. (2015a). False Hope, 21 February.

The Economist. (2015b). A Bigger Stick, 13 June.

The Economist. (2015c). As Safe as Houses, 31 January.

The Economist. (2015d). The Flows Resume, 13 June.

The Independent. (2014). Fat Cats Getting Fatter? Bankers' Bonus Culture Lives on as Millionaires' Club Tops 2,700, 7 November.

The Telegraph. (2009). Bonus Culture to Blame for Banking Crisis, Say MPs, 15 May.

The Telegraph. (2015). Iceland Looks at Ending Boom and Bust with Radical Money Plan, 31 March.

Thoma, M. (2007). What Caused the Great Moderation? Economist's View, 19 January, 2007. http://economistsview.typepad.com/economistsview/2007/01/the_great_moder.html. 17 August 2015.

Thomadakis, S.B. (2007). What Makes Good Regulation, IFAC Council Seminar, Mexico City, 14 November 14.

Thompson, J.R., Baggetts, L.S., Wojciechowski, W.C. and Williams, E.E. (2006). Nobels for Nonsense, *Journal of Post Keynesian Economics*, 29, 3–18.

Thorn, R.S. (1957). Nonbank Financial Intermediaries, Credit Expansion, and Monetary Policy, *International Monetary Fund Staff Papers*, 6(369–383), 1957–1958.

Transparency International. (2015). Incentivising Integrity in Banks, Working Paper. http://www.transparency.org/whatwedo/publication/incentivising_integrity_in_banks. 10 April 2015.

Turk, J. (2009). On the Cusp of Hyperinflation, *Free Gold Money Report*, 2 March. http://www.fgmr.com/on-the-cusp-of-hyperinflation.html. 29 July 2015.

Turner, A. (2009). Mansion House speech, the City Banquet (Mansion House), London, 22 September. http://www.fsa.gov.uk/pages/Library/Communication/Speeches/2009/0922_at.shtml. 6 June 2015.

Turner, A. (2012). Shadow Banking and Financial Instability, Speech at the Cass Business School, 14 March.

Turner, A. (2013). Debt, Money and Mephistopheles: How Do we Get out of This Mess? Speech at the Cass Business School, 6 February.

Utzig, S. (2010). The Financial Crisis and the Regulation of Credit Rating Agencies: A European Banking Perspective, Asian Development Bank Institute Working Papers No. 188.

Valdimarsson, O. (2009). Iceland Parliament Approves Debt Bill, *Reuters*, 28 August.

Valdimarsson, O. (2013). Iceland Lacks Currency for Easy Exit of Krona Creditors, *Bloomberg Business*, 30 April.

Varian, H.R. (1985). Divergence of Opinion in Complete Markets, *Journal of Finance*, 40, 309–317.

Vaughan, L., Finch, G. and Choudhury, A. (2013). Traders Said to Rig Currency Rates to Profit Off Clients, *Bloomberg News*, 12 June. http://www.bloomberg.com/news/articles/2013-06-11/traders-said-to-rig-currency-rates-to-profit-off-clients. 12 June 2015.

Vaughan, L., Finch, G. and Ivry, B. (2013). Secret Currency Traders' Club Devised Biggest Market's Rates, *Bloomberg News*, 19 December.

Volcker, P. (2011). Financial Reform: Unfinished Business, *New York Review of Books*, 24 November. http://www.nybooks.com/articles/archives/2011/nov/24/financial-reform-unfinished-business/. 4 September 2015.

von Ehrlich, M. and Radulescu, D. (2012). The Taxation of Bonuses and its Effect on Executive Compensation and Risk Taking — Evidence from the UK Experience. Working Paper, Warwick University. http://www2.warwick.ac.uk/fac/soc/economics/intranet/calendar/bonus_tax_abstract.pdf. 6 October 2015.

von Mises, L. (1998). *Human Action: A Treatise on Economics*, Auburn (Alabama): Ludwig von Mises institute.

Wade, K. and Bilson, J. (2012). Will Quantitative Easing Lead to Higher Inflation? *Schroders TalkingPoint*, June. http://www.schroders.com/staticfiles/Schroders/Sites/Americas/US%20Institutional%202011/pdfs/Talking-Point-QE-Inflation.pdf. 12 May 2015.

Walker, A. (2014). Has Quantitative Easing Worked in the U.S.? *BBC Business News*, 30 October. http://www.bbc.com/news/business-29778331. 24 September 2015.

Wall Street Journal. (2009). A Triple-A Idea — Ending the Rating Oligopoly, 15 April.

Wallace, T. (2015a). Britain's Biggest Banks to be Forced to Separate Retail Banks from Investment Arms, *The Telegraph*, 15 October.

Wallace, T. (2015b). We Have Better Things to do Than Implement the Ring-Fence, says HSBC, *The Telegraph*, 30 June.

Wallison, P.W. (2012). Does Shadow Banking Require Regulation? *American Enterprise Institute*, 14 June. http://www.aei.org/publication/does-shadow-banking-require-regulation/. 16 August 2015.

Walter, S. (2010). Basel II and Revisions to the Capital Requirements Directive. http://www.bis.org/speeches/sp100503.htm. 4 July 2015.

Wang, F.A. (1998). Strategic Trading, Asymmetric Information and Heterogeneous Prior Beliefs, *Journal of Financial Markets*, 1, 321–352.

Washington Post. (2009a). A Conversation with John Williamson, *Economist*, 12 April.

Washington Post. (2009b). Book Review: 'The Myth of the Rational Market' by Justin Fox, 7 June. http://www.washingtonpost.com/wp-dyn/content/article/2009/06/05/AR2009060502053.html. 19 October 2015.

Washington's Blog. (2009). Fraud Caused the 1930s Depression and the Current Financial Crisis, 29 October. http://georgewashington2.blogspot.com.au/2010/10/fraud-caused-great-depression-and-this.html. 12 July 2015.

Watson, J. (2009). Bonus Culture, International Bar Association. http://www.ibanet.org/Article/Detail.aspx?ArticleUid=0eaccdbe-287b-473c-bbe6-a550508f7804. 19 June 2015.

Waxman, H.A. (2008). Credit Rating Agencies and the Financial Crisis, Hearing Before the House Committee on Oversight and Government Reform. http://oversight.house.gov/images/stories/Hearings/. 23 June 2015.

Weale, M. and Wieladek, T. (2014). What are the Macroeconomic Effects of Asset Purchases? Bank of England, External MPC Unit Discussion Paper No. 42.

Wearden, G. (2010). Goldman Sachs Denies Betting Against Clients, *The Guardian*, 7 April.

Weaver, R.D. and Zhang, Y. (1999). Volatility of Market Prices: The Role of Heterogeneous Expectations. Paper Presented at the Annual Meetings of the American Agricultural Economic Association, Nashville, TN.

Wee, H. (2009). Astonishing That Big Banks are Taking Taxpayer Money, Writing the Rules, Warren Says, 16 October. http://finance.yahoo.com/tech-ticker/article/355983/%22Astonishing%22-That-Big-Banks-Are-Taking-Taxpayer-Money Writing-the-Rules-Warren-Says. 28 September 2015.

Wells Capital Management. (2013). Will "Velocity" Change the Conversation? 11 November. http://www.wellscap.com/docs/emp/20131111.pdf. 26 June 2015.

Wen, Y. and Arias, M.A. (2014). What Does Money Velocity Tell us about Low Inflation in the U.S.? https://www.stlouisfed.org/On-The-Economy/2014/September/What-Does-Money-Velocity-Tell-Us-about-Low-Inflation-in-the-US. 20 July 2015.

Wheatley, M. (2014). We Can't Change Bank Bonus Culture over Night, *The Telegraph*, 3 March.

Wheelock, D.C. (2010). The Monetary Base and Bank Lending: You Can Lead a Horse to Water …, Federal Reserve Bank of St Louis, *Economic Synopses*, No. 24.

White, L. (2002). The Credit Rating Industry: An Industrial Organization Analysis, in R.M. Levich, G. Majnoni and C Reinhart (eds.) *Ratings, Rating Agencies, and the Global Financial System*, New York: Springer.

Williamson, J. (1989). What Washington Means by Policy Reform, in J. Williamson (ed.) *Latin American Readjustment: How Much has Happened*, Washington: Institute for International Economics.

Williamson, J. (2000). What Should the World Bank Think about the Washington Consensus? Paper prepared as a background to the World Bank's World Development Report.

Williamson, J. (2002). Did the Washington Consensus Fail? Speech at the Center for Strategic and International Studies, *Washington DC*, 6 November.

Willsher, K. and Inman, P. (2013). Voters in Swiss Referendum Back Curbs on Executives' Pay and Bonuses, *The Guardian*, 4 March.

Wojcik, D. (2013). The Dark Side of NY–LON: Financial Centres and the Global Financial Crisis, *Urban Studies*, 50, 2736–2752.

Wolf, M. (2008a). Why it is so Hard to Keep the Financial Sector Caged? *Financial Times*, 15 January.

Wolf, M. (2008b). 'Helicopter Ben' Confronts the Challenge of a Lifetime, *Financial Times*, 16 December.

Woodford, M. (2004). Inflation Targeting and Optimal Monetary Policy, *Federal Reserve Bank of St. Louis Review*, July/August, 15–41.

Wray, L.R. (2011). Lessons We Should Have Learned from the Global Financial Crisis but Didn't, Levy Economics Institute of Bard College, Working Paper No. 681, August.

Wyplosz, C. (2009). The ICMB-CEPR Geneva Report: The Future of Financial Regulation, *Vox*, 27 January.

Zandi, M. (2009). *Financial Shock: Global Panic and Government Bailouts — How We Got Here and What Must Be Done to Fix It* (updated edition), Upper Saddle River (NJ): FT Press.

Zumbrun, J. (2009). AIG's Bonus Distraction, *Forbes*, 16 March.

Index

H

H.V. and H.W. Poor Company, 226

HSBC, 82

Hedge funds, 31, 73, 191, 196, 221

Herd behavior, 117

High-frequency trading, 19, 341

Home equity loans, 197

Horse and sparrow theory, 102

House Committee on Government Operations, 64

House of Lords Economic Affairs Committee, 343

House of Representatives Committee on Oversight and Government Reform, 246

Housing bubble, 25, 27, 47, 120, 301

Housing market, 239, 267

Housing policy, 201

Hyperinflation, 278–279

I

Icesave, 320

Icesave bill, 320

Impersonation, 52

Incomplete information, 95

Index funds, 58

Industrial production, 271

Inequality, 103, 145

Inflation doves, 279

Inflation risk, 276

Inflationary expectations, 281

Inflationary pressure, 276

Initial public offering, 30

Insider information, 51, 242

Insider trading, 18, 51, 55, 62, 73, 110, 350

Insurance companies, 221

Intellectual property rights, 110

Internal fraud, 52

Internal models, 38, 75, 260

Internal Revenue Code, 162

International Bar Association, 168

International debt crisis, 210

International Monetary Fund, 319, 321, 339

International Organization of Securities Commission, 126

Investment funds, 196

Investment switching fees, 58

Invisible hand, 105, 313, 334

Irrational exuberance, 302

Issuer-pays model, 232, 256, 258–259

J

Joint stock company, 43

JP Morgan Mafia, 35

Junk bonds, 62, 139

K

Kaupthing, 314, 318–319, 322–323

Kickbacks, 55

L

Laissez faire, 11, 91, 118, 124, 314, 337

Landsbanki, 314, 318–320, 323

Law of unintended consequences, 105

Lehman Brothers, 9, 48, 74, 136, 191, 225, 239, 250

Lender of last resort, 29, 203, 317

Leverage, 18, 56, 263, 267

Leverage ratio, 31, 171, 345